Habermas
Unfinished Project of Mo...

HABERMAS AND THE UNFINISHED PROJECT OF MODERNITY

Critical Essays on
The Philosophical Discourse of Modernity

Edited by

Maurizio Passerin d'Entrèves
and Seyla Benhabib

Polity Press

First published in 1996 by Polity Press
in association with Blackwell Publishers Ltd.

Editorial office:
Polity Press
65 Bridge Street
Cambridge CB2 1UR, UK

Marketing and production:
Blackwell Publishers Ltd
108 Cowley Road
Oxford OX4 1JF, UK

ISBN 0–7456–1452–3
ISBN 0–7456–1570–8 (pbk)

A CIP catalogue record for this book is available from the British Library.

Typeset in 10.5 on 11.5 pt Sabon
by CentraCet Ltd, Cambridge
Printed in Great Britain by
TJ Press Ltd, Padstow, Cornwall

This book is printed on acid-free paper.

CONTENTS

PART II THEMATIC REFORMULATIONS

CONTRIBUTORS

Seyla Benhabib is Professor of Political Theory at Harvard University. She is the author of *Critique, Norm, and Utopia* (1986), *Situating the Self* (1992), *The Reluctant Modernism of Hannah Arendt* (1996), co-author of *Feminist Contentions* (1995), editor of *Democracy and Difference* (1996) and co-editor of *Feminism as Critique* (1987), *The Communicative Ethics Controversy* (1990) and *On Max Horkheimer* (1993).

Jay M. Bernstein is Professor of Philosophy at the University of Essex. He is the author of *The Philosophy of the Novel* (1984), *The Fate of Art* (1989), *Recovering Ethical Life* (1995) and editor of *The Frankfurt School: Critical Assessments* (1994, 6 volumes).

James Bohman is Associate Professor of Philosophy at St Louis University. He is the author of *New Philosophy of Social Science* (1991) and co-editor of *After Philosophy* (1987) and *The Interpretive Turn* (1991).

Diana Coole is Senior Lecturer in Political Theory at Queen Mary and Westfield College, University of London. She is the author of *Women in Political Theory* (1993, 2nd edn) and *Politics and Negativity* (1996).

Fred Dallmayr is Professor of Government at the University of Notre Dame. His numerous publications include *Beyond Dogma and Despair* (1981), *Twilight of Subjectivity* (1981), *Language and Politics* (1984), *Polis and Praxis* (1984), *Critical Encounters* (1987), *Margins of Political Discourse* (1989), *Between Frankfurt and Freiburg* (1991), *Lifeworld, Modernity and Critique* (1991), *G. W. F. Hegel* (1993) and *The Other Heidegger* (1993).

Maurizio Passerin d'Entrèves is Senior Lecturer in Political Theory at the University of Manchester. He is the author *Modernity, Justice,* *and Community* (1990), *The Political Philosophy of Hannah Arendt* (1994) and co-editor of *Public and Private: Legal, Political and Philosophical Perspectives* (1996).

Jürgen Habermas is Professor of Philosophy Emeritus at the University of Frankfurt. His many publications include *The Theory of Communicative Action* (1984–7), *On the Logic of the Social Sciences* (1988), *The Structural Transformation of the Public Sphere* (1989), *The New Conservatism* (1989), *Moral Consciousness and Communicative Action* (1990), *Postmetaphysical Thinking* (1992), *Justification and Application* (1993) and *Between Facts and Norms* (1995).

David Couzens Hoy is Professor of Philosophy at the University of California, Santa Cruz. He is the author of *The Critical Circle* (1978), editor of *Foucault: A Critical Reader* (1986) and co-author of *Critical Theory* (1994).

David Ingram is Professor of Philosophy at Loyola University, Chicago. He is the author of *Habermas and the Dialectic of Reason* (1987), *Critical Theory and Philosophy* (1990), *Reason, History, and Politics* (1995) and co-editor of *Critical Theory: The Essential Readings* (1991).

Christopher Norris is Professor of English at the University of Wales in Cardiff. His many publications include *Deconstruction* (1982), *The Deconstructive Turn* (1983), *The Contest of Faculties* (1985), *Derrida* (1987), *Paul deMan* (1988), *Deconstruction and the Interests of Theory* (1988), *Spinoza and the Origins of Modern Critical Theory* (1990) and *The Truth about Postmodernism* (1993).

James Schmidt is Professor of Political Science at Boston University. He is the author of *Merleau-Ponty: Between Phenomenology and Structuralism* (1985) and editor of *What Is Enlightenment? Eighteenth Century Answers and Twentieth Century Questions* (1996).

Joel Whitebook is a practising psychoanalyst and teaches philosophy and psychoanalytic theory at the New School for Social Research, New York. He is the author of *Perversion and Utopia: A Study in Psychoanalysis and Critical Theory* (1995).

ACKNOWLEDGEMENTS

Chapter 1, 'Modernity: An Unfinished Project', was originally delivered by Jürgen Habermas as his acceptance speech on receiving the Theodor W. Adorno Prize awarded by the City of Frankfurt in September 1980. It was published under the title 'Die Moderne – ein unvollendetes Projekt' in Jürgen Habermas, *Kleine Politische Schriften I–IV* (Frankfurt: Suhrkamp, 1981), pp. 444–64; this is the first complete English translation of that text and appears by kind permission of Suhrkamp Verlag. The translation is by Nicholas Walker.

Chapters 2, 3, 4 and 9 were first published in *Praxis International* 8:4 (Jan. 1989) and chapter 6 was first published in *Praxis International* 9:4 (Jan. 1990); they are reproduced by kind permission of Blackwell Publishers.

The editors and publishers are also grateful for permission to quote extracts from Jürgen Habermas, *The Philosophical Discourse of Modernity: Twelve Lectures*, trans. Frederick G. Lawrence (Cambridge: Polity Press; Cambridge, Mass.: MIT Press, 1987).

INTRODUCTION

Maurizio Passerin d'Entrèves

Since its publication in 1985, *The Philosophical Discourse of Modernity*[1] has been the object of a wide-ranging debate in the disciplines of philosophy and social theory, political science and literary criticism, intellectual history and cultural studies. The reasons for this are not hard to come by. The book presented a broad and imaginative thesis about the unfolding of a philosophical discourse of modernity from Kant to Hegel to Nietzsche and its dramatic dénouement in the writings of Heidegger and Derrida, on one side, and Bataille and Foucault, on the other, coupled with a sophisticated defence of the normative content of modernity. In doing so, it set a challenge to many influential notions about the character of the modern age. Against the depiction of modernity as a spent epoch, as having exhausted the promises and projects of its philosophical mentors in the Enlightenment, Habermas set out to defend the unrealized normative potential of modernity. This defence is based on Habermas's theory of modernity and communicative rationality presented in his earlier two-volume work, *The Theory of Communicative Action*.[2] In that work Habermas offered a systematic theory of societal and cultural modernization capable of explaining both the achievements and the pathologies of modernity. Crucial to that effort was the paradigm shift from the philosophy of consciousness to the philosophy of language, and from a subject-centred to a communicative conception of reason and rationality. The importance of this paradigm shift is crucial in understanding Habermas's criticism of postmodern thinkers and is elaborated at length in the main chapters of *The Philosophical Discourse of Modernity*: only by going beyond the philosophy of subjectivity can Habermas hope to vindicate the rational potential of modernity, to redeem its promise of emancipation and enlightenment, however qualified this may be in the face of the pathologies of the modern age.

A number of crucial issues are at stake in the debate between Habermas and the postmodernists. These have to do not simply with the legitimacy of the modern age,[3] but with questions of rationality, truth, subjectivity, power, justice, morality, and the role of the aesthetic. A fruitful way of addressing the contrast between Habermas and the postmodernists on these issues is by distinguishing two fundamental ethical orientations operating behind their respective positions. These are centred around two different senses of responsibility: a responsibility *to act* vs a responsibility *to otherness*.[4] While Habermas privileges the responsibility to act in the world in a normatively justified way, the postmodernists celebrate the responsibility to otherness, namely, the openness to difference, dissonance and ambiguity.[5] These two senses of responsibility are linked, in turn, to two different understandings of the primary function of language: language can be understood primarily in terms of its capacity to coordinate action (Habermas), or primarily in terms of its capacity to disclose the world (Heidegger and Derrida). The conception of language as action-coordinating goes hand in hand with the priority given to the first sense of responsibility (the responsibility to act), while the view of language as world-disclosing corresponds closely to the priority given to the second sense of responsibility (the responsibility to otherness). While the two senses of responsibility, and their associated conceptions of language, should not be seen as mutually exclusive,[6] it is indeed the case that they represent the polarities around which the debate between Habermas and the postmodernists has been conducted.

The chapters of this book, written by a team of leading philosophers, social scientists, intellectual historians and literary critics, represent the first systematic and detailed assessment of the main theses of *The Philosophical Discourse of Modernity* and of the crucial issues at stake in the debate between Habermas and the postmodernists. They are written from a variety of theoretical standpoints and orientations, and reach each a different conclusion as to the fruitfulness and validity of Habermas's work. But they are all united in their attempt to engage with Habermas by means of a rational dialogue based on critical appraisal and constructive response, that is, by relying on those discursive tools through which the unfinished project of modernity may continue to unfold.

The volume opens with a well-known and influential essay by Habermas, 'Modernity: An Unfinished Project', in which some of the principal themes of *The Philosophical Discourse of Modernity* are discussed in the context of a critical engagement with contemporary neoconservative cultural and political trends.[7] Habermas notes the rise of a neoconservative critique in the 1970s and 1980s that focuses

on the supposedly antinomian consequences of the 'adversary culture'. In the writings of Daniel Bell, modernist culture is accused of
unleashing hedonistic motives incompatible with the rational discipline of economic life and of undermining the moral fabric of society.
Against the anomic forces spurred by cultural modernity, Bell pleads
for a religious revival that would presumably restore faith in tradition, authority and the conventions of everyday life. Habermas
aptly points out that neoconservatism is confused in its understanding
of the relation between culture and society. It attributes to cultural
modernism all those pathological or dysfunctional syndromes, such
as hedonism, narcissism, lack of social identity, withdrawal from
status and achievement competition, that are in reality the product of
a successful capitalist modernization of the economy and society. The
changed attitudes towards work, consumption, achievement and
leisure are rooted in deep-seated reactions against the processes of
societal modernization. The systemic imperatives of an expanding
economy and a bureaucratized state steered by the media of money
and power have penetrated deeply into the communicative infrastructure of the lifeworld, endangering the processes of cultural reproduction, social integration and socialization. The syndromes of loss of
meaning, anomie and personality disorders, as well as the dynamics
of protest, originate in response to the colonizing pressures of the
economy and the state vis-à-vis the lifeworld. But neoconservative
doctrines turn our attention precisely away from such societal
processes: they project the causes, which they do not bring to light,
on to the plane of a subversive culture and its advocates.[8]

By drawing the distinction between *societal* modernization and
cultural modernization, and showing how the former is responsible
for those pathological syndromes mistakenly attributed to the latter,
Habermas is able to rebut the claims of neoconservative critics of
modernity. At the same time, he is able to provide a better diagnosis
of the pathologies originating from within the sphere of cultural
modernity itself. He argues that, while societal modernization is
characterized by the growing autonomy of subsystems of purposive-
rational action steered by the media of money and power (market
economy and administrative state), whose untrammelled expansion
leads to the colonization of the lifeworld, cultural modernization is
characterized by the increasing differentiation of cultural value
spheres (science, morality, art) governed by distinct claims to validity
(truth, rightness, authenticity) and embodying different rationality
structures (cognitive-instrumental, moral-practical, aesthetic-expressive). These differentiated value domains have become the object of
professional discourses (such as theories of science, of morality and
jurisprudence, of art and aesthetic criticism) that have become the
preserve of expert cultures. The elitist splitting off of expert cultures

from the everyday understanding of lay actors, and the relentless erosion of traditions, generate certain cultural pathologies which Habermas describes under the key terms of 'desolation' and 'cultural impoverishment'. Faced with the aporias of cultural modernity, a number of critics have decided to give up the entire project of modernity by recommending either a return to premodernity (neo-Aristotelianism in Germany, some forms of communitarianism in the USA), or a plunge into a technocratic postmodernity (neoconservatives), or an escape into antimodernity (philosophers such as Nietzsche, Heidegger, Bataille, Foucault, Derrida).

In 'Modernity: An Unfinished Project', and more extensively in *The Philosophical Discourse of Modernity*, Habermas provides a number of powerful arguments for retaining a commitment to the project of modernity. He is deeply aware of the distortions, aporias and pathologies of modernity, but believes that they can only be addressed and resolved in a fruitful way by protecting and expanding the sphere of communicative rationality against the systemic imperatives of the economy and the state (that is, reversing the colonization of the lifeworld), and by relinking the differentiated domains of science, morality and art, and their corresponding expert cultures, with the communicative praxis of the lifeworld (that is, reversing cultural impoverishment). Modernity can thus be seen as an unfinished project: it aims at 'a differentiated reconnection of modern culture with an everyday sphere of praxis that is dependent on a living heritage' but would be impoverished by more traditionalism. Such an aim, however, can only be achieved 'if the process of social modernization can *also* be turned into *other* non-capitalist directions, if the lifeworld can develop institutions of its own in a way currently inhibited by the autonomous system dynamics of the economic and administrative system'.[9]

By confronting modernity on its own terms, rather than escaping into a nostalgia for premodern traditions, or enthusiastically embracing a technocratic vision of postmodernity, or invoking an antimodern conception of the 'other' of reason, Habermas can thereby hope to redeem the *unfulfilled* promises of modernity. The cogency of his attempt to redeem the modern project is the subject of the chapters of this book.

Critical Rejoinders

In the opening chapter of part I, Fred Dallmayr provides a broad reconstruction of the main themes of *The Philosophical Discourse of Modernity* and a detailed examination of three central figures of that discourse: Hegel, Nietzsche and Heidegger. The choice of these figures is justified by their role in Habermas's philosophical narrative: while Hegel, in the wake of Kant, inaugurates the broad and multifaceted discourse of modernity, Nietzsche marks the emergence of an antidiscourse that rejects modernity, and Heidegger represents the leading philosophical figure of a postmodern discourse deriving in large part from Nietzsche.

According to Habermas, Hegel was the first philosopher to develop a clear and systematic understanding of modernity. Together with his philosophical precursors, Hegel located the core of modernity in the principle of subjectivity. Such a principle had already been highlighted by Kant, who conceived subjectivity as the foundation of the separate domains of science, morality and art. Yet, in pursuing his analytical task, Kant did not view the differentiation of reason as a problem, or the separation of modern value spheres as a source of diremption (*Entzweiung*). Consequently, he ignored the need for synthesis resulting from his analysis. This was precisely the motive of Hegel's philosophy, his attempt to provide a rational synthesis that would reconcile the dirempted aspects of modern reason and restore the integrity of ethical life. The first attempt at such a synthesis can be found in Hegel's early theological writings, characterized by a romantic or mythopoetic vision of reconciliation which the young Hegel shared with Schelling and Hölderlin. In opposition to both the orthodoxy of positive religion and the abstractness of Enlightenment reason, these writings appealed to a purified public faith or civil religiosity as the ethical bond reconciling the conflicting elements of modern social life. The same writings also spoke of a 'nexus of guilt' or a 'causality of destiny' as the cypher for the experience of common suffering that would bring about a reconciliation of criminally severed relationships. However, as Hegel himself recognized, the ideal of reconciliation embodied in civil religion or in the recognition of a nexus of guilt relies on premodern life-forms, such as the Greek *polis* and the early Christian communities, which modernity has inevitably left behind.

Similar difficulties beset another early work of Hegel, the so-called oldest *Systemprogramm* formulated in Frankfurt while he was still under the influence of Schelling and Hölderlin. In that programme, the function of reconciliation was attributed to art and the aesthetic imagination. Rational religion was presumed to yield to art in order to develop into a popular religion; the monotheism of reason was to be joined to the polytheism of the imagination to produce an aesthetic mythology in the service of ideas. The inadequacy of this programme was soon recognized by Hegel. He argued that since modernity is based on subjectivity and the power of critical reflection, only philosophical reason (*Vernunft*) could achieve the hoped-for reconciliation and overcome the aporias of modern subjectivity. This insight was to find its explicit articulation in Hegel's notion of 'absolute spirit'. Absolute spirit is the 'consuming activity of self-discovery', the 'unconditionally self-productive self-relation' mediating subjectivity and objectivity, nature and spirit, finitude and infinity. In this way, Habermas notes, Hegel utilized the philosophy of subjectivity 'for the purpose of overcoming a subject-centered reason. By means of it, the mature Hegel can convict modernity of its offences without having recourse to anything other than the principle of subjectivity immanent within it' (*PDM*, p. 34).

The self-transcendence of modernity accomplished by 'absolute spirit' is replicated at the level of 'objective spirit' in Hegel's theory of the modern state. The main innovation of *The Philosophy of Right* is to be found in the notion of civil society as a sphere of private needs mediating between the family and the state. In formulating this notion and juxtaposing it to the state, Hegel was able to account both for the advances of modernity and for its divisive effects. Moreover, by showing how civil society was both preserved and sublated in the structures of the modern state, Hegel's *Philosophy of Right* promoted a self-transcendence of modernity which retained at its core the modern principle of subjectivity.

Having outlined Hegel's mature position, Habermas then goes on to criticize it for failing to overcome the diremptions of modernity. In contrast to his previous approbation of Hegel for having adhered to the modern principle of subjectivity, Habermas now criticizes him for remaining hostage to a self-enclosed subjectivity unable to perform a synthetic function.[10] By claiming the power of synthesis for absolute spirit, Hegel merely presupposes what he has to demonstrate, namely, that absolute spirit can reconcile those divisions which modern reason has unfolded. The same problem reappears in Hegel's notion of objective spirit. According to Habermas, the state, as the embodiment of objective spirit, is unable to reconcile the divisions of modern political life. Such a reconciliation can be assumed only on the supposition of an absolute conceived as pure or infinite subjectivity: in the domain of ethical life, this construction results in the priority of the higher subjectivity of the state over the subjective freedom of the individual.

A second line of criticism is directed at the presumed abstractness of Hegel's mature thought: the tendency of objective and absolute spirit to become the object of a passive contemplation entirely removed from critical engagement with the world. Retired into itself or into its own absoluteness, Hegelian *Vernunft* can accomplish at best a partial reconciliation, namely, within the confines of philosophy, rather than between philosophy and the actual. Only latent in his early works, this tendency to passivity is said to emerge strongly in Hegel's later system, including his *Philosophy of Right*. At this point, his thought no longer criticized existing reality but only sought to grasp reality as it is. A modernity grasped in thought thus permits a stoic retreat from it.

Dallmayr finds the division between the young and the mature Hegel, or between a romantic, mythopoetic outlook and an abstract or untainted rationalism, overdrawn; his major objection, however, has to do with Habermas's characterization of Hegelian *Vernunft*. On the one hand, Habermas objects to Hegel's notion of absolute spirit for remaining locked in a self-contained subjectivity, within the confines of monological self-knowledge. Absolute spirit is described as a 'consuming activity of self-discovery', as an 'unconditionally self-productive self-relation'. On the other hand, Hegelian spirit is viewed as a detached realm, as a passively contemplated 'objective reason' that no longer informs or critically shapes the world. Now, this characterization of *Vernunft* as both unceasing activity and passive contemplation is not tenable. As Dallmayr observes, the combination of consuming activity and self-production gives to *Vernunft* a Left Hegelian flavour, while the treatment of spirit as an objective realm amenable only to contemplation carries overtones of Right Hegelianism. Under the pressure of these opposed readings, Hegel's philosophy is liable to be torn asunder. To restore its unity requires the acknowledgement that Hegel's 'spirit' designates a metaphysical or ontological category. As such a category, 'spirit' is not simply a subjective capacity or an objective rational principle, but a dimension presupposed by both which allows for their final reconciliation.

Dallmayr then turns to the second major figure in Habermas's philosophical narrative, that of Nietzsche. According to Habermas, Nietzsche inaugurated a radical antidiscourse that rejected the entire framework of the Enlightenment. Instead of working within the broad parameters of the dialectic of enlightenment as set out by Hegel and his successors, Nietzsche wants to explode the very framework of occidental reason within which the competitors of Left and Right Hegelianism still moved. His antihumanism, continued by Heidegger and Bataille in two different directions, is the real challenge to the discourse of modernity. Habermas lodges two main objections against Nietzsche. First, as opposed to the moderate stance of Wagner and the Romantics, for whom the figure of Dionysus was identified with that of Christ, Nietzsche opts exclusively for the experience of Dionysian frenzy and ends up in an irrational and boundless subjectivism. Closely linked to the charge of subjectivism is Habermas's second objection, directed against Nietzsche's irrationalism and his abandonment of rational standards, especially those of science and morality. For Habermas, 'Nietzsche continues the Romantic purification of the aesthetic phenomenon from all theoretical and practical associations.' By insulating the domain of art from those of knowledge and morality, Nietzsche's aestheticism was bound to drift irremediably into a 'metaphysically transfigured irrationalism' (*PDM*, p. 94). Moreover, removed from all rational standards, Nietzsche's aestheticism was unable to legitimize itself. He could no longer justify the criteria of aesthetic judgement, since he transposed aesthetic experience into the archaic past and separated the critical capacity for assessing value from its grounding in rational argumentation. As a result, the aesthetic domain, viewed as the gateway to the Dionysian, became hypostatized into the other of reason.

With respect to the first charge, Dallmayr argues that it is difficult to sustain. For how can Nietzsche have been the instigator of a radical exit from modernity while at the same time being mired into an undiluted subjectivity (and thus an undiluted modernism)? Habermas characterizes Nietzsche's conception of the Dionysian as the heightening of the subjective to the point of utter self-oblivion.[11] But how can subjectivity be enhanced through self-oblivion? Can Nietzsche have plunged into Dionysian frenzy and simultaneously have worshipped the modern ego?

Similar reservations are voiced with respect to the second objection. Habermas fails to question modern rationalism or his own model of rational discourse. He accuses Nietzsche of having purged aesthetics of all cognitive and moral components, and of having hypostatized art into the other of reason. But isn't the radical separation of art from both science and morality the inevitable outcome of cultural rationalization? Given the increasing differentiation of value spheres, how can we establish that the standards of theoretical and moral-practical reason are applicable to the autonomous domain of art and aesthetic experience? Rather than accusing Nietzsche of irrationalism, Habermas should acknowledge that in his pursuit of the inner logic of avant-garde art Nietzsche steadfastly advanced the discourse of modernity.

In the third part of the chapter, Dallmayr responds to some of the major criticisms levelled against Heidegger. According to Habermas, Heidegger's *Being and Time* suffers from a basic inconsistency vitiating its ontological turn. In dealing with the question of 'authentic *Dasein*' and 'being-toward-death', Heidegger relapses into a form of Kierkegaardian subjectivism, if not solipsism. Having initially undermined the philosophy of the subject through the appeal to the notion of the world as the pre-understood background of all cognition and action, Heidegger subsequently succumbed to the conceptual constraints of subject-centred reason; a solipsistically construed *Dasein* reoccupies in the end the position of transcendental subjectivity. Heidegger's early work thus remains imprisoned by the categories of the philosophy of consciousness, and, in contrast to its original intentions, ends up privileging theoretical knowledge and a cognitive-instrumental relation to the world. Heidegger's later *Kehre* is seen as the attempt to escape from the subjectivist outcome of *Being and Time*. The *Kehre* initiated a radical reversal, the turn from subjectivism to a passive celebration of Being. While *Being and Time* had sponsored 'the decisionism of an empty resoluteness', Heidegger's later philosophy counselled 'the submissiveness of an equally empty readiness for surrender to Being'. This had fateful political consequences. In treating 'Being' as a mode of historical happening, Heidegger transfigured historical events into a fateful dispensation of Being, into an 'ontological destiny' (*Seinsgeschick*). The recommendation of surrender to Being had the practical effect of inducing a diffuse readiness to obedience towards an auratic but undefined authority, towards the edicts of pseudo-sacral powers. In producing this effect, Heidegger's later work militated against a central pillar of modernity, namely, the autonomy of thought and action (or freedom and responsibility). According to Habermas, the surrender to Being and its destiny sponsored a training in a new heteronomy. Heidegger's critique of metaphysics thus culminated in a radical but empty change of attitude: away from autonomy and towards a blind devotion to Being.

Dallmayr provides a nuanced response to these charges. With respect to the charge of subjectivism, he argues that in *Being and Time* Heidegger always retained the primacy of ontological pre-understanding and of the world as the referential context of the various modes of being of *Dasein*. Construed as 'being-in-the-world', *Dasein* is never an isolated ego confronting an independently existing reality; rather, it is ontologically rooted in the world and relates to it through various modalities of care. 'Authentic *Dasein*' does not mean a retreat into an isolated self, but a genuine and caring concern for the world. Even 'being-toward-death' does not cancel *Dasein*'s essential connectedness, its ontological embedment in the world. Moreover, as Heidegger repeatedly stressed in *Being and Time*, the ontological construal of 'being-in-the-world' implies that the world is always already shared with others; the world of *Dasein* is a co-world; being-in-the-world means co-being with others. The charge of subjectivism seems therefore spurious.

Habermas's second main charge, directed at Heidegger's *Kehre*, is also open to doubt. Dallmayr observes that after having criticized the subjectivism of *Being and Time*, Habermas proceeds to rebuke Heidegger's later philosophy for abandoning subjective responsibility in favour of a blind devotion to the destiny of Being. He argues that Habermas is operating with a simple dualism: the dualism of subjectivism versus objectivism, activity versus passivity. Like all other such dualisms, the contrasting terms presuppose each other, and are not helpful in elucidating Heidegger's thought. Finally, he strongly dissents from the view that Heidegger's later works sponsored a new heteronomy, and were thus inimical to freedom and responsibility. He considers this a most unlikely charge, given the centrality of freedom in Heidegger's entire philosophy. As in the case of Hegel's notion of 'Spirit', 'Being' for Heidegger was essentially a synonym for freedom.

In 'Deconstruction, Postmodernism and Philosophy: Habermas on Derrida', Christopher Norris mounts a spirited defence of Derrida against Habermas's charge that he collapses all genre distinctions, especially those between philosophy and literature, logic and rhetoric, concept and metaphor. He believes that Habermas misreads Derrida by identifying his oeuvre with those postmodernist currents that reject the canons and procedures of post-Kantian enlightened reason. Rather than viewing deconstruction as the philosophical offshoot of these postmodernist or counter-enlightenment trends, Norris argues that it should be seen to belong squarely to that same philosophical discourse of modernity that Habermas wants to defend against its present-day detractors. Norris opens his discussion with an account of the radically divergent readings of Derrida's work put forward by leading commentators: on the one hand, there are those, like Rodolphe Gasché, who read Derrida's work as a radicalization of certain Kantian themes, while on the other there are those, like Richard Rorty, who see it as a kind of writing that no longer appeals to such discredited Enlightenment notions of truth, universal reason or the nature of representation. According to the first reading, deconstruction presses certain Kantian antinomies to the point where they demand a radically novel form of analysis, while on the second reading deconstruction dissolves philosophy into a textual or rhetorical genre with no distinctive truth claims of its own. Norris's position is clearly supportive of Gasché's reading, and his main objection to Habermas is that he has identified deconstruction with Rorty's interpretation of it as a species of literary or poetic activity. This is indeed the reading that Habermas puts forward in his 'Excursus on Leveling the Genre Distinction between Philosophy and Literature' (PDM, pp. 185–210), where he accuses Derrida of ignoring the different types of speech acts (constative, regulative, expressive) that have separated out in modernity, and of overgeneralizing the poetic or rhetorical aspect of language to the point where it occupies the entire field of language use.

According to Habermas,

the rhetorical element occurs in its *pure form* only in the self-referentiality of the poetic expression, that is, in the language of fiction specialized for world-disclosure. Even the normal language of everyday life is ineradicably rhetorical; but within the matrix of different linguistic functions, the rhetorical elements recede here ... The same holds true of the specialized languages of science and technology, law and morality, economics, political science, etc. They, too, live off the illuminating power of metaphorical tropes; but the rhetorical elements, which are by no means expunged, are tamed, as it were, and enlisted for special purposes of problem-solving. (*PDM*, p. 209)

By inflating the rhetorical or world-disclosive function of language, Derrida overlooks the peculiar tension between the world-disclosing and the problem-solving functions of language. While this tension is held together within the matrix of ordinary language,

art and literature, on the one side, and science, morality, and law, on the other, are specialized for experiences and modes of knowledge that can be shaped and worked out within the compass of *one* linguistic function and *one* dimension of validity at a time. Derrida holistically levels these complicated relationships in order to equate philosophy with literature and criticism. (*PDM*, p. 207)

Norris has a number of reservations regarding this interpretation of Derrida's work. To begin with, Habermas's criticism only applies to certain texts of Derrida, and even then it can be sustained only through a very partial reading, one that discounts the argumentative rigour with which Derrida undermines the distinction between philosophy and literature. Secondly, Habermas's critique restates the argument made by John Searle in his exchange with Derrida over the nature of J. L. Austin's speech-act theory, to the effect that there is a supposedly self-evident distinction between normal and deviant types of speech act.[12] By restating the argument, Habermas appears to side with Searle against Derrida as the only properly authorized interpreter of Austin's ideas. But this choice fails to register the extent to which Austin invites a deconstructive reading by having himself erected a whole series of obstacles to the project of a generalized and systematic speech-act theory. As Norris points out, Austin (like Derrida) shows a fondness for marginal or problematic cases, for speech acts which cannot be securely assigned to this or that category. What is distinctive of Austin's approach, Norris argues, is his readiness to let language have its way and not to give in to the urge for systematic or clear-cut theory. In this respect Austin is much closer to Derrida than to Searle or Habermas. But it would be wrong to see Austin's approach as a rejection of philosophical 'seriousness' in favour of semantic or rhetorical 'free play'. His approach, like that of Derrida, aims at destabilizing the fixity of our categories and classificatory systems, not at eliminating all distinctions for the sake of a liberating free play.

Finally, Norris contests Habermas's rigid distinction between philosophy and literature. He argues that such a strict separation of discursive genres does not allow for the possibility of a text, like Derrida's *La Carte Postale*, having both literary value and philosophical cogency. Indeed, a whole number of texts, ranging from Plato to Augustine to Hegel to Kierkegaard, would have to be rejected as non-philosophical by Habermas, on account of their mixing of literary form with philosophical argument. A more fruitful reading of Derrida's texts would acknowledge both their ineradicably literary quality and the argumentative force with which they undermine rigid conceptual hierarchies and genre distinctions. Contrary to Habermas, Derrida never abandons the ground of post-Kantian enlightened thought, nor does he renounce philosophical argument in favour of a purely literary or rhetorical style. Rather, his work belongs to those philosophers, like Wittgenstein and Austin, who fought against the habit of erecting rigid dichotomies and who did so by extending or radicalizing a number of Kantian arguments, in particular those having to do with the conditions of possibility of language, meaning and representation. Viewed in this light, Derrida's work belongs squarely to the post-Kantian tradition of critical reason: it does not aim at undoing philosophy at the hands of literature, but at developing a form of criticism that meets the challenge of philosophy at the level of argument, rhetoric and style.

In 'Splitting the Difference: Habermas's Critique of Derrida', David Hoy attempts to overcome the conflict between critical theory and deconstruction by identifying philosophical possibilities that escape a set of binary oppositions, such as history versus theory, modernity versus postmodernity, theory versus method, philosophy versus politics. Such oppositions are shown to be fictitious and an obstacle to a proper appreciation of the debate between Habermas and Derrida. Thus, rather than taking sides in this debate, Hoy endeavours to 'split the difference', not in the sense of finding a median position, but of locating philosophical possibilities that go beyond the logic of mutual exclusion. With respect to the first opposition, that of history versus theory, Hoy argues both that an understanding of history is indispensable to the formation of theory, and that the formation of theory ought to reflect on the history of its formation. He thereby rejects the false dichotomy of *either* history *or* theory, and shows convincingly how the two are interdependent. Similarly, with the second dichotomy, of modernity versus postmodernity, he questions whether it can be sustained either on historical or theoretical grounds. He notes that Habermas describes himself as a modern and Derrida as a postmodern. As a defender of modernity, Habermas may be seen to stand in the tradition of philosophy from Descartes to Kant. But having moved from the philosophy of consciousness characteristic of those thinkers to a philosophy of language and communicative reason, and having rejected their foundationalism for empirical fallibilism, he clearly comes later than modernity. His position is better characterized as *late modern*, since unlike the neo-Nietzschean postmoderns he has not abandoned modern philosophy's goal of formulating and defending universal standards of rationality. The debate, then, is not between modernity and postmodernity, but between a late modern and a postmodern understanding of the tasks of philosophy.

The opposition modernity/postmodernity is also questionable from a theoretical standpoint. According to Hoy, the fundamental philosophical motive of modernity is to think the unthought. From Descartes to Kant, the unthought that modern philosophy tries to think is thought itself. This self-reflexivity generates a number of antinomies, which force successive thinkers to redefine or uncover those aspects of thought that have been left unthought by their predecessors. What the postmoderns are attempting to do is to continue the modern project of thinking the unthought, but with the proviso that the unthought is not a noumenal entity, but something much closer to the surface of things, and thus not in principle inaccessible. Where they really differ from the moderns is in rejecting their desire to make the unthought completely accessible and transparent. Thus the postmoderns continue to try to think what has remained unthought, but they abandon the idea that the unthought can be made entirely transparent. This has a number of consequences, which Hoy describes under six headings: (1) the postmodern outlook accepts rather than laments the inability to make completely manifest the unthought; (2) postmodernists don't believe that the unthought can be captured exhaustively in a theory; (3) there is no single or privileged way to think the unthought; (4) there is no 'master' thought underlying every phenomenon; (5) the unthought itself is no single entity capable of only one correct description; (6) most crucially, postmodernists realize that nostalgia for a premodern age of innocence only makes sense in contrast to the modernist hope for progress, so that abandoning this hope also leads them beyond nostalgia.[13] One sign of their lack of nostalgia, Hoy argues, is their lack of interest in philosophical self-legitimation. If there is no necessary progress in history, the postmodernists cannot claim a normative advantage over the late modernists or any of their modern predecessors. They have abandoned the idea that the present is necessarily better than the past, as well as any nostalgia for the past. So the postmodernists have no argument that could convince the late modernists of the superiority of postmodernism. If this is so, however, the term 'postmodernism' is misleading, since it implies that the postmodern is an advocate of the normative superiority of postmodernism. Thus the genuine issues dividing Habermas from Derrida can only be obscured by thinking that in resolving them we must be partisans of *either* modernity *or* postmodernity.

Having shown the untenability of the first two dichotomies, Hoy turns to an examination of the third, that of theory versus method. Habermas claims that deconstruction, notwithstanding Derrida's repeated denials, still looks like a version of *Ursprungsphilosophie*. It is characterized by a search for origins, for what is primary or foundational, as evidenced in Derrida's claims about archewriting and *différance*. Hoy agrees with Habermas that there is a tone in Derrida's earlier writings that may justify such a reading, but argues that it is too partial and restrictive. He counterposes a broader, hermeneutic reading of Derrida that is less radical than Habermas's, but also less radical than that of some followers of Derrida. On this reading, Derrida is not offering a 'theory' in the strong foundational sense of securing absolute grounds, nor is he offering a systematic explanatory scheme such as Habermas's theory of universal pragmatics. Deconstruction, on the contrary, must be seen as a general strategy of resisting every effort at theoretization and systematic grounding. It is neither foundationalist nor antifoundationalist, since it should not be construed as providing grounds or even as raising the question of grounds. *Différance* is neither a master word nor an arche-synthesis that gathers everything into one word or concept. The aim of deconstruction is, rather, to destabilize the notion of an origin of language, as well as the enterprise of capturing that origin in a 'theory' or 'philosophy' of language.

Thus, on the basis of this reading, it is possible to view Derrida's relation to theory as a double one. On the one hand, deconstruction resists 'theory' in the strong sense by constantly trying to destabilize it; on the other hand, Derrida is not opposed to theory in a weaker sense, that is, the effort to think the unthought or the unsaid, to make (partially) manifest the unstated background assumptions of a theory or a practice. Contrary to Habermas, Derrida believes that what legitimates theory is not problem-solving, but its ability to open up a space, to uncover a multiplicity of problematics. It would be a mistake, however, to identify it simply with world-disclosure: the conception of theory as opening a realm of possibilities is as rich as world-disclosure and as determinate as problem-solving.

The question then arises: is deconstruction a theory or a method?

According to Hoy, deconstruction is best construed as the methodological injunction to keep theories on their guard, since they may
close themselves off from possibilities to which they should remain
open. But Derrida claims that deconstruction is not a method, that
is, a set of rules to be applied algorithmically to every text. The
answer, then, is to split the difference between the opposition, theory
versus method, and to characterize deconstruction as an interpretive
strategy that can be performed on any particular 'theory' or text. As
a strategy of interpretation, deconstruction is neither a universal
theory nor an algorithmic method, and may be applied successfully
to any number of texts, especially those claiming metaphysical
closure.

The final contrast examined by Hoy is that between philosophy
and politics. Habermas maintains that deconstruction cannot be used
constructively to generate a social or political critique of existing
institutions, due to its privileging of the ontological over the ontic, of
philosophy over politics. Hoy, on the other hand, believes that the
critical potential of deconstruction should not be underestimated. He
wants to dispel the worry that deconstruction offers nothing to
replace that which it destabilizes, since any suggested replacement
could always be deconstructed and subverted in turn. He considers
Derrida's remarks on the American Declaration of Independence as
an illustration of the kind of political critique made possible by
deconstruction. Derrida's reading of this text is not a form of ideology
critique; rather, it is an investigation of the status of the Declaration
as a linguistic act, one that is both constative and performative. Since
the Declaration exhibits both aspects at once, its meaning is undecidable. Moreover, Derrida claims that the act of declaring independence
is an instance of a more general phenomenon of founding or
instituting, and that the act of founding is never a purely rational act,
since it always presupposes an institutional framework embodying a
power component. Habermas would resist this reading, with its stress
on indeterminacy and contingency. Derrida, however, might argue
that Habermas's emphasis on rational validity leads him to overlook
the institutional or power-dependent dimensions of discourse. Rather
than opting for one or the other, Hoy suggests that the best option is
to split the difference, by acknowledging that both Habermas and
Derrida are saying something right. If so, however, there is no reason
to assume that Derrida's destabilizing critique is never justified or
that it always leaves us with the status quo. We don't have to know
in advance what alternatives we would prefer to want to destabilize
some of our present practices. The critical potential of deconstruction
is precisely that of allowing us to view our practices in a different
light so that we can become aware of other possibilities. Deconstruction, rather than being a destructive or nihilistic enterprise, can thus

become a productive and liberating interpretive strategy in the service of critical philosophy.

The adequacy of Habermas's critique of Foucault is the subject of James Schmidt's chapter 'Habermas and Foucault'. In the first part he provides a brief reconstruction of Habermas's interpretation of Foucault in *The Philosophical Discourse of Modernity*. Habermas sees Foucault's work as falling into two broad phases: his early studies, which come to an end with *The Order of Things*, aim at an 'unmasking critique of the human sciences', while his later writings articulate a 'theory of power'. Separating these two phases, and motivating the transition from one to the other, are a series of difficulties regarding the status of Foucault's initial critique of the human sciences. Habermas argues that Foucault responded to these difficulties by turning to a Nietzschean theory of power, but that this theory is beset by a number of aporias. Such aporias, Habermas contends, can be attributed to Foucault's failure to transcend the standpoint of the philosophy of the subject.

Against such a reading of Foucault's work, Schmidt advances three main lines of criticism: first, that it misunderstands the approach Foucault adopts in *Madness and Civilization* and thus misrepresents the relationship between *Madness and Civilization* and *The Birth of the Clinic*; second, that it underestimates the centrality of Nietzsche for all the phases of Foucault's work; finally, that Foucault's theory of power is not beset with the aporias Habermas claims to find.

With respect to the first charge, Schmidt argues that Habermas's reconstruction of Foucault's development from the 'depth hermeneutics' of *Madness and Civilization* to the 'structural analysis' of *The Birth of the Clinic* mischaracterizes what Foucault was doing. In *Madness and Civilization* Foucault did not embrace the type of approach he would later criticize in the preface to *The Birth of the Clinic*. In that earlier work he did not attempt to unmask the distortions produced by official discourses about madness so as to give voice to the unspoken elements that 'slumber within speech'. What Foucault was seeking could not be found within the discourses about madness, because such discourses established themselves by excluding and silencing the language of madness. Foucault was not therefore engaged, as Habermas claims, in a 'depth hermeneutics', since he insisted that madness is never present in any of the texts available to the historian. His critical comments at the start of *The Birth of the Clinic*, calling for a 'structural analysis of discourse' that will seek nothing in excess of what has been said, are directed instead at those forms of historiography that see in the works of earlier periods anticipations of subsequent developments.

With respect to the second charge, Schmidt argues that Habermas's explanation of the shift from an archaeology of knowledge to a genealogy of power as having been motivated by a sudden reception of Nietzsche's ideas on the part of Foucault in the 1970s underestimates the central role that Nietzsche's work played throughout Foucault's intellectual career. The notion of the 'overman' figures prominently in Foucault's doctoral dissertation, *Madness and Civilization* is characterized in the opening statement as a Nietzschean inquiry, and *The Order of Things* closes by invoking Nietzsche as the prophet of 'the end of man'. Moreover, while the term 'genealogy' first appears in Foucault's work at the end of the 1960s, the hostility to teleological interpretations of history was present from the very beginning of his work. The turn to Nietzschean genealogy was not prompted by Foucault's belated recognition of insurmountable aporias within his archaeology of the human sciences, but by his acknowledgement that the dimension of power was not sufficiently stressed in his earlier investigations on madness and in the analysis of the rules of discourse in *The Order of Things*.

Schmidt then turns to a consideration of Habermas's most important criticism of Foucault, namely, that his theory of power is plagued by insurmountable aporias. Habermas makes three distinct claims: first, he argues that Foucault's concept of power performs an 'irritating double role', since it is used to advance both empirical and transcendental claims; second, that Foucault's theory of power is necessarily 'presentist', 'relativist' and 'cryptonormative'; thirdly, that Foucault's account of law and sexuality is open to a number of empirical objections.

As regards the first claim, Habermas argues that in *The Order of Things* Foucault gave an account of the emergence of the human sciences that was simultaneously historical and transcendental. He maintained not just that there are certain discernible regularities in the human sciences, but that such regularities function as constitutive rules governing the production of statements. Similarly, in *Discipline and Punish* Foucault gave an empirical account of the development of disciplinary technologies that attempted simultaneously to be a transcendental account of the constitution of the human sciences. Foucault's concept of power, like the concept of 'man' on which the human sciences rest, functions as an 'empirical-transcendental double': its effect is to show that the human sciences have not just arisen historically in conjunction with techniques of surveillance and control, but that they transcendentally constitute their objects of knowledge as objects of manipulation and control. But why assume that Foucault is making a transcendental claim at all? Why should we see him as offering anything more than a genealogical account that shows certain historical or causal affinities between the development of the human sciences and disciplinary technologies? After all, in

Discipline and Punish, all that Foucault claims is that there are certain historical and causal affinities between the human sciences and a network of power technologies epitomized by the prison. He does not claim that this is the only form the human sciences could have taken. Thus, Habermas's charge that Foucault's theory of power incorporates a 'concealed' theory of constitution is misplaced. Moreover, the empirical objections raised by Habermas's third claim, namely, that objectifying approaches to the human sciences have today to compete with hermeneutical and critical approaches, together with his suggestion that the development of penal law and modern notions of sexuality could be analysed in terms of a theory of the evolution of normative structures, are not so much a refutation of Foucault as an argument for a different approach. Such an approach might be more promising than the genealogical analysis Foucault offered, but hardly constitutes an empirical refutation of Foucault's account.

Schmidt then goes on to consider Habermas's second claim, namely, that Foucault's theory of power is necessarily 'presentist', 'relativist' and 'cryptonormative'. Foucault's historical analyses are 'presentist' in so far as they reduce the meaning of past historical epochs to their role in the rise of modern structures of power. Behind the mask of the sober genealogist, Foucault is engaged in a diagnosis of his own time that instrumentalizes the past for the needs of the present. Schmidt notes, however, that in *The Archaeology of Knowledge* Foucault describes his work as a discourse which does not interrogate other discourses in the hope of finding a hidden law or a concealed origin. In his essay 'Nietzsche, Genealogy, History' Foucault praises Nietzsche's genealogy for refusing to succumb to the chimeras of origin. And in *Discipline and Punish* Foucault disavows any interest in writing a history of the past in terms of the present and claims instead to be writing 'the history of the present'. Genealogy views the present as a contingent historical product, as the result of struggles that could have had a different outcome. It alerts us to the utter contingency of what we have become, and thus dispels any comforting notion that we are somehow the end point of a logic intrinsic to history.

With respect to the charge of relativism, Schmidt argues that it is difficult to see why it should represent a problem for Foucault. In *Madness and Civilization* Foucault described his position as 'a sort of relativity without recourse'. This position did not trouble him, because he did not wish (*contra* Habermas's interpretation) to exempt his own research from the claim that it too was an effect of power. His position was quite consistent: it held that all claims to knowledge, including Foucault's own claim about the relation of knowledge and power, implicate us in particular networks of power. Foucault thus remained consistent in his 'relativity without recourse'.

With respect to the charge of 'cryptonormativism', it is again difficult to see why it should present a problem to Foucault. Habermas argues that Foucault provides no answer to the question 'why fight?', since his genealogical analyses lack a normative basis for the critical stance they take towards modern regimes of power. Foucault, however, never saw systems of power as displacing all opposition. He argued, instead, that every form of power inaugurates new forms of resistance. The question 'why fight?' will have many responses, depending on the particular character of the power regime to be opposed. The fact that these responses will be historically contingent, rather than being based on universal criteria, does not detract from their force. Foucault's contextualism, while perhaps troubling, is thus by no means inconsistent. The aporias Habermas claims to find in Foucault's oeuvre are, in the final analysis, not so much internal inconsistencies as fundamental disagreements between two contrasting theoretical approaches.

In 'Intersubjectivity and the Monadic Core of the Psyche', Joel Whitebook analyses the contrasting conceptions of the unconscious in Habermas and Castoriadis in order to bring to light their underlying philosophical differences. In the 'Excursus on Cornelius Castoriadis' (PDM, pp. 327–35), Habermas claims that Castoriadis is unable to account for the mediation between the individual and society: since the unconscious is conceived as a monadic core totally insulated from language and the social world of norms, psyche and society stand in a kind of metaphysical opposition to one another (p. 334). Whitebook shows that such a critique is only partly justified, and that Habermas himself has difficulties in providing an adequate model of interaction between individual and society. He argues that the rationale underlying Habermas's critique can be traced to his 'linguistic turn' of the 1970s, namely, the move from the philosophy of consciousness and subject-centred reason to the philosophy of intersubjectivity and communicative rationality. Anything that would challenge a thoroughgoing philosophy of intersubjectivity, as Castoriadis's notion of the monadic core of the psyche certainly would, poses a threat to Habermas's theory. From his early statement made on the occasion of his Frankfurt Inaugural Address in 1965 that 'language is the only thing whose nature we can know,' Habermas has never deviated from the view that the unconscious is essentially a linguistic phenomenon. He is thus compelled, for strictly philosophical reasons, to dismiss the notion of a prelinguistic unconscious and, a fortiori, the idea of a monadic core of the primal subject.

According to Whitebook, Habermas's linguistic reformulation of Kantian philosophy presents him with a typically Kantian problem, namely, the ineffable character of the ding-an-sich, now recast in linguistic terms. Towards the outside, Habermas's linguistic transcendentalism prevents him from adequately reaching the extralinguistic reality of external (especially living) nature. Towards the inside, it prevents him from adequately reaching the prelinguistic reality of inner nature. Thus, just as the philosophy of consciousness had difficulty transcending the circle of subjectivity and reaching the othersidedness of consciousness, so the philosophy of language has the parallel difficulty of surmounting the larger circle of intersubjectivity and contacting the othersidedness of language in inner and outer nature. If Habermas is satisfied to remain within the circle of language, and is not overly concerned with the paradoxes that emerge as a result, Castoriadis attempts to address that which lies beyond language, but without committing any metaphysical fallacy. He argues that it is incoherent to maintain that extraconceptual or extralinguistic reality is pure chaos, upon which we impose the order or synthesis of our conceptual and linguistic schemes at will. The very fact that we can impose our schemes on reality presupposes that reality, whether inner or outer, is at least amenable to organization, that it is, in some sense, organizable. Unlike Habermas, who refrains from speaking about the *ding-an-sich* altogether for fear of regressing into metaphysics, Castoriadis attempts to develop a discourse, which he calls 'dialectical elucidation', that allows him to say that which would be incoherent *not to say* about the object-in-itself, but to say it in a non-metaphysical manner. It is these philosophical differences between Habermas and Castoriadis which are responsible for their widely divergent analyses of the unconscious.

Both thinkers turned to psychoanalysis in order to overcome the crisis of Marxism. But while Habermas was primarily interested in psychoanalysis for methodological reasons (it was an example of a critical science with an emancipatory intent that combined interpretive understanding with causal explanation), Castoriadis is primarily concerned with Freud's discovery of the unconscious, which he seeks to develop into a theory of the radical imagination. The radical imagination consists in a largely self-generated stream of unconscious representations or images that are not subject to time, causality or contradiction. These representations provide the material for daydreams or private phantasies, and – in a suitably sublimated form – can also provide the symbolic resources for radical historical innovations and the development of novel institutional structures.

Castoriadis's theory of the radical imagination differs from Freud's theory of unconscious phantasy in the degree of autonomy it assigns to phantasy formation with respect to biological-corporeal reality. By being much less rooted in the biological-corporeal, phantasy formation is much more spontaneous for Castoriadis than it is for Freud. This allows Castoriadis to develop a radical social theory based on the notion of historical creation (what he calls 'the imaginary institution of society'), and to avoid the conservative tendencies of orthodox psychoanalysis. To achieve this aim, however, Castoriadis must be able to maintain the required degree of independence for the radical imagination, without disconnecting it entirely from biological-corporeal reality. He does this by enlisting and expanding Freud's doctrine of 'leaning-on' (anaclisis/anlehnung), which stresses the simultaneous relatedness and non-reducibility of the various regions of being. In the case of the relation between psyche and biological-corporeal reality, the doctrine of 'leaning-on' means that the autonomy of the psyche vis-à-vis the biological-corporeal is not absolute, since there can be no oral instinct without a mouth and breast, no anal instinct without an anus. This must not be taken to mean that bodily organs are mere external conditions without which the drive and its related phantasies cannot exist. It means, rather, that the morphology and functioning of the pertinent organs delineate the range of possible forms that drive-related phantasies can assume. As Castoriadis puts it: 'The mouth-breast, or the anus, have to be "taken into account" by the psyche and, what is more, they support and induce [its phantasies].'[14] On the other hand, while these biological-corporeal factors 'support and induce' the phantasy, they do not cause or determine it. A gap of underdetermination separates the biological-corporeal from the drive-related phantasy, and it is precisely in this gap that the creativity of the psyche (or the radical imaginary) functions.

Having established the relative independence and autonomy of phantasy vis-à-vis the real by the creative deployment of Freud's doctrine of 'leaning-on', Castoriadis then advances a very 'undialectical' conception of the relation between the psyche and society. He claims that the 'social institution of the individual' (that is, the process of socialization) consists in the 'imposition' on the psyche by society 'of an organisation which is essentially heterogeneous with it'.[15] As Whitebook correctly points out, this claim is incoherent. If the heterogeneity between psyche and society were as complete as Castoriadis suggests, the process of socialization would not simply be an imposition, it would be impossible. In this respect, there is an evident tension between the heterogeneity thesis and Castoriadis's use of the doctrine of 'leaning-on': while he asserts the essential heterogeneity between psyche and society, Castoriadis also asserts that the social order 'leans-on' the being of the psyche. But this means that there must be something immanent in the psyche upon which socialization can lean.

Unfortunately, Castoriadis never provides an adequate characterization of that element within the psyche that lends itself to socialization, since he holds fast to a monadic view of the unconscious.

Habermas's criticism of Castoriadis is, in this respect, quite justified. His linguistic model of the psyche, however, is open to a number of similar objections. Unlike Castoriadis, who starts with monadic isolation and asks how communication with an extrapsychic reality is possible, Habermas starts with the fact of communication and asks how it can become deformed into a privatized unconscious. The formation of the unconscious is conceived as a process of excommunication of the representation of forbidden wishes or undesired need dispositions from public, intersubjective communication through their degrammaticization and privatization. The therapeutic function of psychoanalysis consists in the regrammaticization of those excommunicated but essentially linguistic representations, and their reintegration into public communication. Habermas's commitment to a linguistic view of the unconscious is so strong that he is forced to reject the existence of any putatively prelinguistic domain by assimilating its apparent prelinguisticality to the linguistic. Remaining squarely within the circle of language, he maintains that, as we only encounter unconscious drives *qua* interpreted, that is, from within the web of intersubjectivity, it is meaningless to talk of a preinterpreted inner nature. Like Lacan, with his structuralist reduction of the unconscious to the rational law of the signifier ('the unconscious is structured *as* language'), Habermas ends up assimilating the realm of drive-related wishes and phantasies to that of language. This, in turn, enables him to provide an account of socialization as a linguistically based process of mediation between individual psyche and society.

However, as Whitebook argues, Habermas does not provide a genuine account of the mediation of individual and society, because he solves the problem in advance through the pre-established harmony between an already linguistic unconscious and an intersubjective public world. What is lost in Habermas's account is a proper acknowledgement of the moment of *non-identity* between individual and society. His model of socialization as simultaneously a process of individuation fails to consider the deeper unconscious aspects of individuation, namely, that core of the psyche which resists full linguistic articulation. Thus, Whitebook concludes, while Habermas may be correct in saying that Castoriadis turns the relationship of psyche and society into a kind of metaphysical opposition, Habermas himself leaves the dimension of prelinguistic inner nature completely unexplored.

Thematic Reformulations

In 'Two Versions of the Linguistic Turn' at the beginning of part II, James Bohman examines the dispute between Habermas and poststructuralist writers such as Derrida and Foucault with respect to their contrasting theories of language and meaning. At the centre of the dispute lies the concept of world-disclosure, a concept whose origins go back to the theories of language of von Humboldt and Herder, and which was later modified and extended in the philosophical writings of Gadamer and Heidegger. In its original meaning, the concept referred to the idea that language has a constitutive function, that it 'discloses' a world made up of distinctive values and meanings which is independent of individuals and into which everyone is socialized. The world disclosed by language is an 'always already' interpreted world of shared meanings and common value orientations. Heidegger radicalized this Humboldtian notion of world-disclosure by claiming that it was dependent on a more primordial sense of disclosure, whose privileged location was to be found in art. If a language already discloses a world, art is more primordial, since it establishes truth, or rather, it 'lets truth originate'. It is this identification of truth with a primordial sense of disclosure, of truth as an 'event', a disclosure of new entities, that lies at the basis of many poststructuralist arguments that Habermas wants to challenge. He points out the impersonal and fateful (*Geschicklich*) character of a history of Being conceived as a succession of 'truth events' over which individuals have no control. He objects to the idea that, since they represent a 'sending of a destiny' (*Geschick*), disclosures lie beyond the purview of critical reflection. Moreover, since they make up a holistic totality, disclosures cannot be justified from any standpoint outside of their own limiting horizon of truth. In this way, world-disclosure is 'raised above any and every critical forum: the luminous force of world-disclosing language is hypostatised.' (*PDM*, p. 154). This hypostatization is the result of a basic fallacy of transcendental argumentation: by identifying disclosure with truth, Heidegger has conflated the conditions of possibility of truth (which are themselves neither true nor false) with truth itself.

The same transcendental fallacy recurs in Foucault and Derrida, when they substitute Heidegger's primordial world-disclosure with the notion of 'episteme' or 'Western logocentrism', each with their own claim of determinate semantic limitation. As a result, historicist descriptions of changes in the conditions of truth replace justification, while extraordinary truth events replace ordinary epistemic standards of validity. Moreover, any interaction between world-disclosure and innerworldly praxis is prejudiced from the start, since the world-disclosing function of language 'is conceived on analogy with the generative accomplishments of transcendental consciousness . . . This constitutive world-understanding changes independently of what subjects experience . . . and independently of what they can *learn* from their practical dealings with anything in the world . . . Any interaction between world-disclosing language and learning processes in the world is excluded' (*PDM*, p. 319).

Having outlined Habermas's criticism of the poststructuralist conception of world-disclosure, Bohman goes on to examine the way Habermas incorporates a modified notion of disclosure in his theory of universal pragmatics. He shows that in order to resist the reductionist view of language characteristic of poststructuralism, whereby language is reduced to rhetoric (Derrida) or power (Foucault), Habermas restricts disclosure to one of the functions of language and confines it to the cultural domain of art and aesthetic experience. Both of these steps are problematic and inconsistent with Habermas's own philosophy of language. By restricting disclosure to the fictional use of language, which is marked by the suspension of illocutionary force, Habermas separates it too drastically from the other illocutionary or action-coordinating functions of language. Moreover, by releasing disclosure from relations to the actual world and its pressure to coordinate social action, it becomes difficult to see how disclosure is to be connected once again to innerworldly learning. Finally, by linking disclosure exclusively to the domain of aesthetic experience, Habermas downplays the world-disclosing powers of ordinary language.

A more fruitful strategy, Bohman suggests, is to view disclosure as a mode of second-order communication or discourse in which the constraints and pressures of action-coordination are suspended in order to test the underlying claims to validity of any first-order communication. Such virtualization of action constraints in discourse is part of the reflective capacities of competent speakers, rather than the exclusive prerogative of art or poetry. Once disclosure is reformulated as a mode of reflective language use employed in second-order communication, and operating in all cultural domains (science, morality, art), it is possible to assimilate it to the role of rhetoric in communication. Like rhetoric, disclosure can play a reflective role in overcoming rigid cultural interpretations and in articulating new ones. It may overcome stalled learning processes or problem-solving capacities by showing new ways of looking at things and new patterns of relevance. In this respect, disclosure (like rhetoric) is about relevant meanings and novel interpretations, rather than truth; it concerns the reflective capacities of agents to transform their cultural context, rather than being an epochal experience to which we have passively to submit.

Bohman then introduces a second important reformulation of the notion of world-disclosure. He argues that, once it is properly reformulated as a hermeneutic theory of truth candidates, Foucault's notion of discursive formation or *episteme* can fruitfully account for genuine differences among the plurality of cultural worlds and historical epochs in which different statements are candidates for truth. The problem of hermeneutic failure that arises in historical and cross-cultural comparison can be partially overcome once we acknowledge that within the meaning horizon of a particular discursive formation there may be, in Ian Hacking's phrase, 'whole other categories of truth-and-falsehood than ours'. In such cases, interpretation requires understanding not what others think is actually true, but what they hold to be possibly true-or-false. Such a reformulation of the notion of disclosure as a hermeneutic theory of truth candidates also makes clear how our interpretations can come to a standstill in solving problems: the solution to a problem is not even a candidate solution, since it cannot be disclosed in a particular cultural context as either true or false. In such cases what are needed are 'new styles of reasoning' or new paradigms which introduce new sentences, that is, new candidates for truth. By being directed to creating new possibilities for truth, novel disclosures can change the conditions under which we make true or false statements about the world and ourselves. They also allow us to change the conditions for possible action. Suitably reinterpreted, the concept of world-disclosure can therefore account for the possibility of freedom and innovation, and restore a sense to the idea of transformative agency.

The question of the place of the aesthetic in modern and postmodern discourses is broached in Diana Coole's 'Habermas and the Question of Alterity'. She notes at the outset that Habermas's hostility to the discourse of postmodernism can be explained in terms of its appeal to alterity. For Habermas, such an appeal appears irrational, anachronistic and out of step with history's evolution. Rather than opening up the field of the prediscursive and non-rational to conscious self-reflection, the discourse of postmodernism ends up retreating into antimodernism, the archaic, the primordial. Whether couched in terms of Nietzsche's appeal to Dionysian frenzy, Heidegger's evocation of Being, Bataille's notion of heterogeneity, Derrida's archewriting or Foucault's concept of power, the discourse of postmodernism fails to provide a plausible vision or criterion of emancipation, and thus cannot be acknowledged as a radical or progressive discourse. Coole's paper attempts to undermine such a negative characterization of postmodernism, to show the positive role that appeals to alterity might play within modernity, and to suggest that a politics supplementary to discursive democracy, based on aesthetic strategies of intervention and an openness to the Other, is both necessary and desirable.

According to Coole, alterity is invoked by practices which can be broadly characterized as aesthetic, which communicate a meaning lying behind or beyond rational discourse. To be sure, such practices can be reflected upon and discussed using rational argument and specialized discourses. In this respect, advocates of alterity tend to employ both aesthetic means (which may be linguistic or non-linguistic) and philosophical or reflective discourses. Even in the case of language and discourse, however, they stress the limits of what can be rationally said. For otherness cannot be translated into rational discourse without remainder or loss, while discursive forms always retain within themselves opaque and ambiguous dimensions of meaning.

The otherness invoked by postmodernists is not an ontological or metaphysical principle. Rather, it alludes to another order characterized by mobility, fluidity, heterogeneity, by the loss of stability, certainty and closure. Its invocation is meant to subvert the rationalizing project of modernity, not through a retreat to the irrational or the archaic, but in order to reveal the limits of reason and the violence it imposes when it aims to make everything knowable, communicable, transparent. The invocation of alterity is meant to alert us to processes of exclusion, marginalization, silencing and repression that operate inconspicuously within the apparently neutral attempt to articulate meaning and to rationally reflect upon it. Postmodernists such as Derrida or psychoanalytic thinkers such as Kristeva do not see themselves pursuing an alternative to reason, but want to open up the rational to those voices it has excluded or cannot accommodate. They do not attempt to set up a reason/unreason dichotomy in order to invert it, but to play along and transgress its boundaries, so as to allow the non-rational to destabilize reason without replacing it. For Coole, it is the subversive thrust of this process that renders postmodernism political.

The political is here associated with relations of power, especially those operating at a prediscursive level. Aesthetic practices intervene at this level, opening up dimensions immune to rational discourse and challenging representations that reproduce relations of privilege and exclusion. Modernity cannot turn its back on this politics, since it operates beneath and within processes of rational negotiation, where it affects the competencies of actors to participate as free and equal beings in democratic deliberation, as well as protecting the lifeworld from rationalistic closure.

Coole then goes on to consider two examples which highlight the political implications of excluding alterity. First, as feminists and the romantic tradition have stressed, the dominant Western attitude to knowledge has tended to suppress the body and emotions, feelings and desires, imagination and the unconscious. This suppression of the non-discursive is both culturally impoverishing and overestimates reason's capacity to render everything reflective and transparent. Invocations of alterity might be politically significant in opening up meaning and disrupting reason's closure. Second, the exclusion of otherness affects those groups associated with it, such as women, blacks, gays, lesbians, and members of ethnic and religious minorities. These groups are marginalized, yet the mechanisms of exclusion remain largely prediscursive. Since such mechanisms are still operative within modernity, a politics supplementary to the formal procedures of discourse ethics is required. This politics would be associated both with an openness to be invoked and a closure to be subverted. It would be broadly synonymous with the non-rational, the pre- or non-discursive, with that which cannot conclusively be reflected upon or subjected to formal validity claims.

After reviewing the contributions of Merleau-Ponty and Kristeva to an understanding of language and the lifeworld as infused with alterity, Coole goes on to examine what happens at a lifeworld level prior to its discursive retrieval. Are there not power relations operative at this level, and by implication a certain politics, which cannot be reflectively mediated and are thus not amenable to discursive redemption? There are two dimensions of this type of prediscursive power which call for attention. The first concerns the translation of meaning from the prereflective level of the lifeworld to the level of discursive articulation. The second concerns those processes which remain prediscursive even in modernity. With respect to the passage from the prediscursive to the discursive, it cannot be characterized simply as a rational process occurring by communicative means, but a process, as Foucault has argued, wherein certain themes or persons are silenced, constituted, displaced or normalized. With respect to the persistence of the prediscursive within modernity, it is not the case that actors enjoy an absolute freedom: they may indeed reproduce the lifeworld through language, but they remain products of their traditions, norms and socialization patterns. If communication opens up traditions, it too has its limits in 'the implicit, the prepredicative, the not focally present background of the lifeworld' (*PDM*, p. 300).

It is here that processes are at work through which subjects are constituted prior to their participation in communicative action and discourse. Such processes have inscribed within them forms of power that engender and exclude alterity and the life forms associated with it. Those who are defined as other are those who do not share modernity's dominant hierarchy between mind and body, conscious and unconscious, reason and non-reason, culture and nature. The empowering of such marginalized groups is one aspect of postmodernists' democratic impulse, which is closely linked to their attempt to subvert the dominant hierarchies on which exclusions of alterity rest. Thus, as well as mobilizing those voices that modernity silences, postmodernists engage in aesthetic practices that transgress the boundary between reason and non-reason, in order to resist the suppression of alterity and allow for the full recognition of the other. As examples of such practices Coole cites the work of Iris Young, Julia Kristeva and feminist art criticism, whose aim is to alert us to the unconscious mechanisms at work in the construction of the other, and to subvert the cultural dualisms on which fear and exclusion of the other are predicated.

Having shown the significance of alterity and the political import of postmodern aesthetic strategies, Coole turns in the final part of her chapter to a detailed examination of Habermas's theory, to show how it is biased against alterity. Focusing on Habermas's accounts of language, the lifeworld, history and subjectivity, Coole shows how in each case there is an exclusion of otherness springing from Habermas's rationalist proclivity. In the case of language, there is little acknowledgement of the ruptures, absences and deferrals at the heart of ordinary language that both derail and enrich attempts at mutual understanding. In the case of the lifeworld, there is nothing in principle which resists thematization, no unredeemable otherness, nothing resistant to linguistification. The same goes for the subject: there is nothing in principle immune to reflection, no structured unconscious, no primary repression or resistance. There is no alternative psychic economy with a logic of its own unamenable to discursive self-reflection. As for history, its logic of development appears to eliminate any otherness that, under the name of the sacred, is associated with premodern life forms and that still pervades modern ones. Rather than a dichotomy modern/premodern, profane and sacred, we should acknowledge more of a continuum and an interweaving of the two.

Habermas has more recently come to recognize the role of alterity within modern life forms, which he identifies with aesthetic experience and avant-garde art. Once the experience of art is related to one's own life problems, it enters into a different language game: '[it] not only revitalizes those need interpretations in the light of which we perceive our world, but also influences our cognitive interpretations and our normative expectations, and thus alters the way in which all these moments *refer back and forth* to one another.'[16] Yet there is still a sense in which such aesthetic experiences are valued by Habermas more for their reintegrative and harmonious qualities than for their disruptive and sublime ones. He is therefore unable to acknowledge the political relevance of postmodern and avant-garde aesthetic practices which subvert reason's closures and open up the domain of alterity.

In 'The Causality of Fate: Modernity and Modernism in Habermas', Jay Bernstein critically interrogates Habermas's defence of modern reason. He notices at the outset that for Habermas rationalization involves both a real increment in rationality and a distortion of reason. The increment in rationality can be seen in the progressive, if always precarious, extension of communicative rationality in the various life spheres of modern societies, while the distortion of reason is the outcome of an illegitimate intrusion of subject-centred reason into a communicatively structured lifeworld. The question that is immediately raised is whether communicative rationality, as Habermas conceives it, is not itself a product of subject-centred reason, and, therefore, a distortion of reason. Could we envisage a form of reason that is neither subject-centred nor communicative, as Habermas understands these terms? Are not the claims of art and aesthetic judgement an intimation of a comprehensive reason that goes beyond the fateful dialectic of subject-centred versus communicative reason?

These questions, going to the heart of Habermas's project, can be answered in the affirmative only by probing deeply into the claims of artistic modernism and the 'extraordinary discourse' of philosophical modernism. Bernstein argues that the claim of aesthetic autonomy embodied in modernist art finds its philosophical analogue in those discourses, such as Derrida's grammatology, Foucault's theory of power, or Adorno's aesthetic theory, that attempt to account for the 'other' of reason in terms, respectively, of *différance*, the non-verbalizable language of the body, the non-identical. *Contra* Habermas, these discourses do not operate outside the horizon of reason, but represent an attempt to articulate a conception of reason more comprehensive than either subject-centred reason or a procedurally conceived communicative reason. Such discourses are the expression of a concern to avoid the silencing of local reason, of sensuous particularity, of discriminating judgement. They attempt to secure for themselves the kind of autonomy from given epistemic or normative conventions that had been the prerogative of modernist art. Like artistic modernism, however, the discourse of philosophical modernism is confronted with an aporia: it can say what it wants to say only by *not saying it*. Since it tries to speak to those experiences that have been silenced or marginalized by modern reason, its speech is paradoxical and aporetic.

Still, there are important claims being made in such discourse, and these claims are simultaneously cognitive, moral and aesthetic. We can begin to understand the claims of philosophical modernism by questioning the strict separation or diremption of modern reason in three mutually antagonistic and exclusive components. Such a diremption has in fact resulted in a distortion: once aesthetic judgement achieved its autonomy vis-à-vis the moral and the cognitive, it became evident that its autonomy entailed a distortion of its claims as well as of those of knowledge and morality. The separation of aesthetic judgement from considerations of truth and rightness was effectively a silencing of the claims of comprehensive reason.

To support this critical reading of the diremption of modern reason, Bernstein turns to Habermas's powerful evocation of the Hegelian motif of the causality of fate. Drawing on Hegel's example of the criminal and his punishment in 'The Spirit of Christianity and Its Fate', Habermas describes the operation of the causality of fate as the fateful dynamic that results from the disruption of a presupposed ethical totality. He writes:

> A criminal who disturbs such ethical relationships by encroaching upon and oppressing the life of another, experiences the power of the life alienated by his deed as a hostile fate . . . In this causality of fate the ruptured bond of the ethical totality is brought to consciousness. This diremted totality can become reconciled only when there arises from the experience of the negativity of divided life a longing for the life that has been lost. (*PDM*, pp. 28–9)

The dynamic of fate originates from the disruption of the conditions of symmetry and reciprocity that characterize an intersubjectively constituted life context. And, as Habermas pointedly remarks, 'this act of tearing loose from an intersubjectively shared lifeworld is what first *generates* a subject–object relationship. It is introduced as an alien element . . . into relationships that by nature follow the structure of mutual understanding among subjects' (*PDM*, p. 29).

According to Bernstein, the criminal act that sets the operation of the causality of fate into motion can be seen as the cypher of the categorial deformation of the ethical totality in modernity. By radically separating the three domains of validity (truth, rightness, authenticity) that are unmetaphorically intermeshed in the lifeworld, rationalization processes have distorted the substantive unity of reason. The claims of comprehensive reason have been, thereby, effectively silenced. More crucially, by being subjected to the imperious claims of subject-centred reason, the communicative structures of the lifeworld, resting on the fragile bond of mutual understanding and reciprocal recognition, have been disrupted and deformed. In such case, Habermas points out, the avenging force of the causality of fate manifests itself indirectly, that is, in symptomatic and displaced ways: the act of diremption is experienced in the end as a collective act, 'an involuntary product of an entanglement that, however things stand with individual accountability, communicative agents would have to ascribe to communal responsibility' (*PDM*, p. 316). Thus it is only in the act of becoming aware of our collective responsibility that we come to recognize that 'any violation of the structures of rational life together, to which all lay claim, affects everyone equally' (*PDM*, p. 324).

Habermas's suggestive reworking of the model of the causality of fate stands, however, in deep tension with his attempt to secure quasi-transcendental grounds for his theory of communicative rationality. According to Bernstein, there is a real incommensurability between the transcendental claims of communicative reason and the logic of the causality of fate. The claims of others to intersubjective recognition register as claims not by virtue of transcendental necessity, but only in so far as we *already recognize them as other selves*. Communicative reason can express this recognition once made, but cannot *ground* it. If the force of the ethical totality could be grounded in universal norms, becoming thus an obligation binding everyone equally, there would be no avenging force acting back upon the subject. That there is such a force, however defused and displaced, is a mark of the resilience, the stubborn power, of the claims of the lifeworld, which Hegel thematized under the names of recognition, love and life.

In 'The Subject of Justice in Postmodern Discourse', David Ingram critically evaluates the contrasting theories of language and politics of Habermas and Lyotard. He characterizes the thinking of both authors as neo-Kantian, in so far as both are attempting to confront the modern diremption of reason and the increasing differentiation of value spheres and cultural lifeworlds by means of a critical rationalism that eschews Hegelian dialectic and the claim to absolute or final reconciliation. Habermas and Lyotard, however, diverge with respect to their conceptions of justice and legitimacy, the former arguing that justice is grounded in a universal consensus whose legitimacy can be derived from the norms of rational speech, the latter arguing that consensus and the primacy of rational speeech are inherently totalitarian and that justice and legitimacy consist in the proliferation of new vocabularies, the plurality of small narratives and the assertion of difference. Rather than simply disputing the disagreement between Habermas and Lyotard over questions of justice and legitimacy, Ingram focuses on the underlying agreement with respect to their assessment of the pathological manifestations of modernity and their shared appeal to Kant's notion of aesthetic judgement. Both thinkers believe that the pluralizing dynamics of cultural rationalization encourage forms of specialization that threaten to impoverish lay persons' capacities for autonomous moral reflection. Both also maintain that the dynamics of societal rationalization in capitalistically modernized societies encourage the one-sided expansion of cognitive-instrumental rationality at the expense of the moral-practical and the aesthetic-expressive. Criticism of such one-sidedness and imbalances requires *clinical judgements* by philosophers and lay actors regarding the proper harmony between different types of rationality, domains of validity, and institutionalized action-systems. The model for such clinical judgements is found, for both Habermas and Lyotard, in Kant's notion of aesthetic judgement. Given that such judgements mediate between conflicting types of rationality, they cannot be discursively demonstrated by way of rational argumentation. Rather, they can be indirectly shown to be valid by appeal to more global intuitions and 'ways of seeing' that feel *authentic* to us.

Habermas's defence of modernity is based on the rejection of the philosophy of consciousness which privileges the cognitive-instrumental relation of subjects to the world, in favour of a pragmatic theory of language which privileges the intersubjective relation between actors attained through mutual understanding. By viewing communicative understanding as a process involving the raising and testing of validity claims in the three domains of validity (science, morality, art), Habermas is able to identify a universal core of communicative rationality. Such a universal core, or what Habermas calls the 'procedural unity of reason', enables him to rebut both the Weberian-inspired value relativism of contemporary ethics and the postmodern scepticism of 'grand narratives'. Moreover, since communicative rationality is based on the free interplay of cognitive with moral-practical and aesthetic-expressive elements, Habermas is able to criticize the one-sided growth of instrumental rationality and the systemically induced phenomenon of reification.

Yet, according to Ingram, there are residual problems concerning the procedural unity of reason that Habermas has not satisfactorily answered. To begin with, even if we accept Habermas's claim that there are three types of validity claim that accompany every speech act, to which there correspond three distinct forms of argumentation (theoretical and practical discourse with respect to truth and moral rightness, aesthetic criticism and therapeutic critique with respect to authenticity and sincerity), there remain significant differences between these forms of argumentation. These are in respect to the *scope* of the anticipated consensus (only in theoretical and practical discourse do participants raise universal validity claims and can thereby aim at a universal consensus), and the *moral symmetry* of the interlocutors (which can be achieved at best in theoretical and practical discourse, but cannot be presumed to obtain in therapeutic critique). Secondly, consensus might not be a necessary feature or aim of practical discourse, whether moral or political. Drawing on Albrecht Wellmer's critique of discourse ethics, Ingram argues that moral reasoning does not primarily involve justifying moral rules, but rather *exceptions* to rules that are usually taken for granted. The reasoning employed in morally dilemmatic situations will always reflect a unique constellation of factors and a unique set of personal circumstances. A similar objection applies to political discourse. Even though one might agree with Habermas that participants in political discourse ought to seek consensus, consensus is not a necessary or sufficient criterion of legitimacy. Rather, as Habermas himself has acknowledged, the legitimacy of a law or of an act of public policy is based on the fairness of the *procedures* through which it is enacted and ratified. Moreover, even when a political consensus is reached, it is often of a different kind from that reached in theoretical discourse among scientists. Unlike scientists, citizens may agree to a specific proposal for different reasons, and what appears to be common linguistic usage often conceals deeper disagreements rooted in incompatible world-views (as in the debate on abortion).

Although Habermas has acknowledged some of these problems in his recent work, *Between Facts and Norms*,[17] we are still left with the question of whether his theory of argumentation provides an adequate normative basis for the critique of reification and the closely related phenomenon of cultural impoverishment. According to Habermas, criticism of reification involves a clinical judgement of *health*, that is, of the equilibrated interplay of the cognitive with the moral-practical and the aesthetic-expressive elements required for the attainment of well-integrated identities. Since Habermas is not able to show that health is a rationally defensible value on a par with truth, justice and sincerity (health is a specific *value content* 'that is by no means internally connected with one of the universal validity claims'[18]), he is forced to appeal to the notion of 'aesthetic truth' in order to redeem his normative critique of reification. How does such an appeal work? The argument, briefly put, is as follows. According to Habermas, works of art function simultaneously as arguments and as idealized anticipations of integral experience. The 'truth' disclosed by works of art, Habermas writes,

> reaches into our cognitive interpretations and normative expectations and transforms the totality in which these moments are related to each other. In this respect, modern art harbours a utopia that becomes a reality to the degree that the mimetic powers sublimated in the work of art find resonance in the mimetic relations of a balanced and undistorted intersubjectivity of everyday life.[19]

Moreover, in *The Philosophical Discourse of Modernity* Habermas links the mimetic disclosure of such a balanced utopia to Kant's notion of aesthetic judgement. In Schiller's appropriation of this notion, 'art operates as a catalyst, as a form of communication, as a medium within which separated moments are rejoined into an uncoerced totality' (*PDM*, p. 50). Art therefore offers a presentiment or prefiguration of a harmonious life experience which can serve as an intuitive yardstick in our clinical judgements on the pathologies caused by reification. However, as Habermas notes, the validity claim associated with the world-disclosing power of art 'stands for a *potential* for "truth" that can be released only in the whole complexity of life-experience'. As such, 'it may not be connected to (or even identified with) just one of the three validity claims constitutive for communicative action.'[20] On the contrary, since works of art symbolize a lifeworld experience in which the three validity claims are unmetaphorically intermeshed, their own truth can only be *metaphorical*. In this respect, Ingram notes, the rationale underlying the claim to aesthetic truth is not simply discursive or argumentative, but is rhetorically compelling in some experiential or intuitive sense. By the same token, the judgement of health and harmony regarding the global well-being of an identity, individual or collective, is only convincing to the extent that it brings agreement in feelings and experiences as well as agreement in judgements (the agreement must thus be intuitively as well as cognitively compelling).

Habermas's appeal to the idea of aesthetic truth as a prefiguration of the harmonious integration of different aspects of rationality and validity has been challenged by Lyotard. He has aptly observed that in Kant's *Critique of Judgement* aesthetic ideas can symbolize sublime incommensurability as well as beautiful harmony. He writes:

> Is the aim of the project of modernity the constitution of sociocultural unity within which all the elements of daily life and of thought would take their places as in an organic whole? Or does the passage that has to be charted between heterogeneous language games – those of cognition, of ethics, of politics – belong to a different order from that? And if so, would it be capable of effecting a real synthesis between them?[21]

As is well known, Lyotard stresses the incommensurability of language games as well as the unconventional, agonistic inventiveness of 'moves' that can be made within them. He argues that there is no metalanguage that can act as a bridge between different languages, no *grand récit* that can mediate between different narratives, since each language, each discourse, is a discrete and self-contained semantic universe. Moreover, he departs from Wittgenstein in conceiving language games as essentially resting on a contest, a *différend*, with each player introducing new moves, rather than on consensus and convention.

However, as Ingram points out, Lyotard's scepticism towards

metanarratives and his linguistic anarchism are qualified by his recourse to the faculty of judgement. Judgement enables one to decide the rightful boundaries separating different discourses and language games. But how can judgement adjudicate boundary disputes between incommensurable language games? Like Habermas, Lyotard looks for an answer in Kant's theory of aesthetic judgement, but finds it, unlike Habermas, in Kant's account of judgements of the sublime rather than the beautiful. Like judgements of beauty, judgements of sublimity are grounded in the experience of pleasure arising from the free interplay of incommensurable faculties (imagination and understanding in the case of judgements of beauty; imagination and reason in the case of judgements of the sublime). However, the pleasure associated with the sublime is mixed with pain, owing to the complexity of the judgement in question. Unlike judgements of beauty, in which the imagination apprehends a formal representation that is in harmony with the understanding, the imagination here apprehends a representation so unlimited and exceeding all form that it discloses not the harmony, but the disharmony between imagination and reason. Yet judgements of sublimity also reflect a harmony between our finite capacities and our infinite power of transcendence in a manner which is analogous to the painful/pleasurable feeling of moral respect.

It is this simultaneous presence of harmony and disharmony, pleasure and pain, in judgements of sublimity, emblematic of the kind of metaphorical linkages connecting literally incommensurable language games – in this case those of aesthetics and morality – that Lyotard finds so appealing and instructive. For him, the judgement dispensed by the critical philosopher mediates abstract ideas and concrete intuitions and metaphorically links the diverse genres of discourse, but not with prescriptive authority. It is like the judgement dispensed by Kant's guardian in *The Conflict of the Faculties*, which – according to Lyotard – listens for the silences that betoken injustice (*différend*) so as to let the suppressed or excluded voice find its proper idiom within a community of discourse. The judgement that issues in justice thus attempts to rescue, as Habermas himself has put it in a recent comment on Lyotard's *Le Différend*, 'moments of the non-identical and the non-integrated, the deviant and the heterogeneous, the contradictory and the conflictual'.[22] Such judgement allows new and unconventional idioms to flourish and reminds us of the injustices that accompany every attempt to silence the voice of the other.

NOTES

1 Originally Jürgen Habermas, *Der philosophische Diskurs der Moderne: Zwölf Vorlesungen* (Frankfurt am Main: Suhrkamp, 1985); in English as

The Philosophical Discourse of Modernity: Twelve Lectures, trans. Frederick G. Lawrence (Cambridge: Polity Press; Cambridge, Mass: MIT Press, 1987), hereafter abbreviated as *PDM*. All citations in brackets in the text refer to the English translation.

2 Originally Jürgen Habermas, *Theorie des kommunikativen Handelns*, vol. 1: *Handlungsrationalität und gesellschaftliche Rationalisierung*; vol. 2: *Zur Kritik der funktionalistischen Vernunft* (Frankfurt am Main: Suhrkamp, 1981); in English as *The Theory of Communicative Action*, vol 1: *Reason and the Rationalization of Society*; vol. 2: *Lifeworld and System: A Critique of Functionalist Reason*, both vols trans. Thomas McCarthy (Cambridge: Polity Press; Boston: Beacon Press, 1984 and 1987).

3 To borrow from the title of a well-known book by Hans Blumenberg, *The Legitimacy of the Modern Age*, trans. Robert M. Wallace (Cambridge, Mass: MIT Press, 1983).

4 See Stephen K. White, *Political Theory and Postmodernism* (Cambridge: Cambridge University Press, 1991), pp. 19–23.

5 For a brilliant articulation of this position, see William E. Connolly, *Politics and Ambiguity* (Madison: University of Wisconsin Press, 1987); *Identity/Difference: Democratic Negotiations of Political Paradox* (Ithaca and London: Cornell University Press, 1991). For a sophisticated response to the postmodernist stance, see Thomas McCarthy, *Ideals and Illusions: On Reconstruction and Deconstruction in Contemporary Critical Theory* (Cambridge: Polity Press; Cambridge, Mass.: MIT Press, 1991); Richard J. Bernstein, *The New Constellation: The Ethical-Political Horizons of Modernity/Postmodernity* (Cambridge: Polity Press; Cambridge, Mass.: MIT Press, 1991); Seyla Benhabib, *Situating the Self: Gender, Community and Postmodernism in Contemporary Ethics* (Cambridge: Polity Press; New York: Routledge, 1992).

6 Habermas, for example, does acknowledge the constitutive function of language as world-disclosure, while Derrida recognizes the crucial role of language as a mechanism of action-coordination. For a discussion of the tension between these two conceptions of language, see chapter 7 below.

7 In this essay Habermas outlines some of the main arguments at stake in the modernity/postmodernity debate that will subsequently receive much fuller articulation in *The Philosophical Discourse of Modernity*. Although the chapters in this book engage primarily with the latter work, Habermas's 1981 essay represents the best succinct statement of his position in the debate.

8 See p. 44 below.

9 See pp. 52–3 below.

10 As Habermas puts it: 'With this concept of the absolute, Hegel regresses back behind the intuitions of his youthful period. He conceives the overcoming of subjectivity within the boundaries of a philosophy of the subject' (*PDM*, p. 22).

11 See *PDM*, pp. 93–4.

12 J. Searle, 'Reiterating the Differences', *Glyph* 1 (1977), pp. 172–208; and Derrida's response, 'Limited Inc. abc', *Glyph* 2 (1977), pp. 162–254.

13 For an extended discussion of these features of postmodernism, see also D. Hoy, 'Foucault: Modern or Postmodern?', in J. Arac (ed.), *After Foucault: Humanistic Knowledge, Postmodern Challenges* (New Brunswick: Rutgers University Press, 1988).

14 C. Castoriadis, *The Imaginary Institution of Society*, trans Kathleen Blamey (Cambridge: Polity Press; Cambridge, Mass.: MIT Press, 1987), p. 290.

15 Ibid., pp. 298, 301.

16 See p. 51 below.

17 Originally Jürgen Habermas, *Faktizität und Geltung: Beiträge zur Diskurstheorie des Rechts und des demokratischen Rechsstaats* (Frankfurt am Main: Suhrkamp, 1992); in English as *Between Facts and Norms: Contributions to a Discourse Theory of Law and Democracy*, trans. William Rehg (Cambridge: Polity Press; Cambridge, Mass.: MIT Press, 1996).

18 Habermas, *The Theory of Communicative Action*, vol. 1, pp. 252–3.

19 Jürgen Habermas, 'Questions and Counterquestions', in R. Bernstein (ed.), *Habermas and Modernity* (Cambridge: Polity Press, 1985), p. 202.

20 Ibid., p. 203.

21 Jean-François Lyotard, *The Postmodern Condition: A Report on Knowledge*, trans. G. Bennington and B. Massumi (Minneapolis: University of Minnesota Press, 1984), pp. 72–3.

22 Jürgen Habermas, *Nachmetaphysisches Denken* (Frankfurt am Main: Suhrkamp, 1988), p. 153; in English as *Postmetaphysical Thinking*, trans. W. M. Hohengarten (Cambridge: Polity Press; Cambridge, Mass.: MIT Press, 1992), pp. 115–16.

1

MODERNITY:
AN UNFINISHED PROJECT

Jürgen Habermas

Following the painters and the film-makers, the architects have now been admitted to the Venice Biennale as well. The response to this, the first architecture Biennale, was one of disappointment. The participants who exhibited in Venice formed an avant-garde with the fronts reversed. Under the slogan of 'the presence of the past' they sacrificed the tradition of modernity in the name of a new species of historicism: 'The fact that the entire modern movement was sustained through its engagement with the past, that Frank Lloyd Wright would be inconceivable without Japan, Le Corbusier without classical antiquity and Mediterranean architecture, and Mies van der Rohe without Schinkel and Behrens, all this is passed over in silence.' With this remark W. Pehnt, the critic on the *Frankfurter Allgemeine Zeitung*, supports his claim, one which provides a significant diagnosis of our times over and beyond its initial occasion: 'Postmodernity decisively presents itself as a form of Antimodernity.'[1]

This claim holds for an affective trend which has seeped into the pores of every intellectual domain and given rise to various theories of post-Enlightenment, of postmodernity, of post-history and so forth, in short to a new kind of conservatism. Adorno and his work stand in marked contrast to this trend.

So unreservedly did Adorno subscribe to the spirit of modernity that in the very attempt to distinguish authentic modernity from mere modernism he quickly sensed the affective response to the affront of modernity itself. It may not therefore be an entirely inappropriate way of expressing my gratitude for receiving the Adorno Prize if I pursue the question concerning the current attitude with respect to modernity. Is modernity as *passé* as the postmodernists argue? Or is the widely trumpeted arrival of postmodernity itself 'phony'? Is 'postmodern' a slogan which unobtrusively inherits the affective attitudes which cultural modernity has provoked in reaction to itself since the middle of the nineteenth century?

The Old and the New

Anyone who, like Adorno, conceives of 'modernity' as beginning around 1850 is perceiving it through the eyes of Baudelaire and avant-garde art. Let me elucidate this concept of cultural modernity with a brief look at its long prehistory, which has already been illuminated by Hans Robert Jausse.[2] The word 'modern' was first employed in the late fifth century in order to distinguish the present, now officially Christian, from the pagan and Roman past. With a different content in each case, the expression 'modernity' repeatedly articulates the consciousness of an era that refers back to the past of classical antiquity precisely in order to comprehend itself as the result of a transition from the old to the new. This is not merely true for the Renaissance, with which the 'modern age' begins *for us*; people also considered themselves as 'modern' in the age of Charlemagne, in the twelfth century, and in the Enlightenment – in short, whenever the consciousness of a new era developed in Europe through a renewed relationship to classical antiquity. In the process culminating in the celebrated *querelle des anciens et des modernes*, the dispute with the protagonists of a classicistic aesthetic taste in late seventeenth-century France, it was always *antiquitas*, the classical world, which was regarded as the normative model to be imitated. It was only the French Enlightenment's ideal of perfection and the idea, inspired by modern science, of the infinite progress of knowledge and the advance towards social and moral improvement that gradually lifted the spell exercised on the spirit of these *early* moderns by the classical works of antiquity. And finally, in opposing the classical and the romantic to one another, modernity sought its own past in an idealized vision of the Middle Ages. In the course of the nineteenth century *this* Romanticism produced a radicalized consciousness of modernity that detached itself from all previous historical connection and understood itself solely in abstract opposition to tradition and history as a whole.

At this juncture, what was considered modern was what assisted the spontaneously self-renewing historical contemporaneity of the *Zeitgeist* to find its own objective expression. The characteristic feature of such works is the moment of novelty, the New, which will itself be surpassed and devalued in turn by the innovations of the next style. Yet whereas the merely modish becomes outmoded once it is displaced into the past, the modern still retains a secret connection to the classical. The 'classical' has always signified that which endures through the ages. The emphatically 'modern' artistic product no longer derives its power from the authority of a past age, but owes it solely to the authenticity of a contemporary relevance that has now become past. This transformation of contemporary relevance into a relevance now past has both a destructive and a constructive aspect. As Jauss has observed, it is modernity itself that creates its own classical status – thus we can speak today of 'classical modernity' as if such an expression were obvious. Adorno opposes any attempted distinction between 'modernity' and 'modernism' because he believes that 'without the characteristic subjective mentality inspired by the New no objective modernity can crystallize at all.'[3]

The Mentality of Aesthetic Modernity

The mentality of aesthetic modernity begins to take shape clearly with Baudelaire and with his theory of art, influenced as it was by Edgar Allan Poe. It then unfolded in the avant-garde artistic movements and finally attained its zenith with surrealism and the Dadaists of the Café Voltaire. This mentality is characterized by a set of attitudes which developed around a transformed consciousness of time. It is this consciousness that expresses itself in the spatial metaphor of the avant-garde – that is, an avant-garde that explores hitherto unknown territory, exposes itself to the risk of sudden and shocking encounters, conquers an as yet undetermined future, and must therefore find a path for itself in previously uncharted domains. But this forward orientation, this anticipation of an indefinite and contingent future, the cult of the New which accompanies it, all this actually signifies the glorification of a contemporariness that repeatedly gives birth to new and subjectively defined pasts. This new consciousness of time, which also found its way into philosophy with Bergson, expresses more than the experience of a mobilized society, of an accelerated history, of the disruption of everyday life. The new value which is now accorded to the ephemeral, the momentary and the transitory, and the concomitant celebration of dynamism, expresses precisely the yearning for a lasting and immaculate present. As a self-negating movement, modernism is a 'yearning for true presence'. This, according to Octavio Paz, 'is the secret theme of the finest modernist writers.'[4]

This also explains the abstract opposition of modernism to history, which thus forfeits the structure of an articulated process of cultural transmission ensuring continuity. Individual epochs lose their own distinctive features, and the present now assumes a heroic affinity either with what is most remote or what is closest to it: decadence recognizes itself immediately in the barbaric, the wild and the primitive. The anarchistic intention of exploding the continuum of history accounts for the subversive force of an aesthetic consciousness which rebels against the norm-giving achievements of tradition, which is nourished on the experience of rebellion against everything normative, which neutralizes considerations of moral goodness or practical utility, a consciousness which continually stages a dialectic of esoteric mystery and scandalous offence, narcotically fascinated by the fright produced by its acts of profanation – and yet at the same time flees from the trivialization resulting from that very profanation. That is why for Adorno

> the wounds inflicted by disruption represent the seal of authen-ticity for modernity, the very thing through which modernity desperately negates the closed character of the eternally invariant; the act of explosion is itself one of the invariants of modernity. The zeal directed against the tradition becomes a devouring maelstrom. In this sense modernity is myth turned against itself; the timelessness of myth becomes the catastrophe of the moment which disrupts all temporal continuity.[5]

The consciousness of time articulated in avant-garde art is not simply an antihistorical one, of course. For it is directed only against the false normativity of a historical understanding essentially oriented towards the imitation of past models, something which has not been entirely eliminated even in Gadamer's philosophical hermeneutics. This time-consciousness avails itself of the objectified pasts made available by historical scholarship, but it simultaneously rebels against that neutralization of criteria practised by a historicism which relegates history to the museum. It is in the same rebellious spirit that Walter Benjamin attempted to construe the relation of modernity to history in a *posthistorical* manner. He recalls the way in which the French Revolution conceived of itself: 'It evoked ancient Rome much as fashion evokes the costumes of the past. Fashion shows a flair for the topical, no matter where it stirs in the thickets of long ago.' And just as for Robespierre ancient Rome represented a past charged with 'nowness', so too the historian has to grasp the constellation 'into which his or her own era has entered with a particular earlier one'. This is how Benjamin grounds his concept of 'the present as the "time of the now" which is shot through with splinters of Messianic time'.[6]

This spirit of aesthetic modernity has aged since Benjamin's time. During the 1960s it was, of course, rehearsed once more. But with the 1970s now behind us, we have to confess that modernism finds almost no resonance today. Even during the 1960s Octavio Paz, a partisan for modernity, observed with some sadness that 'the avant-garde of 1967 repeats the deeds and the gestures of the avant-garde of 1917. We are witnessing the end of the idea of modern art.'[7] In the wake of Peter Bürger's work we now speak of post-avant-garde art, an expression that acknowledges the failure of the surrealist rebellion. Yet what is the significance of this failure? Does it indicate the demise of modernity? Does the post-avant-garde imply a transition to postmodernity?

In fact this is precisely how Daniel Bell, a well-known social theorist and the most brilliant of the American neoconservative thinkers, understands the situation. In an interesting book[8] Bell has developed the thesis that the crisis manifested in advanced Western societies can be traced back to the bifurcation between culture and society, between cultural modernity and the demands of the economic and administrative systems. Avant-garde art has supposedly penetrated the values of everyday life and thus infected the lifeworld with the modernist mentality. Modernism represents a great seductive force, promoting the dominance of the principle of unrestrained self-realization, the demand for authentic self-experience, the subjectivism of an overstimulated sensibility, and the release of hedonistic motivations quite incompatible with the discipline required by professional life, and with the moral foundations of a purposive-rational mode of life generally. Thus, like Arnold Gehlen in Germany, Bell locates the blame for the dissolution of the Protestant ethic, something which had already disturbed Max Weber, with an 'adversary culture', that is, with a culture whose modernism encourages hostility to the conventions and the values of everyday life as rationalized under economic and administrative imperatives.

Yet, on the other hand, this same reading claims that the impulse of modernity has definitely exhausted itself and that the avant-garde has run its course; although still propagated, the latter supposedly no longer represents a creative force. Thus the question which concerns neoconservatism is how to establish norms that will restrain libertinism, restore discipline and the work ethic, and promote the virtues of individual competitiveness against the levelling effects of the welfare state. The only solution envisaged by Bell is some kind of religious renewal that would link up with quasi-naturally given traditions which are immune to criticism, which allow for the emergence of clearly defined identities, and which procure some existential sense of security for the individual.

Cultural Modernity and Social Modernization

Of course, it is not possible simply to conjure up authoritative beliefs from nowhere. That is why analyses of this kind only give rise, as the sole practical recommendation, to the sort of postulate we have also seen in Germany: namely, an intellectual and political confrontation with the intellectual representatives of cultural modernity. And here I quote Peter Steinfels, a perceptive observer of the new style which the neoconservatives succeeded in imposing on the intellectual scene in the 1970s:

> The struggle takes the form of exposing every manifestation of what could be considered an oppositionist mentality and tracing its 'logic' so as to link it to various expressions of extremism: drawing the connection between modernism and nihilism ... between government regulation and totalitarianism, between criticism of arms expenditures and subservience to Communism, between women's liberation or homosexual rights and the destruction of the family ... between the Left generally and terrorism, anti-Semitism, and fascism.[9]

Peter Steinfels is referring here only to the United States, but the parallels with our situation are very obvious. The personalizing of debate and the degree of bitterness that characterize the abuse of intellectuals stirred up by those hostile to the Enlightenment cannot adequately be explained in psychological terms, since they are grounded rather in the internal conceptual weakness of neoconservative thought itself.

Neoconservatism displaces the burdensome and unwelcome consequences of a more or less successful capitalist modernization of the economy on to cultural modernity. It obscures the connections between the processes of social modernization, which it welcomes, on the one hand, and the crisis of motivation, which it laments, on the other, and fails to reveal the sociostructural causes of transformed attitudes to work, of consumer habits, of levels of demand and of the greater emphasis given to leisure time. Thus neoconservatism can directly attribute what appear to be hedonism, a lack of social identification, an incapacity for obedience, narcissism, and the withdrawal from competition for status and achievement to a culture which actually plays only a very mediated role in these processes. In place of these unanalysed causes, it focuses on those intellectuals who still regard themselves as committed to the project of modernity. It is true that Daniel Bell does perceive a further connection between the erosion of bourgeois values and the consumerism characteristic of a society which has become orientated towards mass production. But even Bell, seemingly unimpressed by his own argument, traces the new permissiveness back first and foremost to the spread of a lifestyle which originally emerged within the elite countercultures of bohemian artists. This is obviously only another variation on a misunderstanding to which the avant-garde itself had already fallen prey – the idea that the mission of art is to fulfill its implicit promise of happiness by introducing into society as a whole that artistic lifestyle that was defined precisely as its opposite.

Concerning the period in which aesthetic modernity emerged, Bell remarks that 'radical in economics, the bourgeoisie became conservative in morals and cultural taste.'[10] If this were true, one might see neoconservatism as a return to the old reliable pattern of the bourgeois mentality. But that is far too simple: the mood to which neoconservatism can appeal *today* by no means derives from a discontent with the antinomian consequences of a culture that has transgressed its boundaries and escaped from the museum back into life. This discontent is not provoked by the modernist intellectuals, but is rooted rather in much more fundamental reactions to a process of social modernization which, under pressure from the imperatives of economic growth and state administration, intervenes further and further into the ecology of developed forms of social life, into the communicative infrastructure of the historical lifeworlds. Thus neo-populist protests are merely giving forceful expression to widespread fears concerning the possible destruction of the urban and the natural environments, and the destruction of humane forms of social life. Many different occasions for discontent and protest arise wherever a one-sided process of modernization, guided by criteria of economic and administrative rationality, invades domains of life which are centred on the task of cultural transmission, social integration, socialization and education, domains orientated towards quite *different* criteria, namely towards those of communicative rationality. But it is from just these social processes that the neoconservative doctrines distract our attention, only to project the causes which they have left shrouded in obscurity on to an intrinsically subversive culture and its representatives.

It is quite true that cultural modernity also generates its own aporias. And those intellectual positions which hasten to proclaim postmodernity, to recommend a return to premodernity, or which radically repudiate modernity altogether, all appeal to these aporias. Thus, apart from the problematic social consequences of *social* modernization, it is true that certain reasons for doubt or despair concerning the project of modernity *also* arise from the *internal perspective* of cultural development.

The Project of Enlightenment

The idea of modernity is intimately bound up with the development of European art, but what I have called the project of modernity only comes into clear view when we abandon the usual concentration on art. Max Weber characterized cultural modernity in terms of the separation of substantive reason, formerly expressed in religious and metaphysical world-views, into three moments, now capable of being connected only formally with one another (through the form of argumentative justification). In so far as the world-views have disintegrated and their traditional problems have been separated off under the perspectives of truth, normative rightness and authenticity or beauty, and can now be treated in each case as questions of knowledge, justice or taste respectively, there arises in the modern period a differentiation of the value spheres of science and knowledge, of morality and of art. Thus scientific discourse, moral and legal enquiry, artistic production and critical practice are now institutionalized within the corresponding cultural systems as the concern of experts. And this professionalized treatment of the cultural heritage in terms of a single abstract consideration of validity in each case serves to bring to light the autonomous structures intrinsic to the cognitive-instrumental, the moral-practical and the aesthetic-expressive knowledge complexes. From now on there will also be *internal* histories of science and knowledge, of moral and legal theory, and of art. And although these do not represent linear developments, they none the less constitute learning processes. That is one side of the issue.

On the other side, the distance between these expert cultures and the general public has increased. What the cultural sphere gains through specialized treatment and reflection does not *automatically* come into the possession of everyday practice without more ado. For with cultural rationalization, the lifeworld, once its traditional substance has been devalued, threatens rather to become *impoverished*. The project of modernity as it was formulated by the philosophers of the Enlightenment in the eighteenth century consists in the relentless development of the objectivating sciences, of the universalistic foundations of morality and law, and of autonomous art, all in accord with their own immanent logic. But at the same time it also results in releasing the cognitive potentials accumulated in the process from their esoteric high forms and attempting to apply them in the sphere of praxis, that is, to encourage the rational organization of social relations. Partisans of the Enlightenment such as Condorcet could still entertain the extravagant expectation that the arts and sciences would not merely promote the control of the forces of nature, but also further the understanding of self and world, the progress of morality, justice in social institutions, and even human happiness.

Little of this optimism remains to us in the twentieth century. But the problem has remained, and with it a fundamental difference of opinion as before: should we continue to hold fast to the intentions of the Enlightenment, however fractured they may be, or should we rather relinquish the entire project of modernity? If the cognitive potentials in question do not merely result in technical progress, economic growth and rational administration, should we wish to see them checked in order to protect a life praxis still dependent on blind traditions from any unsettling disturbance?

Even among those philosophers who currently represent something of an *Enlightenment rearguard*, the project of modernity appears curiously fragmented. Each thinker puts faith in only one of the moments into which reason has become differentiated. Karl Popper, and I refer here to the theorist of the open society who has not yet allowed himself to be appropriated by the neoconservatives, holds firmly to the potentially enlightening capacity of scientific criticism when extended into the political domain. But for this he pays the price of a general moral scepticism and a largely indifferent attitude to the aesthetic dimension. Paul Lorenzen is interested in the question as to how an artificial language methodically constructed in accordance with practical reason can effectively contribute to the reform of everyday life. But his approach directs all science and knowledge along the narrow path of justification analogous to that of moral practice and he too neglects the aesthetic. In Adorno, on the other hand, the emphatic claim to reason has withdrawn into the accusatory gesture of the esoteric work of art, morality no longer appears susceptible to justification, and philosophy is left solely with the task of revealing, in an indirect fashion, the critical content sealed up within art.

The progressive differentiation of science and knowledge, morality and art, with which Max Weber characterized the rationalism of Western culture, implies *both* the specialized treatment of special domains *and* their detachment from the current of tradition, which continues to flow on in a quasi-natural fashion in the hermeneutic medium of everyday life. This detachment is the problem which is generated by the autonomous logic of the differentiated value spheres. And it is this detachment which has also provoked abortive attempts to 'sublate' the expert cultures which accompany it, a phenomenon most clearly revealed in the domain of art.

Kant and the Autonomy of the Aesthetic

Simplifying considerably, one can trace a line of progressive autonomization in the development of modern art. It was the Renaissance which first saw the emergence of a specific domain categorized exclusively in terms of the beautiful. Then, in the course of the eighteenth century, literature, the plastic arts and music were institutionalized as a specific domain of activity distinct from ecclesiastical and court life. Finally, around the middle of the nineteenth century, there also arose an aestheticist conception of art which obliged artists to produce their work in accordance with the conscious outlook of *l'art pour l'art*. The autonomy of the aesthetic was thereby explicitly constituted as a project.

In the initial phase of this process, therefore, there emerged the cognitive structures of a new domain, one quite distinct from the complex of science and knowledge and that of morality. And the task of clarifying these structures subsequently fell to philosophical aesthetics. Kant laboured energetically to define the distinctive character of the aesthetic domain. His point of departure here was the analysis of the judgement of taste, which is certainly directed towards something subjective, namely the free play of the imagination, but which manifests more than mere preference, being orientated rather towards intersubjective agreement.

Although aesthetic objects belong neither to the sphere of phenomena knowable by means of the categories of the understanding, nor to the sphere of free acts subject to the legislation of practical reason, works of art (and those of natural beauty) are accessible to *objective judgement*. The beautiful constitutes another domain of validity, alongside those of truth and morality, and it is this which grounds the *connection between art and the practice of art criticism*. For one 'speaks of beauty as if it were a property of things'.[11]

Beauty pertains, of course, only to the *representation* of a thing, just as the judgement of taste refers only to the relationship between the mental representation of an object and the feeling of pleasure or displeasure. It is only in the *medium of semblance* that an object can be perceived *as* an aesthetic object. And only as a fictive object can it so affect our sensibility as to succeed in presenting what evades the conceptual character of objectivating thought and moral judgement. Kant describes the state of mind which is produced through the play of the representational faculties, and which is thus activated aesthetically, as one of *disinterested* pleasure. The quality of a *work* is therefore determined quite independently of any connections it might have with our practical relations to life.

Whereas the fundamental concepts of classical aesthetics already mentioned – namely those of taste and criticism, beautiful semblance, disinterestedness and the transcendent autonomy of the work of art – serve principally to distinguish the aesthetic domain from the other spheres of value and life practice, the concept of the *genius* which is required for the production of the work of art involves positive elements. Kant describes genius as 'the exemplary originality of the natural talents of a subject in the free employment of his or her cognitive faculties'.[12] If we detach the concept of genius from its romantic origins, we could freely paraphrase this thought as follows: the talented artist is capable of bestowing authentic expression on those experiences enjoyed through concentrated engagement with a decentred subjectivity which is released from the constraints of knowledge and action.

This autonomous character of the aesthetic – namely, the objectification of a self-experiencing decentred subjectivity, the exclusion of the spatio-temporal structures of everyday life, the rupturing of conventions attaching to the processes of perception and purposive activity, the dialectic of shock and revelation – could first emerge as a distinct consciousness of modernity only with the gestures of modernism, and only once two further conditions had been fulfilled. These conditions were, in the first place, the institutionalization of artistic production dependent on the market and of a non-purposive enjoyment of art mediated through the practice of art criticism; and in the second place, an aestheticist self-understanding on the part of artists, and also on the part of critics, who conceive of themselves less as representatives of the general public than as interpreters who form part of the process of artistic production itself. Now for the first time in painting and literature we discern the beginnings of a movement which some already see anticipated in the aesthetic criticism of Baudelaire: colours, lines, sounds and movements cease to be primarily for the purpose of representation; the media of representation, along with the techniques of production themselves, advance to become aesthetic objects in their own right. Thus Adorno can begin his *Aesthetic Theory* with the statement: 'It has now become self-evident, as far as art is concerned, that nothing is self-evident any more, either in art itself or in its relation to the whole, not even its right to exist.'

The False Sublation of Culture

Of course, art's right to exist could not have been called into question by surrealism if modern art, and indeed especially modern art, did not also harbour a promise of happiness which concerned its 'relationship to the whole'. In Schiller the promise that aesthetic contemplation makes but fails to fulfil still possessed the explicit form of a utopia which points beyond art. This line of utopian aesthetic thought extends all the way to Marcuse's lament concerning the affirmative character of culture, expressed here as a critique of ideology. But even in Baudelaire, who repeats the *promesse de bonheur*, this utopia of reconciliation had turned into a critical reflection of the unreconciled nature of the social world. The more remote from life art becomes, the more it withdraws into the

inviolable seclusion of complete aesthetic autonomy, the more pain-
fully this lack of reconciliation is brought to conscious awareness.
This pain is reflected in the boundless *ennui* of the outsider who
identified himself with the Parisian rag-and-bone men.

Along such pathways of sensibility all those explosive energies
gather which are finally discharged in rebellion, in the violent attempt
to shatter the illusory autarchy of the sphere of art and thus to
enforce reconciliation through this sacrifice. Adorno sees very clearly
why the surrealist programme 'renounces art, without, however,
being able to shake it off'.[13] All attempts to bridge the disjunction
between art and life, fiction and praxis, illusion and reality, and to
eliminate the distinction between artistic product and objects of
utility, between something produced and something found, between
premeditated configuration and spontaneous impulse, the attempt to
declare everything art and everyone an artist, to abolish all criteria
and to equate aesthetic judgements with the expression of subjective
experience: all these undertakings, well analysed as they have been,
can be seen today as nonsense experiments. They only succeed,
against their own intention, in illuminating even more sharply the
very structures of art which they had intended to violate: the medium
of semblance, the autonomous transcendence of the work, the
concentrated and premeditated character of artistic production, as
well as the cognitive status of the judgement of taste.[14] Ironically, the
radical attempt to sublate art reinstates those categories with which
classical aesthetics had circumscribed its own domain, although it is
also true that these categories have changed their character in the
process.

The failure of the surrealist rebellion sets the seal of confirmation
on a double error of a false sublation. On the one hand, once the
vessels of an autonomously articulated cultural sphere are shattered,
their contents are lost; once meaning has been desublimated and
form dismantled, nothing remains and no emancipatory effect results.
But the second error is even more fraught with consequences. In the
communicative praxis of everyday life, cognitive interpretations,
moral expectations, expressions and evaluations must interpenetrate
one another. The processes of reaching understanding which tran-
spire in the lifeworld require the resources of an inherited culture *in
its entire range*. That is why a rationalized everyday life could not
possibly be redeemed from the rigidity of cultural impoverishment by
violently forcing open *one* cultural domain, in this case art, and
establishing some connection with *one* of the specialized complexes
of knowledge. Such an approach would only substitute one form of
one-sidedness and abstraction with another.

There are also parallels in the domains of theoretical knowledge
and morality to this programme and its unsuccessful practice of false

sublation, although they are admittedly less clearly defined. It is certainly true that the sciences on the one hand and moral and legal theory on the other have, like art, become autonomous. But both these spheres remain closely connected with specialized forms of praxis, the former with a scientifically perfected technology, the latter with an organized practice of law and administration dependent on moral justification. And yet institutionalized scientific knowledge and the activity of moral-practical argument segregated within the legal system have become so remote from everyday life that here too the programme of *elevation* implied by the Enlightenment could be transformed into that of *sublation* instead.

The 'sublation of philosophy' is a slogan that has been current ever since the days of the Young Hegelians, and the question concerning the relationship of theory and praxis has been raised since Marx. And here the intellectuals have allied themselves with the workers' movement, of course. It was only at the margins of this social movement that sectarian groups found room to play out the programme of sublating philosophy in the way the surrealists played out the sublation of art. The consequences of dogmatism and moral rigorism here reveal the same error as before: once the praxis of everyday life, orientated as it is towards the unconstrained interplay between the cognitive, the moral-practical and the aesthetic-expressive dimensions, has become reified, it cannot be cured by being connected with any *one* of the cultural domains forcibly opened up. Nor should the imitation of the lifestyles of extraordinary representatives of these value spheres – in other words, by generalizing the subversive forces which Nietzsche, Bakunin or Baudelaire expressed in their own lives – be confused with the institutionalization and practical utilization of knowledge accumulated through science, morality and art.

In specific situations it is quite true that terrorist activities may be connected with the overextension of one of these cultural moments, that is, with the inclination to aestheticize politics, to replace politics with moral rigorism, or to subjugate politics to dogmatic doctrines.

But these almost intangible connections should not mislead us into denouncing the intentions of an intransigent Enlightenment as the monstrous offspring of a 'terroristic reason'. Those who link the project of modernity with the conscious attitudes and spectacular public deeds of individual terrorists are just as short-sighted as those who claim that the incomparably more persistent and pervasive bureaucratic terrorism practised in obscurity, in the cellars of the military and the secret police, in prison camps and psychiatric institutions, represents the very essence of the modern state (and its positivistically eroded form of legal domination) simply because such terrorism utilizes the coercive means of the state apparatus.

Alternatives to the False Sublation of Culture

I believe that we should learn from the aberrations which have accompanied the project of modernity and from the mistakes of those extravagant proposals of sublation, rather than abandoning modernity and its project. Perhaps we can at least *suggest* a possible escape from the aporias of cultural modernity if we take the reception of art as an example. Since the development of art criticism during the romantic period there have arisen certain contradictory tendencies, and they became more rigidly polarized with the emergence of the avant-garde movements. On the one hand, art criticism claims the role of a productive supplement to the work of art, while on the other it claims the role of an advocate who provides the interpretation required by the public at large. Bourgeois art addressed *both* of these expectations to its audience: on the one hand laypeople who enjoy art should educate themselves to become experts, while on the other they should behave as connoisseurs who are capable of relating their aesthetic experience back to the problems of their own life. Perhaps this second, apparently more innocuous mode of reception lost its radical character because its connection with the former mode remained obscure.

Of course, artistic production will inevitably degenerate semantically if it is not pursued as the specialized treatment of its own immanent problems, as an object of expert concern without regard for exoteric needs. All those who are involved (including the critic as a professionally trained recipient) engage in the problems they treat in terms of just one abstract criterion of validity. This sharply defined separation and the exclusive concentration on a single dimension breaks down, however, as soon as aesthetic experience is incorporated into the context of an individual life history or into a collective form of life. The reception of art by the layperson, or rather the person who is an expert in the field of everyday life, takes a *different course* from the reception of art by the professional critic who focuses principally on developments which are purely internal to art. Albrecht Wellmer has pointed out to me that an aesthetic experience which is not primarily translated into judgements of taste actually changes its functional character. For when it is related to problems of life or used in an exploratory fashion to illuminate a life-historical situation, it enters a language game which is no longer that of art criticism proper. In this case aesthetic experience not only revitalizes those need interpretations in the light of which we perceive our world, but also influences our cognitive interpretations and our normative expectations, and thus alters the way in which all these moments *refer back and forth* to one another.

Peter Weiss narrates an example of the kind of exploratory, life-orientating power which can emanate from the encounter with a great painting at a crucial juncture in an individual's life. He has his protagonist wander through the streets of Paris after his dejected return from the Spanish Civil War and anticipate in imagination his imminent encounter with Géricault's painting of the shipwrecked sailors in the Louvre. A specific variant of the mode of artistic reception I am talking about here is even more precisely captured in the heroic effort of appropriation described by the same author in the first volume of his *Ästhetik des Widerstands* (Aesthetic of Resistance). He depicts a group of young people in Berlin in 1937, politically motivated workers who are eager to learn, who are acquiring the means of inwardly understanding the history, including the social history, of European painting through night school classes. Out of the obdurate stone of objective spirit they hew the fragments they are able to appropriate, drawing them into the experiential horizon of their own environment, one which is as remote from traditional education as it is from the existing regime, and turning them this way and that until they begin to glow:

> Our conception of culture only rarely cohered with what presented itself to us as a gigantic repository of commodities, of accumulated insights and discoveries. As propertyless people, we approached this hoard with initial trepidation, filled with awe, until it became clear to us that we had to supply our own evaluations to it all, that we could only make use of it as a totality if it actually spoke to us about our own conditions of life, about the difficulties and the peculiarities of our own processes of thought.[15]

Examples like this, where the *expert culture is appropriated from the perspective of the lifeworld*, successfully preserve something of the original intention of the doomed surrealist rebellion, and more of Brecht's, and even Benjamin's, experimental reflections on the reception of non-auratic works of art. And similar observations can be made concerning the spheres of science and morality when we consider that the human, social and behavioural sciences have not been *entirely* divorced from the structure of practically orientated knowledge even now, and further that the concentration of universalistic ethics on questions of justice represents an abstraction which cries out to be connected to those problems concerning the good life that it initially excluded.

However, a differentiated reconnection of modern culture with an everyday sphere of praxis that is dependent on a living heritage and yet is impoverished by mere traditionalism will admittedly only prove successful if the process of social modernization can *also* be turned into *other* non-capitalist directions, if the lifeworld can develop institutions of its own in a way currently inhibited by the autonomous systemic dynamics of the economic and administrative system.

Three Conservatisms

Unless I am mistaken, the prospects for this are not encouraging. Virtually throughout the Western world a climate of opinion has arisen which promotes tendencies highly critical of modernism. The disillusionment provoked by the failure of programmes for the false sublation of art and philosophy, and the openly visible aporias of cultural modernity, have served as a pretext for various conservative positions. Let me briefly distinguish here the antimodernism of the Young Conservatives from the premodernism of the Old Conservatives, on the one hand, and the postmodernism of the New Conservatives, on the other.

The *Young Conservatives* essentially appropriate the fundamental experience of aesthetic modernity, namely the revelation of a decentred subjectivity liberated from all the constraints of cognition and purposive action, from all the imperatives of labour and use value, and with this they break out of the modern world altogether. They establish an implacable opposition to modernism precisely through a modernist attitude. They locate the spontaneous forces of imagination and self-experience, of affective life in general, in what is most distant and archaic, and in Manichaean fashion oppose instrumental reason with a principle accessible solely to evocation, whether this is the will to power or sovereignty, Being itself or the Dionysian power for the poetic. In France this tradition leads from Georges Bataille through Foucault to Derrida. Over all these figures hovers, of course, the spirit of Nietzsche, newly resurrected in the 1970s.

The *Old Conservatives* do not allow themselves to be contaminated by cultural modernity in the first place. They observe with mistrust the collapse of substantive reason, the progressive differentiation of science, morality and art, the modern understanding of the world and its purely procedural canons of rationality, and recommend instead a return to positions *prior* to modernity (something which Max Weber regarded as a regression to the stage of material rationality). Here it is principally contemporary neo-Aristotelianism which has enjoyed some success, encouraged by the ecological question to renew the idea of a cosmological ethic. This tradition, which begins with Leo Strauss, has produced the interesting works of Hans Jonas and Robert Spaemann, for example.

It is the *New Conservatives* who relate most affirmatively to the achievements of modernity. They welcome the development of modern science so long as it only oversteps its own sphere in order to promote technological advance, capitalist growth and a rational form of administration. Otherwise, they recommend a politics directed essentially at defusing the explosive elements of cultural modernity. According to one claim, science, once properly understood, has already become meaningless as far as orientation in the lifeworld is concerned. According to another, politics should be immunized as much as possible from the demands of moral-practical legitimation. And a third claim affirms the total immanence of art, contests the idea of its utopian content, and appeals to its fictive character, precisely in order to confine aesthetic experience to the private sphere. One could mention the early Wittgenstein, Carl Schmitt in his middle period, and the later Gottfried Benn in this connection. With the definitive segregation of science, morality and art into autonomous spheres split off from the lifeworld and administered by specialists, all that remains of cultural modernity is what is left after renouncing the project of modernity itself. The resulting space is to be filled by traditions which are to be spared all demands for justification. Of course, it remains extremely difficult to see how such traditions could continue to survive in the modern world without the governmental support of ministries of culture.

Like every other typology, this too is a simplification, but it may be of some use for the analysis of contemporary intellectual and political controversies. For I fear that antimodernist ideas, coupled with an element of premodernism, are gaining ground in the circles of the greens and other alternative groups. On the other hand, in the changing attitudes within the political parties there is evidence of a similar turn, namely of an alliance between the advocates of postmodernity and those of premodernity. It seems to me that no one political party has a monopoly on neoconservative attitudes and the abuse of intellectuals. For this reason, especially after the clarifications you provided in your opening remarks, Mayor Wallmann, I have good reason to be grateful for the liberal spirit in which the City of Frankfurt has awarded me a prize which bears the name of Adorno, a son of this city who as a philosopher and a writer did more to shape the image of the intellectual than almost anyone else in the Federal Republic of Germany, and who has himself become an exemplary model for intellectuals.

NOTES

This is the first complete English translation of the original version of a speech given by Habermas in September 1980, when he was awarded the Adorno Prize by the City of Frankfurt. The German text was published in Habermas's *Kleine*

Politische Schriften I–IV (Frankfurt: Suhrkamp, 1981). Translated by Nicholas Walker.

1 W. Pehnt, 'Die Postmoderne als Lunapark', *Frankfurter Allgemeine Zeitung*, 18 Aug. 1980, p. 17.
2 'Literarische Tradition und gegenwärtiges Bewusstsein der Moderne', in H. R. Jauss, *Literaturgeschichte als Provokation* (Frankfurt: Suhrkamp, 1970), pp. 11ff.
3 T. W. Adorno, 'Ästhetische Theorie', in *Gesammelte Werke*, vol. 7 (Frankfurt: Suhrkamp, 1970), p. 45.
4 Octavio Paz, *Essays*.
5 Adorno, 'Ästhetische Theorie', p. 41.
6 Walter Benjamin, *Gesammelte Schriften* (Frankfurt: Suhrkamp, 1974), vol. 1.2, pp. 701f. In English see 'Theses on the Philosophy of History', in *Illuminations*, trans. H. Zohn (New York: Schocken, 1969), pp. 261, 263.
7 Paz, *Essays*.
8 Daniel Bell, *The Cultural Contradictions of Capitalism* (London: Heinemann, 1979).
9 Peter Steinfels, *The Neoconservatives* (New York: Simon and Schuster, 1979), p. 65.
10 Bell, *The Cultural Contradictions of Capitalism*, p. 17.
11 Immanuel Kant, *The Critique of Judgement* (Oxford: Oxford University Press, 1952), para. 7.
12 Ibid., para. 49.
13 Adorno, 'Ästhetische Theorie', p. 52.
14 D. Wellershoff, *Die Auflösung des Kunstbegriffs* (Frankfurt: Suhrkamp, 1976).
15 Peter Weiss, *Ästhetik des Widerstands* (Frankfurt: Suhrkamp, 1978), vol. 1, p. 54.

PART I

CRITICAL REJOINDERS

2

THE DISCOURSE OF MODERNITY: HEGEL, NIETZSCHE, HEIDEGGER AND HABERMAS

Fred Dallmayr

The status of the 'modern project' is strongly contested today. Under such summary labels as 'modernism vs postmodernism' or 'enlightenment vs deconstruction', champions and critics of the project are embroiled in lively skirmishes both inside and outside of academia. Unfortunately, the salience of the issues is not often reflected in the character of exchanges: more than other contemporary topics the themes of modernity and postmodernity tend to be submerged in trendiness and facile rhetoric. Only rarely does literature devoted to these themes rise above the plane of broad manifestos or petty polemics; Jürgen Habermas's *The Philosophical Discourse of Modernity* is clearly such an exception. First published in 1985, the study lends substance and focus to otherwise often diffuse debates; moving beyond surface changes and technical gadgets it locates the core issues of modernity on the level of philosophy – more specifically of an ongoing 'philosophical discourse'. From Habermas's perspective, modernity is intimately linked with the central aspirations of Reformation and Enlightenment: the aspirations of cognitive rationality, moral autonomy and social-political self-determination. Accentuating this linkage means to underscore the stakes involved in current discussions. For profiled against the backdrop of heteronomy and caprice, how can one blandly dismiss modernity's gains? On the other hand, given the lengthening shadows cast by anthropocentrism and technical prowess, how can one blithely endorse these gains without naiveté or callousness?

One of the chief merits of Habermas's study is the treatment of modernity not as a platform or doctrine but as a discourse or conversation – a conversation made up of different protagonists or voices and stretching over successive historical periods. In Habermas's presentation, the discourse was inaugurated by Enlightenment thinkers from Descartes to Voltaire and first crystallized in the rationalist theories of Kant and Fichte. In Kantian thought, he notes, modernity meant basically the progressive refinement of conscious- ness and subjectivity, specifically the segregation of reason into the domains of science, ethical freedom and aesthetic judgement – a segregation apparently achieved without costs or charring effects. Neglect of these costs soon led to dissent or insurgency within modern discourse, in the sense that the *cantus firmus* of analytical rationalism was joined by the supplementary or 'counterdiscourse' of rational synthesis – an insurgency which found its chief voice in Hegel's system. Countering the divisions and cleavages (*Entzweiun- gen*) resulting from modernity, Hegel – without abandoning the modern project – sought to reconcile the dichotomies of 'nature and spirit, sensuality and reason, *Verstand* and *Vernunft*, theoretical and practical reason, judgement and imagination, finitude and infinity, knowledge and faith'.[1]

While praising Hegel's philosophical élan, Habermas finds Hegel's insurgency flawed and ultimately unsuccessful – mainly because of its 'subjectivist' moorings and its excessively theoretical-contemplative character. During the nineteenth century, the Hegelian legacy was continued by the opposing camps of 'Young Hegelians' and 'Right Hegelians', the first devoted to the implementation of reason on the basis of praxis or productivity, and the second to the maintenance of objective rational structures as embedded in state, economy or technology. As opposed to these internal modulations of modernity, the study shifts attention at this point to another, more radical insurgency or antidiscourse (*Sonderdiskurs*) – one seeking not so much to modify as to 'cancel' the modern project and whose diverse articulations take up the bulk of the volume. The instigator of this radical stance was Nietzsche, who, in the study, figures as the turning point or as the 'turn-table' (*Drehscheibe*) ushering in the move from modernity to postmodernism. As in Hegel's case, Nietzsche's legacy is said to have been continued by two opposing (but also interdepen- dent) camps, one pursuing a more sceptical and quasi-scientific approach, the other attempting an ontological or quasi-ontological reversal of modernity. The chief representatives of the first camp are Bataille, Lacan and Foucault; those of the second camp Heidegger and Derrida.[2]

To be sure, the preceding synopsis does not do full justice to the complexity of the study, particularly to its many sidelines and repeated interludes or 'excursions'; nevertheless, it captures (I believe) the chief strands and counterstrands of the modern discourse (and antidiscourse) as seen by Habermas. It cannot be my ambition in the present context to recapitulate and discuss all the facets of this discursive or conversational fabric; such an effort would require the format of a full-length commentary or counterstudy. At this point I propose to examine three central episodes in the study's historical scenario, episodes connected with the names of Hegel, Nietzsche and Heidegger. The choice of these thinkers seems justified by their role in Habermas's narrative: while Hegel inaugurated the modern discourse in its broad multidimensionality, Nietzsche marks the dividing line between modernity and postmodernism (or between discourse and antidiscourse); Heidegger finally can be seen as (arguably) the leading philosophical representative of a post-Nietzschean perspective. Following a review of these episodes I shall critically assess Habermas's own model of communicative rationality as developed in the study's concluding chapters – with the intent of providing an alternative interpretation of the modern project and of the conversational structure of the 'discourse of modernity'.[3]

I

Renaissance and Reformation (together with the discovery of the 'New World') heralded an implicit break with the classical and medieval past; but the notion of a distinctly 'modern' period emerged only slowly in the aftermath of these events. According to Habermas, it was left to Hegel to grasp the philosophical meaning and import of the modern project. Hegel, he writes, was 'the first philosopher to develop a clear conception of modernity'. Although anticipated dimly by Enlightenment thinkers from Descartes to Kant, it was only towards the end of the eighteenth century that 'the problem of the *self-understanding* of modernity became so acute that Hegel could perceive it *as* a philosophical problem and moreover as *the basic problem* of his philosophy.' Together with his philosophical precursors, Hegel located the core of modernity in the principle of 'subjectivity' – a principle which carried for him mainly the connotations of individualism, critical-rational competence and autonomy of action. The same principle had already been succinctly pinpointed by Kant, who treated subjectivity as the foundation of the segregated modern domains of science, (categorical) ethics, and expressive art. Kant, we read, 'put in place of the substantial rationality bequeathed by metaphysics the notion of a reason differentiated into separate moments whose unity has merely formal character; he distinguished the faculties of practical reason and judgement from theoretical cognition and assigned to each moment its own place.' Yet, while pursuing his analytical task, Kant did not grasp the differentiation of reason as a problem, or the separation of modern 'value spheres' as division or a source of divisiveness (*Entzweiung*); consequently he also ignored the synthetic 'need' emerging from his analysis. Here was precisely the motif of Hegel's insurgency: while accepting the principle of subjectivity he recognized both its emancipatory potential and its ambivalence. In Habermas's words, the principle 'explained for him simultaneously the superiority of the modern world and its crisis character, in the sense that it represents both a world of progress and of alienated spirit. For this reason the first attempt to conceptualize the modern era was at the same time a critique of modernity.'[4]

In the chapter devoted to Hegel, Habermas traces the successive stages of his insurgency within the confines of Enlightenment discourse. As he notes, the initial impulses of his synthetic efforts can be traced back to critical or 'crisis experiences' of the young Hegel himself, experiences which nurtured his conviction 'that reason must be marshalled as conciliatory power against the divided positivities of his age'. Turning first to Hegel's early (especially his theological) writings, Habermas points to a certain romantic or 'mythopoetic' version of reconciliation which Hegel shared with Schelling and Hölderlin, his friends in the Tübingen seminary. Countering both the orthodoxy of 'positive' (or established) religion and the abstractness of Enlightenment ideas, these writings appealed to a purified public faith or civil religiosity as the bond tying together and reconciling the conflicting segments of society. Only when represented in public festivals and cults and linked with myths engaging heart and phantasy – Hegel argued at the time – could a religiously mediated reason 'permeate the entire fabric of the state'. The same writings also spoke of a 'nexus of guilt' or a 'causality of destiny' as the driving motor propelling a reconciliation of criminally severed relationships, a motor revealing the injury inflicted on others ultimately as self-injury. According to the study, Hegel 'opposed to the abstract laws of morality the very different rule mechanism of a concrete nexus of guilt generated by the sundering of a prior ethical totality [sittliche Totalität]'; by suffering the consequences of his action the criminal comes to recognize in the injured alien existence 'his own repudiated nature'. Shifting from narrative to critique, Habermas at this point challenges the character of the invoked totality or social bond: both in the case of civil religion and of the nexus of guilt, he argues, reconciliation relies on premodern life forms which the process of modernization necessarily leaves behind. 'For the fated reconciliation of a divided modernity,' he writes, 'Hegel presupposes an ethical totality which is not germane to modern conditions but rather is borrowed from the idealized past of early Christian communities and the Greek polis'; yet modernity had gained its self-understanding precisely through 'a reflection which bars the systematic regress to such exemplary traditions'.[5]

Similar or related dilemmas – dilemmas soon recognized by Hegel himself – beset another early or transitional work in his intellectual development: the so-called 'oldest system programme' formulated in

Frankfurt and still under the influence of Schelling and Hölderlin. In that programme, the function of reconciliation was attributed to art or artistic-poetic imagination. 'Rational religion', the study comments, 'was presumed to yield to *art* in order to develop into a popular religion; the monotheism of reason and heart was to ally itself with the polytheism of imagination to produce an (aesthetic) mythology of ideas.' As Habermas observes, this programme was clearly reminiscent of Schiller's letters on the 'aesthetic education of mankind' (of 1795), and it was retained in Schelling's transcendental idealism and in Hölderlin's works to the end. According to Habermas's narrative, however, Hegel quickly abandoned this outlook as an insufficient remedy for modern ills and divisions. Given that modernity is based on subjectivity and critical reflection, only philosophical reason or thought – a thought moving within subjective reflection and beyond it – could accomplish the hoped-for reconciliation and subdue the pitfalls of a solipsistic or domineering subjectivism. This insight, Habermas argues, was the crucial stepping-stone to Hegel's notion of 'absolute spirit'. If modern advances are to be taken seriously and yet to be corrected, he writes, 'reason must indeed be construed as self-relation of a subject, but now as a reflection which does not simply impose itself on otherness through the pure force of subjectivity but rather as one which has its essence and motor only in the effort to oppose all finite absolutisms and to overcome all encountered positivities.' In contrast to static metaphysical conceptions of the past, the 'absolute spirit' in Hegel's treatment consisted 'purely in the process of the relation of finitude and infinity and thus in the consuming activity of self-discovery'; moving beyond the level of substances and fragmented subjects, the absolute is construed 'solely as the mediating process of an unconditionally self-productive self-relation'. In this manner, Habermas concludes, Hegel utilized the philosophy of subjectivity 'with the aim of overcoming a subject-centred reason; with this move the mature Hegel can criticize the defects of modernity without appealing to any *other* premise than the immanent-modern principle of subjectivity.'[6]

The self-transcendence of modernity encapsulated in the 'absolute spirit' is replicated, in somewhat different guise, on the level of 'objective spirit', and especially in the theory of the modern 'state'. Turning to the *Philosophy of Right* (and earlier preparatory writings), Habermas finds Hegel's main contribution in his formulation of the notion of 'civil society' as a domain differentiated from, and mediating between, family and state; 'civil society' in this context meant a mode of association governed by private interest and market exchanges. In formulating this notion and juxtaposing it to the state, Hegel took account both of the advances of modernity and its divisive effects. In Habermas's words, the issue confronting Hegel was how civil society could be conceived not only as a *sphere of decay* of substantive ethics but in its negativity at the same time as a *necessary moment* of ethics (*Sittlichkeit*). He took his departure from the premise that the classical ideal of the *polis* cannot be restored in the context of modern, depoliticized social life; on the other hand, he maintained the idea of an ethical totality which he had thematized earlier under the rubric of popular religion.

By separating and simultaneously linking society and state (embodying the 'objective spirit'), Hegel's *Philosophy of Right* promoted a self-transcendence of modernity under modern auspices; in opposing both a homogeneous *polis* and an unlimited sway of private interests, the work set itself apart 'from restorative philosophies of the state as well as from rational natural law' (in the Enlightenment sense). To quote Hegel himself:

> The idea of the modern state has this immense strength and depth that it allows the principle of subjectivity to unfold to the extreme of self-sustained individual separateness while simultaneously guiding the principle back into substantive unity and maintaining the latter within itself.[7]

Having thus outlined Hegel's 'mature' position as reflected in the notions of 'absolute' and 'objective spirit', Habermas immediately proceeds to criticize this position for failing to 'solve' modern predicaments. Two (related) reasons are given for this failure. Although having previously applauded Hegel's firm adherence to the modern 'principle', Habermas now takes him to task for remaining hostage to a self-enclosed subjectivity unable to perform a synthetic function. 'With the notion of the absolute (spirit),' we read, 'Hegel regresses behind the intuitions of his youth: he conceives the overcoming of subjectivity only within the limits of the philosophy of the subject.'[8] By claiming the power of synthesis for absolute reason or subjectivity, Hegel is said to have feigned reconciliation by a sleight of hand: 'He would have had to demonstrate, rather than merely presuppose that (absolute) reason – which is more than abstract *Verstand* – can strictly reconcile or unify those visions which reason also must discursively disassemble.' The same defect is said to be operative in the objective spirit as represented in the Hegelian 'state'. According to Habermas, the state is unable on the face of it to unify or reassemble the divisions of modern social and political life. Such a 'solution' can be assumed only on the supposition of 'an absolute which is construed after the model of the self-relation of a cognitive subject'. Only when the absolute is conceived as pure or infinite subjectivity, he writes,

> can the moments of universality and particularity be thought to be reconciled in the confines of a monological self-knowledge; in the concrete universal (of the state) universal subjectivity thus takes precedence over the individual subject. In the domain of ethical life, this construction yields the priority of the *higher subjectivity of the state* over the subjective freedom of individuals.[9]

The second line of critique takes its aim not so much at self-enclosed subjectivity, but at the presumed abstractness or aloofness of Hegelian thought: the tendency of objective and absolute spirit to become the objects of passive contemplation removed from participation in the actual world process. Retired into itself or into its own absoluteness, Hegelian *Vernunft* is claimed to accomplish at best a '*partial* reconciliation' – namely, within the confines of philosophy but divorced from the shared beliefs of public religiosity which, in his early writings, were meant to link sense and reason, the common people and philosophers. Restricted to its own concerns, Hegelian philosophy – according to Habermas – 'ultimately robbed present actuality of its salience, destroyed its intrinsic interest and denied its promise for self-critical renewal'. Only latent in his early works, this tendency to passivity is said to surface strongly in Hegel's later system, including his *Philosophy of Right*. At this point his thought no longer criticized existing reality but only sought to 'grasp reality as it is'. This 'muffling of critique' was a close corollary of the 'devaluation of actuality' by philosophy; thus, 'the conceptually defined modernity permits the Stoic retreat from itself.' As remedy for Hegel's failings, Habermas's study proposes a different model of reconciliation or of the 'mediation of the universal and the particular': it is the model of communicative interaction (well known from his other writings). Instead of subordinating the freedom of individuals to the 'higher subjectivity of the state', this model relies on the '*higher intersubjectivity of an uncoerced will formation* within a communication community obeying the need for cooperation'. Rather than appealing to the power of *Vernunft*, synthesis here derives from the 'universality of an uncoerced consensus achieved between free and equal individuals'.[10]

Habermas's reprimands clearly call for a critical response or rejoinder (which I can attempt here only in sharply condensed form). As it seems to me, Habermas's interpretation is lopsided both on the level of certain historical nuances and with respect to key Hegelian concepts. Regarding the former, I find the division between the 'young' and the 'mature' Hegel – or between a romantic, mythopoetic outlook and a later pure rationalism – vastly exaggerated if not 'mythopoetic' in turn. In my own reading, Hegel never abandoned his early views on 'ethical totality' in his later works, nor did he dismiss the notions of public religiosity, the 'nexus of guilt' or the function of art as emblems of an ethical-social bond; he simply proceeded to reformulate these notions in accordance with the needs of his overall system. Like Plato he always maintained the correlation of truth, goodness and beauty, and also the linkage of reason and faith (as is evident in the triad of art, religion and philosophy on the level of 'absolute spirit').[11] This leads me to more important conceptual issues. Habermas chides Hegel's *Vernunft* for remaining locked in self-contained subjectivity and even in 'the confines of monological self-knowledge'. Moreover, absolute reason or subjectivity is presented as a 'consuming activity of self-discovery' and as an 'unconditionally self-productive self-relation'. At the same time, however, Hegelian spirit is treated as a detached realm in itself, as a passively contemplated 'objective reason'. Now clearly *Vernunft* cannot be both (that is, ceaseless activity and passivity); in my view it is actually neither. As it seems to me, by stressing self-production Habermas injects into subjectivity a Fichtean flavour of self-constitution. More pointedly, the combination of consuming activity and self-production gives to *Vernunft* a 'Young Hegelian' cast – the cast of a 'praxis philosophy' relying on self-realization and productivity (which the study elsewhere takes great pains to disavow). On the other hand, the treatment of spirit as an objective realm amenable to contemplation carries overtones of 'Right Hegelianism' – a perspective which, as the study indicates, was always bent on transforming *Vernunft* into a set of abstract and heteronomous rational precepts.

To a large extent, Habermas's Hegel chapter thus oscillates precariously between subjective and objective reason, between action and passivity (or else between Left and Right Hegelian vistas). Under the pressure of these opposing trends, Hegel's philosophy is liable to be torn asunder. To restore its unity requires more than patchwork; what is needed, I believe, is an appreciation of the fact that Hegel's 'spirit' (like other key concepts) is a metaphysical or ontological category – and not a partisan idea available for direct political utilization. As such a category, 'idea' or 'spirit' is not simply a subjective capacity (a capacity of self-production) nor an objective rational principle, but rather a dimension presupposed by both and in which both are finally again reconciled. As is well known, the course of Hegelian philosophy leads from 'subjective' over 'objective' to 'absolute spirit', or else from simple consciousness over mediated self-consciousness to a consciousness of self-consciousness. On one level, this course is described in the *Phenomenology of Spirit* as a path of 'experience' – where experience means neither subjective constitution nor passive endurance. More importantly, the dimension of 'absolute spirit' is not a domain produced or constituted as the outcome of a process of self-production (nor is it externally imposed); rather, it is always already presupposed in the movement of thought, permeating the path of 'experience' from beginning to end. As in the case of all great thinkers, Hegel's philosophizing moved in a circle – not a narrowly self-contained circle but one whose spirals meant to embrace everything. This aspect of Hegel's thought has been eloquently articulated by Heidegger (in his lectures on the *Phenomenology of Spirit*). He writes:

> The conclusion of the work has not moved away from its beginning but is a return to it. *The ending is only the transformed beginning which thereby has arrived at itself.* This means, however: the standpoint of the understanding and reenacting reader is from beginning to end, and from the end to the beginning the same – that of absolute reason, of a knowledge which confronts the absolute.[12]

My point here is not to vindicate Hegel's vocabulary or his foundational view of subjectivity. Philosophical developments in our century have amply illustrated the close linkage which always exists between consciousness (or subjectivity) and the unconscious, between enlightenment and processes of darkening or occlusion, between revealment and concealment. My point is simply that no path can possibly be charted beyond Hegel by short-changing the depth of his insights. Regarding the remedial course proposed in Habermas's study, one can reasonably doubt its viability. In pitting the interest and 'subjective freedom' of individuals against the ethical life of the state, Habermas basically invokes Kierkegaardian and Young Hegelian arguments in favour of particularity and concrete-individual praxis. From Hegel's perspective, however, individuals removed from public-ethical life are precisely unfree since freedom is genuinely a public category (and ultimately a synonym for 'spirit' or 'idea'). By presenting the public sphere as deriving from cooperative 'will formation' and the consensus reached between 'free and equal' individuals, Habermas's proposal harks back to the contractarian tradition – a tradition strongly rebuked in the *Philosophy of Right*. If the public realm is reduced or subordinated to society (or the sum of associated individuals), Hegel writes,

> and if its specific end is defined as the security and protection of property and individual freedom, then the interest of the individuals as such becomes the ultimate end of their association, and hence membership in the state something optional.

But the state's relation to the individual is quite different: since the former is objective spirit, it is only as a member that the individual gains concrete objectivity, genuine individuality, and ethical life.[13]

To the extent that – to elude contractarian premises – Habermas stresses the rationality of cooperative will-formation (reflected in an 'ideal speech community'), he merely appeals to a regulative principle which, in Hegel's terms, remains on the level of an abstract 'philosophy of reflection'. On the other hand, if escape from contractarianism is sought in a concrete 'lifeworld', recourse is taken to the same un- or pre-reflective traditions which were chided in Hegel's early writings. Even when not returning to the *cantus firmus* of Enlightenment rationalism, Habermas's proposal thus retains at best the *disjecta membra* of Hegelian philosophy.

II

According to the study, Hegel did not only inaugurate the modern philosophical discourse, focused on the 'critical self-understanding' of modernity; he also specified the 'rules' in terms of which this discursive theme could be modified or transformed – the rules of the 'dialectic of enlightenment'. During much of the nineteenth century, the broad parameters of these rules were maintained by the opposing schools of thought which cast the lot over Hegel's complex legacy.[14] A radical challenge to these parameters arose only in the later part of the last century, and chiefly in Nietzsche's work. While Young and Right Hegelians were rehearsing or playing out the radical and conservative strands in Hegel's thought, Habermas observes, Nietzsche decided to 'unmask the dramaturgy of the entire plot in which both parties – the representatives of revolution and of reaction – play their roles'. In unmasking the structure of the plot, Nietzsche is also said to have challenged its basic thematic content: the themes of reason and enlightenment. Nietzsche's work, we read, relates to the tradition as a whole 'in the same manner as the Young Hegelians related to reason's sublimations: reason now is nothing else but power or the perverted will to power which reason only serves to disguise.' In this manner, Nietzsche initiated not only a moderate counterpoint or counterdiscourse within the confines of Hegelian parameters but rather a radical antidiscourse no longer obeying the rules of the 'dialectic of enlightenment'. Nietzsche, the study affirms, 'wants to bolt the framework of occidental rationalism which still was binding for the opposing Left and Right Hegelian factions. Continued subsequently in two versions by Heidegger and Bataille, this antihumanism constitutes the real challenge to the discourse of modernity.'[15]

While setting off Nietzsche sharply against his precursors, Habermas also acknowledges a certain linkage with earlier, Young Hegelian arguments, a linkage evident particularly in the rebellious-insurgent tenor of his thought. Pointing to the second *Untimely Meditation* ('On the Use and Disadvantage of History for Life'), the study emphasizes Nietzsche's assault on a sterile antiquarianism and a passively contemplative outlook. Against an education relying on a purely 'antiquarian historiography', we read, Nietzsche 'marshals the spirit of modernity in a similar manner as did the Young Hegelians against the objectivism of Hegel's philosophy of history'. The affinity, however, was only limited and superficial. While the praxis orientation of Hegel's heirs was still tied to the dialectic of enlightenment, Nietzsche bid 'farewell' to the Hegelian tradition and to modern rationality as such. In Habermas's words: 'Nietzsche uses the ladder of historical reason only in order to discard it in the end and to take his stand in myth as the otherness of reason.' To be sure, given his anti-antiquarian stance, Nietzsche's departure from modern enlightenment does not simply mean a return or regression to a mythical past, but rather carries a utopian-futuristic cast. In contrast to purely restorative vistas, his opus depicted the future as 'the only horizon for the revival of mythical traditions ... This *utopian* posture – oriented towards a *coming* God – distinguishes Nietzsche's undertaking from the reactionary motto "Back to the origins".' In his futuristic leanings, Nietzsche is said to have pushed modernity towards postmodernism – a circumstance reflected in his treatment of modern art ('which in its most subjectivist expressions carries modernity to the extreme') as the medium linking past and future, utopia and myth. The chief protagonist of this linkage was for the young Nietzsche Richard Wagner with his vision of art as a quasi-religious festival. Thus, an 'aesthetically renewed mythology' was meant to dissolve the blockages or divisions of industrial society, and modern consciousness was to be 'opened to archaic experiences'.[16]

As Habermas recognizes, Nietzsche's vision was not entirely unprecedented, but could be traced broadly to aesthetic views held earlier by Schiller as well as the young Hegel and his friends. In Hegel's early writings and in Schelling's *System of Transcendental Idealism*, he notes, art was granted a mythopoetic quality and assigned a power of synthesis and reconciliation exceeding the competence of a dissecting or analytical reason. This aesthetic outlook was intensified and radicalized by Romanticism – particularly by Schlegel and Hölderlin, who connected the mythopoetic quality of art with quasi-messianic hopes for a historical renewal, hopes which increasingly moved away from Enlightenment rationalism. Schlegel, Habermas asserts, 'conceives the new mythology no longer as a sensual manifestation of reason, as an aesthetic expression of ideas which thus would fuse with the interests of the people'; rather, segregating it from theoretical and practical reason, he sees art alone as the avenue of renewal. In this manner, modernity is dislodged and confronted 'with the "primordial chaos" as the otherness of reason'. A key theme in early romanticist literature was the figure of Dionysus, 'the god of intoxication, madness and ceaseless transformations'. According to ancient myth, Dionysus was an expelled or banished but also an expected or 'coming' god – a feature which could nurture quasi-messianic sentiments. In Hölderlin's presentation, Dionysus was an alien or 'foreign god', a mythical figure whose absence nourished hopes for a transfigured return – in a manner loosely parallel to Christian hopes for a 'second coming'. While thus tracing the historical lineage of a mythopoetic aesthetics, Habermas immediately differentiates Nietzsche from these romantic precedents. Despite a common allegiance to Dionysus, the dividing line from Romanticism is said to reside in Nietzsche's anti-Christian sentiments, which somehow are linked with his radical anti-Enlightenment posture or antirationalism. The key to Nietzsche's departure from Romanticism, Habermas asserts, lies in the 'nexus of Dionysus and Christ' which permeated romantic poetry: 'This identification of the intoxicated wine-god with the Christian saviour God was possible only because romantic messianism aimed at a *rejuvenation* of, not a *farewell* to occidental culture. The new mythology was meant to restore a lost solidarity, not to deny the emancipation' progressively accomplished in that culture – as was Nietzsche's goal.[17]

The line separating Nietzsche from Romanticism was also the source of his rift with Wagner, focused on the latter's Christian proclivities. Wagner, we read, 'remained tied to the romantic nexus of Dionysus and Christ; as little as the Romantics did he regard Dionysus as the demi-god capable of releasing mankind from the curse of identity, of invalidating the principle of individuation, and thus of unleashing polymorphous chaos against the unity of the transcendental God or *anomie* against lawfulness.' As opposed to the moderate stance of Wagner and the Romantics, Nietzsche is said to have plunged himself headlong into Dionysian frenzy and also into an irrational, boundless subjectivism. As Habermas affirms, Nietzsche's conception of the Dionysian element involved an 'intensification of subjectivism to the point of total self-oblivion' – an oblivion shattering 'the categories of reasonable thought and action and the norms of everyday life'. In fact, Nietzschean aesthetics or what he called the 'aesthetic phenomenon' was predicated on the single-minded 'preoccupation of a decentred subjectivity with itself, a subjectivity extricated from the normal conventions of perception and action'. This retreat into subjectivism is a central feature of Habermas's critical indictment, a theme which is reiterated in a number of variations. On one level, the retreat was a crucial motive of Nietzsche's break with Enlightenment traditions. What Nietzsche initiated, we are told, was a 'total rejection of a nihilistically deflated modernity'; in his work 'the critique of modernity renounced for the first time its emancipatory content.' In contrast with Enlightenment aspirations, Nietzsche is said to have conjured up the 'experiences of self-disclosure of a subjectivity removed from all limiting rules of cognition and instrumental activity, from all imperatives of utility and ethics' – experiences, moreover, which were retrojected into an 'archaic past'. On another level, the same retreat surfaced in the notion of the 'will to power', to the extent that the notion pointed to 'subjective power claims of valuations disguised behind validity claims'.[18]

Closely allied with the charge of subjectivism, in Habermas's indictment, is Nietzsche's presumed irrationalism or his abandonment of rational standards – particularly the standards erected by modern epistemology and ethics. According to the study, Nietzsche 'continued the romantic purge of aesthetics of all cognitive and moral ingredients'; on the level of aesthetic experience 'a Dionysian reality is immunized by a "hiatus of oblivion" against the domains of theoretical cognition and moral action, against the world of everyday life'. By segregating itself from these domains Nietzsche's perspective was constrained to drift irremediably into the sphere of a 'metaphysically sublimated irrationalism' – a sphere in which subjective-aesthetic preferences overwhelm and absorb both empirical and moral considerations. As Habermas insists, however, removed from rational standards Nietzsche's perspective was ultimately unable to legitimate itself, with the result that the metaphysics (or aesthetics) of the 'will to power' lacked a philosophical warrant. Nietzsche, he asserts, 'owes his power-focused concept of modernity to a debunking critique of reason which places itself outside the horizons of reason'. While suggestive in many ways, such a debunking operation is self-defeating in the end. Moving beyond a modern aesthetics of 'taste', Nietzsche can no longer 'justify the standards of aesthetic judgement' because of his decision 'to transpose aesthetic experiences into an archaic past' and to separate the critical faculty of art appreciation from its moorings in 'rational argumentation' or a procedurally unified rationality. As a result, treated as 'gateway to the Dionysian realm', aesthetics is 'hypostatized into the otherness of reason'.[19]

As in Hegel's case, Habermas's reading of Nietzsche calls for a critical reply. Given the broad range of the indictment, several points or facets need to be considered in turn. One point has to do with Nietzsche's alleged break with his romantic and classicist precursors, deriving from his anti-Christian stance – an argument which strikes me as odd (if not in poor taste) in the case of an author whose own defence of modernity and rationalization tends to reduce religion largely to a relic of the past. As was true for some of his precursors, one needs to distinguish, I believe, between Nietzsche's attitude towards official (or 'positive') Christianity and towards the person of its founder (for whom he consistently voiced praise); moreover, someone who signed his last writings alternatively or simultaneously as 'The Crucified' and 'Dionysus' can hardly be accused of having sundered the 'nexus of Dionysus and Christ'.[20] More important in the present context is the presumed plunge into Dionysian frenzy and rampant subjectivism. On the face of it, the latter charge is again odd or curious – given that subjectivity is treated as the basic 'principle' of modernity. For how can Nietzsche have been the instigator of a radical exit or exodus from modern discourse, and simultaneously been mired in an undiluted subjectivity (and thus an undiluted modernism)? The charge, however, is blunted and rendered obscure by Habermas's own presentation. As indicated, Nietzsche is said to be addicted to a subjectivity removed from normal, everyday conventions; at the same time, his conception of Dionysus is portrayed as an 'intensification of subjectivism (or the subjective) to the point of total self-oblivion'. 'Only when the subject loses itself,' Habermas writes, the door opens to 'the world of the unforeseen and completely surprising, the domain of aesthetic appearances'. Another passage presents as Nietzsche's exit route from modernity the 'sundering of the principle of individuation' – a claim which follows on the heels of a sentence underscoring his subjectivism. But is subjectivity enhanced through self-oblivion? Can Nietzsche have unleashed 'polymorphous chaos' and *anomie* – and simultaneously have worshipped the modern ego? The same dilemma besets the treatment of the 'will to power' – which Habermas at one point links with 'subjective power claims' and, at another, with a 'trans-subjective will' revealing 'anonymous processes of domination'.[21]

The preceding point is closely connected with Nietzsche's Dionysian leanings or the status of Dionysus in his work. As it seems to me, Habermas's stress on untamed frenzy is vastly excessive and neglects the tensional and multidimensional character of Nietzsche's thought. Even and particularly *The Birth of Tragedy* – a youthful and (in his own admission) somewhat romantic-effusive work – did not simply glorify irrational chaos, but rather culminated in a paean on Attic tragedy seen as combination and reconciliation of Dionysus and Apollo. In Nietzsche's portrayal, the former appeared as a symbol of non-differentiation, of an 'original oneness of nature', while Apollo was the god of moderation and insight, representing the 'principle of individuation'. Reacting against classicist construals of antiquity (emphasizing 'quiet grandeur'), *The Birth of Tragedy* clearly sought to recapture and reinvigorate the Dionysian dimension of

Greek culture – but without neglecting the need for artistic form and aesthetic sublimation. Pointedly the work distinguished the Greek celebrations of Dionysus from their wilder, barbarian counterparts. In the barbarian festivals, Nietzsche wrote, the central trait was a complete 'promiscuity overriding every form of tribal law', an unleashing of 'all the savage urges of the mind until they reached that paroxysm of lust and cruelty which has always struck me as the "witches' cauldron" *par excellence*'. In opposition to these wild excesses, 'what kept Greece safe was the proud, imposing image of Apollo who, in holding up the head of Gorgon to these brutal and grotesque Dionysian forces, subdued them.' As Nietzsche added, this 'act of pacification' represented 'the most important event in the history of Greek ritual': for only now did it become possible 'to speak of nature's celebrating an *aesthetic* triumph; only now has the absorption of the *principium individuationis* become an aesthetic event.'[22]

In my view, Nietzsche never abandoned nor revoked this complex-tensional outlook – a circumstance which foils any attempt at a univocal interpretation (either as a simple modernist or as a Romantic regressing to an 'archaic past'). This continuity is reflected in his self-description or projection as an 'artistic Socrates' and also in his ambivalence towards reason or rationality throughout his life. Although decrying an abstract or lifeless 'Socratism', Nietzsche never renounced philosophical reason or his (ambivalent) admiration for Socrates. What he opposed in traditional rationalism was chiefly a high-flown essentialism or foundationalism – the pretence of being able to absorb concrete, multilayered experience into uniform concepts or unchanging categories. Turning against self-styled rationalists, his *Twilight of the Idols* attacked their blatant 'Egypticism': 'They think that they show their respect for a topic when they de-historicize it, *sub specie aeterni* – when they turn it into a mummy. All that philosophers have handled for thousands of years have been concept-mummies; nothing real has escaped their grasp alive.' Against conceptual abstractions Nietzsche pitted the endeavour of concrete inquiry – an inquiry he did not disdain to call 'science' (despite his aversion to a reductive scientism or naturalism): 'Today we possess science precisely to the extent to which we have decided to accept the testimony of the senses – to the extent to which we sharpen or strengthen them and have learned to think through them.' This attitude towards reason and science also coloured his estimate of modernity and modern enlightenment. As is well documented, Nietzsche opposed obscurantism in every form, especially the obscurantism spreading during the Bismarck era. Noting the danger of a regressive atavism or shallow Romanticism, *The Dawn* observed that – far from being the monopoly of reactionaries – the study of history and interest in the past had fortunately 'changed their nature one fine day and now soar with the broadest wings past their old conjurers and upward, as new and stronger geniuses of that very Enlightenment against which they were conjured up. This Enlightenment we must now advance further.'[23]

Broadly speaking, Nietzsche's thought is the very reverse of dogmatism or a fixed message or doctrine – a doctrine which necessarily would mutilate real life. This antidogmatism is a recurrent theme in all his writings, most notably in *The Joyful Science*, where we read: 'We, however, we others who thirst for reason, want to look our experiences as straight in the eye as if they represented a scientific experiment – hour after hour, day after day. We want ourselves to be our experiments and guinea pigs.' Wedded to this experimentalism, Nietzsche's thought militated against received formulas or 'answers', remaining always open to new vistas – an openness scarcely evident in the reviewed study. Although broadly endorsing the notion of 'fallibilism', Habermas fails to question (or treat as questionable) modern rationalism or his own model of rational discourse. Presumably armed with 'truth', Habermas hurls at Nietzsche the charges of subjectivism, nihilism, and irrationalism – labels which (though I consider them incorrect) *might* well designate the legitimate outcome of sustained inquiry, rather than being signs of corruption. For who or what method can safeguard thinking in advance to preclude this outcome? A case in point is Nietzsche's aesthetics, which Habermas takes to task for eluding the standards of theoretical and practical reason. But where is it established that these standards are applicable to, or binding on, art? Which doctrine secures the primacy of epistemology and ethics? In light of recent developments in the philosophy of science, can one not plausibly argue that some kind of creative or artful inventiveness is presupposed even in the rule-governed domains of science and ethical discourse? And if such inventiveness is treated not as a marginal gloss but as constitutive feature, how can one fault Nietzsche for pursuing the implications of this insight – rather than returning to the *terra firma* of (realist) epistemology? As it seems to me, his genealogical ventures are evidence of this fearless and relentless quest, as are his (posthumously collected) fragments on the 'will to power as knowledge' and the 'will to power as art'.[24] Far from being a renegade, Nietzsche in these and related areas (I believe) steadfastly advanced the discourse of modernity.

III

As noted before, Habermas treats Nietzsche as the 'turn-table' or hiatus separating defenders of modern reason from champions of postmodernism and counter-enlightenment. In the postmodernist camp, his study differentiates in turn between two camps: one attached to Nietzsche's genealogical method as well as his Dionysian zest, the other concerned with his broader metaphysical ruminations. The founder of the first camp was Georges Bataille, the poet or *écrivain* of human excess. In the case of Bataille, we are told, Nietzsche's legacy inspired an attempted regress to a lost oneness accomplished through an 'eruption of antirational elements, a consuming act of self-immolation'; Dionysian frenzy here took the form of an orgiastic revelry manifesting itself 'in play, dance and intoxication just as much as in those sentiments – mingling horror and lust – which are triggered by destruction and the confrontation with suffering and violent death.' The chief spokesman of the second camp was Heidegger with his focus on Nietzschean metaphysics. 'The goals', Habermas writes, 'that Nietzsche pursued through his total, all-embracing critique of ideology – this goal Heidegger seeks to reach through an immanent destruction of occidental metaphyics. . . . In doing so Heidegger faces the task of putting philosophy into the place' occupied by art in Nietzsche's work. In treating the latter explicitly as a philosopher, Heidegger's exegesis assigns or reassigns to philosophy the function ceded by Romanticism to art – the function of synthesis or reconciliation 'countermanding the divisions of modernity'. What links the two camps, in Habermas's view, is their common antirationalism. Both Bataille and Heidegger, he says, 'want to perform a radical critique of reason which attacks the roots of critique itself'. While Heidegger aimed his critique at the objectivist character of science, Bataille concentrated on modern instrumental rationality and efficiency. In both instances, the 'totalizing' thrust of critique catapulted thought towards an 'otherness' entirely outside the bounds of reason: 'While reason is defined as calculating control and utilization, its otherness can only be characterized negatively as the completely non-controllable and unusable – as a medium which the subject can reach only by transgressing and abandoning itself as subject.'[25]

The study's Heidegger chapter offers initially a broad overview, recapitulating general themes involved in his turn to metaphysics or a critique of metaphysics. Four main themes are accentuated at this point. The first theme is Heidegger's commitment to philosophy, that is, his effort to reinstitute philosophy into the position 'from which it had been expelled by Young Hegelian criticism'. A direct corollary of this reinvigoration was his emphasis on 'ontological pre-understanding' as the dimension pre-forming the particular ideas and perspectives of a given society or culture. For Heidegger, this dimension was in the past commonly articulated by metaphysics, with the result that changes in 'pre-understanding' furnished clues for the history of metaphysics. In modern times – and this is the second theme – metaphysics has progressively buttressed or taken the form of a defence of technology. Based on the philosophy of subjectivity inaugurated by Descartes, modernity has increasingly given rise to calculating rationality, instrumental control of nature, and finally to an all-out 'struggle for control of the earth'. This expanding sway of technology has ushered in a crisis in our time – the third theme. As in the case of Nietzsche, countering this crisis requires recollection of a distant past – but in a non-antiquarian sense and with an eye to the future. Following Hölderlin, Heidegger views our period as marked by traces of an 'exiled god' whose absence presages a possible return. In metaphysical language, this absence denotes the withdrawal or oblivion of 'being' – a withdrawal fostering an ontological (not merely psychological) need for recovery. As a guidepost to recovery, Heidegger's later writings appeal to a recollective or 'anamnetic' mode of thinking transgressing the bounds of calculating reason – the fourth theme. Using the notion of 'ontological difference' as a guiding thread, we read, Heidegger's work claims access to a 'cognitive competence located beyond the pale of (traditional) self-reflection and discursive reasoning'.[26]

In an effort to retrace the steps leading to Heidegger's later writings, the study turns attention to his early magnum opus, *Being and Time* (of 1927). As Habermas recognizes, the work formed a watershed in twentieth-century attempts to transgress the bounds of the 'philosophy of consciousness' (or subjectivity). Heidegger confronted the task, he writes, of 'overcoming or supplanting the concept of transcendental subjectivity – dominant since Kant – without cancelling the wealth of differentiations' generated by Husserl's phenomenology. In trying to surpass the subjectivist legacy, Heidegger performed an ontological 'turn' – while at the same time maintaining the transcendental project of a reflective clarification of the conditions of possibility of human *Dasein* or 'being-in-the-world'. In Habermas's portrayal, the opening chapter of *Being and Time* introduced three crucial innovations paving the way to a 'fundamental ontology'. The first step involved an ontological interpretation of transcendental inquiry or epistemology. Instead of relying (with Kant) on the a priori categories of consciousness, Heidegger at this point appealed to the domain of 'ontological pre-understanding' as the matrix underlying different cognitive and practical pursuits. This pre-understanding surfaces, we read, 'when we probe *behind* the categorial structure of things supplied by a (scientifically informed) transcendental philosophy. The analysis of pre-understanding yields those structures of the lifeworld or "being-in-the-world" Heidegger calls "existentials".' The second step has to do with the interpretive or hermeneutical cast of pre-understanding, a cast modifying or undercutting the straightforward, intentional inspection of phenomena. In contrast to Husserl's focus on perception and direct description, Heidegger's 'hermeneutical phenomenology' shifted the accent to textual (or quasi-textual) exegesis. In a third step, this ontological-hermeneutical outlook was applied to the analysis of *Dasein*, construed as that mode of being concerned essentially with the understanding of 'its own being' and its possibilities. These three steps together – and especially the notion of pre-understanding thematized in them – are said to have enabled Heidegger finally to articulate the 'key concept of his fundamental ontology': the concept of 'world'. In his usage, 'world' signifies a non-objective and non-objectifiable background of experience which is 'always already' assumed by subjects relating to objects: 'For it is not the subject that establishes a relation to something in the world, it is the world which initially furnishes the context of pre-understanding in which beings can be encountered.' Several different modes of encountering and 'caring' about beings were distinguished in *Being and Time* – all of them nurtured by a pre-understood world seen as 'referential context' (*Bewandtniszusammenhang*).[27]

Having thus restated the underlying motivation and general tenor of *Being and Time*, Habermas quickly faults the work for a basic inconsistency vitiating its ontological turn. This inconsistency is said to emerge in the analysis of *Dasein* or the 'who of *Dasein*'. In dealing with this question – and especially with 'authentic' *Dasein* and 'being-toward-death' – Heidegger allegedly lapsed back into a Kierkegaardian subjectivism (if not a hopeless solipsism): although initially having reconstructed the 'philosophy of the subject' in favour of an underlying 'referential context', Heidegger subsequently 'succumbed again to the conceptual constraints of subjective philosophizing: for the solipsistically construed *Dasein* reoccupies the position of transcendental subjectivity.' Departing from traditional idealism, it is true, *Being and Time* ascribed to subjectivity an active potency: in exploring its possibilities, *Dasein* performed a 'Fichtean act (of self-constitution) transfigured into a global project'. In more general terms (and despite this activist stance), Heidegger's early work – according to Habermas – remained a prisoner of the philosophy of consciousness, particularly in its Husserlian form. Contrary to Mead and the later Wittgenstein (but in conformity with Husserl) Heidegger never eluded 'the traditional privileging of theoretical cognition, of constative language-use, and of the validity claim of propositional truth' – thus paying tribute to 'the *foundationalism* of the philosophy of consciousness'. In the pages of *Being and Time*, this indebtedness to the past manifested itself in many forms, particularly in an incipient objectivism giving priority to (realist) epistemology:

Regardless of whether primacy is accorded to the question of being or of knowledge, in both cases explanatory inquiry is monopolized by a cognitive world-relation, by constative speech, theoretical reason and propositional truth. This ontological-epistemological primacy of knowable beings levels the complexity of world-relations – evident in the plurality of illocutionary modes of natural languages – in favour of *one* privileged relation to the 'objective world'. This latter relation governs even human praxis: instrumental activity, that is, the monological pursuit of goals, is seen as the primary mode of action.[28]

Heidegger's later *Kehre* is attributed (at least in part) to an awareness of these predicaments, to the realization that *Being and Time* had ended in the 'cul-de-sac of subjectivity'. As remedy the *Kehre* initiated a radical reversal or inversion: namely, the turn from subjectivism to a passive celebration of 'being'. While *Being and Time* – we read – had sponsored 'the decisionism of an empty resoluteness', Heidegger's later philosophy counselled 'the submissiveness of an equally empty readiness for surrender' (to being). According to Habermas, this counsel carried not only metaphysical but practical-political implications. In treating 'being' as a mode of historical happening, he writes, Heidegger stylized historical events and social conditions into 'an unimpregnable ontological destiny [*Seinsgeschick*]'. The recommendation of surrender (to being) thus had the practical 'perlocutionary effect of inducing a diffuse readiness to obedience towards an auratic, but indefinite authority', that is, towards the edicts of 'pseudo-sacral powers'. In producing this effect, Heidegger's later works militate against a central pillar of modernity or the modern discourse: the autonomy of human thought and action. In Habermas's presentation, the turn to being and its destiny sponsored a 'training or socialization (*Einüburg*) in a new heteronomy'; Heidegger's critique of modern reason accordingly culminated in a 'radical, but substantively empty change of attitude – away from autonomy and towards a devotion to being'. Accentuating this feature the study indicts the later work not only of antimodernism but of an illiberal antihumanism: 'Heidegger rejects the existential-ontological concept of freedom.... *Dasein* now submits to the authority of an uncontrollable meaning of being and renounces the will to self-assertion suspect of subjectivism.' As the reinforcing (if not actually dominant) motive of Heidegger's *Kehre* the concluding section of the chapter points to his political debacle, that is, his rectorship under the Nazi regime (in 1933–4). Heidegger, we read, 'interprets the falseness of the movement in which he had been embroiled, not in terms of subjective responsibility or an existential abdication to "the They" (*das Man*), but as an objective lack or failure of truth. . . . This gives rise to the history of being."[29]

Among the thinkers discussed in the study, the treatment of Heidegger is easily the least favourable (or most polemical). Given the broad sweep of the indictment it seems desirable to disassemble the various charges. Before entering into substantive questions, one may wish to register reservations about the manner in which Heidegger is first introduced, namely, in conjunction with Georges Bataille. Being presented as an ally or accomplice of the *écrivain* of excess is unlikely to gain friends for Heidegger among 'right-minded' people averse to irrationalism. More substantive (and hardly congruent with the preceding complicity) is the portrayal of Heidegger as a 'philosopher', that is, as a thinker bent on reinvigorating philosophy and on reinstituting it in the place occupied by art in Nietzsche's writings. I shall not dwell here on the propriety of this move in light of the presumed expulsion of philosophy by 'Young Hegelian criticism' (given that the latter was itself only a strand in Hegelian, that is, modern-philosophical discourse). More important is the juxtaposition with Nietzsche. While Nietzsche had previously been chided for tearing art out of its broader philosophical context – its nexus with truth and goodness – Heidegger is now taken to task for adhering to a 'classicist aesthetics' and for being unable to appreciate the autonomy or separateness of modern art. Quite apart from the fact that I consider the classicist label erroneous, the juxtaposition places both Nietzsche and Heidegger in a 'no-win' position – with either option being tainted with antimodernism.[30] Heidegger's portrayal as a 'philosopher', incidentally, collides also with the heavy emphasis placed on political motives animating his later *Kehre* (I shall return to this point). To the extent that Habermas accords great weight if not actually precedence to those motives, the inner movement of Heidegger's thought clearly had a more psychological or ideological rather than philosophical character.[31]

On a philosophical plane, the most serious issues have to do with the interpretation of *Being and Time* as well as Heidegger's later opus. As indicated, Habermas regards *Being and Time* as an effort to break out of the confines of modern, Cartesian-type philosophizing – but an effort thwarted by Heidegger's relapse into the 'cul-de-sac of subjectivity'. This relapse is said to have spawned a Kierkegaardian existentialism, a Fichtean activism, and also a privileging of (realist) epistemology focused on the 'objective world'. In my view, these charges are highly dubious, both singly and in conjunction. First of all, one should concede, of course, a certain transcendental flavour of *Being and Time* – the study's attempt to continue inquiry into 'conditions of possibility' on an ontological level. This aspect, however – which Heidegger repeatedly admitted (and which was a cause

of subsequent reformulations) – is a far cry from a lapse into
subjectivism, let alone solipsism. The section on the 'who of *Dasein*'
– on which the study focuses – points in the very opposite direction
from a Kierkegaardian or Fichtean self-centredness. The commonsense assumption, Heidegger writes there, that the 'who of *Dasein*' is
'I' (or me) should not stand in the way of further ontological inquiry;
for, 'we might discover that the "who of everyday *Dasein*" is precisely
not I myself' or the 'ego of subjective acts'. As he adds, the ontological
elucidation of 'being-in-the-world' shows that 'there is not initially
and never ever a mere subject or I without a world. And in the same
manner and finally there exists just as little an isolated I without the
others.' Construed as 'being-in-the-world', *Dasein* necessarily (or
ontologically) and not merely accidentally relates to the 'world'
comprising objects, utensils and fellow beings, and 'cares' about these
modalities of being in different ways. 'Authentic' *Dasein* does not
mean a cancelling of the hyphens or retreat into selfhood, but rather
a *Dasein* that genuinely cares about and cultivates its connections,
instead of relating to the world in thoughtless indifference. Even
'being-toward-death' does not negate *Dasein's* connectedness – but
only a spurious mutual identification or reciprocal manipulation.[32]

The 'worldiness' of *Dasein* also entails its interhuman linkage, an
aspect thematized in *Being and Time* under the label of 'co-being' or
'being-with' (*Mitsein*). In Habermas's account, Heidegger's subjectivist moorings preclude genuine access to intersubjectivity (and
especially to communicative interaction in Habermas's sense).
Although recognizing that co-being is introduced as a 'constitutive
trait of being-in-the-world', he charges that the 'primacy of intersubjectivity' escapes a conceptual structure 'held hostage to the solipsism
of Husserlian phenomenology'. In a closely parallel fashion, subject-
centred *Dasein* is said to 'constitute co-being' just as the 'transcendental ego' constitutes intersubjectivity in Husserl's theory. This argument is barely intelligible; for how can co-being be a 'constitutive
trait' of being-in-the-world and yet at the same time be constituted
by *Dasein* (which is itself defined by Heidegger as 'being-in-the-
world')? As *Being and Time* especially insists, the ontological construal of being-in-the-world implies that world is 'always a world
already shared with others: the world of *Dasein* is a *co-world*; being-
in signifies a *co-being* with others.'[33] The lopsidedness of exegesis on
this level is matched by the incongruence of the alleged outcome of
Being and Time: its return to traditional epistemology privileging the
'objective world'. As will be recalled, Habermas's rehearsal of the
opening chapter of the book stressed precisely the non-objective and
non-objectifiable character of the world seen as a 'meaning-disclosing' horizon. World in this sense, he writes, is 'always already
presupposed by subjects relating cognitively or practically to objects';

consequently, cognitive or practical acts performed in an 'objectifying attitude' (or relating to an objective world) can be grasped as derivative modes of a comprehensive lifeworld and its modalities of being-in-the-world. These statements are plainly contradicted by the subsequent summation which speaks of the 'ontological-epistemological primacy of (objective) beings as knowable', of the '*one* privileged relation to the objective world', and even of instrumental activity as the 'primary form of action'. But why should Heidegger be blamed for this contradiction?

The cogency of interpretation is equally doubtful with regard to Heidegger's later opus. First a few additional words on the political context of the *Kehre*. There can be no doubt (in my mind) that Heidegger's involvement in 1933 was an egregious mistake and calamity; I see no need here to compete in professions of antifascism. I question, however, the claim that he never addressed his political mistake 'in a *single* sentence' – a claim which is disavowed by his many system-critical remarks during the Nazi regime and by his repeated attempts to account for his behaviour afterwards.[34] These 'accounts', it is true, were never written in a properly contrite or submissive spirit – which may be regrettable and a source of irritation for many. I only note that this same stubborn non-submissiveness accords ill with the claimed reversal initiated by the *Kehre*, namely the turn from autonomy to passive surrender. Although having first criticized the subjectivism of *Being and Time*, Habermas proceeds to rebuke Heidegger's *Kehre* for abandoning or renouncing 'subjective responsibility' in favour of a blind devotion to being or the 'destiny of being' (*Seinsgeschick*). As mentioned before, the *Kehre* is said to separate the earlier 'decisionism of an empty resoluteness' from the later 'submissiveness of an equally empty readiness for surrender'. Little imagination is required to see a simple dualism operative in this shift: namely, the dualism of subjectivism versus objectivism, or activity versus passivity. The same dualism was present in the earlier treatment of Hegel – which (as I tried to show) alternated precariously between a 'Young Hegelian' exegesis focused on subjective praxis, and a 'Right Hegelian' approach stressing passive contemplation. As in all such dualisms, however, the contrasting terms presuppose each other.

Regarding Heidegger's *Kehre*, I would question first of all the abruptness or radicalness of the change. As is well known, *Being and Time* from its opening pages addressed itself to the 'question of being' – although (in Heidegger's admission) the question was not yet properly focused at that juncture. His subsequent works show a progressive intensification of ontological inquiry, but in a manner which never simply discards earlier formulations. Regarding the meaning or status of 'being', Habermas offers a number of curious and often contradictory assertions. Commenting on the notion of 'ontological difference', he claims: 'Heidegger separates Being – which has always been viewed as the Being of beings – from beings'; thus segregated from beings and rendered 'quasi-autonomous', the 'hypostatized Being can assume the role of Dionysus.' Somewhat later, hermeneutical phenomenology is presented as a movement from surface to depth, towards a 'Being which is disguised or obstructed by beings'. As can readily be seen, segregated into polar components 'ontological difference' is reabsorbed into traditional metaphysical categories (the antitheses of essence and appearance, universals and particulars) – thereby nullifying Heideggers's 'critique of metaphysics'; as the latter has repeatedly observed (not least in his *Identity and Difference*), ontological inquiry probes precisely the 'being of beings' as a mode of differential 'belonging'.[35] Returning to Habermas: the separation of being and its blockage or obstruction by beings would seem to preclude a direct access to being – a conclusion which plainly conflicts with a subsequent passage affirming the opposite. Referring to the temporal but 'undialectical' character of Heidegger's ontology, the study asserts that 'as in the case of metaphysics' being is for Heidegger 'the absolutely immediate or unmediated'. Whether seen as pure immediacy or as separate entity, being has the character of external positivity – which leads to Habermas's most serious charge: namely, Heidegger's denial of freedom in favour of 'heteronomy'. Although confidently stated and reiterated, the charge is also the most spurious – given the centrality of freedom in Heidegger's entire philosophy. As in the case of Hegel's 'spirit' or 'idea', 'being' for Heidegger was essentially a synonym for freedom (although not for arbitrary wilfulness).[36]

The charge of heteronomy is closely allied with the presumed lapse into counter-enlightenment and antirationalism: by abandoning autonomy, ontological thought is also said to step beyond the bounds of reason. In turning towards being and its destiny, Habermas writes, Heidegger's opus assumes 'a cognitive stance or competence *beyond* the pale of self-reflection, beyond discursive reasoning as such'. The recollective or 'essential' thinking practised and recommended in his work allegedly is hostile 'to all empirical and normative questions which can be treated scientifically and historically or discussed in argumentative form'. In the end, ontological thinking is said to submerge in an irrational intuitionism or 'mysticism'. The vehemence of these claims again does not buttress their plausibility. For what are Heidegger's numerous writings in this area – from *What is Metaphysics?* to *What is Called Thinking?* and beyond – if not strings of arguments trying to make sense to readers – although not on the level of calculative-analytical rationality (or *Verstand*)? And how can this rationality be corrected if every step beyond its confines is immediately branded as irrational or mystical? The latter charge, incidentally, has been addressed long ago by Heidegger himself, in his lectures on Hegel's *Phenomenology of Spirit* (of 1930). 'It is becoming customary now', he remarked, 'to label my philosophy as "mysticism". It is equally superfluous and pointless to counter this charge. . . . Not logical – hence mystical; not *ratio* – hence irrational. In this manner one only shows that one has not yet faced up to the question why and with what justification being (*on*) is related to *logos* (or *ratio*).'[37] Habermas's remedy for Heidegger's mysticism is a return to propositional truth and pragmatic efficiency – the same outlook he had castigated as the outcome of *Being and Time*. Like Nietzsche's radical critique of reason, he writes, Heidegger's turn to being and its destiny involves an '*uprooting of propositional truth* and a devaluation of discursive thought'. Despite the role of 'world' and language as horizons of meaning constitution, the actual 'functioning' of sentences is said to depend not on this horizon but on the 'innerworldly success of praxis' relating to factual conditions; far from antedating and enabling cognitive-factual truth, the horizon of world (or being) is actually 'governed' by this truth and its cognitive standards.[38]

<h2 style="text-align:center">IV</h2>

In its concluding chapters the study recapitulates central themes of the preceding discussions, mainly in an effort to profile or set the stage for Habermas's own proposal (of communicative interaction). Returning to his narrative, Habermas recalls the Enlightenment *cantus firmus* epitomized by Kant, and also the emerging counterdiscourse stressing the intrinsic costs of modernity. What united proponents of this counterdiscourse from Schiller to Schelling and Hegel, he notes, was 'the intent of revising the Enlightenment with the means provided by the latter itself'. Pointing to the cleavages or divisions (*Entzweiungen*) of modernity, Hegel in particular invoked the power of synthesis lodged in a totalizing *Vernunft* or absolute spirit. With diverse accents, the strands of the counterdiscourse were continued by Young Hegelians stressing rational praxis and Right Hegelians extolling abstract principles. Starting with Nietzsche, however, the modern discourse and its counterdiscourse were disrupted in favour of a 'totalizing critique of reason'; exiting from the 'dialectic of enlightenment', Nietzsche and his heirs dismiss or brush aside 'that two-hundred-year-old counterdiscourse implicit in modernity itself'. At this point Habermas turns to his own preferred remedy or exit route from the dilemmas of modern subjectivity: the shift from the 'philosophy of consciousness' to the paradigm of communicative reason and interaction. In contrast to a purely 'subject-centred' stance the latter paradigm, in his presentation, conceives 'intersubjective understanding and consensus as the *telos* implicit in linguistic communication'; constitutive for the paradigm is 'the performative attitude of participants in interactions who coordinate their action plans by reaching mutual consensus on something in the world'. By relying on human interaction, the communicative model is said to correct the basic limitation of modern subjectivity (or 'logocentrism'): its exclusive focus on the 'objective world', that is, its tendency to reduce 'the relation of man and world to a cognitive dimension, namely to a relation to the world of (objective) beings as a whole'. Most importantly, the model returns to and reinscribes itself within the modern philosophical discourse: 'Instead of transgressing or overreaching modernity, it resumes the counterdiscourse inherent in modernity, extricating the latter from the hopeless confrontation between Hegel and Nietzsche.'[39]

I shall not dwell here extensively on the details of Habermas's proposal or presumed paradigm shift (which has repeatedly been done in the literature). Instead I wish to point to some quandaries besetting the proposal and its relation to the modern 'discourse'. First of all, one cannot fail to notice the geographical and intellectual restrictedness of this discourse: as portrayed in the study, its chief protagonists or voices are German (with French thinkers mainly continuing or amplifying German initiatives – such as Bataille vis-à-vis Nietzsche, or Derrida vis-à-vis Heidegger). What is chiefly missing is the contribution of Anglo-Saxon thought to modernity – which is hardly negligible. Thus, one misses the legacy of British scepticism and empiricism from Bacon over Berkeley and Hume to Russell; equally absent is English utilitarianism and neo-utilitarianism which, as an alternative to Hegel, construed 'civil society' as a conglomerate of individual interests. The most important gap, in my view, however, is the neglect of the contractarian tradition from Hobbes to Locke (and later refined by Rousseau and Kant) in which the communicative model was largely prefigured. Contractarian thinkers, as one may recall, derived the commonwealth or the state precisely from the agreement or consensus of 'free and equal' individuals. Generally speaking, modern philosophy (with a few exceptions) was by no means subjectivist in a 'solipsistic' manner – one which would have contested the existence of other subjects; on the contrary, it was the recognized plurality of diverse subjects or individuals which raised the problem of public order and peaceful coexistence (to be met through general agreement). On the same level, it is simply not the case – as Habermas suggests – that modern thought was one-sidedly focused on cognition or a one-world relation (namely, to the so-called 'objective world'). Under the rubric of 'natural law', modern philosophy created an elaborate system of normative standards which

– on a par with the 'ideal speech community' – were meant to regulate human interactions. In a similar vein, modernity has been no stranger to intimate self-disclosure – as manifested in literature from Pascal's *Penseés* to Rousseau's *Confessions*.

The most obvious precursor of the communicative model is Kantian rationalism. In his three critiques, Kant thematized precisely the different world relations emphasized by the model: a cognitive-theoretical access to the external world; a practical grasp of normative standards governing human interactions; and an expressive self-relation manifest in art and aesthetics. As Habermas himself states (in a previously cited passage), Kant replaced the substantive reason of the past by a conception of rationality 'differentiated into separate moments', a concept segregating 'practical reason and the critique of judgement from theoretical cognition'. These separate moments provided the underpinnings to the cultural 'value spheres' emerging in modernity, those of science, ethics and art – the same spheres, Habermas says, which Hegel grasped as manifestations of the 'principle of subjectivity'. While modern science disenchants nature, thus liberating the subject from ignorance, modern ethics is grounded in individual autonomy, and modern art in subjective self-expression. Despite the claimed exit from subjectivity, the same spheres or dimensions clearly resurface in Habermas's model with its various divisions or tripartitions – particularly the divisions between truth, rightness and truthfulness (on the level of validity claims); between constative, regulative and expressive utterances (on the level of speech acts); and between objective, social and subjective worlds (on the level of world-relations). In light of this intrinsic continuity, one can reasonably doubt the asserted 'paradigm shift' – away from subject- or ego-centred reason – given that the various dimensions of the model all pay homage to the same centring (being classifiable respectively into subject–object, subject–subject, and subject-to-itself relationships). In his study, Habermas repeatedly contests this continuity – but in formulations which confirm the linkage. Contrary to the privileged position of cognitive subjectivity, the communicative paradigm is said to support a different, performative relation of subjects: 'When ego performs a speech act and *alter* responds, both enter into an interpersonal relation'; at this point ego is enabled 'to relate to himself from the perspective of *alter* as a participant in an interaction.' Similarly, criticizing Heidegger's notion of 'being-in-the-world', the study presents communicative interaction as anchored in 'the structures of linguistic intersubjectivity' and sustained by 'the same medium in which subjects capable of speech and action reach agreement on something in the world'.[40]

To be sure, Kantian rationalism is not simply translatable into communicative interaction. What separates the two modes of reasoning is primarily Habermas's reliance on language and also on the dimension of the 'lifeworld' seen as a matrix overarching segregated value spheres. Relying in part on Wittgensteinian motifs Habermas portrays the paradigm shift of his approach also as a 'linguistic turn' – from a straightforward 'philosophy of consciousness' to the conception of a linguistically nurtured or mediated thought and action. This turn is invoked in the study as the chief dividing line from past forms of rationalism, including Kant's 'purism of reason'. 'There is no such thing', we read, 'as a pure reason only subsequently clothed in linguistic garments. Rather, reason is from the beginning an incarnate reason enmeshed in contexts of communicative action and in structures of the lifeworld.' As an incarnate faculty embroiled in real-life situations, reason cannot simply soar above or cancel space and time, but is always somehow 'in-the-world'. Similarly, given the linguistic character of reason – its inability to be denuded of language – there cannot be a 'pure' or purely rational language, but only an 'interlacing' or 'tensional mixture' of opacity and clarity, of real and ideal elements of discourse. Despite the radicalness of these and similar formulations, however, their import is sharply curtailed in the study: countermanding his ostensible break with Kantian purism, Habermas quickly retreats to the *terra firma* of rational epistemology. His theory of value spheres and corresponding validity claims is entirely erected on this ground; so are the parameters of modern discourse as drawn in the study. Apprehensive of the spectre of contextualism, his approach basically disaggregates the claimed 'mixture' of elements. Despite the 'essentially' incarnate (and impure) character of reason, pure rationality continues to serve as yardstick of opaque or 'real' elements – in a manner relegating the latter to a level of imperfection or inferiority with which we may have to 'make do'.[41] Obviously, it is only on the assumption of a 'pure' or non-contextual language that a 'universal pragmatics' can be formulated; similarly, it is only by discounting the concrete differences among individuals and the multivocity of speech that ego can be assumed to recognize himself 'in the perspective of *alter*' to reach an ideal consensus. More generally, only traditional epistemology provides the basis for subordinating the meaning-disclosing potency of world (or language) to factual or pragmatic claims – as was done in the Heidegger chapter. Returning to the latter issue, Habermas insists that 'meaning must [*darf*] not absorb validity,' adding that 'it is only the prior *conditions* of the validity of statements which change with changing meaning-horizons – but the latter must in turn be *confirmed* through experience and the contact with things encountered in a given horizon.'[42]

The same ambivalence affects the status of the 'lifeworld'. Recapitulating arguments advanced on other occasions, the study depicts the lifeworld as a background context not directly available to inspection or control. In communicating about something in the world, Habermas writes, speakers and hearers 'move within the horizon of a common lifeworld' which remains 'in their backs as an indivisible holistic foil'. As a background matrix, the lifeworld operates 'pre-reflectively' and can 'only be perceived *a tergo*'; from the 'frontal perspective of communicatively acting subjects, the always "co-present" lifeworld escapes thematization.' Another passage speaks of the lifeworld as 'equivalent to the power of synthesis ascribed by subject-centred philosophy to consciousness as such'. These and similar formulations do not prevent Habermas, however, from distancing the lifeworld to a target of analysis and rational reconstruction – an operation basically bracketing its *a tergo* potency (and reducing it to a pliant 'resource'). 'We need a *theoretically constituted* perspective,' he states, 'in order to perceive communicative action as the medium through which the lifeworld as a whole is reproduced.'[43] What emerges from this perspective are formal-pragmatic schemata capturing the general 'structures of the lifeworld' stripped of variable contents. The main structures pinpointed in the study (and elsewhere) are 'culture', 'society', and 'personality' – domains which in turn undergird the tripartition of modern value spheres (science, ethics and self-expression) and corresponding validity claims (truth, rightness and truthfulness). Although first introduced as a simple change of perspective, the distinction of lifeworld and formal structures quickly acquires broader historical connotations, in the sense that modernization involves the growing segregation of value spheres from pre-reflective moorings. According to Habermas, the difference between lifeworld and (communicative) rationality cannot be bridged or reconciled in modernity; on the contrary, the difference is steadily intensified to the degree that the reproduction of the lifeworld 'no longer merely *passes* through the medium of communicative action but *results* from the interpretive accomplishments of actors'. To the extent that taken-for-granted modes of consensus are replaced by cooperatively achieved agreement, '*concrete* life-forms and *general* structures of the lifeworld *move apart*.'[44]

Pursuing the modernization theme, Habermas at this juncture projects a future scenario in which the lifeworld as *vis a tergo* is progressively replaced by formal structures – to the point where pre-reflective existence is virtually absorbed into conscious-rational designs. On the level of culture, the scenario entails the exchange of traditional beliefs for formal modes of argumentation; on the level of society, habitual behaviour gives way to universal principles of ethics, while personality proceeds from receptiveness to self-constructed modes of identity. Although presented as a 'thought experiment', the scenario is said to reflect the 'factual development' of modern lifeworlds, namely the growing 'abstraction of general lifeworld

structures' from traditional contents. Recasting this trend as a story
of emancipation, the study anticipates these (idealized) goal or end
points: 'for culture, a condition of permanent revision of reflectively
liquified traditions; for society, the dependence of legitimate order on
formal-discursive procedures of legislation and norm validation; for
personality, a condition of hazardous self-steering of a highly abstract
ego-identity.' In line with this development, lifeworlds are no longer
replenished unconsciously or pre-reflectively; rather, their reproduction relies essentially on cognitive critique, ethical universalism and
'extremely individualized' forms of socialization. Having sketched
this emancipatory vision, Habermas – almost abruptly – recoils from
its implicit utopianism. Noticing the affinity of his scenario with
Enlightenment ideals and especially with Kant's 'purism of reason',
he redirects attention to the lifeworld and its role of securing 'the
continuity of meaning contexts'. Despite modernity's steady turn to
abstract-formal structures (of thought and speech), tribute is again
paid to ordinary-language communication; despite the trend towards
extreme individualization, identity is said to be possible only within
a 'universal community'. Yet this tribute in turn is almost instantly
qualified (if not revoked). In a developmental sense, the lifeworld is
portrayed as recalcitrant to complete formalization or structural
differentiation; in fact, its interactive and communicative potential is
said to be of limited or 'low elasticity' – too limited for purposes of
effective rationalization. It is as an antidote or corrective to this
deficiency that Habermas in the end resorts to a dualistic scheme: the
scheme of the progressive uncoupling and tensional correlation of
'system' and lifeworld, where 'system' refers to relatively abstract
modes of action coordination capable of 'unburdening' the lifeworld
of various social tasks or functions.[45]

Given the reduced or tenuous status of the lifeworld – its progressive subordination to formal structures and system imperatives – the
claimed nexus of Habermas's model and Hegelian discourse (or
counterdiscourse) is hard to perceive. This nexus is reasserted at
several points. 'The theory of communicative action', Habermas
states, 'can reconstruct Hegel's concept of an ethical life-context
(without relying on consciousness-centred premises)'; like Hegel in
his early writings on guilt and punishment, the theory is 'guided by
an intuition expressible in Old Testament terms as follows: the unrest
of real life conditions nurtures an ambivalence deriving from the
dialectic of treason and revenge.' In other passages, however, Hegelian echoes are muffled if not entirely cancelled. Elaborating on the
difference between lifeworld and formal structures, the study insists
that the contrast eludes Hegelian notions of totality and synthesis. In
pronounced form, the same is true of the uncoupling of system and
lifeworld in the process of modernization. In his conception of a

'divided ethical totality', we read, Hegel (like Marx later) underestimated the 'autonomous logic' (*Eigensinn*) of system domains, their
tendency to extricate themselves from intersubjective relations in a
manner cancelling 'structural analogies' with the lifeworld. Apart
from the charges of irrationalism and antihumanism, the heirs of
Nietzsche are also specifically indicted for failing to accept modern
'value spheres' and their segregation from the lifeworld. What had
been granted to Hegel – to complain about the cleavages (*Entzweiungen*) of modernity – becomes a source of rebuke in the case of
Nietzscheans. In fact, from Habermas's perspective, the divisions of
modernity 'must not *per se* be viewed as symptomatic pathologies of
a subject-centred reason'. While Hegel had still been credited with
perceiving both the advances and the 'crisis character' of modern life,
modernization in Habermas's presentation is no longer intrinsically
crisis-prone but only subject to contingent (and essentially remedia-
ble) imbalances or derailments. The chief type of imbalance is an
'excessive' ascendancy of system imperatives or a certain 'preponderance of economic and bureaucratic, and more generally cognitive-
instrumental modes of rationality'.[46]

If Habermas's Hegelian credentials are dubious, the summary
expulsion of Nietzscheans from modernity is even less plausible. In
fact, parallels can readily be detected between central Nietzschean
motifs and Hegel's counterdiscourse. As recognized in the study,
Hegel and his Tübingen friends subscribed to a strongly imaginative
or 'mythopoetic' conception of synthesis or reconciliation (with
nature and fellow humans); among romantic writers, this outlook
was blended with the mythic fable of Dionysus, the figure of the
absent and expected god – a theme prominently continued by
Nietzsche and Heidegger (and other post-Nietzscheans). More generally, if modern discourse means a process of relentless self-scrutiny
– a scrutiny extending (as the study stays) to the 'sphere of the
ephemeral or impermanent' – then Nietzsche and his heirs would
seem to be prime exemplars of modernity (rather than antimodernism). Nowhere have the presuppositions and underpinnings of modernity itself been more thoroughly and critically explored than in the
Nietzschean 'camp'. Nowhere also has more attention been given to
the effects of modern divisions and cleavages (*Entzweiungen*) – that
is, to the intrinsic ambivalance or 'crisis character' of modern times.
To be sure, such attention may seem exorbitant to more sanguine
observers for whom modernity, as an 'unfinished project', merely
requires completion; Hegel's counterdiscourse must have seemed
equally lopsided to Enlightenment rationalists.[47] As it happens, the
crisis features of modernity have hardly lessened since Hegel's time;
the catastrophes of our age attest to the opposite. Against this background, the 'extremism' of some Nietzschean and post-Nietzschean

formulations may be viewed as a response to the increased hazards or hardships of modern life, that is, as the expression of a concrete 'suffering' – a suffering which Habermas's study only meets with condescending irony. If, as Hegel thought, ethical reconciliation is possible only on the basis of a deeply felt (or suffered) 'nexus of guilt', then Nietzschean counterdiscourse may have a profound ethical significance – as a counterpoint to the optimism and divisiveness of technological mastery and as a signpost to a different lifeform.

Needless to say, Nietzschean and post-Nietzschean discourse does not simply coincide with Hegel's. Like Habermas, spokespeople of this legacy have sought an exit route from the 'principle of modernity'; however, instead of simply multiplying subjects, they have challenged the underlying ontological assumption: the possibility of thinking together in one category ('subjectivity' or 'spirit') the conflicting elements of sameness and otherness, identity and non-identity. This challenge is evident in Nietzsche's attack on 'Platonism' or Platonic 'ideas', in Heidegger's critique of metaphysics, and in Derrida's notion of '*différance*'. Yet, jointly or singly, these moves do not sponsor a simple reversal or an embrace of antithesis (in lieu of Hegelian synthesis). In his study, Habermas distinguishes between two models of reason: an 'inclusive' model epitomized in Hegel's synthetic *Vernunft*, and an 'exclusive' model in which otherness is banished entirely from reason. The two types are also described respectively as '*Entzweiungsmodell*' where cleavages are ultimately reconciled within reason, and '*Ausgrenzungsmodell*' which insists on irremediable conflict. By appealing to 'being', heteronomy or power, post-Nietzscheans are said to rely on elements '*outside* the horizon of reason' (an 'exclusive' strategy) – and thus to lapse into irrationalism.[48] It is easy to see, however, that the mentioned distinction only reflects traditional metaphysical antinomies: the antinomies between inside and outside, immanence and transcendence. A major thrust of Nietzschean discourse (in the broad sense) has been precisely to unsettle these polar oppositions – that is, to give an account of 'difference' which is neither purely inclusive (synthetic) nor exclusive (antithetical). Here is a source of the genuine intellectual excitement of this discourse, an excitement which is not due to a bland rejection of reason, but to the attempt to rethink its meaning and explore the peculiar 'interlacing' of reason and non-reason, positivity and negativity (or 'real' and 'ideal' elements).

Habermas's study shows little sense for this excitement. With a stern and commanding gesture, Nietzsche and his heirs are exiled or banished from the province of reason – a province seemingly entrusted to Habermas's custody. This banishment, however, exacts a price. With his exclusionary policy Habermas inadvertently lends credence to the claim of some Nietzscheans (especially Foucault) that every discourse, including rational discourse, harbours a principle of exclusion, thus attesting to the intrusion of power (or the interlacing of *pouvoir/savoir*). According to the same Nietzscheans, moreover, discourses also betray a certain doctrinaire bias – by favouring certain kinds of arguments over others. In Habermas's study, the favoured argument or perspective is clearly the communicative model of reason. In fact, the model is held in reserve from the opening pages of the study and finally unveiled, in the concluding chapters, as the correct 'solution' of modern predicaments. All the participants of the modern discourse – from Hegel to Heidegger and Foucault – are chided for having missed the correct answer, although some came closer to the mark than others. While approximating the solution briefly during his Jena period, Hegel failed to follow the proper path by resorting to 'absolute spirit' – a failure replicated later by Marx in his reliance on labour. Thus, already at this early juncture or crossroads, modern discourse is said to have taken the 'wrong turn'. The mistake was compounded by Nietzsche and his heirs. In the case of Heidegger, a lecture of 1939 is singled out for show-ing some promising signs – a promise subsequently foiled by Heidegger's ontological leanings. In sum, all or most of the thinkers discussed in the study at some point stood before 'an alternative they did not select': the alternative of the communicative model – which, compared with past fumblings, represents the more solid and 'reliable solution' and the proper corrective to the philosophy of consciousness.[49]

In my view, the notion of 'solution' is not only alien to philosoph-ical inquiry but also hostile to communicative discourse – since it implies a conclusion or terminal point of discussions. My reservations, however, extend from the form of presentation to the character of the proposed answer – to the degree that it is meant to remedy or redress modern ills. In Habermas's account, the remedy – if one is needed at all – consists mostly in a quasi-mechanical balancing act: the coupling and uncoupling of system and lifeworld (with the life-world increasingly shrinking into an enclave among modern-rational structures and systemic units). Few or no substantive changes seem required to accomplish this task or to correct pathological trends. As the study repeatedly affirms, individualization (even in extreme forms) is a pliant corollary of socialization and community life, occasioning few if any frictions – an assumption which is belied by massive collisions in Western societies between private interests and the common good.[50] As it seems to me, modern cleavages (*Entzweiungen*) and pathologies exceed the capacities of a balancing mechanism. In light of rampantly possessive lifestyles and the predatory thrust of technology, exiting from 'subjectivity' involves more than procedural adjustments: namely, a substantive 'paradigm shift' opening the subject to its otherness. Just as philosophical inquiry implies at some point a turning-about or *'periagoge'* (thematized by Plato as 'a kind of dying'), this opening demands an experiential turn-about or transformation of individual life, that is, a process of character formation. Contrary to Habermas's futuristic scenario (the prospect of entirely self-constructed identities), such character-formation or taming of egocentrism can only happen in the context of concrete historical communities – though not necessarily communities bent on self-enclosure or collective modes of solipsism. Neither narrowly communal nor subsumable under abstract principles, the nature of transformative community life or co-being has been pinpointed by another post-Nietzschean, Derrida, in these terms: 'A community of questioning therefore, within that fragile moment when the question is not yet determined enough for the hypocrisy of an answer ... A community of the question about the possibility of the question.'[51]

NOTES

1 Jürgen Habermas, *Der philosophische Diskurs der Moderne* (Frankfurt am Main, 1985), p. 32 (hereafter abbreviated as *Diskurs*).

2 *Diskurs*, p. 120.

3 I have discussed some of the other thinkers included in the study elsewhere (in a manner deviating from Habermas's exegesis); compare my 'Pluralism Old and New: Foucault on Power', in Dallmayr, *Polis and Praxis* (Cambridge, Mass., 1984), pp. 77–103, and 'Hermeneutics and Deconstruction: Gadamer and Derrida in Dialogue', in Dallmayr, *Critical Encounters* (Notre Dame, 1987), pp. 130–58.

4 *Diskurs*, pp. 13, 26–7, 29, 31.

5 *Diskurs*, pp. 33, 37, 40–2. As Habermas adds: 'No matter how forcefully interpreted, the ethos of *polis* and early Christianity can no longer furnish the standard which could guide an internally divided modernity' (p. 43).

6 *Diskurs*, pp. 44, 46.

7 *Diskurs*, pp. 51–2. Compare *Hegel's Philosophy of Right*, trans. with notes by T. M. Knox (Oxford, 1967), p. 161 (par. 260; translation slightly altered).

8 *Diskurs*, p. 33. The applauding comment was quoted above. In a similar vein the study states: 'With the concept of the absolute ... Hegel is able to grasp modernity on the basis of its own principle. In doing so he shows philosophy as the power of synthesis which overcomes all positivities produced by (abstract) reflection.' This does not prevent Habermas from claiming (p. 41) that Hegel 'misses the essential goal for a self-grounding of modernity: namely, to conceive positivity in such a manner that it can be overcome by relying on the same principle through which it is generated – the principle of subjectivity' (p. 49).

9 *Diskurs*, pp. 35, 53.

10 *Diskurs*, pp. 49, 54, 56–7.

11 Regarding public religiosity one might fruitfully compare Hegel's comments on the topic in *Philosophy of Right* which steer a difficult but fascinating course between established (or 'positive') religion and a strict separation of church and state; see *Hegel's Philosophy of Right*, pp. 165–74 (par. 270).

12 Martin Heidegger, *Hegels Phänomenologie des Geistes*, in *Gesamtausgabe*, vol. 32 (Frankfurt am Main, 1980), p. 52. Heidegger presents Hegel's philosophy as an 'onto-theo-logy', because Hegel's 'idea' or 'spirit' (*logos*) is also the designation for the essence of being which coincides with God (pp. 140–1). The lectures caution against approaching Hegel with the 'methods of an *ab ovo* defunct Hegelianism' (p. 121). Compare also Heidegger, *Hegel's Concept of Experience* (New York, 1970).

13 See *Hegel's Philosophy of Right*, pp. 156 (par. 258). While applauding Rousseau's philosophical treatment of the topic, Hegel in the same context criticizes the French thinker for taking 'the will only in a determinate form as the individual will' and for regarding 'the universal will not as the absolutely rational element in the will, but only as a "general" will which proceeds out of individual wills as out of conscious wills' (p. 157).

14 Habermas in this context assigns a broad philosophical significance to the Young Hegelian movement: 'We remain until today in the theoretical state which the Young Hegelians initiated by distancing themselves from Hegel and philosophy as such ... Hegel inaugurated the discourse of modernity; but only the Young Hegelians have established it permanently. For they extricated the idea of an immanent-modern critique of modernity from the weight of Hegel's concept of reason.' See *Diskurs*, p. 67.

15 *Diskurs*, pp. 71, 93. Referring to Hegel and the two Hegelian schools, Habermas adds: 'Three times the attempt to tailor reason to the programme of a dialectic of enlightenment miscarried. In this situation Nietzsche had the option either of subjecting reason once again to an immanent critique – or else of abandoning the programme altogether. He opted for the second alternative, thus renouncing the task of a renewed revision of reason and *bidding farewell* to the dialectic of enlightenment' (p. 106).

16 *Diskurs*, pp. 105–9.

17 *Diskurs*, pp. 110–14.

18 *Diskurs*, pp. 115–18.

19 *Diskurs*, pp. 116–20.

20 I recognize that Nietzsche's position towards Christian faith, and religion in general, was complex and ambivalent – but not much more so than that of many other modern thinkers. Henry Aitken's cautious comments are at least worth pondering: 'Despite Zarathustra's claim or prophecy that "God is dead", neither he nor his creator is, in the root sense, irreligious. In one sense Nietzsche, like James, "*suffered* from incredulity", and it is this fact which distinguishes him from all the dime-a-dozen atheists and agnostics for whom disbelief in the existence of God is hardly more momentous, and no different in essential meaning, than disbelief in the existence of centaurs.' See Henry David Aitken, 'An Introduction to *Zarathustra*,' in Robert C. Solomon (ed.), *Nietzsche: A Collection of Critical Essays* (Notre Dame, 1980), p. 125.

21 *Diskurs*, pp. 116–18. For an alternative interpretation see my 'Farewell to Metaphysics: Nietzsche', in Dallmayr, *Critical Encounters*, pp. 13–38.

22 See Friedrich Nietzsche, *The Birth of Tragedy*, in *The Birth of Tragedy and The Genealogy of Morals*, trans. Francis Golffing (Garden City, N.Y., 1956), pp. 25–6.

23 These comments occur in section 197, entitled 'The Hostility of the Germans to the Enlightenment'. See Nietzsche, *The Dawn* (1881), in *The Portable Nietzsche*, ed. Walter Kaufmann (New York, 1968), p. 85; also *Twilight of*

the Idols (1888) in the same collection, pp. 479, 481 (section on 'Reason in Philosophy').

24 For an extended commentary on these fragments see Martin Heidegger, Nietzsche, vol. 1: The Will to Power as Art, trans. David F. Krell (New York, 1979), and Nietzsche, vol. 3: The Will to Power as Knowledge and as Metaphysics, trans. Joan Stambaugh, David F. Krell and Frank A. Capuzzi (New York, 1987). Compare also The Joyful Science (1882), in The Portable Nietzsche, p. 101 (section 319).

25 Diskurs, pp. 121–4, 126–7.

26 Diskurs, pp. 158–63.

27 Diskurs, pp. 169–76.

28 Diskurs, pp. 165–6, 177–80. Here as elsewhere Habermas distinguishes between an 'objective' (natural) world, and a 'subjective' (inner) world. The validity claim of 'truth' is juxtaposed to the claims of 'rightness' and 'truthfulness'.

29 Diskurs, pp. 123–4, 167–8, 181, 188–9.

30 Diskurs, p. 122. Habermas's claim in the same context that Heidegger was never really 'touched by the genuine experiences of avant-garde art' is contradicted by the philosopher's documented attachment to Cézanne, Klee and other modern artists. The charge of a 'classicist aesthetics' also fails to take into account Heidegger's lectures on 'The Origin of the Work of Art' (of 1935–6); see Heidegger, Basic Writings, ed. David F. Krell (New York, 1977), pp. 149–87.

31 As Habermas states: 'Quite likely the Kehre was in reality the result of the experience of National Socialism, that is, the experience of a historical event that in a sense happened to Heidegger.' See Diskurs, p. 185. My point is not to deny the role of politics but to question the juxtaposition of inner-philosophical and external-political motives and the subordination of the former to the latter.

32 See Heidegger, Sein und Zeit (11th edn; Tübingen, 1967), pp. 115–16 (par. 25) and pp. 263–4 (par. 53). In contrast with Sartre's approach, Heidegger's notion of 'project' (Entwurf) should be seen in close connection with 'thrownness' (Geworfenheit) – not merely as separate categories, but as two sides of the same coin. On the non-subjectivist character of Being and Time see Friedrich-Wilhelm von Herrmann, Subject und Dasein: Interpretationen zu 'Sein und Zeit' (2nd edn; Frankfurt am Main, 1985). Heidegger's early subjectivism is not confirmed (as Habermas claims) in 'What is Metaphysics?' or 'Vom Wesen der Grundes'; on the contrary. The latter essay presents man as a 'being of distance' (Wesen der Ferne), linking the capacity for 'listening into the distance' with the possibility of authentic co-being; see 'Vom Wesen der Grundes'; in Heidegger, Wegmarken (Frankfurt am Main, 1967), pp. 70–1.

33 Heidegger, Sein und Zeit, p. 118 (par. 26). A little bit later Heidegger adds: 'Alone-ness is a deficient mode of co-being, its possibility a proof for the latter.' (p. 120). The thematization of co-being is followed by a discussion of language as speech (par. 34) – a treatment which in striking ways anticipates later speech-act theory. The alleged parallelism between Husserl and Heidegger is borrowed from Michael Theunissen's The Other (Theunissen corrected himself in part in a postscript to the original study). For a critical discussion of Theunissen's approach and an alternative interpretation of co-being see 'Egology and Being and Time' and 'Heidegger and Co-Being' in my Twilight

of Subjectivity (Amherst, Mass., 1981), pp. 56–71. Regarding the theory of language in *Being and Time* compare '*Dasein* and Speech: Heidegger' in my *Language and Politics* (Notre Dame, 1984), pp. 117–20.

34 I have tried to flush out some of these remarks in his lectures on Hölderlin held in the winter of 1934 (less than a year after his resignation as rector); see 'Heidegger, Hölderlin and Politics', *Heidegger Studies* 2 (1987), pp. 81–95.

35 See Heidegger, *Identität und Differenz* (Pfullingen, 1957), pp. 17–20; also *Diskurs*, pp. 162, 172–3.

36 *Diskurs*, p. 181. The equation of being or the 'truth' of being with freedom is clearly stated in 'On the Essence of Truth' (1930), in Heidegger, *Basic Writings*, pp. 117–41; in *Vom Wesen der menschlichen Freiheit: Einleitung in die Philosphie* (1930), ed. Hartmut Tietjen, in *Gesamtausgabe*, vol. 31 (Frankfurt am Main, 1982); and also in *Schellings Abhandlung Über das Wesen der menschlichen Freiheit* (1936), ed. Hildegard Feick (Tübingen, 1971). For a more detailed discussion see my 'Ontology of Freedom: Heidegger and Political Philosophy', in Dallmayr, *Polis and Praxis*, pp. 104–32.

37 See *Diskurs*, pp. 128, 163, 167; also Heidegger, *Hegel's Phänomenologie des Geistes*, p. 143. Habermas's dismissal of recollective thinking is parallel to his dismissal of Hegel's 'absolute spirit'. In my view, Heidegger's philosophy is not opposed to science but only to the reduction of philosophy to science (or to a prevalent scientific paradigm).

38 *Diskurs*, pp. 182–3.

39 *Diskurs*, pp. 346, 353–4, 356, 361–3.

40 *Diskurs*, pp. 28–30, 177, 346–7; the different spheres or dimensions of the model are discussed on pp. 361–8. In another passage (pp. 397–8) Habermas contests that the interactive lifeworld in his model is composed of subjects or individuals – speaking instead of 'communicative agents' or 'subjects capable of speech and action'.

41 *Diskurs*, pp. 374–6. As Habermas writes: 'As little as we can renounce the *supposition* of a purified speech, as much must we make do in real life with "impure" speech' (p. 376).

42 *Diskurs*, p. 372. The statement neglects that the meaning of confirmation and pragmatic experience also changes with changing meaning-horizons. Habermas's treatment of the relation of meaning discovery and validation (especially in his attacks on Heidegger and others) tends to reduce discovery to a mere antechamber whose opacity or noises cannot affect the process of validation. This outcome is hardly obviated by the concession that meaning constitution 'retains the contingent potency of genuine innovation' (p. 373).

43 *Diskurs*, pp. 348–9, 379. Habermas's distinction at this point between agents as 'authors' and 'products' of historical contexts replicates the division between 'producer' and 'product' castigated in the case of Heidegger, Castoriadis and others (p. 370).

44 *Diskurs*, p. 397.

45 *Diskurs*, pp. 399–401, 405–7. The study actually sketches a three-tiered schema of coordination ranging from the habitual lifeworld over formal lifeworld structures to segregated systems or subsystems (p. 407). For a more detailed discussion of Habermas's ambivalent view of the lifeworld see my 'Life-World and Communicative Action', in Dallmayr, *Critical Encounters*, pp. 90–4.

46 *Diskurs*, pp. 368, 378, 393, 396, 403, 407. In the absence of ontological or 'essentialist' assumptions it is unclear how 'excess' or 'preponderance' is to be defined. In a later passage (p. 413) the lifeworld is presented as a domain 'in need of protection' – which again presupposes an essentialist conception.

47 Compare Habermas, 'Die Moderne – ein unvollendetes Projekt', in *Kleine politische Schriften I–IV* (Frankfurt am Main, 1981), pp. 444–64 (chapter 1 above). For an elaborate attack on the 'extremism' of Nietzsche's heirs see Allan Megill, *Prophets of Extremity: Nietzsche, Heidegger, Foucault, Derrida* (Berkeley, 1985).

48 *Diskurs*, pp. 355–8.

49 *Diskurs*, pp. 41–2, 54, 79, 94, 164–5, 178, 345–6.

50 As Habermas asserts, the participant in discourses is as individual 'wholly autonomous only on the condition' that he remains bound or 'embedded in a universal community'; *Diskurs*, pp. 401. But as Hobbes would have asked: who stipulates or secures this condition (beyond the sphere of definitional fiat)? According to a later passage (p. 402), the communicative model is said to explain why 'critique and fallibilism even reinforce the continuity of traditions' and why 'abstract-universalistic methods of discursive will-formation even solidify the solidarity of life contexts.'

51 Jacques Derrida, *Writing and Difference*, trans. Alan Bass (Chicago, 1978). In its concluding pages Habermas's study actually advances arguments reminiscent of Foucauldian or poststructuralist themes: especially the themes of micropowers and of group resistances to centralized state control; *Diskurs*, pp. 420–3.

3

DECONSTRUCTION, POSTMODERNISM AND PHILOSOPHY: HABERMAS ON DERRIDA

Christopher Norris

I

In this essay I propose to contest some of the arguments that Habermas brings against Derrida in *The Philosophical Discourse of Modernity*.[1] It seems to me that he has misread Derrida's work, and done so moreover in a way that fits in all too readily with common-place ideas about deconstruction as a species of latter-day Nietzschean irrationalism, one that rejects the whole legacy of post-Kantian enlightened thought. In short, Habermas goes along with the widely held view that deconstruction is a matter of collapsing all genre distinctions, especially those between philosophy and literature, reason and rhetoric, language in its constative and performative aspects. This is all the more unfortunate since Habermas's book is by far the most important contribution to date in the ongoing quarrel between French poststructuralism and that tradition of *Ideologie-kritik* which Habermas has carried on from Adorno and earlier members of the Frankfurt School. So I will be criticizing *PDM* from a standpoint which might appear squarely opposed to Habermas's critical project. That this is not at all my intention – that in fact I concur with most of what Habemas has to say – will I hope become clear in the course of this article. His book makes out a very strong case for re-examining the character and historical antecedents of postmodernism, and for seeing it not on its own professed terms as a radical challenge to the outworn enlightenment paradigm, but rather as the upshot of a widespread failure to think through the problems bequeathed by that tradition. Where Habermas goes wrong, I shall argue, is in failing to acknowledge the crucial respects in which Derrida has distanced his own thinking from a generalized 'postmodern' or poststructuralist discourse.

More specifically, Habermas misreads Derrida in much the same way that literary critics (and apostles of American neo-pragmatism) have so far received his work: that is to say, as a handy pretext for dispensing with the effort of conceptual critique and declaring an end to the 'modernist' epoch of enlightened secular reason. I have no quarrel with Habermas's claim that the 'post-' in postmodernism is a delusive prefix, disguising the fact that theorists like Foucault, Lyotard and Baudrillard are still caught up in problems that have plagued the discourse of philosophy at least since the parting of ways after Kant. He is right to point out how their work recapitulates the quarrels that emerged between those various thinkers (left- and right-wing Hegelians, objective and subjective idealists) who attempted – and failed – to overcome the antinomies of Kantian critical reason. One need only look to Lyotard's recent writings on philosophy, politics and the 'idea of history' to remark this resurgence of Kantian themes (albeit deployed to very different ends) in the discourse of postmodern thought.[2] And the same applies to Foucault's genealogy of power/knowledge, as Habermas brings out very clearly when he traces its various intellectual antecedents in the line of counter-enlightenment philosophies running from Nietzsche to Bataille. In each case, he argues, thought has suffered the disabling effects of an irrationalist doctrine that can only take hold through a form of self-willed amnesia, a compulsive repetition of similar episodes in the previous (post-Kantian) history of ideas. *PDM* is in this sense an exercise of large-scale rational reconstruction, an essentially thera-peutic exercise whose aim is to provide a more adequate understand-ing of those episodes, and thus to recall the present-day human sciences to a knowledge of their own formative prehistory.

All this will of course be familiar enough to any reader moderately versed in Habermas's work over the past two decades. Where these lectures break new ground is in specifying more exactly the terms of his quarrel with French poststructuralism, deconstruction and other such forms of – as Habermas would have it – militant latter-day unreason. To some extent the ground had already been prepared by debates on and around his work in journals like *Praxis International* and *New German Critique*. One could summarize the issues very briefly as follows. To his opponents it has seemed that Habermas's thinking belongs squarely within the enlightenment tradition of oppressive, monological reason. That is to say, he has sought a means of reinstating the Kantian foundationalist project – the belief in transcendental arguments, truth claims, critique of consensual values and so forth – at a time when that project has at last been shown up as a mere historical dead-end, a discourse premised on false ideas of theoretical mastery and power. In support of this argument they point to such instances as the reading of Freud that Habermas offers in *Knowledge and Human Interests*, a reading that interprets psychoanalysis as a therapy designed to overcome the blocks and distortions of repressed desire by bringing them out into the light of a conscious, rational self-understanding.[3] To this they respond by drawing on Lacan's very different account of the 'talking cure', namely his insistence that language is *always and everywhere* marked by the symptoms of unconscious desire, so that any attempt to escape or transcend this condition is deluded at best, and at worst a technique of manipulative reason in the service of a harsh and repressive social order.[4]

These opposing viewpoints can each claim a warrant in Freud's notoriously cryptic statement: 'where id was, there shall ego be.' For Habermas, on the one hand, this sentence should be read as signalling an alignment of interests between psychoanalysis and the wider project of enlightened or emancipatory thought. For the Lacanians, conversely, it enforces the message that the ego is always a plaything of unconscious desire, and that therefore any version of ego psychology (to which doctrine, in their view, Habermas subscribes) is necessarily a hopeless and misguided endeavour. On their reading the sentence should be paraphrased: 'wherever reason thinks to explain the unconscious and its effects, there most surely those effects will resurface to disrupt such a project from the outset.' In this case there would seem little to choose between Habermas's talk of 'transcendental pragmatics', 'ideal speech-situations', etc., and those previous modes of foundationist thought (the Cartesian *cogito*, the Kantian transcendental subject or Husserl's phenomenological reduction) whose claims – or so it is argued – have now been totally discredited. The fact that he has been at some pains to distance himself from that tradition apparently counts for nothing in terms of the current polemical exchange. So these thinkers bring two main charges against Habermas: firstly that he attempts the impossible (since reason is in no position to legislate over effects that exceed its powers of comprehension), and secondly that his project is politically retrograde (since it clings to a form of enlightenment thinking whose covert aim is to repress or to marginalize everything that falls outside its privileged domain). And their criticisms will no doubt find ample confirmation now that Habermas has offered his response in the form of these recent lectures. He will still be treated as a last-ditch defender of the strong foundationalist argument, despise the very clear signals that Habermas – no less than his opponents – wants to find a basis for the conduct of rational enquiry that will not have recourse to anything resembling a Kantian epistemological paradigm.

It seems to me that Habermas goes wrong about Derrida mainly because he takes it for granted that deconstruction is one offshoot – a 'philosophical' offshoot – of this wider postmodernist or counter-enlightenment drift. In what follows I shall point to some crucial respects in which Derrida's work not only fails to fit this description but also mounts a resistance to it on terms that Habermas ought to acknowledge, given his own intellectual commitments. In fact I shall argue that deconstruction, properly understood, belongs within that same 'philosophical discourse of modernity' that Habermas sets out to defend against its present-day detractors. But it may be useful to preface that discussion with a brief account of the very different readings of Derrida's work that have now gained currency among literary theorists and philosophers. This will help to explain some of the blind-spots in Habermas's critique, based as it is on a partial reading which tends to privilege just one of those rival accounts.

II

Commentators on deconstruction are divided very roughly into two main camps: those (like Rodolphe Gasché) who read Derrida's work as a radical continuation of certain Kantian themes,[5] and those (like Richard Rorty) who praise Derrida for having put such deluded 'enlightenment' notions behind him and arrived at a postmodern-pragmatist stance relieved of all surplus metaphysical baggage.[6] Nevertheless they are agreed in thinking that we can't make sense of Derrida without some knowledge of the relevant intellectual prehistory. Where they differ is on the question whether those debates are still of real interest – 'philosophical' interest – or whether (as Rorty would have it) they have failed to come up with any workable answers, and should therefore be regarded as failed candidates for Philosophy Honours and awarded nothing more than a Pass Degree in English, Liberal Studies or Comp. Lit.

On Rorty's view we can still put together an instructive story about the way that thinkers from Descartes and Kant on down have so misconceived their own enterprise as to think they were offering genuine solutions to a range of distinctively 'philosophical' problems. But we shall be wrong – simply repeating their mistake – if we try to give this story an upbeat conclusion or a Whiggish metanarrative drift suggesting that we have now, after so many errors, started to get things right. The story is just that, a handy little pragmatist narrative, and the most it can do is stop us from believing in all those grandiose philosophical ideas. For Gasché, on the contrary, Derrida is still very much a philosopher, if by this we understand one whose work is both committed to an ongoing critical dialogue with previous thinkers (notably, in this case, Kant, Hegel and Husserl), and centrally concerned with issues in the realm of truth, knowledge and representation. This dialogue may take an unfamiliar or disconcerting form, as when Derrida questions the categorical bases of Kantian argument and sets out to demonstrate what Gasché calls the 'conditions of impossibility' that mark the limits of all philosophical enquiry. But even so his work remains squarely within that tradition of epistemological critique which alone makes it possible to raise such questions against the more accommodating pragmatist line espoused by thinkers like Rorty. These different readings of Derrida are also, inseparably, different readings of the whole philosophical history that has led up to where we are now. And in Hegel's case likewise there is a conflict of interpretations between those (again including Rorty) who would accept a kind of 'naturalized' Hegelianism, a story of philosophy that includes all the major episodes but dispenses with the vantage point of reason or truth, and those who reject this compromise solution and regard the dialectic as something more than a species of edifying narrative.

One could make the same point about all those philosophers whose work has come in for revisionist readings as a consequence of the currently widespread scepticism as regards truth claims and foundationalist arguments of whatever kind. On the one hand this has led to a new intellectual division of labour, a situation where thinkers like Rorty feel more at home in humanities or literature departments, while the 'real' (analytical) philosophers tend to close ranks and leave the teaching of Hegel, Nietzsche, Heidegger, Derrida, etc., to their colleagues with less exacting standards of argument. On the other, it has persuaded literary theorists that philosophy has no good claim to monopolize the texts of its own tradition, since the current guardians seem overly zealous to protect their canon from any form of unauthorized reading (which is to say, any reading that treats it on rhetorical, hermeneutic or 'literary' terms). And so it has come about that 'theory' now denominates an area (not so much a 'discipline') which straddles the activities of philosophy and literary criticism, taking charge of those figures (the Hegel-Nietzsche-Derrida line) who lend themselves to just such a non-canonical approach. But even within this camp one finds disagreements (as between Rorty and Gasché) concerning the extent to which philosophy may yet be conserved as a discipline with its own distinct mode of conceptual or analytic rigour. Thus 'theory' is construed as post-philosophical *either* in the sense that it dissolves philosophy into a textual, rhetorical or narrative genre with no distinctive truth claims whatsoever (the Rorty argument), or in the sense (following Gasché) that it presses certain Kantian antinomies to the point where they demand a form of analysis undreamt of in the mainstream tradition. Both sides have an interest in claiming Kant since he stands at precisely the cardinal point where their histories will henceforth diverge. On the one hand there is the line that leads from Kant via Hegel to the various speculative systems and projects that make up the 'continental' heritage. On the other it is clear that Kant provides the basis for most of those debates about language, logic and truth that have occupied the analytic schools.

One reason why *PDM* seems blind to certain aspects of Derrida's work is that it more or less identifies deconstruction with the Rortyan-postmodern-pragmatist reading, and thus tends to perpetuate the view of it as a species of literary-critical activity, an attempt to colonize philosophy by levelling the genre distinction between those disciplines. Now of course this corresponds to one major premise of Derrida's thought: namely, his insistence that philosophy is indeed a certain 'kind of writing', a discourse which none the less strives to cover its own rhetorical tracks by aspiring to an order of pure, unmediated, self-present truth. Thus a deconstructive reading will typically fasten upon those moments in the philosophic text where some cardinal concept turns out to rest on a latent or sublimated metaphor, or where the logic of an argument is subtly undone by its reliance on covert rhetorical devices. Or again, it will show how some seemingly marginal detail of the text – some aspect ignored (not without reason) by the mainstream exponents – in fact plays a crucial but problematic role in the entire structure of argument.[7] One result of such readings is undoubtedly to challenge the commonplace assumption that philosophy has to do with concepts, truth claims, logical arguments, 'clear and distinct ideas', etc., while literary criticism deals with language only in its rhetorical, poetic or non-truth-functional aspects. What Derrida has achieved – on this view at least – is a striking reversal of the age-old prejudice that elevates philosophy over rhetoric, or right reason over the dissimulating arts of language.

This is the reading of Derrida's work that Habermas offers in his 'Excursus on Leveling the Genre Distinction between Philosophy and Literature' (*PDM*, pp. 185–210). That is to say, he takes it as read that Derrida is out to reduce all texts to an undifferentiated 'free play' of signification where the old disciplinary borderlines will at last break down, and where philosophy will thus take its place as just one 'kind of writing' among others, with no special claim to validity or truth. More specifically, Derrida makes a full-scale programme of ignoring those different kinds of language use that have separated out in the modern (post-Kantian) discourse of enlightened reason. He has privileged just one of these uses (language in its poetic, rhetorical or 'world-disclosive' aspect) and failed to see how the others demand a quite different mode of understanding. Thus, according to Habermas,

> the rhetorical element occurs *in its pure form* only in the self-referentiality of the poetic expression, that is, in the language

of fiction specialized for world-disclosure. Even the normal language of everyday life is ineradicably rhetorical; but within the matrix of different linguistic functions, the rhetorical elements recede here ... The same holds true of the specialized languages of science and technology, law and morality, economics, political science, etc. They, too, live off the illuminating power of metaphorical tropes; but the rhetorical elements, which are by no means expunged, are tamed, as it were, and enlisted for special purposes of problem-solving. (*PDM*, p. 209)

It is the main fault of Derrida's work, as Habermas reads it, that he has failed to observe these essential distinctions and thus overgeneralized the poetic (rhetorical) aspect of language to a point where it commands the whole field of communicative action. The result is to deprive thinking of that critical force which depends on a proper separation of realms, and which has come about historically – so Habermas contends – through the increasing specialization of language in its threefold social aspect. By extending rhetoric so far beyond its own legitimate domain Derrida has not only collapsed the 'genre distinction' between philosophy and literature but also annulled the emancipating promise that resides in the poetic (or 'world-disclosive') function of language. For this promise is likewise dependent on the existence of a 'polar tension', a sense of what specifically differentiates literature from 'everyday' communicative language on the one hand, and those specialized problem-solving languages on the other. Derrida, says Habermas, 'holistically levels these complicated relationships in order to equate philosophy with literature and criticism. He fails to recognize the special status that both philosophy and literary criticism, each in its own way, assume as mediators between expert cultures and the everyday world' (*PDM*, p. 207).

Now I think that these criticisms apply not so much to what Derrida has written as to what has been written about him by various (mostly American) commentators. Or more accurately – on the principle 'no smoke without fire' – they find some warrant in certain of his texts, but can then be made to stick only through a very partial reading, one that sets out quite deliberately to level the distinction between philosophy and literature. The favoured texts for this purpose would include Derrida's response to John Searle on the topic of speech-act theory;[8] the closing paragraph of 'Structure, Sign and Play', with its apocalyptic overtones and Nietzschean end-of-philosophy rhetoric;[9] and more recently the 'Envois' section of *La Carte Postale*, where Derrida goes about as far as possible towards undermining the truth claims of logocentric reason by recasting them in fictive or mock-epistolary form.[10] One could then go back to

Derrida's earliest published work – his introduction to Husserl's essay 'The Origin of Geometry' – and cite the well-known passage where he appears to encounter a moment of choice between 'philosophy' and 'literature', or the quest for some pure, univocal, self-present meaning (Husserl) as opposed to the prospect of a liberating 'free play' of the signifier glimpsed in such writings as Joyce's *Finnegans Wake*.[11] In so far as he has confronted this choice – so the argument goes – Derrida has come out firmly on the side of a literary approach to the texts of philosophy, one that pays minimal regard to their truth claims or structures of logical argument, and which thus frees itself to treat them as purely rhetorical constructs on a level with poems, novels, postcards or any other kind of writing.

So it might seem that Habermas's arguments are fully warranted by the 'levelling' or undifferentiating character of Derrida's generalized rhetoric. What drops out of sight is the complex and highly evolved relationship between (1) everyday communicative language, (2) the mediating discourses of philosophy and criticism, and (3) the various forms of 'expert' or specialized enquiry ('art, literature, science, morality') which would otherwise tend to float free in a conceptual universe of their own creating. Criticism can only perform this essential task so long as it maintains a due sense of its own distinctive role vis-à-vis those other disciplines. Where philosophy occupies the middle ground between 'ordinary language' and specialized questions of ethics, epistemology, metaphysics, theory of science, etc., criticism stands in much the same relation to everyday language on the one hand and artistic or literary innovation on the other. And it is also imperative that criticism and philosophy should not become mixed up one with another and thus produce the kind of hybrid discourse that Habermas thinks so damaging in Derrida's work.

The point is best made by quoting him at length, since this is the passage where the charge is pressed home with maximum force.

> Literary criticism and philosophy . . . are both faced with tasks that are paradoxical in similar ways. They are supposed to feed the contents of expert cultures, in which knowledge is accumulated under one aspect of validity at a time, into an everyday practice in which all linguistic functions are intermeshed. And yet [they] are supposed to accomplish this task of mediation with means of expression taken from languages specialized in questions of taste or of truth. They can only resolve this paradox by rhetorically expanding and enriching their special languages . . . [Thus] literary criticism and philosophy have a family resemblance to literature – and to this extent to one another as well – in their rhetorical achievements. But their family relationship stops right there, for in each of these enterprises the tools

of rhetoric are subordinated to the discipline of a *distinct* form
of argumentation. (*PDM*, pp. 209–10)

What is presented here is a qualified version of Kant's doctrine of the
faculties. It is qualified mainly by Habermas's wish to avoid any hint
of a Kantian foundationalist legacy by reasoning in terms of the
different languages – 'everyday', 'expert', 'specialized', etc. – which
between them mark out the range of communicative options. He can
thus maintain a critical attitude towards Derrida's 'levelling' of genre
distinctions without having to argue that philosophy has access to
some privileged realm of a priori concepts or uniquely self-validating
truth claims. We can afford to give up that outworn tradition, he
argues, just so long as we grasp that *language* itself is oriented
towards a better understanding of those blocks, aporias, misprisions
and so forth which get in the way of our (everyday or specialized)
communicative acts.[12] But on Derrida's account – so Habermas
believes – this process could never make a start, let alone achieve the
levels of complexity and sophistication required by the various
present-day arts and sciences.

This follows from Derrida's extreme form of contextualist doctrine, that is, his argument – enounced in the debate with John Searle
– that (1) meaning is entirely a product of the various contexts in
which signs play a part; (2) that such contexts can in principle be
multiplied beyond any possible enumerative grasp; and (3) that
therefore meaning is strictly undecidable in any given case. But we
are simply not obliged to accept this conclusion if – as Habermas
suggests – we drop the idea of an open-ended general 'context' and
recognize the various *specific* normative dimensions that exist within
the range of communicative action. For Derrida, in short, 'linguistically mediated processes within the world are embedded in a *world-
constituting* context that prejudices everything; they are fatalistically
delivered up to the unmanageable happening of text production,
overwhelmed by the poetic-creative transformation of a background
designated by archewriting, and condemned to be provincial' (*PDM*,
p. 205). 'Provincial', one supposes, in the sense that it seeks to reduce
all language to a single paradigm, and thereby annexes every form of
communicative action to the province of poetic or literary language.
Thus Habermas cites Roman Jakobson and the Prague structuralists
by way of insisting that the poetic function be defined more specifically, that is, in terms of those features (like self-reflexivity or lack of
informative content) that set it apart from other uses of language.
Where Derrida has gone wrong (he argues) is in failing to perceive
the constitutive difference between speech acts engaged in the normative activities of problem-solving, theorizing, giving information,
etc., and speech acts that are not so engaged and can therefore be

construed as fictive, non-serious, parodic or whatever. Otherwise
Derrida would not have been misled into extending the poetic
function so far beyond its proper reach, or discounting those normative constraints upon language that save it from the infinitized 'free
play' of an open-ended contextualist account. 'The frailty of the
genre distinction between philosophy and literature is evidenced in
the practice of deconstructon: in the end, *all* genre distinctions are
submerged in one comprehensive, all-embracing context of texts –
Derrida talks in a hypostatizing manner about a "universal text"'
(*PDM*, p. 190). The result of this confusion is to give language up to
the effects of an infinite regress (or 'unlimited semiosis') which
excludes all possibility of rational understanding.

III

The first point to note about Habermas's critique of Derrida is that it
more or less restates John Searle's basic claims with regard to the
supposedly self-evident distinction between 'serious' and other
(deviant) kinds of speech act.[13] That is, it assumes that Searle has both
common sense and reason on his side of the argument, while Derrida
is content to make 'literary' play with certain marginal or merely
rhetorical aspects of Austin's text. In which case Searle would be the
serious, the faithful or properly authorized exponent of Austin's ideas,
while Derrida would stand to Austin in much the same relation as the
sophists to Socrates: a gadfly rhetorician merely anxious to display his
own ingenuity and wit, and lacking any regard for wisdom or truth.
But this ignores several important points about the three-sided debate
between Austin, Derrida and Searle. It fails to register the extent to
which Austin invites and solicits a deconstructive reading by himself
putting up all manner of resistance to the project of a generalized
speech-act theory. I have written at length on this topic elsewhere – as
have a number of other commentators, including Jonathan Culler and
Shoshana Felman – so there is no need to rehearse the details over
again here.[14] Sufficient to say that Austin, like Derrida, shows a
fondness for marginal or problematic cases, speech acts which cannot
be securely assigned to this or that typecast category. Thus he often
comes up with supposedly deviant instances which then turn out to
be typical of the kind, or to indicate features that necessarily pertain
to all possible varieties of speech act. Or again, he will illustrate a
point with some odd piece of anecdotal evidence, only to find that it
creates real problems for his classificatory system.

What is distinctive about Austin's approach – aligning it with
Derrida as against Searle – is this readiness to let language have its
way with him and not give in to the systematizing drive for method
and clear-cut theory.[15] Partly it is a matter of the 'Oxford' ethos, the

attitude of quizzical detachment mixed with a passion for linguistic detail that Derrida encountered on his trip to Oxford (narrated in *La Carte Postale*). But we would be wrong to see this as a downright rejection of philosophical 'seriousness', an opting out in favour of stylistic 'free play' or the possible worlds of his own fictive devising. Certainly Derrida goes a long way towards deconstructing the terms of this old opposition. Thus *La Carte Postale* takes up a great variety of philosophic themes, among them the relationship of Plato and Socrates, the Heideggerian questioning of Western metaphysics, the status of truth claims in the discourse of Freudian psychoanalysis, and the way that all these topics return to haunt the seemingly detached, almost clinical idiom of Oxford linguistic philosophy. But it does so by way of a fictional *mise-en-scène*, a correspondence carried on by postcard, and specifically through a series of fragmentary love-letters inscribed on numerous copies of a card that Derrida discovered in the Bodleian Library. This card reproduces an apocryphal scene which apparently has Plato dictating his thoughts to Socrates and Socrates obediently writing them down at Plato's behest. It thus stages a comic reversal of the age-old scholarly assumption: namely, that Socrates was the thinker who *wrote nothing* – whose wisdom prevented him from entrusting his thoughts to the perilous medium of writing – while Plato, his disciple, gave in to this bad necessity in order to preserve Socrates' teaching for the benefit of later generations. So one can see why this postcard so fascinated Derrida. What it offered was a kind of zany confirmation of his own thesis (in *Of Grammatology* and elsewhere) that writing is the 'exile', the 'wandering outcast' of the Western logocentric tradition, the repressed term whose disruptive effects are none the less everywhere manifest in the texts of that same tradition.[16]

So *La Carte Postale* is undoubtedly a work of 'literature' in so far as it exploits the full range of fictive possibilities opened up by this scandalous reversal of roles between Socrates and Plato. From here it goes on to develop various other counterfactual, extravagant or apocryphal themes, along with a running debate among the scholars as to the authenticity or otherwise of Plato's letters, a 'correspondence' (by postcard, what else?) between Heidegger and Freud, a quizzical commentary on Ryle, Austin and the Oxford tradition of linguistic philosophy, and a whole series of anachronistic swerves and redoublings which enable Derrida to play havoc with accredited notions of history and truth. His point in all this is to show how philosophy has excluded certain kinds of writing – letters, apocrypha, 'unauthorized' genres of whatever sort – while allowing them a place on the margins of discourse from which they continue to exert a fascination and a power to complicate received ideas. And there is something of this even in the Oxford tradition – for all its analytical 'seriousness' – when thinkers like Austin cite (or invent) their various speech-act examples, and then find their arguments beginning to get out of hand. 'I adore these theorizations, so very "Oxford" in character, their extraordinary and necessary subtlety as well as their imperturbable naivety, "psychoanalytically speaking"; they will always be confident in the law of quotation marks.'[17] Derrida's reference here is to the problem of naming, and more specifically the difference between *using* and *mentioning* a name, as theorized by Russell and Ryle among others. But where this distinction serves analytical philosophers as a technique for avoiding trouble – for resolving the kinds of paradox that emerge when the two linguistic functions are confused – its appeal for Derrida has more to do with the undecidability of names in general, their tendency to migrate across the borderlines of authorized genre, history, etc., and thus to create all manner of intriguing fictive scenarios.[18] 'Psychoanalytically speaking', it is by no means certain that philosophy can control these potential aberrations of language, or lay down rules for the proper conduct of serious debate.

Thus Derrida cites a 'very good book' by one such analytical thinker, a book which advises us not to be misled by the seeming identity of names-as-used and names as merely cited, mentioned or placed between quotation marks. To which Derrida responds by asking: what kind of *de jure* regulation can back up this confident policing operation, designed to cure language of its bad propensity for conjuring up phantom nominal presences? The 'law of quotation marks' could achieve this purpose only on condition that language be treated as *already having attained* what Habermas describes as an 'ideal speech-situation', that is, a transparency of meaning and intent that would admit no impediment to the wished-for meeting of minds. But this condition is impossible – so Derrida implies – for reasons that return us to Freud, Lacan and the arguments of French (post-structuralist) psychoanalysis. That is to say, it ignores the effects of a 'structural unconscious' that forever divides the speaking self ('subject of enunciation') from the self spoken about ('subject of the enounced'). Thus:

> [t]he author of the book of which I am speaking, himself, not his name (therefore he would pardon me for not naming him) is himself reserved as concerns the very interesting 'position of Quine' ('a word-between-quotation-marks is the proper name of the word which figures between the quotation marks, simultaneously an occurrence of the word which is between the quotation marks and an occurrence of the word-between-the-quotation-marks, the latter including the former as a part' – and it is true that this logic of inclusion perhaps is not very satisfying

in order to account for the 'simultaneously', but small matter here), and making an allusion to a 'forgetting', his word, a forgetting 'evidently facilitated by the resemblance that there is between a word and the name of this word formed by its being placed between quotation marks', he concludes, I quote, 'But one must not let oneself be abused by this resemblance, and confuse the two names . . .' Okay, promise, we won't any more. Not on purpose anyway. Unless we forget, but we will not forget on purpose, it's just that they resemble each other so much . . .[19]

This passage is typical of *La Carte Postale* in the way that it picks up numerous themes, cross-references, cryptic allusions and so forth, among them the 'correspondence' between philosophy and psycho-analysis (or Socrates and Freud), staged as a kind of running encounter where reason confronts its own 'structural unconscious' in the form of a promiscuously generalized writing that circulates without origin or proper addressee. Hence the link that Derrida perceives between philosophy as a 'serious', responsible discourse and the postal service (in its 'grand epoch') as a smoothly functioning system of exchange which ensures that letters arrive on time and at the right destination. But there is always the residue of mail that hasn't been correctly addressed, that bounces back and forth between various recipients and ends up in the dead-letter office. Or again, those items that arrive out of the blue with some intimate yet wholly undecipherable message, and thus give rise to all manner of pleasing conjecture. So it comes about that 'the guardians of tradition, the professors, academics, and librarians, the doctors and authors of theses are terribly curious about correspondences . . . about private or public correspondences (a distinction without pertinence in this case, whence the post card, half private half public, neither the one nor the other, and which does not await the post card *stricto sensu* in order to define the law of the genre, of all genres . . .)'.[20]

It is on this level that the 'Envois' can be read as relating to the essays on Freud and Lacan that make up the remainder of *La Carte Postale*. For here also Derrida is concerned with the status of a certain theoretical enterprise (psychoanalysis) which attempts to secure itself on the basis of an authorized truth passed down from founder to disciple, but which runs into all manner of speculative detours and swerves from origin. In each case there is a strong *proprietory* interest at work, a tendency to anathematize those various distortions, misreadings or perversions of the Freudian text that would compromise its original (authentic) meaning. In Freud himself, this takes the form of an obsessive desire to keep psycho-analysis 'in the family', to save it from the egregious falsehoods put about by his erstwhile colleagues and disciples.[21] With Lacan, it produces an allegorical reading of Poe's story 'The Purloined Letter', treated as a virtual *mise-en-scène* of the dialogue between analyst and patient, a dialogue whose meaning can never be fully brought to light, caught up as it is in the shuttling exchange of transference and countertransference, but which none the less points to an ultimate truth identified with the 'letter' of the Freudian text.[22] In both instances, so Derrida argues, this desire takes the form of a putative master-discourse that attempts to put a frame around the various episodes, case histories, speculative ventures, correspondences and so forth that make up the proper, self-authorized legacy of Freud's life and work. But these projects cannot reckon with the undecidability of all such narrative frames, or the way that events from 'outside' the frame – whether textual events, as in Poe's short story, or episodes from the life, as in Freud's troubled correspondence with Wilhelm Fliess – may always return to complicate the record beyond all hope of a straightforward, truth-telling account. Here again, it proves impossible for thinking to master the effects of a generalized writing (or 'structural unconscious'), some of whose canniest adepts – like Freud and Lacan – may yet be caught out by its uncanny power to disrupt their projects at source.

Now it might well seem – from what I have written so far – that Habermas is absolutely right about Derrida, since *La Carte Postale* is a 'literary' text which exploits various philosophical themes merely as a springboard for its own extravagant purposes. This is certainly the reading that most appeals to a postmodern pragmatist like Rorty, one for whom philosophy is in any case a dead or dying enterprise, best treated (as Derrida apparently treats it here) with a fine disregard for the protocols of truth and an eye to its fictive potential or entertainment value. Thus if Rorty has problems with the 'early' Derrida – too serious by half, too argumentative, too much inclined to take a term like *différance* and give it the status of a privileged anticoncept – these problems disappear with *La Carte Postale*, where philosophy receives its final come-uppance at the hands of literature. But Rorty's reading is open to challenge, as indeed is Habermas's assumption (in *PDM*) that Rorty has read Derrida aright, and therefore that the two of them must be saying much the same kind of thing. What this ignores is the extent to which a text like *La Carte Postale* continues to engage with philosophical questions which don't simply disappear when approached from a fictive, apocryphal or 'literary' standpoint. After all, philosophers in the mainstream tradition – from Plato to Austin – have often had recourse to invented case histories, parables, counterfactual scenarios and so forth, in order to make some critical point about our language or commonplace habits of thought. Hence one of the problems that Derrida remarks in connection with Austin's procedure: namely, his exclusion of 'deviant' or 'parasitical' speech acts (such as those merely cited, placed between quotation marks, uttered in jest, on the stage, in a novel, etc.) as not meriting serious philosophical attention. For it is surely the case (1) that *all* speech acts must perform, cite or rehearse some existing formulaic convention (since otherwise they would carry no recognized force); (2) that this creates a real problem for Austin's distinction between 'serious' and 'non-serious' cases; and (3) that the majority of Austin's own examples are speech acts contrived specifically for the purpose of illustrating speech-act theory. Once again, the 'law of quotation marks' turns out to have effects far beyond those allowed for on the standard, unproblematical account.

My point is that Habermas mistakes the character of deconstruction when he treats it as having simply *given up* the kinds of argument specific to philosophy, and opted instead for the pleasures of a free-wheeling 'literary' style. It is true that Derrida's writings can be roughly divided – as Rorty suggests – into two categories. On the one hand there are texts (like the essays collected in *Margins of Philosophy*) that argue their way through a rigorous and consequential treatment of the various blind-spots, aporias or antinomies that characterize the discourse of philosophic reason. On the other there are pieces (like the 'Envois' section of *La Carte Postale* or Derrida's prolix and riddling response to John Searle) where undoubtedly he is making maximum use of 'literary' devices in order to provoke or to disconcert the more self-assured guardians of that mainstream tradition. But we would be wrong to suppose – as Rorty does – that Derrida has gone over from the one kind of writing to the other, renouncing 'philosophy' and its self-deluded claims for the sake of a henceforth uninhibited devotion to 'literature'. This ignores the extent to which 'Envois' and 'Limited Inc.' (the rejoinder to Searle) continue to work within the same problematics of writing, language and representation that Derrida addresses more explicitly elsewhere. And it also fails to recognize the distinct kinship between deconstruction and those passages of offbeat, speculative musing in Austin's text ('so very "Oxford" in character, their extraordinary and necessary subtlety, as well as their imperturbable naivety, psychoanalytically speaking') which Derrida singles out for attention in *La Carte Postale*.

IV

There are, I think, several reasons for Habermas's inability to grasp the philosophical pertinence of Derrida's work. One is the fact that he (Habermas) clearly doesn't have much concern for the finer points of style, writing as he does in a manner that surpasses even Hegel in its heavyweight abstractions, its relentless piling up of clause upon clause, and the sense it conveys that strenuous thinking is somehow incompatible with 'literary' arts and graces. One can therefore understand why he (like Searle) might regard Derrida's stylistic innovations with a somewhat jaundiced eye. But the antipathy goes much deeper than that, as can be seen from those passages in *PDM* where Habermas sets out his reasons for opposing any attempt to level the genre distinction between philosophy and literature. Again, I shall need to quote at some length since – at risk of labouring the point – Habermas's style doesn't exactly lend itself to concise summary statement.

> Derrida and Rorty are mistaken about the unique status of discourses differentiated from ordinary communication and tailored to a single validity dimension (truth or normative rightness), or to a single complex of problems (questions of truth or justice). In modern societies, the spheres of science, morality and law have crystallized around these forms of argumentation. The corresponding cultural systems of action administer *problem-solving capacities* in a way similar to that in which the enterprises of art and literature administer *capacities for world-disclosure*. Because Derrida overgeneralizes this one linguistic function – namely, the poetic – he can no longer see the complex relationship of the ordinary practice of normal speech to the two extraordinary spheres, differentiated, as it were, in opposite directions. The polar tension between world-disclosure and problem-solving is held together within the functional matrix of ordinary language; but art and literature on the one side, and science, morality, and law on the other, are specialized for experiences and modes of knowledge that can be shaped and worked out within the compass of *one* linguistic function and *one* dimension of validity at a time. (*PDM*, p. 207)

It is clear from this passage that Habermas is still working within a broadly Kantian architectonic, a doctrine of the faculties that insists on maintaining the distinction between pure reason, practical reason and aesthetic judgement. In this respect his arguments in *PDM* are continuous with the project set forth in an early work like *Knowledge and Human Interests*, despite what is presented as a crucial shift of emphasis, from an overtly Kantian ('epistemological' or 'foundationalist') approach to one that takes its bearings from speech-act theory, pragmatics and the study of communicative action. The continuity can be seen clearly enough in Habermas's way of separating out those uses of language 'specialized' for the purposes of problem-solving, argument, or rational critique. It is likewise evident in the distinction that Habermas maintains between 'ordinary' and 'extra-ordinary' language games, or those that have their place in 'normal speech' and those that belong more properly to art, literature and the 'world-disclosive' function of aesthetic understanding. Here we have the nub of Habermas's case against Derrida: the charge that he has effectively *disenfranchised* critical reason by allowing this promiscuous confusion of realms within and between the various linguistic orientations.

What this argument cannot countenance is any suggestion that *one and the same text* might possess both literary value (on account of its fictive, metaphorical or stylistic attributes) and philosophic cogency (by virtue of its power to criticize normative truth-claims). Thus Habermas would need to reject as non-philosophical not only a text like *La Carte Postale*, but also those numerous borderline cases – among them Plato, Augustine, Hegel, Kierkegaard, Austin, Borges, Calvino – where fiction and philosophy are closely intertwined. And if the list were then extended to philosophers who had once in a while made use of fictive devices or analogies, then it would also include Aristotle, Kant, Husserl, Frege, Quine, Searle and just about every major thinker in the Western tradition. So Habermas is pretty much out on a limb when he seeks to demarcate the types and conditions of language according to their various specialized roles. And this applies even more to his argument that literary criticism – at least as that discipline has developed since the eighteenth century – should also be regarded as a language apart from those texts that constitute its subject domain. Thus:

> it [criticism] has responded to the increasing autonomy of linguistic works of art by means of a discourse specialized for questions of taste. In it, the claims with which literary texts appear are submitted to examination – claims to 'artistic truth', aesthetic harmony, exemplary validity, innovative force, and authenticity. In this respect, aesthetic criticism is similar to argumentative forms specialized for propositional truth and the rightness of norms, that is, to theoretical and practical discourse. It is, however, not merely an esoteric component of expert culture but, beyond this, has the job of mediating between expert culture and the everyday world. (*PDM*, p. 207)

This last sentence might appear to qualify Habermas's rigid demarcation of realms by allowing that criticism (like philosophy) must have contact with 'ordinary language', at least to the extent of being understood by persons outside the 'expert culture' specifically devoted to such questions. But the passage makes it clear that Habermas conceives this alignment of interests as basically a two-term relationship, holding between 'ordinary language' on the one hand and aesthetics and literary theory on the other. That is to say, he excludes the possibility that this semi-specialized or mediating discourse might also respond to stylistic innovations in literary language, of the kind most strikingly exemplified in Derrida's texts. For Habermas, such developments have exactly the opposite effect. As literature becomes more 'autonomous' – more preoccupied with matters of style, form and technique – so criticism has to insist more firmly on the distance that separates its own language ('specialized for questions of taste') from the language of poetry or fiction. For otherwise – so Habermas implies – criticism will be in no position to claim a knowledge of the text that the text itself has not already made explicit. Only in so far as it maintains this stance can criticism adjudicate in those questions of 'aesthetic harmony, exemplary validity, innovative force, and authenticity' which constitute its own proper sphere of understanding. And in order to do so it will need to be aligned not so much with 'literature' as with 'philosophy', since it is here that such normative validity-claims are most thoroughly tried and tested.

I have already perhaps said enough to indicate just how remote these specifications are from Derrida's practice of a 'philosophical criticism' (for want of any better term) that deliberately mixes the genres of literature and theory. But we should not be misled into thinking that he has thereby renounced philosophy and given himself up to a mode of 'extraordinary' language that severs all links between itself and critical reason on the one hand, or itself and the interests of communal understanding on the other. What Habermas fails to recognize is the extent to which so-called 'ordinary' language is in fact shot through with metaphors, nonce-usages, chance collocations, Freudian parapraxes and other such 'accidental' features that cannot be reduced to any normative account. Henry Staten makes the point well when he describes how Wittgenstein, like Derrida, develops a style that is 'radically errant', one which effectively 'unlids all the accidence concealed by "normal" uses of words in order to show how many different routes it would be possible to take from any given point in the discourse.'[23] Staten is here arguing specifically against those mainstream readings of Wittgenstein which fasten on his talk of 'language-games' and 'forms of life', and use it as a warrant for confining authentic, serious or meaningful discourse to the range of usages sanctioned within some existing cultural community. On the contrary, says Staten, Wittgenstein is just as much concerned as Derrida with the radical 'accidence' of language, the way that it can open up unlooked-for possibilities of meaning precisely through the absence of such binding communal constraints. And the same applies to Derrida and Austin if their texts are read with sufficient regard to these innovative byways of language, routes which 'we had simply not thought of because we were bemused by normality'.[24]

Staten argues a convincing case for Derrida as one who has pushed the project of post-Kantian critical reason to the point of acknowledging its covert involvement in a general problematics of language, writing and representation. This is why his book pays careful attention to Derrida's reading of Husserl, and more specifically to those passages where the claims of transcendental phenomenology are subject to a certain dislocating pressure brought about by the effects of linguistic *différance*. It is here, Staten writes, that Derrida most decisively 'wrests the concept of meaning away from the moment of intuition in order to attach it *essentially* to the moment of signification'. Thus language (or writing, in Derrida's extended sense of the term) cannot be confined to its traditional role as a mere vehicle for thoughts and intuitions that would otherwise exist in a state of ideal self-presence or intelligibility. Rather, it is the signifying structure of language – that system of differential marks and traces 'without positive terms' – that constitutes the very possibility of meaning, and thus creates all manner of problems for Husserl's philosophical enterprise.[25] But again we should be wrong to see in this encounter a straightforward instance of philosophy's undoing at the hands of literature, writing or rhetoric. As Staten says, 'what is both original and problematic about Derrida's own project is that it does *not* pursue Joyce's path, but remains faithful to the problematic of that "univocity" that Derrida sees as underlying Joyce's equivocity, while yet opening out the univocal language in which he works, the language of philosophy, to that spread of meaning Joyce explored.'[26] It is precisely this possibility that Habermas excludes when he takes it that Derrida's levelling of the genre distinction between philosophy and literature deprives thinking of its critical force and thus betrays the very project of enlightened thought.

One could offer many instances from Derrida's work that would count strongly against this reading. Thus his essay on Foucault ('Cogito and the History of Madness')[27] makes exactly the point that Habermas is making when he asks what kind of *argumentative* force could possibly attach to Foucault's critical genealogies. More specifically: what is the status of a discourse that reduces all truths to the level of an undifferentiated power-knowledge; that denounces reason as merely an agency of ever-increasing surveillance and control; and that claims not only to speak on behalf of that madness which reason has constructed as its outcast other, but moreover to speak the very language of madness from a standpoint beyond any rational accountability?[28] For Habermas, this serves to demonstrate the sheer dead-end that thought runs into when it follows the line of reactive counter-enlightenment rhetoric that leads from Nietzsche to Bataille, Foucault and other such present-day apostles of unreason. It also goes to show how much they have in common with that one-sided view of modernity and its discontents adopted by an earlier generation of Frankfurt theorists (notably Adorno and Horkheimer in their book *Dialectic of Enlightenment*). For them, as for Foucault, 'modernity' is more or less synonymous with the encroachment of an instrumental reason that subjugates everything – nature, social existence, art, philosophy, language – to its own homogenizing drive. Thus 'Foucault so levels down the complexity of societal modernization that the disturbing paradoxes of this process cannot even become apparent to him' (*PDM*, p. 291). And he can do so only by ignoring the crucial distinction between instrumental reason – as developed in the service of scientific mastery and power – and those other forms of reason (communicative, critical or emancipatory) which point a way beyond this predicament.

Derrida is arguing to similar effect when he remarks on the strictly *impossible* nature of Foucault's undertaking and the fact that any such discourse on madness will necessarily have resort to a different order of language, logic and validity-claims. Thus:

> if discourse and philosophical communication (that is, language itself) are to have an intelligible meaning, that is to say, if they are to conform to their essence and vocation as discourse, they must simultaneously in fact and in principle escape madness. They must carry normality within themselves . . . By its essence, the sentence is normal . . . whatever the health or madness of him who propounds it, or whom it passes through, on whom, in whom it is articulated. In its most impoverished syntax, logos is reason and, indeed, a historical reason.[29]

Where this differs from Habermas's reading is in its argument that Foucault has *not* in fact achieved what he thinks to achieve, that is, a decisive break with the protocols of reason and truth. Since no such break is possible – since every sentence of Foucault's text betrays an opposite compulsion at work – Derrida can acknowledge the critical force of his writing *despite and against* its avowed purpose. 'Crisis of reason, finally, access to reason and attack of reason. For what Michel Foucault teaches us to think is that there are crises of reason in strange complicity with what the world calls crises of madness.'[30] For Habermas, conversely, Foucault exemplifies that levelling of the difference between reason and unreason which heralds the 'postmodern condition' and the ultimate betrayal of enlightenment values. In short, Habermas takes Foucault at his word as having left behind all the rational criteria, normative truth-claims, standards of validity, etc., which constitute the 'philosophical discourse of modernity'. And this despite his clear recognition elsewhere that 'Foucault only gains this basis [that is, the explanatory matrix of power-knowledge] by not thinking genealogically when it comes to his *own* genealogical historiography and by rendering unrecognizable the derivation of this transcendental-historicist concept of power' (*PDM*, p. 269). For ultimately Habermas cannot conceive that Foucault's project, deriving as it does from the Nietzschean counter-enlightenment lineage, might yet possess a power of demystifying insight that works against its own professed aims and interests.

Derrida can allow for this ambivalence in Foucault's work because (unlike Habermas) he doesn't draw a firm, juridical line between reason and rhetoric, philosophy and literature, the discourse of enlightened critique and the capacity of language (even 'extraordinary' language) to reflect on the inbuilt limits and aporias of that same discourse. But it is simply not the case, as Habermas asserts, that Derrida has thereby abandoned the ground of post-Kantian critical thought, or gone along with that 'drastic levelling of [the] architectonic of reason that results from the Nietzsche-inspired reading of Kant' (*PDM*, p. 305). On the contrary, several of his recent essays are concerned with questions in precisely this sphere. They include Derrida's writings on the modern university and its division of intellectual labour, especially as this relates to Kant's doctrine of the faculties and their role vis-à-vis the cardinal distinction between 'pure' and 'applied' forms of knowledge.[31] Here, as in Habermas, philosophy is assigned to its proper place as the discipline that legislates in questions of validity and truth, while the other, more practical or research-oriented disciplines have their separate domains marked out according to their own specific ends and interests. Certainly Derrida calls this system into question, remarking on the various conflicts, aporias or boundary disputes that arise within and between the faculties. Moreover, he does so by way of a rhetorical reading that suspends the privileged truth claims of philosophy and asks more specifically what *interests* are served by this policing of the various faculty limits. All the same there is no question of simply revoking the Kantian paradigm and declaring a break with that entire heritage of enlightened critical thought. In fact Derrida repeatedly insists on the need to keep faith with this 'vigil' of enlightenment, a vigil whose term is not ended (as 'postmodern' thinkers would have it) on account of these constitutive blind-spots in its own project. Those who profess to deconstruct Kant's doctrine of the faculties 'need not set themselves up in opposition to the principle of reason, nor need they give way to "irrationalism"'.[32] While questioning the modern university system and its forms of self-authorized knowledge, they can nevertheless assume, 'along with its memory and tradition, the imperatives of professional rigor and competence'.

V

Perhaps the most interesting text in this regard is Derrida's essay 'Of an Apocalyptic Tone Recently Adopted in Philosophy'.[33] The title is borrowed almost verbatim from Kant, who used it for a piece of philosophical polemics against those who saw fit to reject the dictates of enlightened reason, and who relied instead on their own unaided intuition as to questions of truth and falsehood or right and wrong. Kant has nothing but scorn for these enthusiasts, these adepts of the 'inner light', imagining as they do that one can bypass the critical tribunal of the faculties and arrive at truth without benefit of reasoned debate. And of course their presumption has religious and political overtones, laying claim to a freedom of individual conscience that goes far beyond Kant's prescription for the exercise of citizenly virtues in a liberal-democratic state. In short, this text bears a close resemblance to Habermas's critique of Derrida, especially those passages where he locates the origins of deconstruction in a 'subject-centred' pre-enlightenment discourse which in turn goes back to the 'mysticism of being', and which thus provides a starting point for Heidegger and Derrida alike. 'If this suspicion is not utterly false, Derrida returns to the historical locale where mysticism once turned into enlightenment' (PDM, p. 184). On this reading, deconstruction is the upshot of a fateful swerve in the history of thought, a path wrongly chosen at precisely the point where philosophy might have set out on the high road of rational self-understanding.

Thus Habermas takes Derrida to task – just as Kant once chastised the fake illuminati and apostles of unreason – for rejecting that alternative, far preferable course which led *through and beyond* Kant and Hegel to the theory of communicative action. In short, Derrida's deconstructive reading of Heidegger 'does not escape the aporetic structure of a truth-occurrence eviscerated of all truth-as-validity' (PDM, p. 167). And again:

> unabashedly, and in the style of *Ursprungsphilosophie*, Derrida falls back on this *Urschrift* [viz. *arche-écriture*] which leaves its traces anonymously, without any subject ... As Schelling once did in speculating about the timelessly temporalizing internest-ing of the past, present and future ages of the world, so Derrida clings to the dizzying thought of a past that has never been present ... He too [like Heidegger] degrades politics and contemporary history to the status of the ontic and the fore-

ground, so as to romp all the more freely ... in the sphere of
the ontological and the archewriting. (pp. 179–81)

This passage tends to confirm the impression that Habermas has
based his arguments on a very partial knowledge of Derrida's work.
It is a reading that conspicuously fails to take account of his more
recent texts on the 'principle of reason', the politics of representation
and the role of the modern university system as a site where Kant's
doctrine of the faculties is both reproduced and subjected to forms of
destabilizing pressure and critique. But the point can be made more
specifically with reference to Derrida's essay 'Of an Apocalyptic
Tone', and the way that it rehearses not only Kant's quarrel with the
mystagogues but also – at least by implication – the issue between
Habermas and Derrida.

For it is simply not the case (or *not simply* the case) that Derrida
here 'deconstructs' the pretensions of enlightenment discourse in
order to gain a hearing for those sophists, rhetoricians or purveyors
of an occult wisdom whose extravagant teachings Kant holds up to
ridicule in the parliament of plain-prose reason. Thus when Derrida
offers his own free paraphrase of Kant's case against the mystagogues
it could easily be taken for a passage from one of Habermas's
chapters on Derrida in *PDM*. 'This cryptopolitics is also a crypto-
poetics, a poetic perversion of philosophy' (*AT*, p. 14). And again:
'this leap toward the imminence of a vision without concept, this
impatience turned toward the most crypted secret sets free a poetico-
metaphorical overabundance' (p. 12). For Kant, 'all philosophy is
indeed prosaic,' since it is only by submitting to the democratic rule
of reason – to the various 'faculties' duly assembled in parliament,
along with all their delegated powers and provisions – that thinking
can avoid the manifest dangers of a direct appeal to individual
conscience or naked, self-advocating will. Hobbes is a warning
presence in the background here, as he is in those passages where
Habermas reproaches Foucault for abandoning the ground of enlightened critique, as evolved through the various forms and procedures
of civil-administrative reason. What is most to be feared is a
wholesale levelling of the faculties which would deprive reason of its
moderating role and thereby reduce history, philosophy and politics
to a mere force-field of contending interests or rhetorical strategies.
And according to Habermas deconstruction is complicit in this
process, since it overextends the province of rhetoric to the point of
annulling reason itself, along with all those crucial distinctions that
emerged in the sphere of sociopolitical debate.

Again, these are arguments that Derrida rehearses – and the term
seems just right in this context – when he speaks up for Kant and the
values of enlightenment, as against the purveyors of a false knowledge

vouchsafed by mere intuition. Thus the mystagogues 'scoff at work, the concept, schooling ... To what is given they believe they have access effortlessly, gracefully, intuitively or through genius, outside of school' (AT, p. 9). Where these characters offend most gravely is in 'playing the overlord', in 'raising the tone' of philosophy (or pseudo-philosophy) to such a pitch that it rejects all rational obliga-tions, all the rules of civilized exchange among equals that make up an emergent and developing public sphere. In so doing they seek 'to hoist themselves above their colleagues or fellows and wrong them in their inalienable right to freedom and equality regarding everything touching on reason alone' (AT, p. 11). And the signs of this attitude are there to be read in the various forms of *rhetorical* overreaching – hyperbole, multiplied metaphor, prosopopeia, apostrophe and other such tropes – whose effect is to disrupt the parliament of faculties by giving voice to a language that respects none of its agreed-upon rules and protocols. As Derrida writes, again paraphrasing Kant: 'they do not distinguish between pure speculative reason and pure practical reason; they believe they *know* what is solely *thinkable* and reach through feeling alone the universal laws of practical reason' (p. 12). Hence their resort to an 'apocalyptic tone' that takes effect through its sheerly *performative* power, its use of an oracular, 'inspired' or prophetic style of speech where the truth claims of reason (or of language in its constative aspect) have no part to play.

Now it is clear that Derrida is not unambiguously taking Kant's side in this attack on the pretensions of any philosophy that thinks to place itself above or outside the jurisdiction of plain-prose reason. For one thing, his essay is itself shot through with apocalyptic figures and devices, among them various mystical injunctions from Jewish and Christian source texts. To this extent Derrida is asking us to see that the ethos of Kantian civilized reason has sharp juridical limits; that it has only been able to impose its rule through a constant policing of the border-lines between reason and rhetoric, concept and metaphor, 'genuine' philosophy and a discourse that lays false claim to that title. But we should be wrong to conclude that the essay comes out squarely *against* Kant, or that Derrida's use of an apocalyptic tone signals yet another 'postmodern' break with the discourse of enlightened reason. What sustains this project, he writes, is the 'desire for vigilance, for the lucid vigil, for elucidation, for critique and truth' (AT, p. 22). Of course it may be said that Derrida is here not speaking 'in his own voice'; that this essay is a kind of ventriloquist performance, mixing all manner of citations, intertextual allusions, contrapuntal ironies and so forth, so that anyone who instances this or that passage as evidence for their own preferred reading is surely missing the point. But this objection is itself wide of the mark in so far as it ignores the distinctly Kantian form of Derrida's argument, namely, his questioning of enlightenment values and truth claims through a debate whose terms are inescapably set by that same Kantian tribunal. That is to say, Derrida is asking what might be the *conditions of possibility* for the exercise of a critical reason that thinks to keep itself pure by excluding or denouncing all other forms of discourse.

To regard this essay as a mere assemblage of 'literary' tricks and devices is to make the same error that Habermas makes when he criticizes Derrida for supposedly levelling the genre distinction between philosophy and literature. It involves the kind of typecast binary thinking that refuses to see how a 'literary' text – or one which exploits a wide range of stylistic resources – might yet possess sufficient *argumentative* force to unsettle such deep-laid assumptions. Derrida belongs very much with those philosophers (Wittgenstein and Austin among them) who resist this habit of compartmentalized thinking. He wants to keep open the two-way flow between so-called 'ordinary' language and the various extra-ordinary styles, idioms, metaphorical usages, 'expert' registers and so forth, which help to defamiliarize our commonplace beliefs. But he also sees – unlike Habermas or Searle – that 'ordinary language' is a gross misnomer, since there is no possibility of laying down rules (or extracting a generalized speech-act theory) that would separate normal from deviant instances. It is the idea that such rules *ought* to be available – and that philosophy is the discipline specialized (as Habermas would say) for the purpose of producing them – that actually prevents philosophy from perceiving how manifold, inventive and remarkable are the varieties of 'ordinary' language. The result of such thinking is to isolate philosophy in a realm of metalinguistic theory and principle where it can have no contact with those energizing sources.

Derrida's point – to put it very simply – is that philosophy is indeed a 'kind of writing', but a kind which (contrary to Rorty's understanding) cannot be collapsed into a generalized notion of rhetoric or intertextuality. It is unfortunate that Habermas takes his bearings in *PDM* from a widespread but none the less fallacious idea of how deconstruction relates to other symptoms of the so-called 'postmodern condition'. What Derrida gives us to read is *not* philosophy's undoing at the hands of literature but a literature that meets the challenge of philosophy in every aspect of its argument, form and style.

NOTES

1 Jürgen Habermas, *The Philosophical Discourse of Modernity: Twelve Lectures*, trans. Frederick Lawrence (Cambridge and Cambridge, Mass., 1987). Hereafter cited as *PDM*.

2 See for instance Jean-François Lyotard, 'The Sign of History', in Derek Attridge, Geoff Bennington and Robert Young (eds), *Post-structuralism and the Question of History* (Cambridge, 1987), pp. 162–80.

3 Habermas, *Knowledge and Human Interests*, trans. Jeremy J. Shapiro (Cambridge, 1972).

4 For a useful account of these differences, see Rainer Nägele, 'Freud, Habermas and the Dialectic of Enlightenment: On Real and Ideal Discourses', *New German Critique*, no. 22 (1981), pp. 41–62.

5 See Rodolphe Gasché, *The Tain of the Mirror: Derrida and the Philosophy of Reflection* (Cambridge, Mass., 1986).

6 Richard Rorty, 'Philosophy as a Kind of Writing', in *Consequences of Pragmatism* (Minneapolis, 1982), pp. 89–109. See also Richard Rorty, 'Deconstruction and Circumvention', *Critical Inquiry* 11 (1984), pp. 1–23.

7 See especially Jacques Derrida, *Margins Of Philosophy*, trans. Alan Bass (Chicago, 1982).

8 Jacques Derrida, 'Limited Inc. abc', *Glyph* 2 (1977), pp. 162–254.

9 Jacques Derrida, 'Structure, Sign and Play in the Discourse of the Human Sciences', in Derrida, *Writing and Difference*, trans. Alan Bass (London, 1978), pp. 278–93.

10 Jacques Derrida, *The Post Card: From Socrates to Freud and Beyond*, trans. Alan Bass (Chicago, 1987). I have slightly modified Bass's translation in some of the passages cited.

11 Jacques Derrida, *Edmund Husserl's 'Origin of Geometry': An Introduction*, trans. John P. Leavey (Pittsburgh, 1978).

12 In this connection see especially Jürgen Habermas, *Communication and the Evolution of Society*, trans. Thomas McCarthy (Cambridge, 1979).

13 John Searle, 'Reiterating the Differences', *Glyph* 1 (1977), pp. 198–208.

14 See Christopher Norris, *Derrida* (Cambridge, Mass., 1987), pp. 172–93; also Jonathan Culler, 'Convention and Meaning: Derrida and Austin', *New Literary History* 13 (1981), pp. 15–30, and Shoshana Felman, *The Literary Speech-Act: Don Juan with J. L. Austin, or Seduction in Two Languages*, trans. Catherine Porter (Ithaca, N.Y., 1983).

15 See J. L. Austin, *How to Do Things with Words* (London, 1962) and *Philosophical Papers* (London, 1961), especially the essay 'A Plea for Excuses', pp. 123–52.

16 Jacques Derrida, *Of Grammatology*, trans. Gayatri C. Spivak (Baltimore, 1976).

17 Derrida, *The Post Card*, p. 98.

18 On this topic see also Jacques Derrida, *Signsponge*, trans. Richard Rand (New York, 1984).

19 Derrida, *The Post Card*, p. 99.

20 Ibid., p. 62.

21 Jacques Derrida, 'To Speculate – on "Freud"', in *The Post Card*, pp. 257–409.

22 Jacques Lacan, 'Seminar on "The Purloined Letter"', trans. Jeffrey Mehlman, *Yale French Studies*, no. 48 (1972), pp. 38–72. Derrida's essay, 'Le facteur de la vérité', appears in *The Post Card*, pp. 411–96.

23 Henry Staten, *Wittgenstein and Derrida* (Lincoln and London, 1984), p. 75.

24 Ibid., p. 75.

25 See Jacques Derrida, *'Speech and Phenomena' and Other Essays on Husserl's Theory of Signs*, trans. David B. Allison (Evanston, Ill., 1973).

26 Staten, *Wittgenstein and Derrida*, p. 48.

27 Jacques Derrida, 'Cogito and the History of Madness' in *Writing and Difference*, pp. 31–63.

28 Michel Foucault, *Madness and Civilization: A History of Insanity in the Age of Reason*, trans. Richard Howard (New York, 1965). Foucault responded to Derrida's essay in his appendix to the second edition of *Folie et déraison* (Paris, 1972), pp. 583–603.
29 Derrida, 'Cogito and the History of Madness', pp. 53–4.
30 Ibid., p. 63.
31 See for instance Jacques Derrida, 'The Principle of Reason: The University in the Eyes of its Pupils', *Diacritics* 19 (1983), pp. 3–20.
32 Ibid., p. 17.
33 Jacques Derrida, 'Of an Apocalyptic Tone Recently Adopted in Philosophy', trans. John P. Leavey, *Oxford Literary Review* 6:2 (1984), pp. 3–37. Hereafter cited in the text as AT.

4

SPLITTING THE DIFFERENCE: HABERMAS'S CRITIQUE OF DERRIDA

David Couzens Hoy

Jürgen Habermas and Jacques Derrida are arguably the living European philosophers who are best known to academics in the US and the UK today. Each has a different audience, with Derrida receiving attention more from literary critics and Habermas from social theorists, for instance. This difference of audience is not merely a sociological feature, however; it reflects the underlying philosophical differences between the two. I doubt that among those specialists who study both thinkers there are many who find both acceptable. Instead, there are 'Habermasians' and 'Derrideans', depending on whether their intuitions are that one or the other is wrong-headed. There is good reason for this response since each thinker represents not simply a different set of ideas, but more broadly, a different sense of what philosophy (or what is now called 'theory') can be at the current stage of history. Or perhaps I should put the term 'history' in scare-quotes, since a crucial part of the debate about theory is whether the idea of history can be taken seriously any longer.

But obviously 'theory' must be put in scare-quotes as well. Part of the debate is whether there can be 'theory' that somehow transcends the phenomenon of historical change by stating conditions that are universal and therefore unhistorical. Another part of the debate is whether there is any such thing as 'history', given that the unity required to tell a single story about complex events may merely be a fiction imagined by the historian. My own activity in this paper will be to take Habermas's critique of Derrida as a chapter in the history of late twentieth-century philosophy. Admittedly, then, my activity may seem to beg the question of history versus theory by assuming both that an understanding of history is indispensable to the formation of theory, and that the formation of theory ought to reflect on the history of its formation. Since I do think that history and theory are interdependent, and that Habermas's and Derrida's positions strike some critics as disconnecting history and theory, my own standpoint is neither Habermasian nor Derridean. I am therefore not begging the question in a fallacious way but am constructing a philosophical opposition for the further purpose of going beyond it.

I will therefore point out in advance that taking the Habermas–Derrida debate as a chapter that is already part of a history, and therefore in the recent past, conflicts with another message of this chapter, which is that the debate is really part of the present and will be constitutive of what philosophy becomes, especially since both thinkers are still alive and evolving. Any 'history' I sketch will therefore be in the future perfect tense, projecting how things will have been. Writing the Habermas/Derrida debate as a chapter in the history of twentieth-century philosophy before rather than after the fact is a deliberate way of avoiding Habermas's emplotment, and especially its implication that we must take one side or the other. The point of constructing a fictional history in the future perfect tense is to suggest that the opposition is itself fictional. There may be other alternatives, and these alternatives may involve splitting the difference between the two. 'Splitting the difference' is not the same, however, as synthesizing the two or of finding some third position between them.[1] Instead, it identifies philosophical possibilities that are left open instead of being closed off by two theoretical positions construing themselves as mutually exclusive.

Modernity vs Postmodernity?

To write this history of the present I cannot avoid invoking two problematic terms, 'modern' and 'postmodern'. I have doubts about the usefulness of these labels, but they feature in Habermas's *The Philosophical Discourse of Modernity*. These labels are more historical than theoretical, but they provide the general frame within which Habermas's particular criticisms are placed. I shall therefore question this historical frame in this section and leave the details of the theoretical arguments for the next section.

Habermas sets himself as a modern and casts Derrida as a postmodern. The postmodern line begins with Nietzsche, who 'renounces a renewed revision of the concept of reason and *bids farewell* to the dialectic of enlightenment'.[2] As a defender of modernity Habermas stands in the tradition of philosophy from Descartes to Kant, but of course he cannot be modern in the same sense that they are. Habermas acknowledges that the modern philosophy of consciousness had reached a state of exhaustion by the nineteenth century, and the task ever since has been to find ways around this exhaustion.[3] Habermas's stance is later than the modern one, for it recognizes the failure of the modern philosophers to ground the possibility of knowledge in the self-certainty of subjectivity. The modern philosophers privilege subjectivity as the paradigm of philosophical efforts to discover the foundations of knowledge. Habermas claims to have moved beyond the philosophy of subjectivity into the philosophy of language. Doing so also means that he is not a foundationalist as the modern philosophers were. Instead, he thinks that philosophy must recognize that its claims are fallible instead of absolute. Having substituted language for the moderns' philosophy of the subject, and rejected their absolutism and foundationalism for empirical fallibilism, means that in central ways he comes later than modernity. So it is tempting to think of Habermas himself as a postmodern. Yet supposedly unlike the neo-Nietzschean French postmoderns, he has not abandoned modern philosophy's goal of formulating and defending rationality and universality. I would therefore characterize him as a *late* modern. But I wish to stress that both 'late' and 'post' suggest 'after', and thus the contrast is not between modernity and postmodernity, but between a late-modern and a postmodern sense of what to do next, given that in central ways modern philosophy has reached a state of exhaustion, and not just recently.

These terms are more historical than theoretical, and are difficult to use precisely. As a result Habermas's account would be easy to deconstruct, if a Derridean wanted to turn the tables on Habermas's critique. Habermas characterizes Derrida as a postmodern, because Habermas sees Derrida abandoning modern philosophy's ambitions to be universal and thus to assure itself of its own rationality. But at the same time Habermas's message is that there is no successful postmodern stance, and further that such a stance would be impossible anyway. So Derrida's theory is postmodern (says Habermas as historian of the present), and yet there really cannot be any postmodern theory (says Habermas as a theorist). Habermas then explains Derrida's motivation by suggesting that the postmodern effort to overcome modern enlightenment disguises a desire to return to a premodern anti-enlightenment tradition. In Derrida's case the tradition influencing his thought is said to be Jewish mysticism.

The Derridean could object to this apparently *ad hominem* line of argument that explains and attacks Derrida's text by appeal to biographical features of Derrida's personal history. To the Derridean, Habermas's reasoning would resemble the 'kettle logic' that Derrida notices in Freud's account of the logic of dreams: 'In his attempt to arrange everything in his favor, the defendant piles up contradictory arguments: (1) The kettle I am returning to you is brand new; (2) The holes were already in it when you lent it to me; (3) You never lent me a kettle, anyway.'[4] Analogously, Habermas's argument seems to be:

(1) Postmodernism represents a radical break with the history of modern rationalism; (2) To break with rationality and universality is impossible and philosophy without the aspirations of modernity would be unrecognizable, so Derrida is incoherent to the point of unintelligibility: (3) Derrida is not doing anything new, anyway, since his moves are already familiar ones recognizable and intelligible from the tradition of Jewish mysticism, which is out of date because it is premodern.

In response to this attempt to deconstruct Habermas's critique of Derrida, a Habermasian could say that his argument is misinterpreted. Habermas's text is unfortunately vague about exactly what sort of explanation of Derrida's theory is being offered when Habermas writes that Derrida's stance 'may have something to do with the fact that Derrida, all denials notwithstanding, remains close to Jewish mysticism'.[5] The Habermasian could insist that Habermas is using the method of *Ideologiekritik*, adapted from the Critical Theory of the Frankfurt School. Habermas's argument is not *ad hominem*, appearances to the contrary, but depends on the difference between the *desire* to create a postmodern theory, and the success in doing so. If the desire fails and is frustrated, the Critical Theorist can give an account of the difference between what the desire seems to be on the surface, and what it really represents, given its failure and frustration. Thus Habermas's analysis is that Derrida is attempting to break with modernity, and his desire is to be postmodern. But Derrida is unsuccessful in doing so, and his attempt at postmodernism is a failure. Derrida's desire to transcend the aspirations of modern reason is in reality a frustrated desire for a return to the premodern traditions where reason has not yet undermined the mystery of hidden religious authority. Since the quarrel is between the Enlightenment's faith in reason and the counter-enlightenment rebellion against reason, what Habermas is objecting to is the vestige of Jewish mysticism (not because it is Jewish, of course, but because it is mystical to the point of being not only mysterious but also unintelligible).

A central point of this defence is that Habermas's goal is not simply to show that Derrida's theory is incoherent. Critical Theory differs from traditional theory in that the goal of the former is not simply to destroy a theory by showing its incoherence, but to *explain* how the adherents to the theory could have failed to perceive their own incoherence. This explanation depends on identifying how their real desires or interests were different from what the adherents thought they were. The explanation would also presumably be one that the adherents themselves could accept once their desires were unmasked.

So the conflict in theory today is also a conflict of methods. Textual deconstruction is one method, but the Critical Theory of the later

Frankfurt School is another. Both claim to show what is really going on in a theoretical text, but the latter posits an extratextual reality (such as social conflict, real interests, frustrated desires, basic needs) as an explanation for the blindness of the text or the theory to its own inadequacy and inconsistencies.[6]

So Habermas's analysis of Derrida is not simply a form of kettle logic but can be properly understood only as the methodological consequence of the tradition of Critical Theory. With that much said in Habermas's favour, however, where I would also agree with my hypothetical deconstructivist defender of Derrida is that Habermas's use of the term postmodern does set the scene in his favour from the start. Derrida, as far as I know, does not see himself as a postmodern, so applying the label to him seems simply to use a term of abuse.[7] I would therefore like to offer a different model of what postmodernity might mean. This model is intended to be neutral, and thus 'postmodern' will be a term neither of abuse nor of approbation. I adapt this account from Foucault (who is neutral in the exchange between Habermas and Derrida, although Habermas considers him to be a postmodern as well), but I hasten to point out that Foucault also does not claim to be a postmodern. (The label is explicitly adopted mainly by J. F. Lyotard.)[8]

The fundamental drive of modernity, on Foucault's analysis, is to think the unthought. In particular, modern philosophy is obsessed with the question not of what sorts of beings can be known, but how knowledge itself is possible. So the unthought that modern philosophy tries to think is thought itself. This self-reflectivity produces antinomies, which force successive modern theorists to redefine what about thought has been left unthought by their predecessors. While Foucault spells out these antinomies (or 'doubles') at great length (in *The Order of Things*), I do not want to follow his exposition further, but will ask instead how we might construe postmodern thinking, given this characterization of modern thought.

Foucault himself seems to be beyond the modern thinking that he is describing, yet he too seems to be trying to think the unthought. Sometimes postmoderns are criticized for trying to think the unthinkable. If this is what they are doing, then Habermas is correct in rejecting their project as impossible. (Even to try to think the unthinkable is impossible, since one could not try to do what one knew one could not do, such as finding the last value of π.) Since this definition rules out postmodernity from the start, however, a more sympathetic approach is to see the postmoderns as continuing the modern project of thinking the unthought, but changing the enterprise such that the unthought is no longer some noumenal entity or an inexperienceable transcendental ego, but something more on the surface of things, and thus not in principle inaccessible. Nevertheless, the postmoderns do not share the desire of the moderns to make the unthought completely accessible.

For the postmoderns the mistake of earlier moderns lies not so much in their efforts to think the unthought, but in the moderns' belief that they could think the unthought completely. Moderns aim at *transparency* in a strong sense because they aim to attain self-transparency. In a weak sense transparency is the generally acceptable idea that how knowledge works or how ethical practices work should not be misunderstood by knowers or by moral agents. Enlightenment rationalism leads to the much stronger sense of transparency whereby we do not understand ourselves or our epistemological, moral and social practices unless we can identify and state systematically the rules, principles or beliefs that make them possible.[9] The postmoderns continue to try to think what has remained unthought, but they abandon the idea that the unthought can be made completely transparent.

The difference, then, between moderns and postmoderns will not be in what they are doing so much as in their attitude towards what they are doing. Let me propose six features that typify the postmodern attitude. (1) The first feature of the postmodern outlook is that it accepts rather than laments the inevitable inability to make completely manifest the unthought or unsaid. Moderns assume that a great unthought runs throughout the world in all its forms and events, and we cannot claim really to understand anything about the world until we understand this unthought. For postmoderns, however, thinking can never be complete and self-transparent, but always generates further complexity and complications. Their acceptance of this point is not simply a nihilistic resignation to it, but because of the further features, it is a positive and liberating action.

(2) Postmoderns therefore do not give up trying to think the unthought altogether. The second feature thus concerns how they continue to try to think the unthought. They need not become idealists and deny the reality of what has been left unthought but still seems to be governing thought. They can accept that the kinds of unthought that they are trying to get at are real or genuinely operative, without believing that they can capture them in a theory that would make them completely transparent. The unthought might include background conditions and a general style of organization of a way of thinking, and thus will not be theorizable in the same way that particular objects, contents or ideas are. (Thus Foucault does not claim to have a 'theory' of power, which is the unthought he pursues in some of his writings, and, as I will argue, Derrida also does not have a *theory* of writing, of the 'trace', or of *différance*, the latter being neither a word nor a concept.)

These differences in how the unthought is to be approached lead to three further corollaries that explain the postmodern conception of what the unthought is like: (3) there is no single, privileged or uniquely paradigmatic way to think the unthought; (4) there is not a single, unique, 'master' unthought running through every phenomenon; and (5) no unthought is itself a single thing (that is, capable of only one correct description or of one level of analysis). In short, postmoderns are pluralists, and can find more than one unthought to talk about. Foucault moves from analysing discourse as the unthought, to power, to sexual self-fashioning. Derrida similarly addresses a different unthought with each text he analyses (such as trace, supplement, graft or parergon).[10] The postmoderns' pluralism contrasts with the drive of a late modern like Habermas to find in a single phenomenon – communicative competence – the unique a priori structure from which to derive the universal rationality to which the modern tradition aspires.

The final feature follows from these, and captures the difference in attitude between the late modern and the postmodern. The late modern thinks that the Enlightenment ideal of progress through the advance of reason cannot really be abandoned. The late modern will interpret the postmoderns' lack of belief in progress as a despair suggesting nostalgia for a premodern age of innocence. But I interpret the postmodern attitude differently, and the final feature I suggest is, (6), that the postmoderns realize that nostalgia only makes sense in contrast to the hope for progress, so that truly abandoning this hope also leads them beyond nostalgia. Thinkers like Heidegger and perhaps Adorno do seem nostalgic in this sense, and thus do not strike me as genuine postmoderns (despite Habermas's tendency to group them with Nietzsche, Foucault and Derrida). Like postmodern architecture, postmodern thought is best understood not as nostalgic exhaustion, but as a more forward-looking cheerfulness that manages to recombine and play with the elements of modernity in unanticipated ways.

One sign of a lack of nostalgia is a lack of interest in philosophical self-legitimation. Of course, Foucault and Derrida do not want their views and methods to be internally inconsistent. But they are not seeking the foundations of thought so much as alternative methods for thinking about and interpreting texts (and other worldly phenomena, such as ourselves). I do not see either Derrida's strategy of dissemination or Foucault's genealogy as claiming to be the only correct method of interpretation. Methods are not 'true' or 'false', but only more or less useful, and thus the main legitimation of a method of interpretation is its heuristic value.

This lack of concern for self-legitimation may make postmoderns seem playful even to the point of being unserious and irresponsible, especially about their own enterprises.[11] However that may be in particular cases, I would suggest that it would be contradictory for them to be so concerned with self-legitimation as to attack late modernism and to defend postmodernism as the only viable attitude in the present context. Lyotard perhaps falls into a trap in so far as he does explicitly avow the label of postmodernism, and defends it. However, if the postmodern attitude is as I have described it, then the postmodern would be inconsistent in thinking that postmodernism is the most advanced, most rational, or in general, the only possible attitude. If there is no necessary progress in history, the postmodern cannot claim a normative advantage in being later in time or a sign of the future. Such a normative advantage is implied in the notion of 'modernity', and is still assumed by the late modern. But the postmodern seems to have abandoned the idea that the present is necessarily better than the past, as well as any nostalgia for the past. So the postmodern should not claim to be better or more advanced or more clever than the late modern, and has no argument that the late modern should become a postmodern. Since the true postmodern could not be an advocate of postmodernism, I think that the label is not really a useful one. If there are genuine issues separating Habermas and Derrida, these issues can only be obscured by thinking that in resolving them we must be partisans of either modernity or postmodernity.

Deconstruction: Theory or Method?

I suggest, therefore, that the historical label of postmodernity is *not* the crux. Habermas may have been using the modern/postmodern contrast only as a convenient fiction, but when pressed, the device threatens to become counterproductive. Furthermore, the idea of progress is itself a red herring. If the postmoderns are accused of abandoning rationality because they do not believe that we are better off now than human beings were in the past, it should be noted that the postmoderns need not claim that there are *no* respects in which people are now better off. They need only affirm that in some particular respects (including crucial ones about which people often deceive themselves) people are not better off. So to the question as to whether the world ever gets better, they can answer reasonably: never entirely.

To the further question as to whether history *as a whole* can be said to be necessarily progressive, their answer is that there is no possible standpoint from which this judgement can be made. So they are not denying the rationality and progressiveness of history as a whole so much as questioning whether the belief in the growth of reason makes sense, or has any content. On this point, even Habermas recognizes that progress can be spoken of only in some subsystem or other, and that there is no point to speaking of the progress of the whole of history. So the issue is not whether there is progress, but is instead to locate where the belief in progress in some areas of social life might be covering up insidious oppression in other areas.

Given this problem, there is a genuine question as to whether Derrida's method of dissemination or deconstruction can help. Habermas is not alone in arguing that Derrida's approach has not been and cannot be applied to such a concrete issue. Foucault also accuses Derrida of being overly preoccupied with texts and ignoring their social context. Foucault suspects that Derrida's method tacitly claims authority for itself as a result of the authority and primacy it grants to the text. Furthermore, Foucault believes that a text is not autonomous from the social practices to which it is tied both in its own time and in the time of its later interpretation. Foucault suggests that deconstruction is blind not only to the ways in which the text reflects social practices, but also to the extent to which deconstruction is itself a social practice.

I think that what may be troubling Foucault is that deconstruction may appear to have the status of being a philosophy because it claims universal applicability. There is no form of text, no genre of discourse, nothing that can be said, thought or done that escapes its purview. Yet this appearance of universality may be the result of its inability to apply itself to itself, even if only because it refuses to make any theoretical assertions. Unlike Foucault's own willingness to avow that his histories are the product of the needs of the moment, and therefore not objective or neutral studies (although Habermas thinks that they do aspire to such neutrality), Derrida's deconstructions take place as if in a vacuum, showing what could have been seen earlier and what will presumably have to be seen from now on. This vacuum probably seemed particularly apparent to Foucault and Habermas by the refusal (until more recently) to reflect on the social and political implications of the deconstructive method.

Habermas too thinks that Derrida's theory still looks like *Ursprungsphilosophie*, the search for what is really primary.[12] He finds this dimension particularly in Derrida's claims about archewriting. More strongly than Foucault, Habermas accuses Derrida of being like Heidegger in maintaining that politics and history are merely ontic, everyday matters that can be ignored in favour of the more important ontological investigations. Unlike Heidegger, however, Habermas thinks that Derrida's practice is subversive and anarchistic, with no redeeming theory, but simply a desire to blow up and trash tradition and continuity.[13] As Derrida says about *différance*, 'It governs nothing, reigns over nothing, and nowhere exercises any authority. It is not announced by any capital letter. Not only is there no kingdom of *différance*, but *différance* instigates the subversion of every kingdom.'[14] But although Derrida denies claiming any authority, philosophical or otherwise, for *différance*, Habermas thinks that Derrida is suggesting that *différance* is really the primary feature of language. So Habermas believes that there is an appeal to authority after all, if not to the authority of holy scripture (expressing the direct voice of God, and thus phonocentric, onto-theology), then to that of an exiled scripture (the Torah). Habermas thinks that the 'a' in *différance* is to be understood as a mystical symbol, like the *aleph* with which the first commandment in the Hebrew text begins, and which is the only part of the commandments that the Hebrew people was supposed to have really heard, such that everything else is a matter of interpretation.

Habermas presses this point to show that Derrida fails in his attempt to take the linguistic turn and falls back into the paradoxes of philosophies relying on subjectivity.[15] Derrida's linguistic turn supposedly relapses into mysticism despite Derrida's intention of taking the linguistic turn precisely to avoid not only the later Heidegger's *Seins*-mysticism but also the earlier detour through *Sein und Zeit* that replaces subjectivity with *Daseins*-analysis. The philosophical issue separating them is Habermas's charge that Derrida's aesthetic contextualism ignores how the idealization procedures built into the communicative action of everyday practices require us to redeem and prove the validity of our claims. In seeming to deny that validity claims can be redeemed or proved, Derrida's view is blind to the social learning processes through which we change and improve our understanding of ourselves and our world. Because of this blindness, deconstruction implies that we are stuck in our context, and caught fatalistically in the forces of textual production. We are doomed to provincialism by the overpowering background of the archewriting.[16] Derrida's Heideggerian privileging of the ontological over the ontic is seen by Habermas in the way Derrida denies or at least overlooks the point that judgements and experience require criticizable validity claims. Derrida focuses too much on the (ontological) question of whether texts can disclose the world and forgets the (ontic) dimension of texts as solving problems and aiming at hermeneutical consensus (*Einverständnis*).

There are thus two basic charges against Derrida by Habermas. First, Derrida's linguistic turn is still a form of *Ursprungsphilosophie*, one that seeks the safety of pure theory. Second, Derrida's Heideggerian preference for the ontological over the ontic, philosophy over politics, is still a nostalgic desire to return to an archaic premodernism. Let me discuss the first charge, leaving the second charge for the concluding section.

I agree that there is a tone in Derrida's earlier writings that does invite Habermas's first charge. Habermas's interpretation may thus be a possible one, but not the most favourable one, or the one that makes the best sense of many other elements in Derrida's text. Given my strategy of splitting the difference between Habermas and Derrida, I will offer a moderate, hermeneutic reading of Derrida that is less radical than Habermas's, but also less radical than that of some Derrideans. A hermeneutical defender of Derrida has the option of showing that Derrida is not directly asserting philosophical claims, but alluding to them indirectly because he knows how problematic they are. Derrida may not even be offering a 'theory', at least in the strong sense of theory that Habermas has in mind when he constructs his own theory of universal pragmatics as the best explanation of human communication. In the strong sense of 'theory' that we inherit from the time since Galileo, a theory should have concepts, principles, and arguments based on evidence, and it should organize all the relevant phenomena in a single explanatory system. Deconstruction is not itself 'theory' in this sense, but is more the general operation of resisting efforts at such theorization.

If deconstruction is not a theory, the term *différance* should not be taken as the essence or *origin* of language, as Habermas interprets it by seeing Derrida as falling back into the dream of *Ursprungsphilosophie*. Deconstruction is neither foundationalist nor antifoundationalist, Derrida asserts, since it should not be construed as a grounding or even as raising the question of grounds. Derrida therefore denies that *différance* is a master word or arche-synthesis that gathers everything into one word.[17] Habermas's interpretation does not take seriously claims in Derrida's essay '*Différance*' that are intended to dispel the illusion of *Ursprungsphilosophie*. Derrida uses the image of a bottomless chessboard to suggest that his remarks about trace and *différance* are not an attempt to ground writing or language. Neither a word nor a concept, *différance* is said not to be a name at all, let alone a substitute for a lost origin, for which Heidegger's master-name was 'Being':

> What we know, or what we would know if it were simply a question here of something to know, is that there has never been, never will be a unique word, a master-name. . . . There will be no unique name, even if it were the name of Being. And we must think this without *nostalgia* . . .[18]

Habermas reads nostalgia back into Derrida's enterprise by dismissing these qualifications and seeing Derrida as pointing to the origins of language, when Derrida's point is instead to destabilize both the notion of an origin of language in this sense, as well as the enterprise of capturing that origin in a 'theory' or 'philosophy' of language.

Derrida is thus not well served either by friends or by critics who read him as if he were attempting to offer a new theory of language, or as attempting to invert the traditional philosophical distinction between logic and rhetoric. This distinction between logic and rhetoric leads to the distinction between philosophy and literature, which Habermas defends in the face of attacks on that distinction by literary critics such as Jonathan Culler. I think Habermas is right that there are some differences between philosophy and literature, but I think Derrideans could agree that these are differences *in degree*. Habermas maintains more strongly, I believe, that there is a difference *in kind* both between philosophy and literature and between logic and rhetoric. Here again I do not think that Derrida is best defended by interpreting him as collapsing entirely the difference between these terms. Instead, he can be interpreted as suggesting that the question whether there is a difference *in kind* is not answerable, or even fully intelligible. He can be *agnostic* about this question because his aim is to show that the traditional distinction between these terms is not simply a neutral distinction but a value-laden hierarchy. This hierarchy informs the philosophical tradition, where logic effaces rhetoric and philosophy asserts itself as the domain in which the relation between itself and literature is to be determined.

In challenging this distinction in kind, Derrida may give the impression that he rejects philosophy, truth, logic and reason altogether, and turns everything into rhetoric. However, his style is designed to 'show' the paradoxes following from any attempt to 'say' these things. Contrary to Habermas's reading, then, Derrida does not deny truth, reason, or the seriousness of philosophical discourse. He knows he cannot deny that there is truth (or what Habermas would call validity claims), and he says of his enterprise:

Finally, it goes without saying that in no case is it a question of a *discourse against truth* or against science. (This is impossible and absurd, as is every heated accusation on this subject) . . . I repeat, then, leaving all their disseminating powers to the proposition and the form of the verb: *we must have [il faut]* truth.[19]

I interpret his nuanced view as suggesting that truth is a trivial notion, in that there are many statements that are true ('the grass is green,' 'the sky is blue,' etc.). The question is why some statements are taken to be not only true, but more significant than others. Truths only ever appear in a context of interpretation, and interpretations select subsets of truths. Derrida therefore can question cogently whether any interpretation can claim to have captured 'the truth' of a given text or author, where 'the truth' means the single correct way in which to see all the things that are true.[20]

Similarly, Derrida denies being an enemy of reason. He may want to challenge the rationality of many established conceptual distinctions or institutional practices. The task of criticism involves a double gesture of formulating rationally questions about the limits of rational endeavours. Derrida explicitly acknowledges that his own efforts conform to the principle of reason, and he does not recommend that others who would share in these efforts try to contest reason: 'Those who venture along this path, it seems to me, need not set themselves up in opposition to the principle of reason, nor need they give way to "irrationalism".'[21] Since philosophy has always been the 'place' where reason must be respected, Derrida recognizes that his own discourse is subject to the constraints and rigours of philosophical (as opposed to those of 'literary') expression. Early in his career he opposed the interpretation of deconstruction as advocating the death of philosophy.[22] More recently, he has acknowledged that his own discourse is institutionally framed by the philosophical profession. Although he wants to reflect critically on the institution of philosophy, he also admits (with a playful paraphrase on his famous earlier and controversial claim that 'il n'y a pas de hors-texte') that 'il n'y a pas de hors-philosophie.'[23]

Can Derrida be interpreted as doing philosophy at the same time that he is denying that he is doing 'theory'? Could the Habermasian urge that if Derrida is a philosopher, then he must tell us what the theoretical standpoint is from which he generates his deconstructive critique? Habermas formulates a theory of communicative action called universal pragmatics as a standpoint from which to do social theory and to generate social criticism. He thus sees Derrida's grammatology as a rival effort to do the same thing. For Habermas only a theory can provide the conceptual clarity needed to explain and criticize. History, for instance, will not suffice, since from its standpoint developments are only ever contingent. On his view, only theory (for instance, a theory of cognitive or moral or social development, in the manner of Piaget or Kohlberg) gives us the principles to say why a particular stage represents an advance towards a more mature and reasonable position in comparison to previous stages. Theory thus tells us that developments are rational successes if there is a learning process that results from solving problems.[24]

Habermas thinks that Derrida does not see that philosophy can recognize the problem-solving capacity of theory, and that as a result Derrida falls back into an older conception of philosophical theory as world-disclosing. He sees Derrida as holistically trying to get a global picture of how everything hangs together with everything else, and thus sharing in Heidegger's preference for the ontological over the ontic, philosophy over science, the speculative and poetic over the empirical and practical, world-disclosure over problem-solving.

A Derridean could try to turn the tables on Habermas by suggesting that a good deconstruction *is* a form of problem-solving, since it shows that a text has more than one side, and that problems in reading the text are best explained by the deconstructive exposure of its tensions. However, to say this would be to buy into Habermas's model. Another strategy would be to ask why problem-solving would be preferred to world-disclosure anyway. Even though this response suggests a different preference from Habermas's, it still accepts Habermas's distinction.

The best defence would therefore be for the Derridean to urge that Derrida is not taking the side of world-disclosure against problem-solving, but is challenging the distinction and splitting the difference. This separation, as that between history and theory, ignores the phenomenon of theory formation by concentrating exclusively on the phenomenon of theory verification. Habermas's emphasis on problem-solving draws on a narrow, late-empiricist conception of scientific method, whereas Derrida thinks of theory differently. Any observation, whether of physical events, historical actions or textual features, will be theory-laden, but theory itself is conditioned by background assumptions and practices that are never completely articulated.

So again, Derrida's relation to 'theory' is a double one (which is why the quotation marks around the word are necessary). On the one hand, deconstruction resists 'theory' in the strong sense by constantly trying to destabilize it, and show it what lies outside its parameters. On the other hand, Derrida is not opposed to theory in a less strong sense (that therefore need not be put in quotes). Theory in this weaker sense should welcome deconstruction's efforts since theory must always remain open to what it has left unexplored, in the hope that it will confirm itself by explaining these further features, but always recognizing the possibility of being disconfirmed. Contrary to Habermas, Derrida believes, however, that what legitimates theory is not problem-solving. The phenomenon of theory change suggests that while from the inside a theory may seem to be viably solving problems, from the outside it may have stagnated and even degenerated. Derrida thinks that what legitimates theory is instead its ability to open a space, which should include opening up a multiplicity of problematics more than (as on Habermas's model) the elimination of particular problems.

The strategy of splitting the difference leads to the conclusion, then, that Habermas's distinction between world-disclosure and problem-solving is not an adequate 'theory of theory', and does not capture either the complexity of theory formation or Derrida's conception of deconstruction. Derrida's conception of theory as opening possibilities is as rich as world-disclosure (without being holistic in a Hegelian manner) and as determinate as problem-solving (without falling into verificationist difficulties).

Is deconstruction a theory, then? Or is it a method? The answer depends on which theory of theory gives sense to the word. Deconstruction is best construed, I believe, by suggesting that theories must always be on their guard against themselves, since they may close themselves off from possibilities to which they should be open. But Derrida insists that deconstruction is not a method. I believe he means that it is not a set of rules, like those postulated for the so-called 'scientific method', to be applied algorithmically to every text. So again, I split the difference between the opposition, theory or method, by suggesting that deconstruction is an interpretive strategy or operation that can be performed on any particular 'theory'. The deconstructive operation puts the quotation marks around the theory in question by suspending the application of the theory and interrogating it instead.

If deconstruction is a strategy of interpretation instead of either a universal theory or an algorithmic method, can it always be applied successfully? Here I would think that the best answer is to admit that to claim universal applicability is to make a theoretical assertion, which deconstruction is not capable of if it is not a 'theory' in the strong sense. If Habermasians object that Derrida does claim universality for deconstruction in asserting that *différance* can be found in all metaphysical texts, an appropriate response is to point out that deconstruction is not thereby claiming to be able to dissolve all texts, for instance, non-metaphysical ones. Radical deconstructionists might believe that all texts are metaphysical, but I do not know how they could argue that. What I suspect is that texts that did not have some vestiges of metaphysics would not be of much interest either to Derrideans or to Habermasians. Hence, what both groups are doing can be described as 'philosophy', whether they agree on what the term means or not.

Deconstruction: Philosophy or Politics?

More topical right now than the first general criticism raised by Habermas's reading of Derrida is the second one: can deconstruction be used constructively in social and political contexts? Habermas believes that Derrida is like Heidegger in preferring the realm of pure philosophy to that of politics, except that unlike Heidegger's fascistic allegiance to authority, Derrida's stance is anarchistic. As in the contrasts of history versus theory, modernity versus postmodernity and theory versus method, bifurcations between which I have tried to split the difference, Habermas's polemical opposition between philosophy and politics may be more of a problem than a solution. While I agree that the relation of deconstruction to social and political critique needs to be clarified, I think that its critical potential should not be underestimated. To make sure that the issue is presented fairly, let me first state what I take to be Habermas's legitimate worry, and then see whether more recent texts by Derrida than Habermas could have considered help dispel these worries.

Habermas and Foucault both allege that Derrida has not paid enough attention to the social practices that surround textuality. I would express their worry as follows. The practice of deconstruction appears to be subversive. But in reality it offers nothing to replace that which it destroys, and it suggests that nothing could serve as a replacement that could not be deconstructed and subverted in turn. At the same time, the deconstructionist's admission that we cannot think in any other terms than those metaphysically laden ones being deconstructed, that we cannot get beyond metaphysics, seems to leave thought in the same situation, and not to change anything. So deconstruction is not even subversion, since subversion implies a desire to change, and deconstruction demurs from thinking about how things could be different, let alone better. (Foucault thinks that things will be different once genealogy reveals the arbitrariness of our present beliefs and norms, although he refuses to say that 'different' necessarily means 'better'. Paradoxically enough, deconstruction seems to deny us the hope even for significant change or difference.)

To consider this charge I will take as an example of political deconstruction Derrida's remarks on the American Declaration of Independence.[25] Contrary to the way he is often interpreted, Derrida's deconstruction of this text is not a form of ideology criticism, or of finding substantive contradictions in texts or between texts and practices. He does not assert, for instance, that the Declaration of Independence is an indispensable hypocrisy, as the Frankfurt School might have. Instead, he is investigating the status of 'declaration' as a linguistic act. He finds that it falls somewhere between a constative and a performative act. This act of declaration is neither a single act in itself, nor a third kind of act different from these other two, but is instead the undecidable play back and forth between these two kinds of act. This undecidability is not something philosophy should take as a challenge to resolve by deciding. Instead, Derrida is suggesting that we know (even if only implicitly) about the paradox of what declaration is, and that declaration as a linguistic act depends on this undecidability for its effects.

His larger point is that the act of declaring independence is an instance of a more general phenomenon of 'founding' or 'instituting'. Some of his recent essays investigate institutions, especially academic ones, such as the university, or philosophy itself. 'Institution' has a double sense, much like *différance*, which means both different and temporally deferred. Similarly, 'institution' means on the one hand, the existing social edifice or structure, and on the other hand, the coming into being of that structure. The reason he chooses academic institutions is partly because he believes that deconstruction does have a political application in that it can bring out how in any text, discourse, seminar or argument some conception of institution is at work.[26] This claim must be true about acts of deconstruction themselves, hence Derrida's own focus particularly on academic institutions. But Derrida does not believe that foundings are purely rational acts. The structure of *différance* is echoed in that the founding of a university is not an academic event (but, presumably, a social event), and the founding of a state is not a legal event (at least, not in the same sense that the laws are legal once the state is founded). Derrida's point comes to more, therefore, than saying that acts of declaration or founding or originating are at once both constative and performative. He believes that more is involved than 'speech acts' in the narrow, technical sense. Deconstruction is the enterprise of revealing the lack of clear boundaries between terms like constative and performative, as well as the indeterminacy that lies at the beginnings of efforts to mark out the determinate boundaries of different kinds of texts and institutional discourses.

More problematically, however, he also states that the origin of the principle of reason is not in itself rational. I assume that he is not attacking the principle of reason (given his statement that I cited earlier), but what 'origin' and 'rational' mean is not clear. In so far as he is engaged in a general critique of enlightenment thinkers like Kant, he is probably urging that the founding cannot be 'rational' in the sense of a purely cognitive and self-transparent act. Derrida is presumably agreeing with Kantians (like Habermas) that in any discursive act what is implied is an ideal conception of the conditions under which that discursive act should take place successfully. Against Kantians, however, Derrida thinks that there is more going on than constating what is true. He is not denying the constative element, but he thinks that other elements, such as the performative features, ought not to be ignored. In so far as the discourse presupposes an institutional framework, and institutions have as much to do with power as with knowledge, Kantians are wrong to exclude power and authority in favour of ideal models of coercion-free truth.

Here is, I believe, the crux of the conflict between Habermas and Derrida. Habermas is not objecting to deconstruction because it is subversive. Habermas thinks that philosophy will always be subversive. In addition to philosophy's role of explaining the theoretical basis of science, morality and law, Habermas believes that it 'maintains just as intimate a relationship with the totality of the lifeworld and with sound common sense, even if in a subversive way it relentlessly shakes up the certainties of everyday practice.'[27] Philosophical reflection must be able to show the irrationality of some practices, but it must also be able to see that others are rational. Habermas thinks that his own model of communicative interaction as attempting to reach understanding and consensus supplies a model for seeing the rationality as well as the irrationality of social practices, but he fails to find any basis for making this same discrimination from deconstructivist premises.

With this model Habermas thinks he can see the rationality of the separation of the domains of science, morality and art from one another. He thinks that Kant was correct to argue for the differentiation of these spheres from one another, and he sees the deconstructivist attack on the separation of philosophy and literature as the beginning of an attack on this Kantian separation of questions of truth, value and taste. This rationalized differentiation is worthy of being preserved, according to Habermas. Derrida's analysis of foundings finds indeterminacy at the beginnings of such differentiation, and thus suggests that whatever the benefits of such differentiation, one cannot say that such differentiation is rational and therefore a necessary learning process, but only that it is contingent.

Habermas resists the suggestion of indeterminacy and contingency. He believes, for instance, that the deconstructionist claim that the same text can be open to different readings forgets that identical ascriptions of meaning must be possible for readers to talk to one another about the same text. Some readings must be right and others wrong, and 'wrong interpretations must in principle be criticizable in terms of consensus to be aimed for ideally.'[28] Consensus in the present is not enough, because our understanding of our reasons is never transparent, given the tacit background that conditions our utterances. Only the idealizations implied in communication, including what Habermas has called the ideal of arriving at consensus in a coercion-free speech situation, will enable us to say that what looks *historically* like exhaustion is in reality (that is, according to the correct *theory*) '*deficient* solutions to problems and *invalid* answers'.[29]

Several lines of rebuttal are open to Derrida here. First, on the point about identical ascriptions of meaning, I think that Derrida could ask Habermas for an argument for this claim that disagreement is possible only when the words are understood in the same way by the parties to the dispute. This claim seems false about some disputes in which the opponents disagree about how to interpret a certain phenomenon because they contest the meaning of the central terms involved. There may be essentially contested concepts on which consensus should not be expected but about which there could be genuine debate. For instance, as Ronald Dworkin has argued in *Law's Empire*,[30] to have genuine disagreements about how to interpret the law, differing lawyers do not need to use the same criteria for employing the term 'law'. Their disagreements are often theoretical, and disagreement about what 'law' means is precisely what leads to their differing interpretations, just as disagreement about whether to count a photograph as art may depend on different construals of what art is (and whether 'art' can include the genre of photography). Similarly, in *Power: A Radical View*, Steven Lukes argues that social theorists who disagree about whether a particular social power configuration has been analysed properly disagree precisely because they understand 'power' differently.[31]

Second, even if meanings did have to be ascribed identically for genuine disagreement to be possible, Derrida could still ask Habermas whether the postulation of an ideal consensus follows. Why does Habermas draw such a strong conclusion about ideal consensus? My guess is that, in short, he is committed to the rationalistic transparency aimed at by 'traditional theory', while Derrida is not. Third, the poststructuralists could ask whether Habermas's search for a guarantee that the paradigm of enlightenment is not exhausted is not itself a sign of exhaustion. Postmoderns may be simply those who can live without such a guarantee.

Finally, on the charge that Derrida is still caught in the philosophical paradigm of subjectivity that deconstruction wants to overcome, Derrida could ask in turn whether Habermas has really freed himself from the philosophy of the subject. Derrida might think that Habermas is still too theoretical in the Kantian sense, and that Habermas (especially in chapter 7 of *PDM*) privileges the constative, truth-telling function of language in his idealized speech situation.[32] Stressing idealization will lead, Derrida might argue, to overlooking the institutional dimensions of texts, and to ignoring the contingency lurking behind the rationality that the texts might project but never achieve. Furthermore, Habermas may have overreacted to Derrida in thinking that Derrida is dismissing subjects altogether from language, or turning language as a self-sufficient, self-stabilized system into an 'event without any subject'.[33] Models of communicative interaction may be intersubjective instead of subjective, but the appeal to many subjects instead of an isolated subject is still an appeal to subjects. To argue that an account of language is not necessarily the same as an account of communicative speech actions, Derrida need not assert that there could be language even if there were no speakers or writers.

On this point, I believe that Habermas misinterprets Derrida's analysis of writing in the following passage:

> Writing guarantees that a text can always repeatedly be read in arbitrarily changing contexts. What fascinates Derrida is this thought of an *absolute readability*: Even in the absence of every possible audience, after the death of all beings with an intelligent nature, the writing holds open in heroic abstraction the possibility of a repeatable readability that transcends everything in this world. Because writing mortifies the living connections proper to the spoken word, it promises salvation for its semantic content even beyond the day on which all who can speak and listen have fallen prey to the holocaust.[34]

The page that Habermas cites need not be read as making this radical a claim. A more sympathetic reading would see it as suggesting, in the spirit of Wittgenstein's attack on private language, that writing must be legible by others than those to whom it is addressed.[35] Derrida's point would then be that we can say of any particular reader that the text could function in the absence of that reader. But this means only that some other readers could still read the text, not the nonsensical claim that the text could be read in the absence of all possible readers.

The difference can be split here by acknowledging that they are both saying something right. Habermas is insisting on context to say that meaning is not arbitrary. Meaning is tied to context, and contexts cannot be merely willed. The right theory will show us that the contexts in which we find ourselves have developed rationally as a result of learning processes, such that some parts are rational advances. In contrast, Derrida is insisting that texts can be taken up and interpreted differently in different contexts, so that no context is necessary or definitive. But this is not to say that the text could make sense in the complete absence of context (or in some 'absolute context' that includes all possible contexts, since this absolute would be equally contextless). Derrida need not appeal either to a lost original or Ur-context to which all written texts point backwards in time, or to a contextless *telos* towards which any text points ideally. What *would* be contextless is the counterfactual, coercion-free, ideal speech-situation.

Furthermore, Derrida need not deny the existence of speaking, writing and communicating subjects. Thus he does not deny that the intentions of subjects or agents play a role in contexts. He simply does not think that subjects are clear enough about what their intentions are, or that 'intention' is a sufficiently clear notion to make intention the decisive criterion for interpreting the range of possible meanings in a context or across contexts.

If I am right to read Derrida along these lines, deconstruction can be defended against the allegation that in principle deconstruction cannot be used effectively as destabilizing critique. There would be no reason to assume that such destabilization (the term I prefer to Habermas's term 'subversion') is never justified or that it only ever leaves us with the status quo. We do not have to know what alternatives we would prefer to want to destabilize some of our present practices. If we deplore them, we can try through such indirect means (since we do not know what direct means to try) to shake up ways of thinking sufficiently so that we can start to see what would be preferable instead. We can try to see our practices in a different light so that we can become aware of other possibilities. That is how Nietzsche and Heidegger understood critical history, and Foucault's genealogy is also an example of one way of doing critical history. Another way is deconstruction, when informed by the critical attitude that Horkheimer contrasts to 'traditional theory'. The deconstruction of texts could thus become one more strategy to be used by critical philosophers. Specifying the universal categories of all thought need no longer be the primary task for critical philosophers who are trying to understand, both historically and theoretically, who we have become, where we are now, and what we can be.

NOTES

1 Splitting the difference is an interpretive operation used by Richard Rorty in 'Habermas and Lyotard on Postmodernity', in *Habermas and Modernity*, ed. Richard J. Bernstein (Cambridge, 1985).
2 Jürgen Habermas, *The Philosophical Discourse of Modernity: Twelve Lectures*, trans. Frederick G. Lawrence (Cambridge and Cambridge, Mass., 1987), p. 86. Hereafter also cited as *PDM*.
3 *PDM*, p. 296. Habermas hopes that the symptoms of exhaustion will dissolve with his own shift from the philosophy of consciousness to his paradigm of mutual understanding.
4 Jacques Derrida, 'Plato's Pharmacy', in *Dissemination*, trans. Barbara Johnson (Chicago, 1981), p. 111.
5 *PDM*, p. 182. Habermas suggests further that

> Derrida's grammatologically circumscribed concept of an archewriting whose traces call forth all the more interpretations the more unfamiliar they become, renews the mystical concept of tradition as an ever *delayed* event of revelation. Religious authority only maintains its force as long as it conceals its true face and thereby incites the frenzy of deciphering interpreters. Earnestly pursued deconstruction is the paradoxical labor of continuing a tradition in which the saving energy is only renewed by expenditure: The labor of deconstruction lets the refuse heap of interpretations, which it wants to clear away in order to get at the buried foundations, mount ever higher. (p. 183)

Habermas is here varying a famous image from Benjamin to make fun of deconstructionist literary critics.

6 These are not the only methods currently employed in contemporary philosophy, or even in continental philosophy alone. A third competitor is genealogy, a method normally attributed to Nietzsche and Foucault, but which goes back to British moralists like Hume. I have discussed the genealogical method in several papers, including 'Nietzsche, Hume, and the Genealogical Method', in *Nietzsche, Genealogy, Morality*, ed. Richard Schacht (Berkeley, 1994), and 'Power, Repression, Progress: Foucault, Lukes, and the Frankfurt School', in *Foucault: A Critical Reader*, ed. D. C. Hoy (Oxford, 1986).

7 At a conference on 'The States of "Theory"' at the University of California, Irvine (24–5 April 1987), Derrida distanced himself from the use of the prefix 'post', as in, for instance, 'poststructuralism' (but also, by implication, in 'postmodernism'). He thinks deconstruction should not be identified with any such -ism because terms like 'after', 'new', and 'post' imply a global rewriting of history (which is what we should have learned to avoid from Derrida's earlier readings of Nietzsche and Husserl).

8 For a more detailed discussion of whether Foucault is a modern or a postmodern, as well as of the differences between Foucault's and Lyotard's postmodernism, see my essay, 'Foucault: Modern or Postmodern?' in Jonathan Arac (ed.), *After Foucault: Humanistic Knowledge, Postmodern Challenges* (New Brunswick, 1988).

9 In *Ethics and the Limits of Philosophy* (Cambridge, 1985), Bernard Williams challenges theorists like Rawls for such a strong notion of transparency:

> One significant point is that while transparency is a natural associate of liberalism, it falls short of implying rationalism. It is one aspiration, that social and ethical relations should not essentially rest on ignorance and misunderstanding of what they are, and quite another that all the beliefs and principles involved in them should be explicitly stated. That these are two different things is obvious with personal relations, where to hope that they do not rest on deceit and error is merely decent, but to think that their basis can be made totally explicit is idiocy. (p. 102)

10 While I derived these particular categories in thinking about Foucault, I found them confirmed by Derrida's remarks at the meeting of the American Philosophical Association in March 1987. In a discussion of Heidegger, who believes great thinkers each have one central thought (which eludes them and which remains unthought, until it is revealed by a later great thinker like Heidegger himself), Derrida rejected three central premises of Heidegger's way of reading the history of thought: (1) the idea of the great thinker; (2) the idea that there is only one thought for any such thinker; and (3) the idea that there is only the one unthought that runs through the earlier great thinker but that can necessarily not be thought except by the later great thinker.

11 For instance, Derrida suggests that his own interpretation of Nietzsche's undecidability is itself undecidable. See Jacques Derrida, *Spurs: Nietzsche's Styles*, trans. Barbara Harlow (Chicago, 1979), pp. 135–9.

12 *PDM*, pp. 179, 296.

13 *PDM*. p. 182.

14 Jacques Derrida, *Margins of Philosophy*, trans. Alan Bass (Chicago, 1982), p. 22.

15 *PDM*, p. 166.

16 *PDM*, p. 205.

17 Derrida made these remarks in response to Rodolphe Gasché and Stanley Cavell at the March 1987 meeting of the Pacific Division of the American Philosophical Association. On 'arche-synthesis', see Rodolphe Gasché, *The Tain of the Mirror: Derrida and the Philosophy of Reflection* (Cambridge, 1986), p. 273.

18 Jacques Derrida, '*Différance*', in Derrida, *Margins of Philosophy*, p. 27.

19 Jacques Derrida, *Positions*, trans. Alan Bass (Chicago, 1982), p. 105

20 See Derrida in *Spurs*: 'there is no such thing either as the truth of Nietzsche, or of Nietzsche's text. . . . Indeed there is no such thing as a truth in itself. But only a surfeit of it. Even if it should be for me, about me, truth is plural' (p. 103).

21 Jacques Derrida, 'The Principle of Reason: The University in the Eyes of its Pupils', *Diacritics* 13 (Fall 1983), p. 17.

22 Derrida, *Positions*, p. 6.

23 Jacques Derrida, 'Les antinomies de la discipline philosophique: lettre préface', in *La Grève des Philosophes* (Paris, 1986), p. 12.

24 See Jürgen Habermas, 'Geschichte und Evolution', in Habermas, *Zur Rekonstruktion des Historischen Materialismus* (Frankfurt, 1976). I discuss Habermas's claims at greater length in 'Two Conflicting Conceptions of How to Naturalize Philosophy: Foucault versus Habermas', in *Metaphysik nach Kant?*, ed. Dieter Henrich and Rolf-Peter Horstmann (Stuttgart, 1988).

25 Jacques Derrida, *Otobiographies* (Paris, 1984), pp. 13–32. For a more extensive discussion of his analysis of the Declaration of Independence see my article, 'Dworkin's Constructive Optimism v. Deconstructive Legal Nihilism', *Law and Philosophy* 6 (1987), pp. 321–56, esp. pp. 333–7.

26 See Jacques Derrida, 'The Conflict of Faculties: A Mochlos', trans. Cynthia Chase, Jonathan Culler and Irving Wohlfarth, in Deborah Esch and Thomas Keenan (eds), *Institutions of Philosophy* (Cambridge, Mass., 1992).

27 *PDM*, p. 208.

28 *PDM*, p. 198.

29 *PDM*, p. 206.

30 Ronald Dworkin, *Law's Empire* (London, 1986), pp. 31–46.

31 Steven Lukes, *Power: A Radical View* (London, 1974).

32 Certainly Habermas deals at length with the performative dimensions in chapter 3 of vol. 1 of his *Theory of Communicative Action*, trans. Thomas McCarthy (Cambridge, 1984). In the chapter on Derrida in *The Philosophical Discourse of Modernity*, however, the focus is primarily on truth, which Derrida could interpret as an implicit privileging of the constative, cognitive dimension, as well as of the 'theoretical' in general.

33 *PDM*, p. 178. See Derrida, *Positions*, p. 88: 'I have never said that *there is not* a "subject of writing". . . . It is solely necessary to reconsider the problem of the effect of subjectivity such as it is produced by the structure of the text.'

34 *PDM*, p. 166.

35 Derrida, *Margins of Philosophy*, p. 315.

5

HABERMAS AND FOUCAULT

James Schmidt

In *The Philosophical Discourse of Modernity*, Jürgen Habermas takes stock of a critique of reason that 'has not substantially changed from Hegel and Marx down to Nietzsche and Heidegger, from Bataille and Lacan to Foucault and Derrida'.[1] This critique charges that the Enlightenment ideal of freeing humanity from all forms of repression, exploitation, degradation and alienation paradoxically results in a new, and insidious, form of control that produces a 'thoroughly concealed domination' under the 'false absolute' of a subject-centred reason (*PDM*, p. 59). Attempts at enlightenment lead only to the triumph of new forms of mythology, efforts at humanistic reform lead only to ever more crafty forms of domination, and each of the alleged triumphs of reason has led only to new and more pervasive forms of enslavement.

Against these critics Habermas marshals one basic counter-argument: they have fallen prey to the same tendency they diagnose in others. Their efforts to conceive of reason as something other than the self-assertion of an isolated subject typically culminate in more complex and concealed forms of the very same rationality that is under attack. Habermas finds this same pattern repeated in the career of Michel Foucault. Like others who sought to break free from the snares of subject-centred reason, he wound up trapped within it (*PDM*, p. 294).

In the face of this unhappy history of botched escapes from the stranglehold of subject-centred reason, Habermas suggests that he will follow 'a more trivial path'. He proposes to take up 'the ordinary perspective of a participant who is recalling the course of the argument in its rough features' and notes some of the difficulties encountered by those engaged in the critique of modernity (*PDM*, p. 59). This modest strategy pays off handsomely. Habermas's exploration of the aporias that plague efforts to transcend the standpoint of subject-centred reason uncovers traces of a 'philosophical counter-discourse which, from the start, accompanied the philosophical discourse of modernity . . .' This counterdiscourse, he argues, 'already drew up a counterreckoning for subjectivity as the principle of modernity'. All that is necessary now is 'to retrace the path of the philosophical discourse of modernity back to its starting point – in order to examine once again the directions once suggested at the chief crossroads' (p. 295). At these crossroads we can find the escape route out of subject-centred reason. Conveniently enough for Habermas, this path leads straight to his own notion of communicative rationality.

The strategy Habermas adopts in *The Philosophical Discourse of Modernity* is a familiar one. In both *The Theory of Communicative Action* and *Knowledge and Human Interests* Habermas's own position emerged only in the course of a consideration of the positions others had taken. This approach is not without its dangers. The attempt to show how one's own insights emerge from the efforts of earlier thinkers always runs the risk of reducing one's predecessors to a series of failed attempts at answering the questions that we somehow are able to resolve with ease. 'Dialogue' with others can easily degenerate into a ventriloquist's act where the dummy never gets the last word.

Such is the complaint that has been raised against Habermas by John Rajchman, one of Foucault's ablest defenders:

> The law of Habermas' narrative is that while all the actual roads in modern philosophy lead nowhere, all the possible ones lead to him . . . The 'philosophical discourse of modernity' thus turns out to be a strange sort of discourse. Everyone who takes it up . . . ends in error, self-contradiction, and 'exhaustion'; and yet everyone *might* have found the correct Habermasian solution.[2]

Rajchman suggests that one of the more questionable steps in Habermas's construction of this narrative is the assumption that Foucault's work can be read as a response to the problem that Habermas regards as constitutive of the 'philosophical discourse of modernity': the question of how modern society can provide a foundation for itself without appealing to earlier traditions. Rajchman argues that if Habermas is to provide a convincing critique of Foucault for having failed to provide an adequate response to this problem, he must first make a compelling case that this, indeed, was what Foucault was trying to do. Otherwise he will not have shown us the aporias in which Foucault and others are trapped, he will have simply demonstrated that they fail to answer a question that *he* regards as essential. In Rajchman's words, Habermas 'must first show that they were responding to a question they didn't realize they were asking, before showing that they didn't answer it'.[3]

A Genealogy of the Genealogist

The main outline of Habermas's discussion of Foucault in *The Philosophical Discourse of Modernity* is simple enough. Habermas sees Foucault's work as falling into two broad phases: his early studies mount an 'unmasking critique of the human sciences', while his later writings articulate a 'theory of power'. Separating these two phases, and providing the motivation for the transition from one to the other, are a series of difficulties regarding the status of Foucault's initial critique of the human sciences. Habermas suggests that Foucault responded to these difficulties by turning to a Nietzschean 'theory of power' but that this theory ultimately proves to be plagued by its own aporias. Habermas's exploration of the difficulties facing Foucault's 'theory of power' concludes that they can be attributed to a failure to transcend the standpoint of the philosophy of the subject (*PDM*, pp. 274–5).

Habermas argues that in the first phase of Foucault's career – which comes to an end with *The Order of Things* – he was engaged in 'a radical critique of reason in the form of a historiography of the human sciences' (*PDM*, p. 247). This critique links the development of the human sciences to practices of 'supervisory isolation' found in asylums, clinics and prisons. In these settings the gaze of the rational subject objectifies and analyses, reducing other subjects to mute objects that are classified and controlled (*PDM*, pp. 242–5). Thus a work like *Madness and Civilization* must not be read as simply an account of changes in the way the insane were treated. 'In Foucault's hands,' Habermas observes, 'the history of science is enlarged into a history of reason because it studies the constituting of madness as a reflex image of the constituting of reason' (pp. 239–40).

While Foucault's early works pursue a common aim, Habermas suggests that *Madness and Civilization* differs significantly in its methodology from the works that follow. *Madness and Civilization* practised what Habermas characterizes as a 'depth hermeneutics', which sought to reach back 'to the initial branching off of madness from reason in order to decipher what is unspoken in what is said'.[4] The preface to *The Birth of the Clinic*, however, rejects such an approach and proposes to replace a 'commentary' that attempts to 'uncover the deeper meaning of speech' with a 'structural analysis of discourses'.[5]

This shift, Habermas argues, has serious consequences. The 'hermeneutics of unveiling' employed in *Madness and Civilization* 'always still connects a promise with its critique' – the hope that by returning to the point where reason excluded madness it might be possible to give voice once again to the 'excluded and the outlawed'. The 'chastened archaeology' of *The Birth of the Clinic* harbours no such hope (*PDM*, pp. 240–1). But if archaeology can no longer claim to unearth what the human sciences have silenced, in what sense can it retain a critical force?

Habermas suggests that it was in search of a solution to this problem that Foucault turned to a Nietzsche-inspired concept of power. Foucault's works until *The Order of Things* had focused on the 'specific will to knowledge' and the particular truths that are 'constitutive for the modern form of knowledge in general and for the human sciences in particular' (*PDM*, p. 261). But in the works that follow *The Order of Things* this 'will to knowing self-mastery' is generalized into 'a will to power *per se*'. Foucault now maintains that '*all* discourses (by no means only the modern ones) can be shown to have the character of hidden power and derive from practices of power.' It is this generalization that marks the transition from Foucault's early structuralist 'archaeology of knowledge' to his subsequent Nietzschean 'genealogy'. An archaeology that had maintained the autonomy of systems of discourse is now subordinated to an account that traces the emergence of knowledge from the practices of power (*PDM*, p. 268). The 'ensemble of rules according to which true and false are separated' is now viewed as the creature of a 'will to knowledge' that is now generalized to 'all times and all societies' (*PDM*, pp. 269–70).

This concealed derivation of the concept of power from the will to knowledge accounts for what Habermas characterizes as the 'irritating double role' played by power (*PDM*, pp. 273–4, 270). It attempts to be both empirical analysis of power technologies (and thus part of a functionalist social science) and an element of a theory of constitution (and thus a transcendental account of how discourse about man is possible at all). Thus, in Habermas's accounting, Foucault's turn to his 'theory of power' does not free him from the aporias he had analysed at the close of *The Order of Things*. His concept of power, like the concept of 'man' on which the human sciences rest, functions as an 'empirical-transcendental double'. Foucault's theory of power does not move beyond the confines of the theory of the subject since it allows for only two stances towards a world of manipulable objects: cognitive relations regulated by the truth of judgements or practical relationships regulated by the success of actions. Instead of transcending the standpoint of the philosophy of the subject, Foucault simply reconfigures relationships within it when he 'abruptly reverses power's truth-dependency into the power-dependency of truth' (*PDM*, p. 274).

Such, in its broad outlines, is Habermas's critique of Foucault. In what follows, I will argue that this critique is vulnerable at three points. First, it misunderstands the approach Foucault adopts in *Madness and Civilization* and as a result misrepresents the relationship between *Madness and Civilization* and *The Birth of the Clinic*. Second, Habermas's suggestion that Foucault 'turns' to Nietzsche in response to unresolved difficulties facing his archaeology underestimates the centrality of Nietzsche's thought for all phases of Foucault's career. Finally, and most importantly, it is by no means clear that Foucault's account of the relationship between knowledge and power is beset with the aporias Habermas purports to find.

From 'Depth Hermeneutics' to 'Structural Analysis'

In Habermas's reconstruction of Foucault's development, particular stress is placed on the alleged replacement of the 'depth hermeneutics' of *Madness and Civilization* with the 'structural analysis' of *The Birth of the Clinic*. Since Habermas maintains that Foucault's forsaking of 'depth hermeneutics' robs his archaeology of the human sciences of its critical force and thus forces him down the path to Nietzschean genealogy, it is worth being a bit clearer as to what is done in *Madness and Civilization* and what is repudiated in *The Birth of the Clinic*.

At the start of *The Birth of the Clinic*, Foucault criticizes approaches that question a text 'as to what it says and intended to say' and attempt 'to uncover the deeper meaning of speech', by giving voice to the 'unspoken element' that 'slumbers within speech'. In place of 'commentaries' such as this he calls for a 'structural analysis of discourses' that will seek 'nothing in excess of what has been said' and will content itself with an analysis of 'only the fact of its historical appearance'.[6] Habermas reads this as a repudiation of the approach taken by *Madness and Civilization*:

> He no longer seeks madness itself behind discourse about madness, or the mute contact of body with eyes, which seemed to precede any discourse, behind the archeology of the medical gaze. . . . A hermeneutics of unveiling always still connects a promise with its critique; a chastened archeology should be rid of that . . . (*PDM*, p. 241)

But did *Madness and Civilization* embrace the sort of approach that Foucault criticized in *The Birth of the Clinic*?

Habermas argues that *Madness and Civilization* offers 'an analysis of discourse that, in the manner of depth hermeneutics, probes its way back to the original point of the initial branching off of madness from reason in order to decipher what is unspoken in what is said.'[7] Foucault, however, was a good deal less certain as to whether we can come into contact with 'madness itself' by examining what has been said *about* madness. Arguing that 'the constitution of madness as mental illness' at the close of the eighteenth century suspends any possible dialogue between madness and reason, Foucault wrote: 'The language of psychiatry, which is a monologue of reason *about* madness, has been established only on the basis of such a silence. I have not tried to write the history of that language, but rather the archaeology of that silence.'[8] *Madness and Civilization* differs markedly in focus from Foucault's subsequent efforts at an 'archaeology of the human sciences'. As an attempt to write an 'archaeology of a silence', it investigates a realm which 'is neither the history of knowledge, nor history itself', since the division between madness and reason that it scrutinizes is alleged to be more primitive than any of the established discourses *about* madness.

For this reason it is difficult to see how Foucault's 'archaeology of a silence' can be likened to the exercises in 'commentary' that he criticizes at the start of *The Birth of the Clinic*. In *Madness and Civilization* the task is not to work back from what has been said about madness in order to give voice to something that 'slumbers within speech'. This misses the real difficulties Foucault faces in *Madness and Civilization*: what he seeks cannot be found *within* the discourse about madness. Once madness has been drawn into the discourse of reason 'all those stammered, imperfect words without fixed syntax in which the exchange between madness and reason was made' are thrust into oblivion.[9] Commentaries on 'works' are incapable of giving voice to madness because 'madness is precisely the absence of work [*l'absence d'oeuvre*].[10] How, then, is it possible to characterize Foucault's work as a 'depth hermeneutics' when he insists that madness is never present in any of the texts available for us to interpret?[11]

The project sketched in *Madness and Civilization* may well be fraught with difficulties, but the criticism of 'commentary' at the start of *The Birth of the Clinic* does not speak to them. Foucault's comments would seem to be aimed either at the tendency in writing histories of the human sciences to see in the works of earlier periods 'anticipations' of subsequent discoveries, or perhaps even at his critic Jacques Derrida, whose work Foucault would criticize along these same lines in a postscript added to the second edition of *Madness and Civilization*.[12] While Foucault himself expressed misgivings in subsequent writings about the emphasis placed by *Madness and Civilization* on the experience of 'madness in itself', he never repudiated the work as emphatically as Habermas would have us believe.[13] Hence, while Habermas may see in the transition from *Madness and Civilization* to *The Birth of the Clinic* a loss of the 'promise' associated with a 'depth hermeneutics' – a loss which necessitates a recasting of Foucault's approach – there is no reason to believe that Foucault himself saw matters this way.

From 'Archaeology' to 'Genealogy'

For Habermas the shift from 'depth hermeneutics' to 'structural analysis' is only a prelude to a more fundamental change: the supplanting of an 'archaeology' that regards forms of discourse as autonomous entities that must be understood in terms of their own particular rules of constitution by a 'genealogy' that analyses the emergence of forms of discourse in terms of a Nietzschean account of power. Habermas finds the motive for the turn to genealogy in the difficulties Foucault faces after the alleged abandonment of the 'depth hermeneutic' approach of *Madness and Civilization* for the 'structural analysis' of *The Birth of the Clinic*. Once Foucault has ruled out the 'romantic motif' of giving voice to that which reason has silenced, he must now face 'the methodological problem of how a history of the constellations of reason and madness can be written at all, if the labor of the historian must in turn move about within the horizon of reason' (*PDM*, p. 247).

In *L'Ordre du discours*, Foucault's 1970 inaugural lecture at the Collège de France, Habermas finds evidence of how Foucault thought this problem might be overcome. The separating of madness from reason is now viewed as but one of three 'mechanisms of exclusion' that give rise to rational speech. The opposition between truth and falsehood, no less than the opposition between folly and reason and the distinction between what can be said and what is prohibited, is now understood as the consequence of a process of exclusion. Indeed, Foucault argues that the prohibition of the discussion of certain matters, most typically those having to do with sexuality or politics, and the rejection of the speech of the insane tend to be assimilated into the division between truth and falsehood.[14] Foucault thus regards truth, in Habermas's words, as 'an insidious mechanism of exclusion, because it only functions on condition that the *will to truth* prevalent within it remains hidden' (*PDM*, p. 248).

Habermas argues that Foucault sought to retain a critical dimension for his project by setting himself the task of unveiling the functioning of this 'will to truth'. An 'archaeology of knowledge' (which proceeds with what Foucault terms a 'studious lack of deference') reveals the truth-constitutive rules at work in a discourse. 'Genealogy' (which takes the attitude of what Foucault calls a 'happy positivism') 'studies how discourses are formed and why they emerge and disappear again' by tracing conditions of validity to their institutional roots.[15] If archaeology can maintain this studious indifference and if genealogy can proceed in the manner of an 'innocent positivism', then, Habermas concludes, 'the methodological paradox of a science that writes the history of the human sciences with the goal of a radical critique of reason would be solved' (PDM, p. 248). Archaeology would investigate the rules of exclusion by which truth is created, while genealogy would trace how different systems of discourse replace one another. Foucault's critique of the human sciences is now said to rest on a concept of power 'that lends both the archeological prospecting and the genealogical disclosures their dimensions of being a critique of modernity' (PDM, p. 249).

Habermas attributes Foucault's new 'erudite-positivistic historiography' [gelehrtsam-positivistischen Geschichtsschreibung] to a 'reception' of Nietzsche that is first manifested in the introduction to The Archaeology of Knowledge (1969) and the essay 'Nietzsche, Genealogy, History' (1971) (PDM, pp. 248–9). But in what sense can Habermas speak of a 'reception' of Nietzsche at this particular point in Foucault's development? Nietzsche, after all, had long been a central influence on Foucault.[16] The notion of the 'overman' played an important role in Foucault's discussion of Kant in his 'Secondary Thesis', a translation and commentary on Kant's Anthropology.[17] Madness and Civilization opened by describing the work as part of the 'great Nietzschean inquiry' of discovering the divisions upon which our culture has been created.[18] The Order of Things closed by invoking Nietzsche as the prophet of the 'end of man'.[19] To claim, as Habermas does, that Foucault turned to Nietzsche for inspiration as a consequence of his 'disappointment with the failure of the 1968 revolt' is to overlook the ways in which Foucault's entire career was influenced by Nietzsche's work.[20]

The changes in terminology and emphasis in the works that follow The Archaeology of Knowledge cannot, therefore, be attributed to a 'reception' of Nietzsche. It might be argued that with the appropriation of the term 'genealogy', Foucault began to make use of a different aspect of Nietzsche's legacy. In the works up to and including The Archaeology of Knowledge Nietzsche had been invoked as a check on the anthropologizing tendencies of modern philosophy.[21] In the period after The Archaeology of Knowledge the notion of 'genealogy' was pressed into service to oppose dialectical interpretations of history that postulate a meaningful telos to history.[22] But this, too, underestimates the continuity of Foucault's work. While the term 'genealogy' first begins appearing in Foucault's work sometime between 1969 and 1970, an aversion to teleological interpretations of history was present in his work from the start. The preface to *Madness and Civilization* argued that Nietzsche's great achievement was to have confronted 'the dialectic of history' with the 'immobile structures of tragedy'.[23]

It is thus difficult to argue that the arrival of the term 'genealogy' signals a radical recasting of Foucault's approach prompted by a recognition of aporias within his archaeology of the human sciences.[24] To be sure, Foucault did express dissatisfaction with some aspects of *The Order of Things*. In a 1975 interview he noted that the book tended to overlook 'the effects of power peculiar to the play of statements' because it 'confused this too much with systematicity, theoretical form, or something like a paradigm'.[25] This difficulty, however, is easily corrected, since, as Foucault also noted, 'When I think back now, I ask myself what else it was that I was talking about in *Madness and Civilization* and *Birth of the Clinic*, but power?'[26] The 'turn' to Nietzsche and to genealogy is thus less a matter of Foucault's recasting his approach in the face of insurmountable aporias than of his realizing that there were important dimensions of his earlier analyses that had been neglected in *The Order of Things*.

The Ambiguity of the Concept of 'Power'

Thus far this chapter has focused on Habermas's account of Foucault's development. The major concern of *The Philosophical Discourse of Modernity*, however, is with the aporias that Habermas argues plague Foucault's 'theory of power'.[27] Habermas advances his critique of Foucault's theory of power in three stages. First, he argues that Foucault's concept of power is inherently ambiguous in that it is used to advance both empirical and transcendental claims. Second, he examines the 'metatheoretical' implications of Foucault's theory of power for the human sciences, and argues that its stance is necessarily 'presentist', 'relativist', and arbitrarily partisan. Finally, he voices a few 'empirical' reservations about the adequacy of Foucault's discussion of law and sexuality. Since these 'empirical' criticisms are at best fleeting and rather general in character, the discussion here will focus on Habermas's first and second lines of attack.

In Habermas's view the substitution of genealogy for archaeology does not resolve what some commentators have seen as one of the more troubling aspects of *The Order of Things*: the tendency of Foucault's archaeology of the human sciences to become, like the human sciences it criticizes, an 'empirical-transcendental double'. *The Order of Things* traces the process by which the human sciences come to constitute the notion of 'man' and argues that because the notion of man serves as both empirical object and transcendental ground, the human sciences are ultimately incapable of establishing themselves as sciences. In making such a critique, Foucault provided an account that is simultaneously historical and transcendental. He maintained not merely that there are certain regularities observable in the human sciences, but also claimed that these regularities function as constitutive rules governing the production of statements in the human sciences. In speaking of a 'historical apriori', his archaeology thus commits that same mingling of the empirical and transcendental for which the human sciences were criticized.[28]

Habermas extends this criticism to Foucault's more recent 'genealogical historiography'. It too attempts to be both 'functionalist social science' and 'historical research into constitutive conditions [*historische Konstitutionsforschung*]' (*PDM*, p. 274). Foucault's genealogy explicitly employs the concept of power 'descriptively' in an '*empirical analysis* of power technologies', but at the same time 'the category of power preserves from its concealed genesis [*verheimlichten Enstehungsgeschichte*] the meaning of a basic concept within a *theory of constitution*' (*PDM*, p. 270). Hence Habermas argues that Foucault's genealogy surreptitiously carries on the programme of *The Order of Things* by providing, in the guise of an empirical historical account of the development of the human sciences, an account of the constitution of the human sciences (*PDM*, p. 273).

It is not clear, however, what Habermas means by his characterization of Foucault's concept of power as a 'concealed' theory of constitution. In maintaining that Foucault's account of the relationship between the human sciences and techniques of 'disciplinary power' advances 'concealed' transcendental claims Habermas would seem to be underlining the difference between the argument that the human sciences have, 'historically' or 'causally', arisen in conjunction with the development of technologies of observation and control, and the argument that the human sciences 'transcendentally constitute' the objects of their knowledge in such a way that 'the formation of power and the formation of knowledge compose an indissoluble unity' (*PDM*, p. 272). While the first claim does not argue that the human sciences must necessarily take the form of technologies of observation and control, the second maintains that the human sciences necessarily constitute their object domain as a field of objects to be surveyed and controlled.

If Foucault is seen as advancing transcendental as well as historical claims, his account is open to the objection that it does not adequately account for approaches in the human sciences that do not proceed via objectification and manipulation. To vindicate the claim that strategies of power prejudice the meaning of object domains in the human sciences, Habermas suggests that Foucault would have had to attempt something akin to the 'transcendental-pragmatic epistemology' that Habermas offered in his *Knowledge and Human Interests* (*PDM*, pp. 272, 416). Were he to provide such an argument, he would discover (as Habermas himself did) 'that in the 1970s objectifying approaches no longer dominated the field in the human sciences; they were competing instead with hermeneutical and critical approaches that were tailored in their forms of knowledge to possibilities other than the manipulation of self and of others' (*PDM*, pp. 272–3).

To argue that Foucault's concept of power functions as a 'concealed' theory of constitution is thus to suggest that Foucault advances an argument for the necessity of the human sciences constituting a world of objects to be manipulated and controlled, but supports this transcendental claim with the merely empirical fact that historically the human sciences developed in conjunction with mechanisms of surveillance and control. But why assume that Foucault is making a transcendental claim at all? Why should we see him as offering anything more than a 'historical' or 'causal' account that points to certain affinities between the development of the human sciences and disciplinary technologies? Nothing in this account suggests that this is the only possible form the human sciences could have taken.[29] In *Discipline and Punish*, all that Foucault ultimately claims is that there is an affinity between the human sciences and the network of power relations epitomized by the prison.

> I am not saying that the human sciences emerged from the prison. But if they have been able to be formed and to produce so many profound changes in the episteme, it is because they have been conveyed by a specific and new modality of power: a certain policy of the body, a certain way of rendering the group of men docile and useful. . . . The carceral network constituted one of the armatures of this power-knowledge that has made the human sciences historically possible. Knowable man (soul, individuality, consciousness, conduct, whatever it is called) is the object-effect of this analytical investment, of this domination-observation.[30]

It is, of course, possible that Foucault is mistaken about the affinity between the flourishing of the human sciences and the carceral system. But refuting his argument would involve more than simply noting, as Habermas does, that 'objectifying approaches' to the human sciences now must compete 'with hermeneutical and critical approaches'. Habermas would either have to show that this competition has had practical consequences in transforming the general relationship between power and knowledge that Foucault claims to have revealed, or he would have to provide evidence that undermines Foucault's 'causal' or 'historical' account of the genesis of the human sciences. His brief discussion of 'blind-spots' in Foucault's writings on the prison and on sexuality is less an empirical critique of Foucault's account than an argument for a different approach, which would focus on the ways in which the development of penal law and of modern notions of sexuality could be analysed in terms of a theory of the evolution of normative structures (*PDM*, pp. 288–92). It is possible that such an approach would be more promising than the analysis Foucault offers. But a suggestion of an alternative line of analysis hardly constitutes an 'empirical' refutation of Foucault's account.

Presentism, Relativism and Cryptonormativity

Habermas's critique of Foucault thus ultimately rests on his 'meta-theoretical' criticisms of Foucault's approach for human sciences. He sees Foucault's 'happy positivism' as resting on three 'substitutions': (1) in place of attempts to understand the meanings that historical documents and events might have had for historically situated agents, Foucault proposes an analysis of structures 'that are meaningless in themselves'; (2) in place of attempts at assessing the truth of validity claims advanced by historical agents or historical documents, Foucault proposes that validity claims be understood as 'functions of power complexes'; and (3) in place of efforts to advance and justify criticisms of the theories and practices of the societies under scrutiny, Foucault proposes 'value-free historical explanations' (*PDM*, p. 275). Habermas argues that these substitutions can be viewed as involving three 'reductions': 'the understanding of meaning by interpreters participating in discourses is reduced to the explanation of discourses; validity claims are functionalistically reduced to the effects of power; the "ought" is naturalistically reduced to the "is"' (p. 276). Habermas speaks of Foucault's procedures as 'reductions' because 'the internal aspects of meaning [*Bedeutung*], of validity [*Wahrheits-geltung*] and of value [*Wertens*] do not go without reduction into the externally grasped aspects of practices of power.'[31]

There is a price to be paid for these reductions. The communicative dimension that Foucault 'filtered out and suppressed' returns with a vengeance in the 'metatheoretical' aporias of 'presentism', 'relativism' and 'cryptonormativism' (*PDM*, p. 276). Habermas charges that Foucault's historical analyses are presentist in that they ultimately reduce the meaning of all historical epochs to their role in the rise of the particular structure of power that defines the modern era (pp. 276–8). They are relativist in that their decision to interpret truth claims simply as the consequence of power relations deprives Foucault of any criterion for distinguishing true from false statements (pp. 279–82). Finally, his analyses are cryptonormative in that they lack a basis for the critical stance they take towards modern norms and institutions (pp. 282–6).

Such criticisms of Foucault's work are, of course, not unique to Habermas.[32] What distinguishes Habermas's argument from that of other critics is his insistence that the problems plaguing Foucault's enterprise can ultimately be traced to a single source: the suppression of communicative rationality in favour of an approach to the human sciences that treats historical documents as if they were mute objects to be studied and classified without ever raising the question of what they meant to historically situated agents. Habermas's critique draws on one of the more ambitious arguments of *The Theory of Communicative Action*, the claim that descriptions of reasons for actions require the interpreter to take up the standpoint of a participant and come to a yes or no decision on the validity claims that provide the grounds for these actions.[33] He insists that approaches in the human sciences that attempt to interpret historical documents without passing judgement on their truth or falsehood are fundamentally misconceived since 'It is part of understanding a sentence that we are capable of recognizing the *grounds* through which the *claim* that its truth conditions are satisfied *could be redeemed.*'[34] Unless we take up the position of participant-interlocutors with regard to the past, we will never be able to understand it.

Foucault's 'presentism' is thus viewed as a consequence of his attempt to avoid the question of what meaning historical actors might have attached to the documents under consideration and instead to reduce the 'meaning' of historical documents to the role they played in systems of power relations. For Habermas, the intelligibility of the past rests on the capacity of the present-day historian to take up the standpoint of a participant in a conversation that binds together the past and the present. It is precisely this possibility that Foucault forecloses when he rejects any reference to 'the self-understanding of actors' and attempts to account for the meaning of historical documents through an analysis of '*underlying* practices'. The genealogist regards history as a series of meaningless rearrangements of kaleidoscopic patterns with nothing in common save for 'the single characteristic of being protuberances of power in general'. Habermas maintains, however, that in practice Foucault does not treat individual configurations of power as self-enclosed totalities, but instead 'inevitably connects the viewpoints under which the comparison is proposed with his own hermeneutic point of departure'. Behind the mask of the sober, objective genealogist, Foucault is engaged in a diagnosis of his own time that 'is narcissistically oriented toward the standpoint of the historian and instrumentalizes the contemplation of the past for the needs of the present' (*PDM*, pp. 277–8).

In support of this charge, Habermas notes that Foucault himself, at the close of *The Archaeology of Knowledge*, raises the question of how his own studies can claim objectivity vis-à-vis the discursive systems they analyse. 'For the moment,' Foucault confesses, 'and as far ahead as it can see, *my* discourse, far from determining the locus in which *it* speaks, is avoiding the ground on which it could find support.'[35] Habermas argues that *The Archaeology of Knowledge* raises the problem of objectivity 'only to avoid it'. It is only in Foucault's discussion of Nietzsche's notion of 'effective history' that he finally surrenders 'to the familiar melody of a *professed* irrationalism', admitting that genealogy, like the various forms of historical consciousness that it explores, is but another manifestation of a 'will to knowledge' that reveals that 'all knowledge rests upon injustice.'[36] There is thus no possibility of doing justice to other epochs, since all interpretations are irredeemably partisan.

It is important to note, however, how the passage Habermas cites from *The Archaeology of Knowledge* concludes. Foucault goes on to characterize his work as 'a discourse about discourses' and stresses that it does not interrogate other discourses in hopes of finding 'a hidden law, a concealed origin' that it alone can free. Instead, the goal is 'to deploy a dispersion that can never be reduced to a single system of differences'. Archaeology, thus, seeks 'to *make* differences: to constitute them as objects, to analyse them, and to define their concept'.[37] If we turn to Foucault's discussion of Nietzsche with this passage in mind, we find that Foucault sees this same attempt to 'record the singularity of events outside of any monotonous finality' as central to Nietzsche's notion of genealogy.[38] As in his earlier discussions of Nietzsche, what Foucault finds most attractive about Nietzschean genealogy is the way it makes use of history to ward off the 'chimeras of the origin'.[39] Genealogical historiography rests on a refusal to view history as a cumulative learning process in which the same questions are posed and reposed until they are finally given an adequate answer.[40] We cannot understand how the terms 'good' and 'bad' are employed in heroic societies – to take Nietzsche's famous example from *The Genealogy of Morals* – if we regard them as anticipations of modern notions of 'good' and 'evil'. The assumption that we can take up the standpoint of the participant-interlocutor vis-à-vis earlier ages runs the risk of reducing other epochs to pale reflections of our own age by assuming that their questions in some sense anticipate our own. Genealogy inoculates against such a stance by advising the historian to seek 'not the anticipatory power of meaning, but the hazardous play of dominations'.[41]

Habermas's claim that genealogy 'instrumentalizes the contemplation of the past for the needs of the present' (PDM, p. 278) thus misses what Foucault takes to be the central lesson of Nietzsche's conception of effective history:

> History becomes 'effective' to the degree that it introduces discontinuity into our very being – as it divides our emotions, dramatizes our instincts, multiplies our body and sets it against itself. 'Effective' history deprives the self of the reassuring stability of life and nature ... It will uproot its traditional foundations and relentlessly disrupt its pretended continuity.[42]

At the beginning of Discipline and Punish, when Foucault questioned his motivation for undertaking a history of prison, he disavowed any interest in 'writing a history of the past in terms of the present' and instead described himself as writing 'the history of the present'.[43] Read against his comments on Nietzsche, this somewhat cryptic comment becomes a bit clearer. Genealogy does not, as Habermas charges, use the present as the key to an understanding of the past. Rather, it seeks to view the present as a contingent historical product, as the fragile result of struggles that could easily have had a different outcome. It teaches us the utter contingency of what we are, and thus deprives us of any comfort that might come from seeing ourselves as somehow grounded and rooted in history. While Habermas insists that we understand history only to the extent that we engage in a dialogue with it, the lessons Foucault took from Nietzsche result in a dramatically different conclusion: 'knowledge is not made for understanding; it is made for cutting.'[44]

While it is difficult to square Habermas's charge of presentism with Foucault's understanding of genealogy, his characterization of Foucault's work as relativist is a good deal more persuasive. Indeed, in the preface to the first edition of Madness and Civilization Foucault himself described his stance as 'a sort of relativity without recourse' that demanded a 'language without support' – a language that bracketed scientific, moral or social commitments.[45] The issue, then, is not whether Foucault's stance involves a relativism towards the truth claims of the sciences he studies, but rather whether this stance poses any particular difficulties for Foucault's undertaking. The problem, as Habermas sees it, is that Foucault's relativism undermines his own inquiries. Genealogy reduces the truth claims advanced by the various sciences under scrutiny to 'the functional contribution they make to the self-maintenance of a given totality of discourse'. But, since Foucault cannot exempt his own research from being treated in the same way, his approach must ultimately 'destroy the foundations of the research inspired by it as well'. The meaning of this research would also be reduced to its 'power effects' (*PDM*, p. 279).

It is not obvious, however, that this need trouble Foucault. Foucault's position could be likened to that of classical scepticism. Just as scepticism did not attempt to secure a position that is free from doubt, but rather used doubt to free individuals from the hold that various beliefs might have over them, so too Foucault could be seen not as claiming a special status, uncontaminated by power, for his arguments, but rather as urging us to see that our assent to knowledge claims of any sort – including his own claim about the relation of knowledge and power – implicates us in particular networks of power.[46] The 'aporia' of self-reference does not emerge unless Foucault seeks to have his own work exempted from his general claims about the relationship between truth and power.

Habermas's argument that Foucault did, in fact, seek to exempt his work in this fashion is striking both for the assurance with which he explains Foucault's intentions and the uncharacteristic weakness of the evidence he offers in support of this reading.

> Foucault pursues genealogical historiography with the serious intent of getting a science underway that is superior to the mismanaged human sciences. . . . he would like to single out his genealogy from all the rest of the human sciences in a manner that is reconcilable with the fundamental assumptions of his own theory. To this end, he turns genealogical historiography upon itself; the difference that can establish its preeminence above all the other human sciences is to be demonstrated in the history of its own emergence. (*PDM*, p. 279)

All that Habermas offers in support of this reading of Foucault's intentions is a discussion of Foucault's characterization of the relationship between genealogy and 'subjugated knowledges'. Habermas argues that genealogy claims superiority over other disciplines because it is able to articulate the 'implicit knowledge of "the people" who form the bedrock in a system of power . . .' Habermas maintains that Foucault seeks to 'gain a perspective that is supposed to go beyond the perspectives of the given possessors of power' by taking up the standpoint of those who first experience new technologies of power 'whether as the ones suffering or as the officials manning the machinery of suffering'.[47] Suggesting that this position parallels Lukács's argument in *History and Class Consciousness* that Marxism was able to transcend ideological bias by articulating the standpoint of the wage labourer, Habermas stresses that Foucault, unlike

Lukács, cannot appeal to a philosophy of history that locates universal interests in the standpoint of a particular group or class. Thus Foucault's 'counterdiscourses' are in the same position as the discourses that currently hold sway: 'they too *are* nothing more than the effects of power they unleash.' Habermas concludes that 'Foucault sees this dilemma, but once again evades any response,' explicitly avowing a stance of 'embattled perspectivism' only in his interpretation of Nietzsche (*PDM*, p. 281).

The question, of course, is whether Foucault in fact 'sees' yet 'evades' this dilemma or whether the entire problem is a creature of a misunderstanding of Foucault's intentions. At the centre of Habermas's critique stands the curious picture of Foucault as a failed Lukács who sought to ground genealogy in the 'subjugated knowledges' of the 'people', but ultimately could not. While it is undeniable that Foucault cannot make an argument like that of Lukács, it is not at all obvious that this was his goal. Foucault characterizes 'subjugated knowledges' as 'naive', 'discredited', 'unqualified or even directly disqualified knowledges'; he sees them as involving 'a popular knowledge [*le savoir des gens*] though it is far from being a general commonsense knowledge'.[48] Formulations such as these suggest that Foucault does not see 'subjugated knowledges' as providing access to a common experience shared by all those who are subjugated to power. He stresses instead that genealogy studies 'a particular, local, regional knowledge, a differential knowledge incapable of uniformity . . .' As examples of such 'low-ranking knowledges' Foucault refers to the knowledge 'of the psychiatric patient, of the ill person, of the nurse, of the doctor – partial and marginal as they are to the knowledge of medicine – that of the delinquent, etc.'[49] The point of recalling such long-discredited forms of knowledge is not that they provide us with a more adequate purchase on the truth than those forms of knowledge which proved victorious. Rather, by reminding us that matters were once described differently than they are now, they lead us to see that distinctions which are now taken for granted are the always contingent and problematic victories of certain ways of describing the world over others. Genealogies are 'antisciences' not in the sense that they oppose 'the contents, methods or concepts of a science' but rather because they resist 'the centralizing powers which are linked to the institution and functioning of an organized scientific discourse . . .'[50] Nothing about these 'antisciences' provides them with greater warrant of truth than that of the ruling sciences that they oppose. Foucault thus remained consistent in his 'relativity without recourse'.

In his final 'metatheoretical' objection Habermas suggests that even if it were possible for Foucault to maintain a consistently neutral stance towards the truth claims of the various forms of knowledge scrutinized by his genealogy, the entire undertaking would still be plagued by a 'cryptonormativity' in that it evaluates regimes of power but fails to provide an adequate grounding for its normative stance. Unlike Max Weber, who counselled a rigorous segregation of normative value judgements from value-neutral empirical analyses, Habermas notes that the very 'style and choice of words' in Foucault's writings testifies to his opposition to 'modern thought and humanistically disguised disciplinary power' (*PDM*, p. 282). Yet Foucault is not engaged, like Marx, in a critique that unmasks the humanistic pretensions of modern society by 'suing for the normative content of bourgeois ideals' (ibid.). His aim is not to salvage 'true humanism' from its current, distorted manifestations, but rather to reject the entire vocabulary of humanism.

Habermas grants that genealogy may be capable of serving 'as a tactic and a tool for waging a battle against a normatively unassailable formation of power'. Nevertheless, he insists, Foucault provides no answer to the question of why we should muster any resistance at all to the systems of power that genealogy analyses. 'It makes sense that a value-free analysis of the strengths and weaknesses of the opponent is of use to one who wants to take up the fight – but why fight at all?' (*PDM*, p. 284). While this criticism is, by now, a familiar one, it is not entirely clear what Habermas and other critics see as lacking.

Foucault never saw systems of power as stifling all opposition. Indeed it is central to his argument that every form of power inaugurates new forms of resistance. Consider, for example, his account of the relationship between 'governmentality' and 'critique'.[51] Foucault sees the early modern period as marked by 'a veritable explosion of the art of governing men' involving a 'laicization' of the Christian pastoral concern with the 'meticulous and detailed' direction of individual lives. What had been a relatively limited practice, linked to monastic experience and typically exercised over small groups, was taken up by political authorities and applied to families, armies, cities, the poor, and ultimately to all the groups that constitute the state.[52] Foucault argues that from the sixteenth century onwards attempts to respond to the question 'How to govern?' were accompanied by another question: 'How not to be governed?'

> I do not mean by this that governmentalization would be opposed, in a kind of inverted contrary affirmation, to 'We do not want to be governed, and we do not want to be governed *at all*.' What I mean is that in the great anxiety surrounding the way to govern and in the inquiries into modes of governing, one detects a perpetual question which would be: 'How not to be

governed *like that*, by that, in the name of these principles, in view of such objectives and by the means of such methods, not like that, not for that, not by them.'[53]

It is in this line of questioning that Foucault finds the origins of the 'critical attitude'.

For Foucault, then, there will be no shortage of answers to the question 'Why fight?' Foucault sees biblical criticism, from Wycliffe to Bayle, as an attempt to question the governing authority of the ecclesiastical magisterium, just as natural law theories responded to demands for obedience by insisting on the 'universal and indefeasible rights to which every government – whatever it might be, whether it has to do with the monarch, the magistrate, the educator, or the father of the family – will have to submit'.[54] The question 'Why fight?' has no single response. Answers will vary depending on the particular character of the claim to govern. Criticism is thus 'at once partner and adversary of the arts of governing . . . a way of suspecting them, of challenging them, of limiting them . . .'[55]

Habermas would presumably regard such a characterization of criticism as much too particularistic and contingent. Any reasons for resistance offered by such criticism would be so closely linked to the particular way in which political power is exercised that it would always be possible to open another round of questioning in which the premises shared by both efforts to govern and efforts to resist governance would be called into question. Hence, particular disputes about whether a certain interpretation of Scripture is valid can always be trumped by posing a more general question, for example the question of why Scripture should matter in the direction of the life of the individual, a question that will remove us from the domain of biblical criticism and inaugurate reflection on the relationship between divine revelation and natural reason. For Habermas, the ability to initiate further consideration of the warrants offered for any given action rests ultimately on the always present presupposition that the validity claims advanced by speakers are open to argumentation and redemption.

The question, then, is not whether Foucault can provide answers to the question 'Why fight?' – he can, and does – but rather what is to count as an acceptable answer to the question. The answers Foucault offers will describe the claims that were made in support of the right to govern in any given historical period (including our own) and note the criticisms such claims received. What counts as an 'acceptable' reason will be answered by looking at the rules governing argument that are in force at this particular time. At least initially, Habermas's answer to the question 'Why fight?' might be no different than Foucault's. He, too, could point to particular criticisms advanced against particular claims. But before these criticisms can be certified as 'acceptable' Habermas would require that they be subjected to universalization tests to assure that the reasons advanced for resistance are compelling to other rational agents.[56] Habermas's charge of 'cryptonormativity' thus rests ultimately on the argument that historical and contingent reasons such as those offered by Foucault ought to be viewed as an inadequate justification for the normative rightness of an action.

There may well be good reasons for agreeing with Habermas.[57] But it is significant that when framed in this way his argument falls a good deal short of the claim that Foucault's theory of power is beset by aporias that can be resolved only by embracing Habermas's notion of communicative rationality. There is no contradiction in Foucault's arguing that particular constellations of power relations are intimately linked with certain criticisms of these power relations and yet at the same time finding these historically contingent criticisms to be compelling.[58] What, after all, is Foucault's alternative? A thinker who holds that there are reasons for action that transcend particular constellations of power may maintain that the only really compelling criticisms are those that are justified through arguments that appeal to principles that transcend the terms in which a debate is currently waged. In the absence of such reasons, such a thinker might well ask 'Why fight at all?' But since Foucault holds that these historically contingent criticisms are the only sort of criticisms that we are ever going to be able to mount, the fact that more universal defences of the reasons for resistance cannot be offered does nothing to detract from the force of the historically contingent criticisms that *can* be offered. Here, too, Foucault embraced a relativism that, while perhaps troubling, was by no means inconsistent.

The Aporia

In *The Philosophical Discourse of Modernity* Habermas attempts to reconstruct the path that led Foucault from his early archaeological inquiries into the formation of the human sciences to his subsequent genealogical accounts of the relationship between power and knowledge. In reconstructing this development, he searches for alternative theoretical options that were not explored. His goal is thus to provide an account that argues that despite Foucault's various reformulations of his approach, Foucault's critique of Western rationality remains caught in a series of aporias that can only be resolved by taking up the options that Foucault foreclosed. Habermas's critique thus insists that Foucault's systematic exclusion of communicative rationality – evident as early as his rejection of the 'depth hermeneutics' of *Madness and Civilization* in favour of a 'structural analysis' of *The Birth of the Clinic* – not only accounts for the particular aporias in which Foucault's thought is caught, but also suggests that the resolution to these difficulties would have to take the form of something resembling Habermas's own account of communicative rationality.

I have argued that Habermas's account provides neither a plausible reconstruction of Foucault's development nor a convincing argument that Foucault's 'theory of power' is subject to fatal contradictions. Habermas's account of Foucault's development is plausible only if one assumes that Foucault was attempting to respond to a set of problems that he does not appear to have been asking. The aporias that allegedly plague Foucault's account of the relationship between knowledge and power vanish once it is recognized that Foucault is willing to live with the consequences of a view of history that sees values as contingent and historical.

It is, of course, quite possible to argue that Foucault *ought* to have addressed the questions Habermas assumed that he was answering, just as it is quite reasonable to suggest that Foucault's 'relativism without recourse' may be too hasty in foreclosing the possibility that there are compelling arguments in support of certain of the norms that define modernity. In this case, there might be good reasons for preferring Habermas's approach to that of Foucault. The reasons that would dispose us to opt for Habermas over Foucault, however, would depend largely on what we see as the proper questions for social theorists to be addressing and what we see as a valid reason for taking up certain normative commitments. But in this case the reasons that would dispose us to choose Habermas's approach over that of Foucault would not derive from internal inconsistencies within Foucault's account that, when probed, lead us neatly to Habermas's standpoint. In the end, we are faced, not with aporias *within* Foucault's work, but rather with a set of fundamental disagreements *between* Foucault and Habermas.

NOTES

1 Jürgen Habermas, *The Philosophical Discourse of Modernity: Twelve Lectures*, trans. Frederick Lawrence (Cambridge: Polity Press; Cambridge, Mass.: MIT Press, 1987), p. 55. Hereafter also cited as *PDM*.
2 John Rajchman, 'Habermas' Complaint', in Rajchman, *Philosophical Events: Essays of the '80s* (New York: Columbia University Press, 1991), p. 28.
3 Ibid., p. 27.
4 *PDM*, p. 240. Habermas suggests that Adorno's work may be seen as taking a different tack in pursuing this question. See *PDM*, p. 241.
5 Michel Foucault, *The Birth of the Clinic: An Archaeology of Medical Perception*, trans. A. M. Sheridan Smith (New York: Vintage, 1975), pp. xvi–xvii.
6 Foucault, *The Birth of the Clinic*, pp. xvi–xvii.

7 *PDM*, p. 240. Habermas's characterization of this position as a 'depth hermeneutics' is taken from Hubert Dreyfus and Paul Rabinow, *Michel Foucault: Beyond Structuralism and Hermeneutics* (Chicago: University of Chicago Press, 1983), pp. 11–12.

8 Michel Foucault, *Madness and Civilization: A History of Insanity in the Age of Reason*, trans. Richard Howard (New York: Vintage, 1973) pp. x–xi.

9 Ibid., p. x.

10 Ibid., p. 287 (translation modified).

11 This problem was noted by Foucault's former student Jacques Derrida in his critique of *Madness and Civilization*. See Jacques Derrida, 'Cogito and the History of Madness', in Derrida, *Writing and Difference* (Chicago: University of Chicago Press, 1978), pp. 35–6.

12 See the conclusion of Foucault's response to Derrida, 'My Body, This Paper, This Fire', trans. Geoff Bennington, *Oxford Literary Review* 4:1 (Autumn 1979), pp. 9–28, where Foucault places Derrida within a tradition that is defined by

> the reduction of discursive practices to textual traces; the elision of the events produced therein and the retention only of marks for a reading; the invention of voices behind texts to avoid having to analyse the modes of implication of the subject in discourses; the assigning of the originary as said and unsaid in the text to avoid replacing discursive practices in the field of transformations where they are carried out. (p. 27)

As further evidence that Foucault seems to use 'commentary' to describe positions taken by *others*, see his essay on Bataille, 'A Preface to Transgression', where he contrasts Bataille's philosophy to that of 'the age of commentary in which we live'. See Michel Foucault, *Language, Counter-Memory, Practice: Selected Essays and Interviews*, trans. D. F. Bouchard and S. Simon (Ithaca, N.Y.: Cornell University Press, 1977), p. 41.

13 In a passage in *The Archaeology of Knowledge* that, as Foucault explains in a footnote, was 'written against an explicit theme of my book *Madness and Civilization*, and one that recurs particularly in the Preface', he rejects the notion of 'writing a history of the referent' and insists 'we are not trying to reconstitute what madness itself might be, in the form which it first presented itself to some primitive, fundamental, deaf, scarcely articulated experience . . .' But even here Foucault immediately goes on to state that 'Such a history of the referent is no doubt possible' and to insist that he has no desire 'to exclude any effort to uncover and free these "prediscursive" experiences from the tyranny of the text'. See Michel Foucault, *The Archaeology of Knowledge*, trans. A. M. Sheridan Smith (New York: Harper, 1976), p. 47. For a discussion of this passage see Gary Gutting, *Michel Foucault's Archaeology of Scientific Reason* (Cambridge: Cambridge University Press, 1989), pp. 264–5.

14 Michel Foucault, 'The Discourse of Language', in *The Archaeology of Knowledge*, pp. 217–19. It is interesting to note that at this point Foucault still speaks of sexuality in terms of the 'repression hypothesis' that he would subsequently question in his own work on the history of sexuality.

15 *PDM*, p. 248. In the passages on Foucault, the English translation of Habermas's book makes use of the rather clumsy terminology employed in the English translation of *L'Ordre du discours*, so that the terms Foucault

employs to describe the stances of the archaeology and genealogy suffer greatly. The description of the stance of the archaeologist as one of 'désinvolture studieuse' (suggesting a studious – or studied – lack of deference to or involvement in the truth claims made by the documents the archaeologist examines, since the archaeologist seeks to understand the rules by which the statements are produced, not the claims that they make) – which Habermas renders as 'gelehrter Ungeniertheil' (studious casualness) – thus appears as 'erudite ingenuity'. Likewise, 'positivisme heureux' ('happy positivism', suggesting an untroubled willingness to regard discursive formations as 'positivities' to be explained in terms of the play of forces rather than as the expressive utterances of a subject) – which Habermas renders as 'glücklichen Positivism' – appears as 'felicitous positivism'. For a discussion (and better translation) of this section of L'Ordre du discourse see Dreyfus and Rabinow, Michel Foucault, p. 105.

16 For a careful analysis of Foucault's reading of Nietzsche, see James Miller, The Passion of Michel Foucault (New York: Simon and Schuster, 1993), pp. 66–72, 142, 213–19. See also Foucault's brief discussion in the interview 'How Much Does It Cost for Reason to Tell the Truth?' in Foucault/Live (New York: Semiotext(e), 1989), pp. 238–40.

17 For a summary of the argument of this work, see Miller, The Passion of Michel Foucault, pp. 137–42.

18 Michel Foucault, Folie et déraison (Paris: Librairie Plon, 1961), p. v. This passage is not included in the English translation.

19 Michel Foucault, The Order of Things: An Archaeology of the Human Sciences (New York: Vintage, 1970), pp. 340–3.

20 PDM, p. 249. It is also to misunderstand Foucault's reaction to the events of May 1968, which were hardly 'disappointing' to him. In the 1977 interview 'Truth and Power', for instance, Foucault states that 'it was only around 1968, and in spite of the Marxist tradition and the PCF' that questions about the relation of knowledge and power 'came to assume their political significance, with a sharpness that I had never envisaged, showing how timid and hesitant those early books of mine had been. Without the political opening created during these years, I would surely never have had the courage to take up these problems again and pursue my research in the direction of penal theory, prisons and disciplines.' See Michel Foucault, Power/Knowledge: Selected Interviews and Other Writings, ed. Colin Gordon (New York: Pantheon, 1980), p. 111.

21 Foucault, The Archaeology of Knowledge, pp. 12–13.

22 See Foucault's rejection of 'linear' history and the discussion of 'monumental' history in 'Nietzsche, Genealogy, History', in Language, Counter-Memory, Practice, pp. 138, 161, and his discussion of the differences between monuments and documents in Archaeology of Knowledge, p. 7.

23 Foucault, Folie et déraison, p. v (this passage is omitted from the English translation).

24 In this context it is worth recalling Dreyfus and Rabinow's admonition that 'There is no pre- and post-archaeology or genealogy in Foucault' (Michel Foucault, p. 104).

25 Foucault, Power/Knowledge, p. 113.

26 Ibid., p. 115.

27 Since Habermas's account of Foucault's development effectively ends with Discipline and Punish and La Volonté de savoir, there is no discussion of the

final phase of Foucault's career, in which questions of ethics and 'technologies of the self' move to the fore. For an application of some of Habermas's criticisms to Foucault's last work, see Thomas McCarthy, 'The Critique of Impure Reason: Foucault and the Frankfurt School', *Political Theory* 18:3 (1990), pp. 437–69.

28 See the discussion in Dreyfus and Rabinow, *Michel Foucault*, pp. 90–100.

29 The argument of *The Order of Things* is thus a good deal more ambitious, insisting that the human sciences must forever remain immature sciences. This is precisely the sort of claim that Foucault cannot make in *Discipline and Punish*.

30 Foucault, *Discipline and Punish: The Birth of the Prison*, trans. Alan Sheridan (New York: Vintage, 1979), p. 305.

31 My translation, see *PDM*, p. 276.

32 See, for example, Nancy Fraser, 'Foucault on Modern Power: Empirical Insights and Normative Confusions', *Praxis International* 1.3 (1981), pp. 272–87, and Charles Taylor, 'Foucault on Freedom and Truth', *Political Theory* 12.2 (1984), pp. 152–83.

33 Jürgen Habermas, *The Theory of Communicative Action*, vol. 1, trans. Thomas McCarthy (Cambridge: Polity Press, 1984), pp. 115–17. For a discussion and critique of this argument, see Thomas McCarthy, 'Reflections on Rationalization in *The Theory of Communicative Action*', in Richard Bernstein (ed.), *Habermas and Modernity* (Cambridge, Mass.: MIT Press, 1985), pp. 183–6.

34 Habermas, *The Theory of Communicative Action*, vol. 1, p. 317.

35 Foucault, *The Archaeology of Knowledge*, p. 204. This passage is discussed by Habermas in *PDM*, on p. 278.

36 *PDM*, p. 278, Habermas citing Foucault, 'Nietzsche, Genealogy, History', pp. 162–3. In his discussion of Habermas's critique, Gary Gutting suggests that there is no reason to assume that Foucault's characterization of Nietzsche's work reflects his own position. See Gutting, *Michel Foucault's Archaeology of Scientific Reason*, pp. 277–8. Although it is true that Foucault never explicitly associates himself with Nietzsche's position, Foucault's comments on Nietzsche are congruent enough with his discussions of his own work to suggest that they can aid in explaining Foucault's own stance.

37 Foucault, *The Archaeology of Knowledge*, p. 205.

38 Foucault, 'Nietzsche, Genealogy, History', p. 139.

39 Ibid., p. 144.

40 See ibid., pp. 139, 151.

41 Ibid., p. 148.

42 Ibid., p. 154.

43 Foucault, *Discipline and Punish*, p. 31.

44 Foucault, 'Nietzsche, Genealogy, History', p. 154.

45 Foucault, *Folie et déraison*, pp. ix–x (this passage is not translated in the English edition).

46 For an interpretation of Foucault's work along these lines, see John Rajchman, *Michel Foucault: The Freedom of Philosophy* (New York: Columbia University Press, 1985), pp. 2–7.

47 *PDM*, p. 280. Habermas is summarizing Foucault's argument in *Power/Knowledge*, p. 82.

48 Foucault, *Power/Knowledge*, p. 82. Habermas's phrase 'implizite Wissen "der Leute"' carries connotations that are foreign to Foucault's 'le savoir des

gens'. *Der Leute*, like the French *peuple*, does have the Marxian resonance
Habermas is looking for. But *gens* has a much more diffuse range of
application, occurring most frequently in compounds such as *gens de lettres*
(men of letters), *gens du monde* (men of the world) and *le droit des gens* (law
of nations). The attraction of the term for Foucault may rest with the Latin
root of the word – *gens* (family) – and hence its close relationship to
'genealogy': 'genealogy' recovers *le savoir des gens*.

49 Ibid.
50 Ibid., pp. 82–3.
51 See Michel Foucault, 'Qu'est-ce que la critique? [Critique et *Aufklärung*]',
    Bulletin de la Société Française de Philosophie 84 (1990), pp. 35–63. This
    text is a transcript of a 1978 lecture.
52 Ibid., p. 37.
53 Ibid., pp. 37–8.
54 Ibid., p. 39.
55 Ibid., p. 38.
56 See Jürgen Habermas, *Moral Consciousness and Communicative Action*,
    trans. Christian Lenhardt and Shierry Weber Nicholsen (Cambridge: Polity
    Press; Cambridge, Mass: MIT Press, 1990), pp. 62–8.
57 For an argument along these lines, see the closing section of James Schmidt
    and Thomas Wartenberg, 'Foucault's Enlightenment' in Michael Kelly (ed.),
    Critique and Power: Recasting the Foucault–Habermas Debate (Cambridge,
    Mass: MIT Press, 1994).
58 For an examination of what is involved in taking up such a stance, see
    Richard Rorty, *Contingency, Irony, and Solidarity* (Cambridge: Cambridge
    University Press, 1989), pp. 44–69.

6

INTERSUBJECTIVITY AND THE MONADIC CORE OF THE PSYCHE: HABERMAS AND CASTORIADIS ON THE UNCONSCIOUS

Joel Whitebook

I

Habermas's attacks on Nietzsche, Heidegger, Derrida and Foucault in *The Philosophical Discourse of Modernity* are easily understood. These thinkers, in so far as they raise the spectres of irrationalism, nihilism and political regression for Habermas, represent the enemy; as such, they must be defeated, and the book, which consists in a series of lectures, contains many brilliant polemics to that end. The attack on Castoriadis, however, which centres on the interpretation of psychoanalysis, is more difficult to comprehend, both with respect to its vehemence and to its externality to Castoriadis's position. If he had wanted to criticize Castoriadis's theory of the monadic core of the subject properly[1] – which, to be sure, is not immune from criticism – Habermas should have at least fulfilled Hegel's requirement of stepping into the strength of an opponent's position. Instead, we are given a superficial 'excursus'[2] which hardly does justice to Castoriadis's deep and original appropriation of Freud. If it is to be criticized, a theory of this depth deserves a more serious critique.

The situation is all the more curious given the fact that, vis-à-vis poststructuralism, postmodernism, neoconservatism, etc., Habermas and Castoriadis are, as it were, on the same side of the theoretical barricades, despite the fact that the latter makes his home in Paris. Indeed, with respect to their *most general intentions*, Habermas and Castoriadis perhaps have more in common with each other than either has with many of the central theorists in political and philosophical thinking today. At a time when various forms of contextualist relativism dominate the political-philosophical landscape, their stubborn defence of the Occident's rationalist and democratic traditions – what Habermas calls 'the project of Enlightenment' and Castoriadis refers to as 'the project of autonomy'[3] – almost borders on the eccentric. I believe the similarities go so far that, in the final analysis, it could be shown that Habermas, his claim to have provided a strictly formal argument notwithstanding, defends the 'project of Enlightenment' as a 'project of autonomy'.[4] Yet, despite this agreement at the most general level of programmatic intentions, there are substantive differences in the modes of philosophizing each employs in pursuing those intentions. Whereas Habermas combines a modified form of transcendental philosophy with results from the empirical social sciences to formulate a theory of communicative rationality, Castoriadis proceeds through a mode of what he terms dialectical 'elucidation'.[5] And it is the difference in their modes of philosophizing – which, to be sure, must ultimately have consequences for their more general programmatic intentions as well – that surfaces in the controversy concerning Freud.

Castoriadis's doctrine of the monadic core of the subject touched a theoretical raw nerve in Habermas not only because it poses a profound challenge to the interpretation of Freud in *Knowledge and Human Interests*,[6] but to the very heart of Habermas's general philosophical construction (of which the Freud interpretation is in fact one paradigmatic aspect). The centrepiece of that construction, including the earlier reformulation of Critical Theory and the more recent defence of modernity, has been the 'linguistic turn',[7] that is, the move from the philosophy of consciousness and 'subject-centred reason' to the philosophy of intersubjectivity and communicative rationality.[8] Anything that would challenge a thoroughgoing philosophy of intersubjectivity, as a monadic core of the psyche certainly would, poses a threat to the heart of Habermas's theory.

Let me develop this point by contrasting the (modified) Kantian transcendentalism of Habermas to the, if not fully Hegelian, at least anti-Kantian realism of Castoriadis. Habermas's linguistic reworking of Kantian philosophy – which attempts to establish the scope and validity of the different spheres of rationality through a reflection on the condition of the possibility of the types of communicative action – predictably results in the quintessential Kantian problem: namely, the *Ding-an-sich*, only now recast in linguistic terms. *Towards the outside*, Habermas's linguistic transcendentalism prevents him from adequately reaching the extralinguistic reality of external (especially living) nature.[9] Considered from the other direction, *towards the inside*, I will try to show it also prevents him from adequately reaching the prelinguistic reality of inner nature, which is to say, the unconscious.[10] And, in general, the move from the philosophy of consciousness to the philosophy of language, despite its successes in resolving certain philosophical problems concerning the relationship of subject to subject, does not prove to be the all-encompassing philosophical panacea that Habermas and his followers often hope it will be; much of the old, that is to say, *perennial* baggage comes along in the transition. Just as the philosophy of consciousness had difficulty transcending the *circle of subjectivity* and reaching the *othersidedness of consciousness*, to paraphrase Marx, so the philosophy of language has the parallel difficulty in surmounting the larger *circle of intersubjectivity* and contacting the *othersidedness of language* in inner and outer nature. Habermas's statement that language 'is the only thing whose nature we can know', which he made in his Frankfurt Inaugural Address in 1965, holds for him every bit as much today as it did then.[11] The problem becomes particularly apparent in his treatment of a prelinguistic unconscious, and, *a fortiori*, of a monadic core of the primal subject. He is compelled for systematic reasons simply to dismiss the notion of a prelinguistic unconscious *ex cathedra*. Such a thicket of non-linguisticality at the centre of the subject would be an anathema to his entire philosophy.

If Habermas is content to remain at the Kantian moment, that is, to remain on this side of language, and is not particularly troubled by the paradoxes that emerge as a result, Castoriadis, in contrast, is preoccupied with and repeatedly returns to the question that necessarily arose the instant the transcendental move has been made: what are we to make of this *Ding-an-sich* which we are forced to posit, but about which we can say nothing? A central thesis of Castoriadis's, that, in this respect, sets him in opposition not only to Kantianism but to contemporary contextualism as well – which, in any case, is basically the Kantian problematic of the categorical scheme writ large – is the following: it is incoherent to maintain that extraconceptual or extralinguistic reality is pure chaos, 'amorphous clay',[12] upon which we can impose the order, synthesis, form, etc., of our conceptual/linguistic grids at will. (After all, the history of science demonstrates that nature 'rejects' some of our grids.) It follows from the very fact that we can impose our conceptual/linguistic grids on the object, can organize it, that the object is at least *amenable to* that organization, is in some sense *organizable*. Thus the attempt to maintain the claim that all synthesis is on this side of thought/language cannot itself be sustained and already, to a certain extent, propels us to the other side of thought/language. For example, the fact that the history of science proceeds through a succession of largely incommensurate paradigms is, of course, often adduced as prime evidence for contextual relativism. Castoriadis, however, goes further and inquires into the conditions of the possibility of this fact itself, thus raising the anticontextualist question that underlies it: namely, what must the organization of nature be 'that allows [the succession of paradigms] to exist and makes them occur in the order that they do, and not in some other quite arbitrary order . . .'?[13] This is not to imply that Castoriadis attempts to speak about the object in-itself in a direct, pre-Kantian, and naively metaphysical manner. The point rather is this: unlike Habermas, who abstains from speaking about the object altogether for fear of a regression into metaphysics, Castoriadis attempts to forge a discourse which allows him to say *that which would be incoherent not to say* about the object in-itself, but to say it in a non-metaphysical fashion. This is the mode of discourse he calls elucidation.[14] As we shall see, then, these general philosophical differences which separate Habermas and Castoriadis apply *mutatis mutandis* to their analyses of the unconscious. It represents a test case, of sorts, for their different philosophical approaches.

II

Habermas and Castoriadis turned to psychoanalysis, as Adorno, Horkheimer, Marcuse and others had before them, partly in response to the crisis of Marxism. Both sought to overcome the impasse of Marxian thought by adding a second dimension to Marx's materialistic monism; the second dimension which each elaborated, however, reflects the differences in philosophical styles separating the two thinkers. Whereas Habermas sought to locate that second dimension in *a communicatively conceived notion of practical reason*, Castoriadis sought to locate it in *phantasy*, or what he terms *the radical imagination*. Habermas is primarily interested in psychoanalysis for methodological reasons; it is a 'tangible example'[15] of a successful emancipatory science which combines communicative rationality with explanatory procedures, and as such can be used to clarify the foundations of critical theory. Castoriadis, on the other hand, is primarily concerned with Freud's discovery of the unconscious, which he seeks to develop into a theory of the radical imagination. And he uses the doctrine of the radical imagination, in turn, to counter the reductionism not only of orthodox Marxism, but also of orthodox Freudianism, which, of course, is not entirely dissimilar from it. Each, in so far as it attempts to reduce the symbolic to the real (economic and biological-corporeal reality respectively) excludes the possibility of authentically autonomous thought and action and of genuine historical creation, which is to say, the emergence of radically novel meanings in history. To the extent that the radical imagination intervenes between the real and the symbolic as a potentially inexhaustible source of new meanings, that reduction is impossible. The radical imagination, as Castoriadis describes it in *The Imaginary Institution of Society*, consists in a *largely self-generated* stream of unconscious representations of images which are 'not subject to determinacy', that is, not subject to time and contradiction (*IIS*, p.

274). These representations provide the material for the daydreams of the person-on-the street as well as for the private hallucinations of a Daniel Paul Schreber. But, in sublimated form, they can also be injected into public institutions and become the source of radically novel historical innovations, that is, of 'new figures of the thinkable'.[16]

Castoriadis's theory of the radical imagination differs from Freud's theory of unconscious phantasy in the degree of autonomy it assigns to the formation of those phantasies vis-à-vis biological-corporeal reality; phantasy formation is, in other words much less rooted in the biological-corporeal, and therefore much more spontaneous, for Castoriadis, than it is for Freud. This allows Castoriadis to appropriate Freud to radicalize social theory by offering a theory of historical creation, while at the same time avoiding the conservative tendencies of orthodox psychoanalysis, which tends to view phantasies (and the social institutions deriving from them) as the eternal repetition of an 'old medley' (*IIS*, p. 311) based on a few drive-related motifs. To pull this off, however, Castoriadis must face another, complementary difficulty: namely, *how to maintain the degree of independence for the radical imagination required by his theory of historical creation without loosing its moorings in the real altogether.* He remains too much of a Marxist and a Freudian – and rightfully so – to disassociate the radical imagination from the real completely. As we shall see, he enlists Freud's doctrine of 'leaning-on' (German *Anlehnung* or Greek *anaclisis*) in an attempt to solve this difficulty.

For the moment, however, let us note that Castoriadis's central criticism of Freud is that he devoted 'a large part of his work' to trying to mitigate the radicalness of his break-through, which consisted in the 'discovery of the imaginary element in the psyche', by seeking 'real' factors that would account for the history of the psyche, its organization, and finally, even its being' (*IIS*, p. 281), for instance, in the biological, infantile seduction, the primal scene, historical events, etc. Against this tendency, Castoriadis wants to assert 'the *relative* independence and autonomy of phantasizing' (p. 282) vis-à-vis the real. *Everything turns, of course, on how the relative autonomy is understood.*

The dilemmas Castoriadis encounters in trying to determine that relative autonomy 'are by no means proper to Freud alone', but, on the contrary, 'have a venerable tradition in philosophy' (ibid.). On the one hand, if too much independence is assigned to the productive imagination, one runs the risk of a psychoanalytic version of subjective idealism: 'If the psyche produces everything out of itself, if it is sheer and total production of its own representations with respect to their form (organization) and to their content, we can wonder how and why it should ever meet anything other than itself and its own products' (ibid.). While Castoriadis is certainly aware of this danger, as the foregoing passage indicates, I shall try to show that ultimately he is not entirely successful in avoiding it. If, on the other hand, the psyche 'borrows' the material *and* organization for its representations from the real, the question arises as to how the real can make an impression on or register in the psyche which is heterogeneous to it. Castoriadis argues that the answer to the paradox of representation cannot be found 'outside representation itself' and that an 'original representation' must be posited which, as a 'schemata of figuration', would 'contain within itself the possibility of organizing all representations', and, as such, would be the condition of the possibility of all further representations in the psyche (*IIS*, p. 283).

Freud, as we know, maintains that the real first announces itself in the psyche through the unpleasurable affect associated with hunger. The child, drawing on previous experiences of satisfaction, which is to say, drawing on traces of the real, forms a hallucinatory representation of the breast in an attempt to restore the 'state of psychical tranquillity' that existed prior to the intrusion of the real through the unpleasurable affect. This hallucinated breast becomes, for Freud, the original phantasmic representation, and hallucinatory wish fulfilment becomes the prototype for all further phantasy- and dream-formation. Castoriadis argues, however, that the hallucinated breast is already a secondary or 'constituted' phantasy which itself presupposes a prior '"constituting" phantasy-phantasmatization' (*IIS*, p. 285). He maintains that we cannot rest content with hallucinatory wish fulfilment as an ultimate datum, but must inquire into that state of psychic tranquillity that obtained prior to the intrusion of the unpleasurable affect and which the child seeks to restore through the hallucination. Castoriadis posits the existence of an original *Ur-Vorstellung*, proto-representation or phantasmatization, which cannot be traced to the real, and which cannot be a representation in the ordinary sense, for it is not the representation *of* anything; rather, it is a 'phantasmic scene', or a 'unitary subjective circuit' (p. 298), which does not admit any externality, and where the difference between inside and outside, subject and object, infant and breast, etc., has yet to emerge. After all, 'the "discovery" of the breast as absent ... is made only in relation to and on the basis of the requirement that nothing is to be absent, nothing is to be lacking' (p. 291).

How, then, does this 'monadic core of the primal subject' or state of 'initial autism' (p. 294), as he calls it, 'contain within itself the possibility of organizing all representations'? Castoriadis argues that the requirement for complete unification 'posited by [this] original representation' (p. 283) continues to operate after the break-up of the initial state – and we shall have to inquire into the nature of that break-up – when it is transferred to the 'monadic pole' of the psyche. The monadic pole exerts a 'tendency towards unification' over the rest of psychic life which has the most diverse and even contradictory effects, ranging from the complete irrationality of the unconscious to the highest achievements of Reason. On the level of unconscious mentation, where the demand for complete unification continues to 'reign in the fullest, rawest, most savage and intractable manner' (p. 287), it accounts for the utter indeterminacy of the primary processes: on this level, the monadic pole attempts to 'short circuit' all difference 'in order to carry it back to an impossible monadic "state" and failing to do so, to its substitutes, hallucinatory satisfaction and phantasizing' (p. 302). In the more conscious, socialized strata of the psyche, the unifying intention of the monadic pole is enlisted to synthesize the manifold of contents emanating from the outside into the relative unity of experience. It is in this sense that it provides the schemata for assimilating all representations coming into the psyche; it is not simply the synthetic function of the ego but of the psyche in general. In a manner similar to the transcendental unity of apperception, it is the source of the 'I think' which accompanies all representations and makes them *my* representations. And, like the transcendental unity of apperception, as it is the precondition for all other representations, it cannot itself be represented; we only infer it through its effects. At an even higher level yet, this intention towards unification, transformed into the demand for 'universal cognitive connection' and 'universal significance', becomes a source of the highest achievements of mental life:

> The sperm of reason is also contained in the complete madness of the initial autism. An essential dimension of religion – this goes without saying – but also an essential dimension of philosophy and of science derive from this. One does not put reason where it should be, and, what is even more serious, one cannot reach a reasonable attitude with respect to reason . . . if one refuses to see in it something other than, of course, but *also*, an avatar of the madness of unification. Whether it is the philosopher or the scientist, the final and dominant intention – to find, across differences and otherness, manifestations of the *same* . . . is based on the same schema of a final, that is to say, primal unity . . . (*IIS*, p. 299)

Finally, as it is the opposite of Habermas's position, mention should be made of the fact that, for Castoriadis, the monadic pole of the psyche is a source of individuation. As a kind of Aristotelian prime matter which cannot be exhaustively informed by the socialization process and therefore resists complete absorption into the common world (*kosmos koinos*) it 'assures the individual a *singular identity*' (p. 302).

Thus far we have examined Castoriadis's attempt to conceptualize the autonomous aspect of the psyche's functioning vis-à-vis the real. We must now examine the problem from the other direction, namely, with respect to its non-autonomous relationship to extrapsychic reality. To conceptualize the relationship between the radical imagination and the real, or, more specifically, between phantasy formation and biological-corporeal reality, Castoriadis, as I have already indicated, employs Freud's notion of 'leaning-on', which he expands into an almost quasi-ontological category. To be sure, as Laplanche and Pontalis have pointed out, the central and pervasive role of the notion of *Anlehnung* in Freud's thinking is often missed by the non-German reader, who generally associates it only with a type of object choice.[17] But Castoriadis wants to go further. He insists that the concept of 'leaning-on', along with the notion of the radical imagination, is both 'as original and irreducible' a concept as cause or symbol, and absolutely necessary for '[thinking] otherwise': the simultaneous relatedness but non-reducibility which characterizes the 'gaps' separating the various regions of being,[18] such as between vital and inanimate phenomena, society and nature, and psyche and soma, cannot be conceptualized within the 'inherited logic-ontology' (*IIS*, p. 290), but requires the concept of leaning-on. In each case, the first member of the pair leans on the second.

With respect to our topic, then, what does it mean for the psyche to lean on biological-corporeal reality? In the first instance, the psyche's autonomy vis-à-vis the biological-corporeal is not absolute because 'there can be no oral instinct without mouth and the breast, no anal instinct without an anus.' By this statement, Castoriadis does not simply mean that the bodily organs are mere *external conditions without which* the drive and its related phantasies cannot exist:

> the existence of the mouth and breast, or the anus, is not a mere 'external condition', without which there would be no oral or anal instinct, or more generally, no psychical functioning as we know it – in the same way as it is clear that without oxygen in the atmosphere or circulatory system there would be no psyche, no phantasies or sublimation. Oxygen contributes nothing to phantasies, it 'allows them to exist' . . .

He means, rather, that the morphology and mode of functioning of the pertinent organs contribute to the drive-related phantasies in that they delineate the range of possible forms those phantasies can assume:

The mouth-breast, or the anus, have to be 'taken into account'
by the psyche and, what is more, they support and induce . . .
The privileged somatic data will always be taken up again by
the psyche, psychical working out will have to 'take them into
account', they will leave their mark on it . . . (*IIS*, p. 290)

From the other side, however, while these biological-corporeal
factors necessarily 'support and induce' the phantasy, they do not
cause or determine it. It is therefore impossible, within the 'identitary
frame of reference of determinacy', to state with 'which mark and in
what manner' these 'privileged somatic data' will affect the phantasy.
A gap of underdetermination separates the biological-corporeal substratum from the drive-related phantasy, and it is precisely in this gap
that the 'creativity of the psyche' functions; this gap also makes the
reduction of the drives to the biological-corporeal impossible. Thus,
while we know that every individual and society will necessarily take
up these privileged somatic factors and rework them in its formation,
we can predict nothing about the determinate form they will assume
in a given individual or society. The attempt to comprehend the
relationship of the drive to its biological substratum from within the
identitary logic thus leads to the paradoxical violation of one of the
central canons of scientific thinking: 'In the name of the scientific and
rigorous mind, one ends up once again with this scientific monstrosity
as a consequence: constant factors produce variable effects' (*IIS*, p.
316).

Finally, we must address the question of the break-up of the
psychic monad. Castoriadis's thesis stated in its sharpest (or most
rhetorical) form – and this is where Habermas lodges his main
objection – is as follows: the 'social institution of the individual',
which is simultaneously a process of psychogenesis (*idiogenesis*) and
sociogenesis (*koinogenesis*), consists in the 'imposition on the psyche'
by society 'of an organization which is essentially heterogeneous with
it' (*IIS*, pp. 298, 301). As the psyche is 'in no way "predestined"
[*sic*] by nature' for socialization, this imposition 'amounts to a violent
break, forced [on it] by its "relation" to others . . .' (pp. 300–1).

*Stated in this form, however, the thesis is incoherent: if the
heterogeneity between psyche and society were as complete as
Castoriadis suggests in these, his most extreme formulations, the
socialization process would not simply be violent, it would be
impossible.* In this respect, there exists a tension between the heterogeneity thesis and Castoriadis's use of the doctrine of *anaclisis*. At
the same time as he asserts the essential heterogeneity between psyche
and society he also asserts – *as he must* – that the social order '"leans
on" the being of the psyche' (p. 298). *But this would mean that there
is already something immanent in the monad upon which socializa-*

tion can lean, that is, it is not the absolute other of society. And, indeed, this follows from Castoriadis's anti-Kantian use of *anaclisis* as a central doctrine of his entire philosophy: in order for any region of being to lean-on another, we must posit something within the second region which, while '*not* thoroughly or ultimately *congruent*' with the first, nevertheless '*lends itself to*' that *anaclisis* (p. 273). Concerning our topic, Castoriadis never, however, adequately theorizes that element within the psyche that 'lends itself to' socialization.

Empirically, as it were, the break-up of the monad commences at the point where hunger first announces itself into the monad. However, hunger, in and of itself, 'explain[s] nothing, for the "canonical" response to need is hallucination and phantasmatic satisfaction,' (p. 302). To illustrate the relative strength and independence of the imaginatory factor in this context, Castoriadis adduces the example of anorexia: 'To be sure, the imagination does not provide calories and if nothing else were to take place the infant would die – as indeed he does die as a result of his imagination and despite the food he is offered, if he is anorexic' (ibid.). Somewhat ironically, the example of anorexia points to the very difficulties in Castoriadis's position I have been attempting to bring out. For if he has not located something within the monad which makes it capable of opening up to and registering external reality, he cannot explain how hallucinatory wish fulfilment is ever renounced.[19] To be fair, this is not a problem just for Castoriadis, but one he shares with no less a figure than Freud, who begins with an equally monadic starting point. Freud could never explain how a 'psychical apparatus' operating according to the pleasure principle alone could renounce hallucinatory wish fulfilment and 'decide to form a conception of the real circumstances in the external world and endeavour to make a real alteration in them'. A psyche operating only according to the pleasure principle cannot decide anything.[20]

There is, however, a less extreme formulation in Castoriadis where he does not assert that psyche and society are radically heterogeneous, but only that the psyche 'can never generate' sociability 'out of itself', which is a different story indeed. The more extreme formulation is the result of a faulty inference from the weaker one: Castoriadis wants to conclude from the fact 'that the psyche's entry into society could never occur *gratuitously*' (*IIS*, p. 311) that the psyche is 'in no way "predestinated" by nature' for socialization. All that follows, however, from the fact that psyche can never autochtonously generate a socialized individual out of itself is only that a 'facilitating environment'[21] is necessary for socialization to unfold. Indeed, there are passages in Castoriadis himself which deny the inherent asociability of the psyche: 'This is the history of the psyche in the course of which the psyche alters itself and opens itself to the social-historical world, depending too, on its own work and its own creativity' (p. 300). This statement presupposes the existence of a potentiality immanent in the psyche – dare we say an *Anlage?* – which not only 'lends itself to' socialization but which can 'support and induce it' as well. I believe Castoriadis could not incorporate the significance of these *Anlagen* which lend themselves to socialization into his theory, as he should have, for two reasons. The first is the general hostility in the French psychoanalytic tradition (both Lacanian and non-Lacanian) towards American psychoanalysis:[22] ego *Anlagen* constitute one of the central topics of ego psychology. The second is his commitment to the monadic starting point, which he apparently feels he has to defend in a radical form in order to defend, in turn, the autonomy and creativity of the radical imagination.

III

For Castoriadis, then, the starting point is monadic isolation, and the 'great enigma' which has to be accounted for 'once we find ourselves within . . . the imaginary-representative magma of the unconscious' is 'the emergence of separation' (*IIS*, pp. 276, 301). *He begins with isolation and asks how communication is possible.* Starting from within an *originary* and *irreducible* 'representive/affective/intentional flux' (p. 274) of the unconscious, Castoriadis must, like Freud, explain both how that self-enclosed stream of representations could possibly communicate with an extrapsychic reality which is heterogeneous to it, and also how those images could be translated into words. Habermas's starting point is precisely the opposite: *he begins with the fact of communication and asks how it can become deformed into the privatized unconscious*; for Habermas, in short, the unconscious is a *derivative* phenomenon.

Habermas's criticisms of Castoriadis could have been predicted on the basis of his interpretation of Freud in *Knowledge and Human Interests*, where he emphatically rejects the distinction between word-presentations and thing-presentations and *ipso facto* the existence of a non-linguistic unconscious consisting in a stream of imagistic representations: 'Now the distinction between word-presentations and asymbolic ideas is problematic, and the assumption of a non-linguistic substratum in which these ideas severed from language are "carried out", is unsatisfactory.'[23] This rejection, in turn, is closely connected with one of the central theses of his Freud interpretation, namely, that repression is an intralinguistic phenomenon in and through which the unconscious is constituted. Habermas bases this thesis on the fact that repression is undone and the unconscious is translated to consciousness in the actual process of psychoanalysis.[24] He argues that 'the ego's flight from itself is an operation that is carried out in and with language. Otherwise it would not be possible to reverse the defensive process hermeneutically, via the analysis of language.'[25] Habermas conceives of repression as a process of *excommunication*. When, in the course of development, 'the infantile ego' is confronted with the social prohibition of forbidden wishes personified in the form of frightening parental figures, it has no choice, because of its inherent weakness, but to take 'flight from itself and objectivate itself in the id'.[26] (To the detriment of his analysis, Habermas does not systematically distinguish between the unconscious and the id.) This flight consists in the excommunication of the representation of those wishes from public, intersubjective communication through their degrammaticization and privatization: 'The psychically most effective way to render undesired need dispositions harmless is to *exclude from public communication the interpretations to which they are attached*.'[27]

As a psychic realm, the unconscious is constituted as the repository for all those excommunicated *qua* distorted, degrammaticized and privatized representations, and, as such, assumes the character of an internal foreign territory. Its foreignness, however, is only *relative* and not *absolute*, for, despite the distortions, it remains essentially a linguistic domain.'[28] 'The communication between the two systems', as Freud called it,[29] is for Habermas, *in principle* at least, not a problem; whatever *technical* difficulties such translation may present, the talking cure consists in the regrammaticization of those excommunicated but *essentially linguistic* representations and their reintegration into public communication.

Habermas's commitment to the linguistic position is so strong that he is *compelled to eliminate systematically the existence of any putatively prelinguistic phenomena by assimilating their apparent prelinguisticality to the linguistic*. This strategy is evident in the following passage, which is not only so inaccurate as to be almost bizarre, but which also points to the fundamental difficulty with Habermas's approach:

> Only in the medium of language is the heritage of man's natural history articulated in the form of interpreted needs: the heritage of a plastic impulse potential, which, while pre-oriented in libidinal and aggressive directions, is otherwise undefined, owing to its uncoupling from inherited motor activity. On the human level, instinctual demands are represented *by interpretations, that is, by hallucinatory wish-fulfillments*.[30]

In this passage, Habermas's Kantianism is in full view. Remaining squarely on this side of language, he wants to maintain that, as we only encounter the drives *qua* interpreted, that is, from within the web of intersubjectivity, it is meaningless to refer to a preinterpreted inner nature. Freud's entire drive theory, however, consisted precisely in the attempt, if not to theorize inner nature *an sich*, at least to theorize the *'frontier'* (*Grenze*)[31] between soma and psyche (not to mention the frontier between the image and the word). Indeed, it would not be excessive to assert, as Grossman has,[32] that Freud was essentially a theorist of frontiers; and, as Hegel already argued against Kant, to attempt to determine the limit of a frontier is already to cross over it.

Habermas, in contrast, rather than theorizing the frontier between the prelinguistic and the linguistic, that is, rather than theorizing the coming-to-be of language, extends the web of intersubjectivity so far as to incorporate the prelinguistic into it; hence the strange equation of hallucinatory wish fulfilments with interpretations (the most that could possibly be said is that they are both *representations*). Were such an equation correct, a central distinction of Freud's entire theoretical construction, namely, between the progressive and regressive functioning of the psyche, would be obliterated. When the psyche operates in a 'progressive' direction, excitation moves towards the 'motor end of the apparatus', and the individual seeks gratification through action in the external, public, linguistically mediated world. Hallucinatory wish fulfilment, however, is the result of the psyche's tendency to work in 'a *backward* direction';[33] excitation moves towards the 'sensory end' of the apparatus, the individual eschews the external world as a source of gratification and seeks pleasure through private, asocial, phantasms. Habermas ignores 'the most general and the most striking psychological characteristic' of a dream (the prototype of hallucinatory wish fulfilment), namely, that 'a thought of something that is wished is represented,' not as a statement, but, pictorially, 'as a scene'.[34] In so far as they are *linguistic, and therefore public and intersubjective*, interpretations are precisely the opposite of pictorial, private and autistic hallucinations. However, if wishes were in fact linguistically interpreted via their hallucinatory representation, as Habermas asserts, they would *ipso facto* be linked with public, culturally defined interpretations and the requirements of his philosophical programme would be met: drive representations would be included in the web of intersubjectivity and 'rooted in the meaning structures of the life-world, no matter how elementary . . .'[35] from the start.

Given the foregoing considerations, Habermas's criticisms of Castoriadis should come as no surprise. He argues that, having posited 'the stream of the imaginary dimension' and the 'monadic core of subjectivity', Castoriadis cannot solve the problem which plagued 'the philosophy of consciousness from Fichte to Husserl', namely, 'the intersubjectivity of social praxis that is compelled to begin from the premise of isolated consciousness'. He proceeds to argue that, in Castoriadis's conception, 'socialized individuals do not enter into intersubjective relationships with one another in any genuine sense of the term.' Ultimately, *and this is Habermas's main point*, 'Castoriadis cannot provide us with the figure of mediation between the individual and society.' In Castoriadis, the socialized individual remains 'divided into monad and member of society', and 'psyche and society stand in a kind of metaphysical opposition to one another.'[36] As I have already indicated, these criticisms are not entirely unfounded, and I shall return to them below.

For now, however, I would like to point out that the main charge Habermas levels against Castoriadis, namely, that he cannot provide the mediation between individual and society, can itself be turned against Habermas, but from the opposite direction. Habermas himself does not provide a *genuine* account of the mediation of individual and society, because he solves the problem, at least in principle, in advance through the pre-established harmony between *an already linguistic unconscious and an intersubjective social world. The problem of mediation only arises when there is a sufficient difference to be mediated. Habermas, in short, purchases the mediation between psyche and society by deradicalizing Freud's notion of the unconscious.* Habermas is correct in arguing that 'language functions as a kind of transformer'[37] which draws the individual into the intersubjective social world. But it does not do so without a residuum of private in-itselfness – without which we would all be pre-coordinated clones – and it is this residuum that does not adequately appear in Habermas's account.

Adorno, as we know, praised the orthodox psychoanalytic theory of the drives, even with its biologism, for preserving the moment of non-identity between individual and society. And whereas he (as well as Castoriadis), after having dramatized the moment of difference, has difficulty in accounting for the moment of identity between psyche and society, Habermas is in danger of losing sight of the moment of non-identity altogether. Habermas believes he has solved the problem by rejecting Castoriadis's *techne* model of socialization, in which social form is imposed on asocial matter, in favour of a model that views *socialization as simultaneously a process of individuation*:

language has to be conceived of as a medium that both draws each participant in interaction into a community of communication, as one of its members, and at the same time subjects him to an unrelenting compulsion toward individuation. That is to say, the integration of perspectives of speaker, hearer and observer, as well as the intermeshing of this structure with a system of world perspectives that coordinates the object world

with the social and the subjective worlds, are pragmatic presuppositions of a correct use of grammatical sentences in speech
acts.[38]

The concept of individuation employed in this passage remains on
the surface: it consists merely in the *external* Piagetian mapping of
one's viewpoint against a variety of other viewpoints, which is
undoubtedly an important cognitive component of decentring and
individuation. However, it fails to consider the deeper unconscious
meaning of individuation, that is, 'the strain of relating ... self-
representatives and object-representatives ... that no human being is
free from'.[39] As always, Habermas's account 'screens out the
psychodynamics'[40] of the situation. While Habermas may be correct
in arguing that Castoriadis tends to turn the relationship of 'psyche
and society' into a 'kind of metaphysical opposition ...',[41] Habermas
leaves the dimension of private subjective interiority completely
unplumbed.

IV

Habermas's error of equating hallucinations and interpretations
results from the overextension of the translatability thesis. Like all
the linguistic reformulators of Freud, as Ricoeur refers to them,[42]
Habermas argues from the fact that psychoanalysis is a 'talking cure',
that is, that the unconscious can be made conscious via speech, that
the unconscious *must already be linguistic ab initio*. This argument,
while possessing a certain plausibility, *infers too much*: logically, all
that is required to account for the *factum* of the talking cure is the
assumption that the unconscious is *amenable to translation into
words*, not that it is *wholly linguistic at the start*. It does not follow
from the fact that unconscious discourse is *translatable* into conscious
discourse that the unconscious is already linguistic, any more than
the fact that French is *translatable* into English establishes that
French is *already* English: 'That these [unconscious] complexes
should have an affinity for discourse, that they are sayable in principle
is not to be doubted. Therefore the analytic situation itself establishes
a semiotic aspect. . . . But none of this proves that what thus comes
to language – or better, is brought to language – is or must *be*
language.'[43] The central contribution of Habermas and the reformulators has been to elucidate the linguistic dimension of psychoanalysis, that is to say, to elucidate the element of homogeneity between
the two systems which makes the translation from unconscious to
conscious possible. The corresponding shortcoming is to overextend
their discovery and undervalue the moment of heterogeneity between
the two systems.

By simply dismissing thing-representations as 'asymbolic', Habermas fails to make a crucial distinction which would have allowed for a more differential treatment of the problems at hand. Ricoeur, in contrast, makes such a distinction, and the greater subtlety of his Freud interpretation can, in large part, be traced to this fact. Ricoeur distinguishes between 'a signifying power that is operative prior to language', on the one hand, and language *stricto sensu*, which is a subspecies of that larger category of signification, on the other.[44] This allows Ricoeur to account for the moment of both identity and difference in the mediation between unconscious and conscious, private and public. In so far as it is already significant, the pictorial language of the unconscious would be homogeneous with the language *stricto sensu* of consciousness in that it could potentially be translated into the latter. But in so far as it is not yet language *stricto sensu*, and in so far as it requires an enormous amount of *work* by both analyst and analysand to translate the language potential of the unconscious into language *stricto sensu* (a fact that is largely underappreciated by the linguistic reformulators), the language of the unconscious is heterogeneous with the language of consciousness and is separated from it by a bar of repression, that is, by force.[45] Hence, the necessity of economic and dynamic categories.

Castoriadis's problem, then, is precisely the opposite of Habermas's. Because he refuses to theorize adequately the way in which the psyche 'lends itself' to socialization, he cannot ultimately provide the moment of identity in the mediation between psyche and society. In this context, the fact that Castoriadis repeatedly returns to one of the central scandals of Kantian philosophy is suggestive, for, ultimately, he shares Kant's problem.[46] Could Castoriadis's preoccupation with this scandal indicate that he is intuitively struggling with one of the central difficulties of his own thinking under the guise of a discussion of Kant? Kant, in *The Critique of Judgement*, is forced into the embarrassing admission that the fit between the categories of our thinking (and language) and the being-thus of the world rests on no more than a 'lucky accident' (*glücklicher Zufall*);[47] after God could no longer be invoked to underwrite that fit, as he could be in Descartes and Leibniz, it proved impossible to find an equally secure transcendental guarantor for it.[48] While Castoriadis adduces this remarkable admission to rub Kant's nose in the ultimate shortcomings of critical philosophy, a similar criticism can be made of his own position: as long as he completely abstains from examining the 'predestination' of psyche for socialization, the fit between psyche and society also rests on no more than a 'lucky accident'.

Interestingly enough, Freud addresses this question in the final paragraph of *The Future of an Illusion*. Displaying his characteristic impatience with the 'empty abstraction[s]' of perennial philosophy, he provides a rather prosaic answer, which consists of little more than a mix of common sense and Darwinian empiricism. It does, nevertheless, possess a certain plausibility. Freud argues that the attempt 'to discredit scientific endeavour in a radical way, on the ground that' it is tied to the subjective organization of our 'mental apparatus' is mistaken on the following count: the organization of our mental apparatus 'has been developed precisely in the attempt to explore the external world, and it must therefore have realized in its structure some degree of expediency.'[49] In other words, there must be some fit between the organization of our mental apparatus and the world, because that organization has developed in the course of evolution in order to adapt to that world. This idea, of course, became the point of departure for the research programme of the ego psychologists who went on to investigate the 'preadaptiveness' of the psyche to the world.'[50] Much has been made, within both the Frankfurt School and Lacanian psychoanalysis, concerning how this concentration on adaptation provided the theoretical underpinnings for the social and cultural conformism of the American Ego Psychologists who stressed the moment of identity in the mediation between psyche and society to the almost complete exclusion of the moment of difference. And there is undoubtedly truth to this accusation. A conformist attitude, however, need not necessarily follow from a theory of adaptation, and the question of the fit between psyche and society remains unsolved without it or, at least, without an alternative theory to carry the same conceptual load.

In conclusion, in his treatment of the unconscious, Castoriadis is not sufficiently faithful to the anti-Kantian element of his philosophy as it is formulated in the theory of leaning-on. The reason for this is undoubtedly his *legitimate* eagerness to preserve the radicalness of Freud's discovery of the unconscious, which has been softened by almost all the recent interpreters, such as the linguistic reformulators who try to assimilate 'the operations of the unconscious to *secondary* modes of functioning belonging to waking life' (*IIS*, p. 275) and thereby lose its radical distinctiveness. We saw that Castoriadis objected to the excessive 'constitutivism' of both the Kantians and contextualists who view the object as no more than 'amorphous clay' upon which our conceptual/linguistic grids can be imposed at will. But doesn't his notion of the magma, which must be posited at the base of the unconscious and which is approached at the navel of the dream, itself resemble such amorphous clay? 'A magma is that from which one can extract (or in which one can construct) an indefinite number of ensemblist organizations . . .' (*IIS*, p. 343).

Castoriadis does not identify any potentiality towards language and sociability within the magma; it merely passively tolerates their (violent) imposition on it. Ricoeur's 'archaeology of the subject' results in a similar posit at the deepest layer of the psyche, namely, the posit of what he terms 'desire'. And, in fact, the characteristics that Ricoeur ascribes to desire come closer to fulfilling the requirements of Castoriadis's philosophical construction than does Castoriadis's own notion of the magma. For Ricoeur defines desire, 'which is at the origin of language and prior to language', as the 'potency to speech'. If, like the magma, 'desire is the unnameable,' we must nevertheless posit that 'it is turned from the very outset toward language',[51] and can therefore 'support and induce' socialization. Philosophically, this posit of 'potency to speech' provides a minimal notion 'predetermined by nature' which Castoriadis's position requires.

NOTES

1 See Cornelius Castoriadis, *The Imaginary Institution of Society*, trans. Kathleen Blamey (Cambridge, Mass., 1987), pp. 294–9. Hereafter also cited as *IIS*.

2 See Jürgen Habermas, 'Excursus on Cornelius Castoriadis: The Imaginary Institution,' in *The Philosophical Discourse of Modernity: Twelve Lectures*, trans. Frederick Lawrence (Cambridge and Cambridge, Mass., 1987), pp. 327–35.

3 See Habermas, 'Modernity: An Unfinished Project', ch. 1 above; *IIS*, pp. 101ff.

4 Habermas claims to argue for the relative superiority of modern Western rationality over premodern world-views *on strictly formal grounds*, i.e. in terms of the decentration of the modern world-view and its differentiation into cognitive-instrumental, moral-legal and expressive-aesthetic rationality. He hopes thereby to avoid the charge of Eurocentrism, with its imperialist implications, that was levelled against nineteenth-century philosophy of history and classical anthropology. On close inspection, however, Habermas does not praise that differentiation itself on strictly formal grounds, but because it, in turn, makes the achievement of another, more *substantive* good possible, i.e. an 'open society' (which, for the present purposes, we can take as more or less equivalent with an autonomous society). The institutionalization of the differentiation of an external world, a social world and an inner world, and the forms of cognitive-instrumental, moral-legal and expressive-aesthetic cognition which correspond to them, is *a necessary precondition* for the penetration and criticism of the sacred realm which characterizes closed societies. It is the autonomous critique of dogmatic tradition which is structurally impossible in closed societies, and not the formal conditions that make it possible, which is the final value. Furthermore, I would argue that, far from being a formal and 'context-independent standard for the rationality of world-views', the notion of an open society, in so far as it excludes all societies constructed on a sacred core, which is to say, the vast majority of societies that have existed historically, carries with it *enormous substantive content*. While the notion of an open or autonomous society must be defended, the immense problems involved in such a defence cannot be avoided by retreating into formalism. See Jürgen Habermas, *The Theory of Communicative Action*, vol. 1: *Reason and the Rationalization of Society*, trans. Thomas McCarthy (Cambridge, 1984), pp. 61ff.

5 See Cornelius Castoriadis, *Crossroads in the Labyrinth*, trans. Kate Soper and Martin Ryle (Cambridge, Mass., 1984), p. xxviii. For a discussion of the concept of elucidation, see Joel Whitebook, 'Review of *Crossroads in the Labyrinth*', *Telos* 63 (Spring 1985), pp. 231ff.

6 Jürgen Habermas, *Knowledge and Human Interests*, trans. Jeremey J. Shapiro (Cambridge, 1972), chs 10, 11, 12.

7 See Albrecht Wellmer, 'Communication and Emancipation: Reflections on the Linguistic Turn in Critical Theory', in John O'Neill (ed.), *On Critical Theory* (New York, 1976), pp. 231–62.

8 It is significant that the excursus on Castoriadis immediately follows a chapter entitled 'An Alternative Way out of the Philosophy of the Subject: Communicative versus Subject-Centered Reason'.

9 See Joel Whitebook, 'The Problem of Nature in Habermas', *Telos* 40 (Summer 1979), pp. 41–69, and Jürgen Habermas, 'A Reply to my Critics', in John Thompson and David Held (eds), *Habermas: Critical Debates* (Cambridge, Mass., 1982), pp. 238ff.

10 This particular argument, as well as much of the current paper, was anticipated in Joel Whitebook, 'Reason and Happiness: Some Psychoanalytic Themes in Critical Theory', in Richard Bernstein (ed.), *Habermas and Modernity* (Cambridge, 1985), pp. 151ff. It is also interesting to note that, according to Castoriadis, the two topics which 'radically question inherited logic and ontology' and demand new, radicalized forms of thinking are 'the auto-organization of living organisms and the unconscious', i.e. biology and psychoanalysis. These are two areas where the application of Habermas's philosophical programme, I would say, has not produced the most conspicuous successes. *IIS*, p. 340.

11 'Appendix: Knowledge and Human Interests: A General Perspective', in Habermas, *Knowledge and Human Interests*, p. 314.

12 *IIS*, p. 333.

13 Cornelius Castoriadis, 'Modern Science and Philosophical Interrogation', in *Crossroads in the Labyrinth*, pp. 168–9. Thus, whereas Castoriadis's 'refutation of contextualism' proceeds through reference to the being-thus of the extracontextual object, Habermas's remains strictly within the circle of transcendental intersubjectivity and operates completely on this side of language. That is, Castoriadis attempts to refute the insurpassability of the context by demonstrating the necessary being-thus of an extracontextual object to which contextual framework can refer. Habermas, on the other hand, attempts to show that the *factum* of human communication as such indicates the existence of universal validity claims, specific to each domain of cognition, which transcend all particular contextual schemes. The refutation of contextualism thus would be achieved exclusively by way of the consensus achieved *by the communication community in referring to the object*, that is, completely from this side of language and independently from the object.

14 In this respect, he is close to Adorno, who, despite his modernistic, postmetaphysical consciousness which bars access to the object, nevertheless – with his notion of 'the preponderance of the object' – continually strained to reach it. Indeed, this can be viewed as the central tension animating his entire philosophy.

15 Habermas, *Knowledge and Human Interests*, p. 214. This emphasis on the 'scientific' side of Freud, rather than on his discovery of the unconscious, is fully consistent with the particular way Habermas defends modernity. As

has often been pointed out, Habermas does not primarily formulate his defence in terms of aesthetic modernism, but in terms of the threefold differentiation of rationality, of which aesthetic modernism (i.e. the aesthetic-expressive sphere) is but a subordinate moment. Habermas does not emphasize the restless, explosive, experimental moment of aesthetic modernism and the avant garde, what McCarthy terms 'radical experience' – which would correspond to the discovery of the unconscious – but the greater differentiation of Reason. In this respect, Castoriadis's concentration on the radical imagination incorporates more of the impulses of aesthetic modernism. See Tom McCarthy, 'Introduction', in *The Philosophical Discourse of Modernity*, p. viii, and Martin Jay, 'Habermas and Modernism', in Bernstein (ed.), *Habermas and Modernity*, pp. 125–39.

16 Castoriadis, *Crossroads in the Labyrinth*, p. xx. Castoriadis's notion of the radical imagination can be compared to Hannah Arendt's notion of natality, which she too uses to combat historical determinism and account for the possibility of radically new beginnings in history. See Hannah Arendt, *The Human Condition* (Chicago, 1958).

17 Jean Laplanche and Jean-Baptiste Pontalis, *The Language of Psychoanalysis*, trans. Donald Nicholson-Smith (New York, 1973), pp. 29–32.

18 Castoriadis 'Modern Science and Philosophical Interrogation', pp. 217ff.

19 Beginning with the posit of primary autism, Castoriadis is shackled with all the insoluble dilemmas which confronted Freud's notion of primary narcissism, and which are, as Laplanche has argued, simply the insurmountable aporia of Cartesian solipsism recast in psychoanalytic terms. On the assumption of a totally closed, monadic starting point, with complete and utter irrelation between internal consciousness and the external world, there is no way out: it is as impossible for Freud to distinguish between perceptions and hallucinations as it was for Descartes to distinguish between veridical and adventitious ideas. See Jean Laplanche, *Life and Death in Psychoanalysis*, trans. Jeffrey Mehlman (Baltimore, 1976), pp. 70ff.

20 Sigmund Freud, 'Formulations on the Two Principles of Mental Functioning', in *Standard Edition of the Complete Psychological Works of Sigmund Freud*, ed. James Strachey (London, 1953–74) vol. 12, p. 219. This problem, stated in psychological terms, is exactly parallel to the central problem of social contract theory. A group of individuals living in a state of nature would never have the structures available to them to enter into a contract. Just as the 'decision' to form a contract and enter into an institution presupposes the existence of institutions, so the 'decision' to renounce the pleasure principle and recognize reality principles already presupposes the renunciation of the pleasure principle.

21 See D. W. Winnicott, *The Maturational Process and the Facilitating Environment: Studies in the Theory of Emotional Development* (New York, 1974), pp. 223, 239.

22 See Marion Michel Oliner, *Cultivating Freud's Garden in France* (Northvale, New Jersey, 1988), p. 13.

23 Habermas, *Knowledge and Human Interests*, p. 241.

24 'How are we to arrive at a knowledge of the unconscious? It is of course only as something conscious that we know it, after it has undergone transformation or translation into something conscious. Psycho-analytic work shows us every day that translation of this kind is possible.' Sigmund Freud, 'The Unconscious', in *Standard Edition*, vol. 14, p. 166.

25 Habermas, *Knowledge and Human Interests*, p. 241. For the purposes of this chapter, I must leave aside the critical question of whether Habermas, or any of the linguistic reinterpreters of Freud for that matter, can adequately account for the dynamic, economic and affective elements involved in analysis, e.g. working-through, within the theoretical confines of their linguistic reformulations.
26 Ibid., p. 258.
27 Ibid., pp. 223–34.
28 In its broad outlines, Habermas's position invites a comparison with Lacan's. Not only does the latter maintain that the unconscious is essentially a linguistic entity, but he also argues that only a sophisticated linguistic theory, which was unavailable to Freud, can overcome the anachronisms in Freud's theorizing, rid psychoanalysis of biologism and place it on firm methodological foundations. The linguistic theories that Habermas enlists, hermeneutics and universal pragmatics, are, of course, different from the one to which Lacan turned, i.e. structuralism. See Habermas, *Knowledge and Human Interests*, p. 241.
29 Freud, 'The Unconscious', p. 190.
30 Habermas, *Knowledge and Human Interests*, p. 239 (emphasis added).
31 See Sigmund Freud, 'Instincts and their Vicissitudes', in *Standard Edition*, vol. 14, p. 122.
32 William Grossman, 'Hierarchies, Boundaries and Representation in a Freudian Model Organization', Thirty-first Sandor Rado Lecture, Columbia Psychoanalytic Institute, 7 June 1988 (unpublished).
33 Sigmund Freud, *The Interpretation of Dreams*, in *Standard Edition*, vol. 5, p. 534.
34 Ibid.
35 Habermas, *Knowledge and Human Interests*, p. 256.
36 Habermas, *The Philosophical Discourse of Modernity*, pp. 333–4.
37 Jürgen Habermas, 'A Postscript to *Knowledge and Human Interests*', *Philosophy of the Social Sciences* 3 (1970), p. 170.
38 Habermas, *The Philosophical Discourse of Modernity*, p. 334.
39 D. W. Winnicott, 'Transitional Objects and Transitional Phenomena', in *Through Paediatrics to Psycho-Analysis*, ed. Masud Khan (London, 1958), p. 240.
40 Jürgen Habermas, 'Moral Development and Ego Identity', *Communication and the Evolution of Society*, trans. Thomas McCarthy (Boston, 1979; Cambridge, 1991), p. 91.
41 Habermas, *The Philosophical Discourse of Modernity*, p. 334.
42 See Paul Ricoeur, 'Image and Language in Psychoanalysis', in *Psychoanalysis and Language: Psychiatry and the Humanities*, vol. 3, ed. Joseph Smith (New Haven, 1978), p. 303. Ricoeur includes Lacan, Edelson, Chomsky and Katz in his list, and I would add Schafer and Habermas.
43 Ibid., p. 312.
44 Paul Ricoeur, *Freud and Philosophy: An Essay on Interpretation*, trans. Denis Savage (New Haven, 1970), pp. 398–9. See also Ricoeur, 'Image and Language in Psychoanalysis', pp. 314ff.
45 See Ricoeur, *Freud and Philosophy*, pp. 400ff, and 'Image and Language in Psychoanalysis', p. 312.
46 See *IIS*, p. 342, *Crossroads in the Labyrinth*, p. 169, and 'The Greek Polis and the Creation of Democracy', *Graduate Faculty Philosophy Journal* 9 (Fall 1982), p. 85.

47 Immanuel Kant, *The Critique of Judgement*, trans. J. C. Meredith (Oxford, 1952), p. 23.
48 Kant, of course, finally smuggled God in through the back door as a postulate of pure practical reason.
49 Sigmund Freud, *The Future of an Illusion*, in *Standard Edition*, vol. 21, p. 55.
50 See Heinz Hartmann, 'On the Reality Principle', in *Essays on Ego Psychology* (New York, 1964), p. 264. See also, of course, Heinz Hartmann, *Ego Psychology and the Problem of Adaptation*, trans. David Rapaport (New York, 1961).
51 Ricoeur, *Freud and Philosophy*, pp. 455–7.

PART II

THEMATIC REFORMULATIONS

7

TWO VERSIONS OF THE LINGUISTIC TURN: HABERMAS AND POSTSTRUCTURALISM

James Bohman

In *The Philosophical Discourse of Modernity*, Jürgen Habermas provides a rich and complex defence of modern universal reason against its antimodern and postmodern detractors. Unlike his earlier essays on the 'unfinished project of modernity', his criticisms here are primarily philosophical and only indirectly political. He argues that a conception of communicative action and intersubjectivity provides the only real way out of the 'philosophy of consciousness' and 'subject-centred reason'. At the same time, he demonstrates how thoroughly postmodernism repeats many nineteenth-century mistakes in its total rejection of reason and its abstract negation of modernity. Particularly convincing are Habermas's identification and criticism of the underlying assumptions of anti-Enlightenment thinking from Nietzsche and Heidegger through Derrida and Foucault. In analysing the Nietzschean search for the 'other' of reason – whether identified as life, art, Being, the other, the body or *différance* – the strength of Habermas's historical argument is to show systematically the remarkable continuity of postmodernism with previous totalizing criticisms of modern subjectivist forms of rationality.[1] The argument that emerges in this historical presentation of the 'counterdiscourse' to modernity is complex, multi-faceted and often pointedly polemical. Habermas discovers many simple conceptual confusions, unwarranted logical implications and false empirical generalizations, as well as standard self-referential contradictions underlying all of postmodern scepticism and its 'totalizing', rather than dialectical, critique of modern Enlightenment reason.

But is there an underlying, philosophical basis that unifies Habermas's diverse criticisms of poststructuralism? Both sides of the dispute reject the 'philosophy of consciousness' and take a linguistic turn of sorts: in the one case, in order to underwrite a revised version of

Kantian regulative ideals; and in the other case, in order to deepen
the sceptical predicament of modern universal reason. I shall argue,
first, that it is this disagreement about the turn to language and
meaning that is fundamental to *The Philosophical Discourse of
Modernity*, and second, that the basis of most of Habermas's
arguments against various poststructuralists is his pragmatic theory
of meaning and its notion of interpretation.[2] Habermas's dispute
with poststructuralism turns on the character of 'the linguistic turn'
and the role of 'world-disclosure' within it. Surprisingly, behind the
polemical surface, his argument often makes remarkable concessions
to this alternative version of the linguistic turn as he tries to overcome
the false antinomy behind much of the debate: the tension between a
holistic and historical notion of disclosure and a pragmatic and
presentist theory of speaker's meaning.

Habermas undermines the false antinomies that are at the heart of
postmodernist criticisms of the philosophy of language in two ways:
first, he makes world-disclosure one of the 'functions' of language;
and second, he tries to tame it philosophically by confining it to the
delimited cultural domain of art and aesthetic experience. I shall
argue that both of these lines of argument are neither entirely
successful nor fully consistent with Habermas's own philosophy of
language. The problem is that Habermas's deeper concessions do not
sufficiently enrich his philosophy of language in ways that they might.
The difficulty is that he is too quick to limit his own concept of
disclosure, primarily because of its implications for meaning and
agency. But disclosure can be delimited by an entirely different, more
powerful argument than the one Habermas gives: rather than link
disclosure to art, it has to do with meaning, that is, with conditions
for making true utterances and statements rather than with truth
itself. Once a clearer demarcation and connection between validity
and disclosure is established, Habermas has nothing to lose in simply
accepting some of those broader implications which he fears for the
theory of meaning. Indeed, this broader pragmatic theory of meaning,
with weaker connections between meaning and validity, would
enable Habermas to make stronger arguments against the philosophically inflated versions of world-disclosure that underpin all of
poststructuralist scepticism.

My aim here is to reconstruct both Habermas's criticisms of the
poststructuralist conception of world-disclosure and his indirect,
positive appropriation of it. The reconstruction has three steps. In
the first section, I will consider the central role that disclosure plays
in Habermas's arguments against poststructuralism: after showing
the parallels between the Heideggerian and poststructuralist concepts,
Habermas then deflates disclosure and delimits its scope to art in
general and fictional discourse in particular. I shall argue that the

second, demarcating step of this main argument is unconvincing and does not effectively address the main issues at stake in making room for disclosure and innovation in pragmatics. In the second section, I shall return to Derrida's deconstruction of literal meaning and discuss the problems that it raises for pragmatics. These criticisms are instructive in that they show the need to distinguish between disclosure as a type of language use and as a level of reflection in language. Rhetoric and non-literal expression can play a reflective role in overcoming rigid cultural interpretations and in disclosing new ones. In the third section, I turn to Habermas's discussion of Foucault's archaeology for the next step of my positive reconstruction. Properly reinterpreted without Heideggerian confusions and as a hermeneutic theory of truth candidates, Foucault's archaeology helps us understand the role of disclosure in analysing and overcoming various forms of interpretive failure, including those in historical and cross-cultural comparisons. Properly interpreted, disclosure helps us to understand freedom and innovation after the linguistic turn.

Limiting World-Disclosure to Art: Habermas's Humboldtian Argument against Poststructuralism

In its original sense, world-disclosure was the central category of an entire tradition of the continental philosophy of language and of the social theory of meaning, beginning with von Humboldt and Herder.[3] It is only with Heidegger that it becomes the basis of an alternative conception of truth as *aletheia*. While Heidegger certainly based his conception of truth on a strong interpretation of some ill-defined practical-linguistic constitution of the world, truth and meaning are entirely separable in Humboldtian analysis of language and culture. There is no reason why we cannot accept world-disclosure in the constitutive features of social language use while at the same time holding some entirely different theory of truth. In other words, we can (and should) separate Humboldt from Heidegger. This is precisely Habermas's main strategy in arguing against poststructuralism, particularly against both Derrida and Foucault, who do not seem to be aware of such a possibility. He hopes thereby to undercut the force of poststructuralist objections to the theory of meaning by incorporating a more restricted and tamer Humboldtian notion of world-disclosure into formal pragmatics. Disclosure, Habermas wants to argue, is not an omnipresent and determining feature of a language, but instead is domain and site specific. In modern culture, it is explicit only in the aesthetic sphere. This argument for demarcating a limited domain of art as a way of incorporating world-disclosure into a theory of meaning is, I believe, more a fatal concession than an effective counterargument.

What does it mean for a language to constitute and hence to 'disclose' a world? Although it is in part Habermas's somewhat idiosyncratic interpretation of poststructuralism to see its diverse thinkers in terms of this concept, a brief history of the concept shows why it is so significant. In *Truth and Method*, Gadamer credits von Humboldt with freeing the anthropology of language from the 'dogmatism of the grammarians', precisely by recognizing that each among the plurality of human languages discloses its own 'world'. As Gadamer puts Humboldt's insight: 'Language is not just one of the many human possessions in the world; rather, on it depends the fact that human beings have a *world* at all.'[4] Such a world is an already articulated and shared orientation and interpretation of the world, which is independent of individuals and into which each of us is socialized. But this very notion of a whole language or culture 'disclosing' a world gives rise to a problem, a problem that Heidegger tries to resolve in the second phase of the development of the concept: if everything is experienced within such a linguistic-cultural world, how are innovations, new facts, values or interpretations possible?

To answer this question, Heidegger introduces the problematic of truth into the concept of disclosure. The world constituted by language in Humboldt's sense is dependent on a more primordial sense of disclosure, which, although still present in the exceptional case of poetry, has 'already happened unnoticed in language'.[5] Art is the special activity of ongoing and explicit disclosure, in that it 'lets truth originate'. If a language already discloses the world, art is more primordial in that it establishes truth, 'by bringing forth a being such as never was before and will never come to be again'.[6] In this strong contrast between poetry and ordinary language, we see that truth is disclosure in a special sense, an event within which new possibilities open up. Heidegger goes beyond the Humboldtian notion of the linguistic articulation and constitution of the world; on its basis, he constructs a theory of truth as an event, a disclosure of 'new' entities that is sometimes so profound that it transforms the linguistic world and 'founds' a new one and, with it, a new cultural destiny.

It is precisely this Heideggerian identification of disclosure with truth that is an assumed premise of the poststructuralist arguments that he is challenging. Habermas points out the impersonal, fateful character of the history of Being, as one truth event after another, in which human agency is part of the 'will of planetary domination' and truth merely the 'will to knowledge'. Conceiving of truth as disclosure is central to Heidegger's attempt to overcome the humanism of modern subjectivity in ethics and epistemology.

But along with 'subjectivism' and 'humanism', Heidegger and Heideggerians also jettison critical reflection on our supposed 'destiny': disclosures are simply self-verifying and overwhelming. Furthermore, to the degree that 'every truth is also primordially untruth,' they cannot be justified from any critical standpoint outside of their own determining-limiting horizon of truth. In this way, world-disclosure is 'raised above any and every critical forum: The luminous force of world-disclosing language is hypostatized' (*PDM*, p. 154). According to Habermas, this hypostatization depends on a crucial equivocation in Heidegger's argument. Heidegger has simply reversed the relative priority of disclosure and justification: as a condition of truth, 'the horizon of the understanding of meaning brought to bear on beings is not prior to, but rather subordinate to, the question of truth' (ibid.). Heidegger has made a basic error of transcendental argumentation: he has confused the conditions of possibility of truth, which are themselves neither true nor false, with truth itself. Without some possibility of critical justification, truth events can have no authority proper to them. Heidegger 'transfers the epistemic authority proper to the validity of truth to the process of the formation and transformation of world-disclosing horizons. The conditions making truth possible can themselves be neither true nor false, and yet a paravalidity is ascribed to the process of their changing' (*PDM*, p. 255).

World disclosure acquires 'paravalidity' in two senses: it now resembles validity (as parapsychology resembles psychology) and makes a claim on those who undergo it; but it is also a form of extraordinary validity, one that determines and goes beyond ordinary truth. But this extraordinary validity is possible at all only if meaning determines validity in some strong sense. Thus all ordinary standards, including reflective standards of justification (or 'correctness'), must be relativized to the constitutive and concealed horizon of a disclosure.[7] This claim about concealment cannot itself, however, escape problems of self-reference. Such a limiting-concealing horizon and its paravalidity becomes the 'concrete historical a priori' of Foucault's archaeology or 'Western metaphysics' in deconstruction, each with their own claims of determinate limitation. Historicist descriptions of these changes in the conditions of truth replace reflective justification for the Heideggerian critics of modernity, while extraordinary truth events beyond the tribunal of critical judgement replace ordinary epistemic validity and reasoning.

The transcendental fallacy underlying the identification of truth with disclosure can be put in an even stronger way than Habermas does. A related error common to both Heidegger and poststructuralism is the claim that world-disclosing horizons somehow limit truth claims in some determinate way. Rather, they are always *both* enabling, with limiting conditions.[8] Such limits are established only from a mysterious third-person, observer perspective on changes in the limiting cultural conditions of truth in the 'history of metaphysics' or 'discursive formations'. Against such Heideggerian historicism, Habermas insists that the real recognition of the finite, conditioned character of human knowing would lead to the recognition of the inevitability of a participant, first-person perspective on understanding meaning. Here Habermas effectively makes common cause with Gadamer and turns the inevitability of the hermeneutic circle against the later Heidegger and poststructuralists. This hermeneutic argument plays a large role in Habermas's criticism of both Derrida and Foucault.

The next step in Habermas's argument is to show that these same Heideggerian fallacies underlie poststructuralist claims about language and culture. This step is easy work, since for Habermas disclosure in our two senses (as truth event and meaning horizon) is everywhere in poststructuralist writings. Indeed, Habermas's interpretation shows how a variety of poststructuralist concepts do the same work as Heideggerian disclosure in Derrida, Foucault and Castoriadis. It is easy to see the twin errors that I have just outlined in Habermas's criticism of all ontologies of language: the ontological difference between the constitutive 'metahistorical' understanding of the world and what is constituted in the world, between the ontic perspective of practical agents and the ontological perspective of deconstructive philosophers.

> This constitutive world-understanding [an understanding of the world as a concrete a priori] changes independently of what subjects experience concerning conditions in the world interpreted in the light of this preunderstanding, and independently of what they can *learn* from their practical dealings with anything in the world. No matter whether this metahistorical transformation of linguistic world views is conceived of as Being, différance, power, or imagination ... What all these concepts have in common is the peculiar uncoupling of the horizon-constituting productivity of language from the consequences of an intramundane practice ... Any interaction between world-disclosing language and learning processes in the world is excluded. (*PDM*, p. 319)

This long quotation shows not only the remarkable unity of Habermas's criticisms of all the poststructuralists, but also the positive task that is the next step of his argument. Given that his own version of hermeneutics is highly cognitive and evaluative, Habermas next needs to show how world-disclosure can interact with learning processes, in order to reconnect it to critical judgement and learning, to agency and truth. He makes this connection by giving disclosure its own linguistic function and then limiting its role in learning to art. In this last step, Habermas's argument is unnecessarily restrictive as well as inconsistent with his own theory of meaning.

Before his encounter with poststructuralism, Habermas followed Buehler in outlining three basic 'functions' or types of uses of language. This schema follows from the three minimal elements of any utterance: that a speaker says something to a hearer.[9] He now speaks of world-disclosure as a distinct function and has even chastised Peirce's semiotics in a recent essay for ignoring it altogether.[10] World-disclosure is roughly equivalent in *The Philosophical Discourse of Modernity* to Jakobson's 'poetic function', the metalinguistic relation to the message aspect of speech. The poetic function is thus not limited to poetry and is indeed 'always fulfilled together with other linguistic functions' (*PDM*, p. 200), as is also the case with the simultaneous presence of all linguistic functions for Habermas. The pure case of speech acts of this type for Habermas is literary fiction, marked by 'the suspension of illocutionary force' and the release from relations to the actual world and its pressure to coordinate social action (pp. 200–2).

Whatever the merit of this analysis of fictional discourse, it seems inconsistent with the general thrust of Habermas's own arguments against poststructuralism. First, it implies that there is some sharp distinction between world-disclosure and the other, illocutionary-action coordinating functions of language, a separation Habermas explicitly rejects in his criticism of Heidegger's ontological difference. Such fictional speech acts would be entirely exceptional and extraordinary, since in all other cases Habermas argues that *all* functions of language are operative at once. Second, with the release of such disclosure from 'the relation to the world', it is still unclear how disclosure is to be related once again to 'innerworldly learning'.[11] Nor does this analysis of fictional discourse give any clue as to how ordinary language might have a world-disclosive function. By Habermas's own argument surely it must, since, as we already saw in his argument against Heidegger, 'world-disclosure' in ordinary language has been made an enabling condition of possibility for any true statement whatsoever. The suspension of relations to the world and of the action situation are better seen as continuous with Habermas's well-developed analysis of second-order communication, or discourses. Such virtualization of context in discourse is part of the everyday reflective and expressive capacities of competent speakers, not restricted to special qualities of art or poetry.

The appeal to art as a unique location or domain of world-disclosure fares no better, especially if, on a pragmatic interpretation, disclosure in a broad sense is a cultural condition of possibility of truth. Habermas's analogy between art and other culturally differentiated spheres of knowledge in modernity simply fails him here, since there are no specialized validity claims or forms of argumentation in art that correspond with the 'function' of disclosure. It also seems difficult to isolate world-disclosure as a distinct activity. If the point of Habermas's criticism of Heidegger is to debunk any extraordinary events and to make disclosure ordinary again, it is hard to know how 'art and literature' are supposed to 'administer capacities for world-disclosure' in the same way that morality and science 'administer problem-solving capacities' (*PDM*, p. 207). Art, then, is better seen as a sphere which interacts with all the others. As such, it uses reflective capacities similar to the general and ordinary conditions of discourse rather than unique, specialized or extraordinary capacities. But then the question remains: where does world-disclosure fit in, if not in the aesthetically domesticated and administered confines of Weberian value spheres?

This delimiting step of Habermas's argument fails, although not because poststructuralism gives us a better account of art. What was it meant to accomplish? As we shall see in the next section, it was supposed to resist the reductionist aspects of Derrida's and Foucault's reinterpretations of Heideggerian world-disclosure. Based on the ineliminability of cultural horizons of disclosure, the poststructuralists reduce all language use to rhetoric or power. Habermas's attempt is a plausible counterargument to such levelling and reductionism. If confined to art, disclosure is no longer a plausible basis for such reductionistic views of culture. It is true that Derrida and Foucault have such one-sided and reductionist views of modern culture. However, I want to claim that the aesthetic step in Habermas's argument is not only unnecessary, but it also gives the misleading impression that he has not faced squarely the challenge of the poststructuralist view of language. By recasting his criticism of poststructuralist conceptions of language in light of his decisive criticisms of Heidegger's theory of truth, Habermas can meet these similar challenges. None the less, this reconstruction is not without its cost. It might introduce a wider role for rhetoric in speech, as well as greater recognition of the plurality of cultural worlds and the potential for hermeneutic failures into Habermas's theory of linguistic meaning and understanding.[12] Both are residual problems for Habermas's theory, problems that I think these modifications in the notion of world-disclosure and linguistic constitution resolve in a manner internal to Habermas's overarching theory of meaning and social learning. It is by taking Habermas's criticism of Derrida further that the gains of such a deflationary reinterpretation of disclosure can best be seen.

Rhetoric and Disclosure: Against Deconstruction

In considering his criticisms of Derrida in *The Philosophical Discourse of Modernity*, it is important to emphasize that Habermas rejects two distinct sorts of 'levelling' in the theory of meaning: first, among *types* of speech acts and genres of discourse, such as between philosophy and literature, and second, between *levels* of language use, such as between argumentation and rhetoric. Although the chapter on Derrida is perhaps the least developed in the book, Habermas does effectively employ the general anti-Heideggerian strategies outlined above. Against the deconstruction of Western reason as logocentric, he shows that Derrida clearly employs the same sort of anti-hermeneutic, impersonal world-disclosure as Heidegger.[13] While it is fairly easy to answer Derrida's critique of all genre and type distinctions in pragmatics, Habermas has a more difficult time arguing for distinctions between levels of language use. The problem here is that he changes his critical strategy when he introduces a version of his disclosive view of art, here fiction. Rather than limit disclosure to non-literal or fictional uses of language, Habermas could more effectively undercut Derrida by showing that world-disclosure can itself be assimilated to the domain of rhetoric. It is *one* type of reflective language use among many. As in Derrida's debate with Searle, Habermas somewhat misleadingly frames his own criticisms in terms of the distinction between literal and non-literal meaning, or normal and parasitic uses of language. However, this is only one of the distinctions that Habermas needs to defend here. Habermas's intervention in this argument is interesting, since it provides one of the few instances, other than Lyotard's *Postmodern Condition*, in which a potential deconstructive critique directly aims at the core of Habermas's own philosophical project.

Derrida's first volley against a pragmatic theory of meaning, which he believes shows it to be in the thrall of 'logocentrism', is a criticism of Austin's account of performatives in *How to Do Things with Words*. It has some initial plausibility. It resembles Gilbert Ryle's criticism of the 'use theory of meaning', as well as Strawson's criticism of both intentionalist and conventionalist approaches. How could the meaning of a word be its use, Ryle argued, if each word can be used in a non-denumerable number of sentences, and each sentence in turn in an infinite number of contexts?[14] If this is the case, meaning is context dependent and thus no formal theory of sentence meaning (in which sentences are identical across contexts, or usages) is possible. Derrida makes a similar criticism at the level of utterances, citing 'the iterability of statements', including quotations and theatrical utterances. However, to think that this is a criticism of speech-act theory is to make a serious logical error: unlike Ryle, Derrida's criticism confuses type and token. Speech-act theory, even Austin's conventionalist variety, is a theory of utterance *types*: the mere fact that token identical sentences are uttered in different contexts with different meanings ('I hereby marry you' by an actor in a play, by an official in a ceremony, or in a quotation) is no criticism of the analysis of the identity conditions of utterance meaning. The sentence tokens are not necessarily being used in utterances of the same type: quoting someone's promise and actually uttering a promise to a hearer are entirely different *types* of speech acts (since the former is a report). Such criticism is simply a red herring and gets us no closer to Derrida's ultimate conclusion that these phenomena show that the very idea of speech genres is incoherent or that all discourse is mere rhetoric. The real point here is nothing more than an unsupported and dogmatic scepticism about all abstractions and conceptual analysis as such.[15] Similarly, Derrida's distinct criticisms of intentionalist and conventionalist approaches do not rule out the plausibility of some combination of approaches, as Strawson argues for in his continuum of speech acts.[16] Derrida never considers this possibility.

Even if Derrida's criticisms of Austin were coherent, they would not get him very far towards criticizing either Habermas's or Searle's speech-act theory. For neither theorist are types of speech acts logically primitive for the theory of meaning. It is hard to see why the sorts of phenomena described by Derrida (such as quotation, context dependency, irony and metaphor) would be sufficient to establish the sweeping claims that Derrida makes in light of them: that there are no distinctions of types employed by competent speakers themselves, or that 'every reading is a misreading,' or that 'serious speech is role playing.' Habermas is right to say that Derrida's appeal to these phenomena simply begs the question by failing to provide any analysis of them (*PDM*, p. 195).

But Derrida has one more argument: that because of the pervasiveness of such phenomena as metaphor and indirect speech, different speakers can always understand the same utterances differently. Because of such changes in contexts, written texts in particular can be subject to interpretation of any sort. As Culler puts it, 'If a text can be understood, it can in principle be understood repeatedly by different readers in different circumstances. These acts of reading or understanding are not, of course, identical.'[17] From this fact about the uncontrollability of effective history, it is supposed to follow that 'understanding is a special case of misunderstanding.' As Habermas argues, this is a *non sequitur* on hermeneutic grounds alone: nothing of the sort follows from the fact of the variability of effective history, other than that misunderstanding is always a possibility. As usual, Derrida and Culler tell only half the story of the productivity of understanding. As Gadamer has argued, this same productivity is guided by the ideal of possible agreement, even over historical and cultural distances in the present (*PDM*, p. 198). It is only against the background of some understanding that we can identify what and when we do not understand. Once again, the poststructuralist view of linguistic understanding works only by ignoring such hermeneutic insights and ultimately by adopting an observer perspective on the process of effective history, as an anonymous process of world-disclosure without agents. From this third-person perspective, the effective history of interpretations of a text may well be a random process. From the perspective of agents engaged in interpretation, however, it is constrained by various idealizing presuppositions and epistemic constraints, including the identity of shared meanings and some minimal possibility of ongoing agreement in interpretations.

This epistemological shift to the actor's perspective allows Habermas to make his final criticism of the attempt to collapse the notion of literal meaning into sheer indeterminacy. Not only does Derrida confuse type and token identity, according to Habermas, he begs the question concerning literal meaning by absurdly considering ordinary speech to be a specific *type* of discourse rather than a *level* or mode of communication. Literal meanings are to be found in everyday speech, in which speech is 'binding' on actors in coordinating their actions with each other. Austin's whole analysis is an attempt to specify the conditions under which this 'illocutionary binding force' operates in everyday practice as a mechanism for coordinating action. These constraints define 'the domain of "normal" language' and 'can be analyzed as the kinds of idealizing assumptions we have to make in communicative action' (*PDM*, p. 196). Among these idealizing and constraining assumptions is literal meaning, understood not as something fixed and ahistorical, but as the presupposition of intersubjectively identical ascriptions of meaning, an inevitable presupposition if we are to communicate and actually coordinate action in everyday practice. Certainly, these assumptions are 'idealizing' in the sense that they may not, as a matter of fact, be present in actual communication.[18] But in so far as they are made in contexts of ongoing communicative action, other uses of language can be understood as 'parasitic' upon this 'normal' use, as second-order reflection is upon first-order uses.

Although I think Habermas's argument is here basically correct, it would be more consistent for him to say that *some* of these other uses of language are second-order and reflective uses, in which these constraints are 'suspended' or reflectively modified by competent speakers, including literal meaning. For Habermas, literature can be analysed as just such a suspension of the 'pressures' of everyday practice and the assumptions of action coordination. It should also be noted that Habermas's category of 'distorted communication' denotes situations of communication in which ideology or power disrupts these idealizing suppositions and undermines the possibility of communicative success (but not in the sense that communication might not go on).[19] Some sort of analysis of 'normal' conditions of intersubjectively binding communication is necessary in order to develop a contrast to cases of latent power or violence in communicative practice, if these distinctions, too, are not simply to disappear with all others into an anonymous ontology.

If this objection identifies the main difficulty in Derrida's discussion of pragmatics and literal meaning, then it is a small step to see that Habermas's *own* treatment of world-disclosure in art commits a different, but analogous, error. By attempting to limit disclosure to art, Habermas also sees disclosure as a *type* of communication rather than as a *level* of reflective communicative practice. It is remarkable that Habermas does not refer to other forms of second-order communication in his discussion of fiction: all discourses 'suspend' the constraints and pressures of action coordination, precisely in order to test the underlying claims to validity of any first-order communication. If the identification of disclosive suspension of 'the world' with discourse does have the consequences that Habermas deplores in Heidegger's theory of truth, what then could its reflective role be? Disclosure has to do with the role of rhetoric in communication for changing rigid interpretations, for cases of blocked learning and problem-solving, for making interpretive processes fluid when they have come to a standstill, whether by power, ideology or other forms of collective bias.

Such a role is indicated, but not developed explicitly, by Habermas in recent remarks on Peirce's neglect of world-disclosure as a function of language. Problem-solving can run up against cultural-linguistic limits, as Peirce himself noted in his notion of 'blockages in the road of inquiry'. As Habermas puts it:

> In extreme cases we run up against the limits of our understanding, and the interpretations which we use in vain to solve difficult problems come to a standstill. But they become fluid again when familiar facts are seen in a *different* light in a *new* vocabulary, so that the fixated problems can be put in a new and more fruitful way.[20]

Here disclosure is neither a *function* of language nor a *type* of speech nor the provenance of artists or poets; it is described in terms of the *effect* of new vocabularies on the background set of beliefs and interpretations that bring learning and communication to a standstill. Disclosure then designates a certain sort of rhetorical effect on the background assumptions of the hearer, an effect which can be greater or lesser in degree depending on its scope. It may overcome stalled learning processes or problem-solving by showing new ways of looking at things and new patterns of relevance, which in turn may affect a few or a larger set of beliefs. Disclosure then concerns the rhetorical effect of introducing new perspectives and assumptions into the background set of common knowledge, so that the audience of the utterance comes to acquire a new interpretive framework to modify the rigidities of the old one. Should these assumptions be sufficiently in conflict with entrenched existing ones, the whole common world, and not just the initial problem or interpretation, must be repaired or altered.

Social critics in particular engage in this sort of rhetorical activity as they attempt both to disclose things about the initial interpretations of the common world and to recontextualize them in new patterns of relevance. For example, Martin Luther King Jr and others extended the assumptions about constitutional equality relevant to the statement 'all men are created equal' so as to have the effect that the racist 'world' of beliefs and practices was no longer acceptable to large segments of the American public.[21] This racist world was pathologically rigid in its cultural meanings and capacities to solve social problems, and critics expanded currently available forms of meaning, communication and expression. Since unjust critics may 'disclose' their versions of the world as well, we cannot automatically assume that disclosure leads to some new sense of moral responsibility to others.[22] Rather, disclosures must be tested in the discourses in which we reflect upon them, once we are released from rigid interpretive frameworks. But disclosure can *enable* such new truths or moral norms to emerge in the discourses that they make possible in reflection upon the *limits* of the current 'world'. Disclosure then is about relevant meanings and interpretations, not about truth; it is about the reflective capacities of agents to change their cultural context, not about epochal experiences that we passively undergo and submit ourselves to in history.

Disclosure and Truth Candidates: Making Foucault's Archaeology Hermeneutic

Besides many social scientific and empirical objections, Habermas has two basic philosophical criticisms of Foucault. His most extended criticisms here are more internal and involve showing how Foucault himself no more escapes the 'doublets' of transcendental subjectivity than the rest of modern philosophy (when he argues that the intersubjectivity of communicative action does escape these difficulties in Lecture XI). But Habermas's other main line of criticism once again finds the underlying problem of world-disclosure and meaning in Foucault. This is not surprising, since much the same set of hermeneutic arguments can be brought to bear on Foucault's early archaeological analyses of language and discourse as were made against Derrida's deconstruction. As a historian who claims that his historical-archaeological analyses 'eschew all interpretations', Foucault can certainly be criticized with good hermeneutic arguments against his many claims to provide interpretation-free descriptions.[23] As a historicist epistemologist whose analysis of basic changes in the structure of knowledge draws on explicit analogies between epistemes and 'ontologies', he also certainly must be operating implicitly with some concept of disclosures as truth events to explain discontinuities between epochs.[24] As an analyst of discourse, he employs a concept of rules without agents, of 'regularities which regulate themselves'.[25] The archaeological approach is supposedly historical, while leaving utterly unexplained how discourses and practices are to be related in historical cases. Genealogy emerges to fill this gap. This move 'beyond hermeneutics' in yet a different way leads to Habermas's criticism of Foucault's defective social theory, its reductionist methodology and one-sided notion of power. When the all-pervasive panopticon replaces the constitutive force of the disclosure of the modern world in the 'anthropological' episteme in Foucault's totalizing critique of modernity, Foucault has not given his criticisms any better empirical or theoretical warrant.[26]

Habermas traces both archaeology and genealogy back to their common origin in their common critique of metaphysics: to the ontological difference between the world horizons and the things that appear in them. Both world horizons or discourse formations undergo change. But in these changes, Habermas argues, 'they maintain their transcendental power over whatever unfolds within the totalities shaped by them' (PDM, p. 254). For Habermas, this implicit problematic in Foucault explains 'systematic ambiguities' that remain even in his later concept of power, ambiguities between the transcendental constitution of objects and the empirical-historical analysis of contingent events. But Foucault develops the notion one step further by rejecting the 'paravalidity' of Heidegger's identification of truth and disclosure; he 'strips the history of discursive-constitutive rules of any authority based on validity and treats the transformation of transcendentally powerful discourse formations just as conventional historiography treats the ups and downs of political regimes' (PDM, p. 255). Once again, a historicist concept of disclosure underlies an observer perspective (which Foucault calls 'ethnographic distance' in the very odd, structuralist sense of the term) and is disconnected from learning within a horizon by competent, knowledgeable agents. But did Foucault have to think of the relation of disclosure and validity in terms of the ontological difference? Does he have to see the disclosive power of discursive formations as supplying a determinate semantic framework for interpretations of the world? One need only think of the monochrome pictures that Foucault paints of various epistemes as endlessly repeating very simple underlying structures, such as resemblance in the Renaissance and tables in the classical episteme. Is there anything that Foucault might contribute to rethinking the concept of disclosure from a situated actor's perspective?

In a series of articles, Ian Hacking has developed just such an alternative reading of the archaeological aspect of Foucault's project, against his explicit anti-hermeneutic intentions.[27] In such a reading, the disclosive power of discursive formation can be indirectly tied to truth not through the constitution of objects that appear within the world, but instead through cultural possibilities for making true-or-false statements. Such an account of 'truth candidates' could uncover why only certain solutions to problems emerge within certain frameworks, and why interpretation sometimes comes to a standstill, in Habermas's phrase. Such an account of meaning and intelligibility also makes sense of genuine differences among the plurality of cultural worlds in which different statements are candidates for truth. Such an account supplements, rather than contradicts, Habermas's account of meaning and validity, in the same way that viewing disclosure as a form of critical rhetoric supplements, rather than contradicts, his account of literal meaning and discourse.

Habermas's emphasis on the participant's perspective and the irreducibility of the intentional gives him a powerful tool in criticizing poststructuralism, including Foucauldian archaeology. From the participant's perspective, interpretation requires 'taking a position'.[28] But as his treatment of Foucault's archaeology shows, he makes this argument too strong: he sometimes slides from the well-justified claim that the evaluative participant's perspective is necessary and unavoidable in matters of interpretation to the false and unsupported conclusion that a third-person perspective on cultural meanings is impossible. This inference is clearly unwarranted, since such a quasi-objective perspective could be the reflective achievement that builds on the participant's perspective. Once it is suitably reinterpreted by Hacking to eliminate its unnecessary anti-hermeneutic methodology, Foucault's archaeology represents one such social scientific, reflective and objectivating approach to strange and distant cultural expressions that resist hermeneutic work and produce hermeneutic failures. Here what Foucault actually does in his archaeology, and not what he says he does, is helpful in illuminating relations of world disclosure and intelligibility at a reflective level when dealing with difficult comparative work.

The performative stance poses difficulties for cross-cultural and historical comparisons due to these very same inevitable suppositions about the relations between 'our' standards of rationality and 'theirs'. As Davidson puts it, we make others intelligible from this intentional perspective 'only to the extent that we can recognize something like our own reasoning powers at work' as well as our own norms of truth.[29] This sort of ordinary, practical interpretation works well in most cases, particularly for standard intentional actions. The problem is that it makes no allowance for hermeneutic failures. For that reason, it also does not give an adequate account of cross-cultural comparisons. Davidson admits that from within this practical stance there is no clear way to distinguish successful interpretation from mere imposition.

Habermas makes the same epistemological point about the 'performative attitude' in order to undercut any pernicious sceptical consequences for the hermeneutic circle. In such an attitude, the interpreter inevitably takes a position vis-à-vis the validity of the reasons that others give for their utterances or to justify their actions. Given this consequence of the situated character of social scientific knowledge, Habermas puts the comparative element of social scientific interpretation across cultural and historical distance in the strongest possible terms: 'An interpreter cannot, therefore, interpret expressions connected through criticizable validity claims with a potential of reasons (and thus represent knowledge) without taking a position on them.'[30] In this way, the relativist consequences of the hermeneutic circle within which participants are caught are blunted, while the possibility of specific and recognizable differences are supposed to be preserved. While going beyond both mere imposition and uninterpreted conceptual relativism, such a participant will inevitably see sufficiently different sorts of reasons as unjustified or irrational without a clear test for the intelligibility of 'their' reasons; this test cannot simply be the correctness of 'our' reasons without begging the question of imposition.

My point is that the strong claim of the *identity* between evaluation and interpretation cannot be sustained, since some interpreters may not be in the position to identify the expressions of others as having any recognizable justification at all, or to know what makes their reasons count as reasons. It is here that the observer perspective of world-disclosure might be helpful in weakening this identity of evaluation and interpretation. None the less, we can still avoid the relativist and anti-hermeneutic consequences that motivate Habermas's argument by connecting interpretation closely to validity and truth, but now in a different way through the concept of modality:

what is needed is a notion of *possible* truth claims. Without introducing such modality into taking stock of reasons, evaluation, too, can suffer hermeneutic failures similar to Davidsonian imposition: it must find all unintelligible utterances of others false, and their odd actions irrational. They might become intelligible if only we could interpret them in terms of how it could be *possible* for them to be true or rational.

According to Hacking's interpretation, Foucault's archaeology does just that, without denying the necessity of presupposing our norms of rationality in interpretation. In order to avoid both Davidson's and Habermas's overly strong conclusions about this idealizing presupposition, it is not necessary to abandon the connection of truth and interpretation (since this is tantamount to giving up the intentional stance for an observer one). Rather, it is necessary to introduce a new predicate: what Hacking calls being 'true-or-false', or a 'candidate for truth'. On this view, disclosure is not linked to truth, but to truth candidacy (or any number of disjunctive, truth-like predicates for actions, expressions and so on). Within the horizon of a particular discursive formation, or 'style of reasoning' in Hacking's phrase, 'there might be whole other categories of truth-or-falsehood than ours.'[31] The point here is to introduce reflective modalities into the participant's stance: archaeology does not analyse what speakers of a certain age or culture actually consider to be true, but what Foucault called 'positivity' within a discourse, its feasible set of possible candidates for true statements, correct actions or authentic expressions.

Such a notion of discursive modality introduces a further aspect to the concept of disclosure originally present in Heidegger: that of novelty or innovation. It also makes clear how our interpretations 'come to a standstill' in solving problems: the solution to the problem is not even a candidate solution, since it cannot be disclosed in a particular cultural background as either true or false. In such cases what is needed are 'new styles of reasoning' or 'new paradigms' which bring with them 'new sentences, things quite literally never said before'.[32] Hacking's historical analysis of the 'emergence of probability' required uncovering cultural assumptions about events as 'signs' that are deeper than agents' own explicit knowledge. The archaeology of such a concept shows the way such an assumption excludes the possibility of statistical reasoning, and why learning to do so requires a learning process that transforms deep and pervasive cultural assumptions. It may also help us appreciate better the role of modality and how it supplements the notion of translation in understanding the beliefs of other cultures or historical periods, as the work of Paul Veyne also shows.[33] Thus the archaeological method helps us to understand the relation of rationality and intelligibility without reducing the historical and cultural scope of each concept.

But in the end, the test of such interpretations will be from the perspective of the participants: whether they expand the horizon and modalities of 'our' discourses, as well as our practical capacities for mutual understanding and dialogue with others. This mutual interplay of hermeneutic horizons provides a purpose to archaeology as one of many different forms of reflective participation, a purpose much richer than Foucault's artificial, and ultimately impossible, 'reflectionless objectivity of a nonparticipatory, ascetic description' (*PDM*, p. 275).

Conclusion: Disclosure, Reflection and Freedom

The discussion of Derrida and Foucault in the last two sections shows the centrality of the concept of world-disclosure in *The Philosophical Discourse of Modernity*. Habermas's criticisms of poststructuralism focus on the intersubjective and interpretive character of language as a way out of 'the philosophy of consciousness' and 'subject-centred reason'. Habermas puts forth powerful epistemological and methodological arguments against poststructuralism, in which he enlists the aid of hermeneutics to give a more adequate account of the socially and historically situated interpreter and actor than does poststructuralist scepticism about understanding and reflection. His point is neither to dispute that different worlds are disclosed in language nor simply to contrast disclosure to a more originary, action-coordinating language use. Rather, he gives a non-Heideggerian account of disclosure, one that is to free it from both an objectivist and impersonal account of meaning and from the false identification of truth with events beyond an agent's reflective capacities.

In his analysis of Castoriadis's Heideggerian social and political theory, Habermas ends by setting out the twin desiderata of this reinterpretation of disclosure: that 'world-disclosure and proven, shared social practice presuppose one another' (and are not independent, extraordinary, impersonal 'events') and that 'meaning-creating innovations are intermeshed with learning processes' (and thus are not the 'other of reason'). An important part of Habermas's criticism of poststructuralism is therefore an appropriation and transformation of its main concept into his philosophy of language and notion of critical reflection.

Even if these criticisms of the Heideggerian basis of such scepticism succeed, Habermas's own positive account of disclosure in *The Philosophical Discourse of Modernity* ultimately needs revision. First, he attempts to restrict disclosure to the aesthetic domain in order to avoid the deconstructive overgeneralization of rhetoric. But this worry is unfounded, even on his own view. Disclosure is not a *type* of speech, but a *level* of reflection on the conditions of meaning. Disclosive speech acts are thus a type of reflective rhetoric, rhetoric that overcomes fixed and rigid patterns of cultural meaning and interpretation in second-order communication. Social critics best exemplify this sort of use of language in their attempt to establish new systems of relevance and relations of meaning. Second, Habermas's attempt to connect disclosure to learning through an intrinsic relation between meaning and validity also fails, because it is too strong. A weaker connection is all that Habermas needs and indeed better accounts for the possibility of comparative interpretation and hermeneutic failure. By reinterpreting Foucault's notion of discursive formation, we can modify the identity of interpretation and evaluation into a weaker connection between intelligibility and truth candidacy. This introduces modality as an important feature of interpretation in comparative contexts, since interpretation in these contexts requires understanding not what others think is actually true but, more importantly, what they hold to be possibly true-or-false. By incorporating this revised Foucauldian version of disclosure within discursive formations or styles of reasoning, Habermas can better account for the plurality of cultural worlds that his own hermeneutic perspective demands. In these cases, a less restrictive notion of disclosure enriches Habermas's own theory of meaning and interpretive methodology.

Once emptied of postmodern aestheticism, disclosure becomes a useful way of talking about cultural change and learning. Disclosures open up rigid interpretations to new possibilities and restore the plasticity to the cultural world necessary for learning and problem-solving. By being directed to creating possibilities for truth, novel disclosures change the cultural conditions under which we make true or false statements about the world and ourselves. But this emphasis on truth is also too narrow: conditions of agency are also at stake in these debates. As in the case of innovative learning, disclosure indicates a necessary condition for the autonomy of an agent within the context of cultural meanings, that is, a free and open reflective relation to the conditions of intelligible action. There is no reason to restrict disclosure in this sense to linguistic expression and understanding; it concerns the whole domain of the intentional, including actions and expressions. Such an open relation permits reflective agents to change the cultural conditions for possible action as well, even if not all at once. If the holism about cultures as disclosing a world is correct, then sometimes introducing some new possibility for intelligible action might change the world. Such reflective and transformative capacities related to meaning are important features of culturally situated freedom and responsibility. Suitably expanded, Habermas's appropriation of the concept of disclosure helps him to account for the plurality of cultural worlds and for the possibility of transformative agency within them. Poststructuralist scepticism and political defeatism provide the proper foil for Habermas to reincorporate these themes of plurality and transformation into his dialectical critique of modern reason.

NOTES

1 Others have made similar historical arguments. On the positive side, Rodolphe Gasché has interpreted Derrida in terms of the radicalization of the philosophy of reflection in German Idealism, particularly Schelling; see Gasché, *The Tain of the Mirror* (Cambridge: Harvard University Press, 1986), especially his discussion of post-Hegelian 'philosophy of reflection' in chapters 5 and 6. Nothing in Gasché's account shows how Derrida can answer the good Hegelian charges of dogmatism in his 'heterology'. On the critical side, Peter Dews has used this same argument quite effectively to show the fundamentally metaphysical character of Derrida's explication of *différance* as 'the identity of identity and non-identity', the exact rendering of Schelling's conception of the absolute as well; see Dews, *Logics of Disintegration* (London: Verso, 1987), p. 26. Far from escaping Western metaphysics, Derrida betrays a metaphysics of the worst sort: indeed, Dews shows how he collapses *différance* into the absolute identity of the most extreme metaphysical idealism. My claim here is that Habermas shows quite well why what is at stake in poststructuralist critiques of the theory of meaning is simply a dispute over how to describe the linguistic constitution of the social world. The impersonal, yet constitutive, character of world-disclosure no more escapes transcendental philosophy than *différance* does metaphysics; indeed, it betrays a holistic 'transcendental philosophy without a subject', to borrow Ricoeur's phrase, not its overcoming.

2 Jürgen Habermas, *The Philosophical Discourse of Modernity* (Cambridge: Polity Press; Cambridge, Mass.: MIT Press, 1987), hereafter cited as *PDM*; here I am especially concerned with the lectures on Derrida and Foucault (Lectures VII–XI) and with the 'Excursus on Cornelius Castoriadis' in Lecture XI.

3 Charles Taylor calls this the 'HHH view', including Herder, Humboldt and Heidegger; I think that he too quickly assimilates articulation and disclosure in his analysis of this tradition. See his 'Theories of Meaning', in *Philosophical Papers*, vol. 1 (Cambridge: Cambridge University Press, 1985), pp. 248–92. It is also hermeneutically too swift to claim the Fregean tradition has a simple 'denotative' view of language. However, Taylor's analysis is correct in that this tradition (including Heidegger) is based on a conception of the constitutive character of language. Habermas calls his own conception of language 'Humboldtian' in his reply to Taylor's criticisms in *Kommunikatives Handeln* (Frankfurt: Suhrkamp, 1986), p. 328; my claim here is that Habermas's dispute with the poststructuralists about language shows the fissures in the constitutive conception of language between the pragmatist Humboldtians (such as Wittgenstein, Taylor and Habermas) and the strict Heideggerians (such as Derrida and the early Foucault). I shall argue for the superiority of the pragmatic view of disclosure. For Habermas's explicit avowal of his Humboldtian debts, see his 'Individuation through Socialization', in *Postmetaphysical Thinking*, trans. William Mark Hohengarten (Cambridge: Polity Press, 1992), p. 162.

4 Hans-Georg Gadamer, *Truth and Method* (New York: Seabury Press, 1992), p. 443.
5 Martin Heidegger, 'The Origin of the Work of Art', in *Basic Writings* (New York: Harper and Row, 1977), p. 186.
6 Ibid., p. 181.
7 See Martin Heidegger, 'On the Essence of Truth', in ibid, p. 134. According to Heidegger, common sense and the ordinary intuitions of the public world are hopelessly conformist and rule-bound. Reflection remains caught in the familiarity of common sense, until the concealment of beings 'announces itself', beyond the control of the reflective subject. Justification, or correctness, is therefore always relative to such a concealed/unconcealed world horizon.
8 I develop this general argument against all forms of Heideggerian, strong holism (including postmodern ethnography) in my 'Holism without Scepticism', in D. Hiley, J. Bohman and R. Shusterman (eds), *The Interpretive Turn* (Ithaca: Cornell University Press, 1991), pp. 129–54. Interpretive or hermeneutic holism, I argue, does not have the implications for practical agency and critical judgement within a cultural context that Heideggerians and postmodernists think it does.
9 See Jürgen Habermas, *The Theory of Communicative Action*, vol. 1 (Cambridge: Polity Press, 1984), pp. 275–8.
10 See Jürgen Habermas, *Texte und Kontexte* (Frankfurt: Suhrkamp, 1991), p. 28; English translation 'Peirce and Communication', in Habermas, *Postmetaphysical Thinking* (Cambridge: Polity Press, 1992), pp. 88–112.
11 Nikolas Kompridis has argued that this is because Habermas takes over too much of the Heideggerian ecstatic model of art; this notion of art in turn distorts his view of world-disclosure and its relation to learning. For an excellent discussion of disclosure and Habermas's remarks on aesthetics, see his *Decentration, Disclosure and Reconstruction*, Ph.D. Diss. York University. My understanding of the weaknesses of Habermas's attempt to limit disclosure to art in this section has profited greatly from our discussions. For an excellent discussion of disclosure as the basis for a possible Habermasian aesthetics, see Martin Seel, *Kunst der Entzweiung* (Frankfurt: Suhrkamp, 1985); I am sceptical of his view of art as the 'disclosure of disclosure', since on my view disclosure is already second-order communication. For a statement of this view, see Martin Seel, 'Kunst, Wahrheit, Welterschliessung', in F. Koppe (ed.), *Perspektiven der Kunstphilosophie* (Frankfurt: Suhrkamp, 1991), pp. 36–80.
12 Once again, Habermas is willing to grant to art what he withholds from language in its ordinary uses. Habermas argues that works of art can function as arguments, not in the sense that they can replace them, but in that they are rhetorically and experientially compelling. In this context, disclosure refers to 'the potential for truth' that can be released in the 'whole complexity of life experience'. See Jürgen Habermas, 'Questions and Counterquestions', in *Habermas and Modernity*, ed. Richard Bernstein (Cambridge: Polity Press, 1985), p. 203. My argument is that if disclosure is possible in art, then it is possible as a reflective achievement of ordinary language use: both have the same 'potential for truth', or changing truth candidates, as I put it in the next section. In *The Postmodern Condition*, Lyotard criticizes such passages on art in Habermas, but mistakenly believes that Habermas is referring to some actual totality of experience; moreover, he ignores how

such disclosure for Habermas disrupts the holistic background of assumptions and makes learning possible. It is not the experience of harmony that is
disclosive. I am not dealing with Lyotard's version of the postmodern
linguistic turn in this chapter; it has more to do with the lack of unity of
reason, not with some 'other' of reason. See David Ingram in chapter 10
below for this more Wittgensteinian, rather than Heideggerian, attempt at
the postmodern linguistic turn.

13 Habermas does think that the problem with the development of Western
rationality is that it has been one-sidedly cognitivistic and instrumental; in
this sense, he agrees with aspects of the notion of logocentrism and would
even link the one-sided character of this development to Western ideologies
of Western domination and exploitation. However, logocentrism for Derrida
is not merely that Western reason is one-sided; what this really means in
social and political terms remains mysterious and must always remain so.

14 Ryle puts it this way: 'Understanding a word or phrase is knowing how to
use it, i.e., how to make it perform its role in a wide range of sentences. But
understanding a sentence is not knowing how to make it perform its role.'
There is no constraint on how the same sentence token may be used in
different contexts; hence, if meaning is use there is no one semantically
specifiable meaning to a sentence. Gilbert Ryle, 'Ordinary Language Philosophy', *Philosophical Review* (1953), pp. 171–2. Austin's insight is, however,
to switch from a semantic to a pragmatic analysis for just these reasons.

15 Derrida's writings abound with such simple scepticism. For example, in
'Signature, Event, Context' Derrida implies that the conventionality of signs
by itself undermines Austin's identification of utterance meaning: 'Austin
seems to consider only the conventionality that surrounds the circumstances
of the statement, its contextual surroundings, and not a certain intrinsic
conventionality of that which constitutes locution itself.' See Jacques Derrida,
Margins of Philosophy (Chicago: University of Chicago Press, 1982),
pp. 322–3. What difference would this conventionality of locutions or signs
really make? How does the conventionality of the sentence token 'radicalize
the difficulty'? Why is it a problem for a theory of the meaning of utterance
types that I can give a promise in Morse code, German, English, or a thousand
different ways? That this is one of Derrida's central criticisms is evident in its
repeated use in *Limited Inc.* (Evanston, Ill.: Northwestern University Press,
1988). Here Derrida claims that not just 'binary oppositions' are typical of
Western logocentrism, but the idealization inherent in abstract concepts
(p. 117). This sort of argument seems absurd when one considers the very
simple fact that all existing languages have such abstract concepts as class
nouns and general terms. Derrida certainly cannot do without abstract types,
including 'Western metaphysics', which is used repeatedly without regard to
context in *Of Grammatology* from its opening paragraphs onwards. Moreover, Derrida overestimates what Saussure's notion of the arbitrary nature of
the sign can do in the criticism of theories of meaning. On this point, John
Ellis is correct in his criticism of Derrida's misguided use of the 'arbitrary
nature of the sign'. See John Ellis, *Against Deconstruction* (Princeton: Princeton University Press, 1989), ch. 2. For similar criticisms of this and other
'readings' in Derrida, see J. Claude Evans, *Strategies of Deconstruction*
(Minneapolis: University of Minnesota Press, 1991).

16 See P. F. Strawson, 'Intention and Convention in Speech Acts', in *Logico-
Linguistic Papers* (London: Methuen, 1971), pp. 149–69.

17 Jonathan Culler, *On Deconstruction* (Ithaca: Cornell University Press, 1982), cited by Habermas, *PDM*, p. 198.

18 For a discussion of this notion of ideals embedded in practices and its relevance to poststructuralism, see Thomas McCarthy, *Ideals and Illusions* (Cambridge: MIT Press, 1991), pp. 1–10.

19 I have attempted to develop this pragmatic interpretation of ideology as communicative failure in my 'Critique of Ideologies', in *International Handbook of the Philosophy of Language*', vol. 1 (Berlin: de Gruyter, 1992), pp. 689–704. Such a structural analysis of distorted communication is superior to Habermas's own more limited notion of 'latent strategic action' precisely because my revisions no longer make it necessary to see ideology as a specific type of communication with specific latent intentions.

20 Jürgen Habermas, 'Charles Peirce über Kommunikation', in *Texte und Kontexte*, p. 28, see 'Peirce and Communication', in *Postmetaphysical Thinking*, p. 106 (translation modified).

21 For an analysis of the use of such rhetoric by social critics, see my 'Welterschliessung und Radikale Kritik', *Deutsche Zeitschrift für Philosophie* 41:3 (1993), pp. 563–74. For a general discussion of rhetoric and social criticism from the point of view of speech-act theory, see my 'Emancipation and Rhetoric: The Perlocutions and Illocutions of the Social Critic', *Philosophy and Rhetoric* 21:3 (1988), pp. 185–204.

22 Here I am disagreeing with Stephen White's otherwise excellent analysis of Habermas's dispute with postmodernism in *Political Theory and Postmodernism* (Cambridge: Cambridge University Press, 1991). Not only does he see disclosure and action coordination as two 'types' of language use, he also tries to correlate them with contrasting senses of moral responsibility (pp. 19–28). But 'otherness' is simply too vague to denote anything intrinsically moral, and if disclosure is a rhetorical effect, it can disclose both just and unjust worlds. Disclosure has to do with the cultural conditions of responsibility and is not itself a type of responsibility; the truth of disclosure may not be moral at all, as Heideggerians have only recently discovered.

23 See Michel Foucault, *The Archeology of Knowledge* (New York: Pantheon, 1972), part III, ch. 3; Foucault sounds just like a nineteenth-century historicist about meaning, claiming that archaeology can 'provide a description of things said, just as they were said', or a 'neutral' analysis of 'facts of language' that 'avoids all interpretations' (p. 109). It is hard to justify this as a 'methodological stance' even as a fiction, unless there is some recognition that such a description is impossible, and there is none in this book. A 'happy positivist' (as Foucault describes himself in this work) is a deluded one.

24 See Foucault's discussion of the 'analytic of finitude' in *The Order of Things* (New York: Random House, 1970); even in his specific historical analysis, Foucault uses ontological terms such as 'mode of being' to describe various epistemes, as in his discussion of the 'mode of being of economics' (p. 256) common to both Marx and Ricardo.

25 Here Habermas is following Hubert Dreyfus and Paul Rabinow's critique of Foucault's early works; see Dreyfus and Rabinow, *Michel Foucault: Between Structuralism and Hermeneutics* (Chicago: University of Chicago Press, 1983), pp. 133ff. Foucault's conception of rule is remarkably naive and subject to a devastating Wittgensteinian critique, since he has rules that, inexplicably and quite mysteriously, govern their own application. In inter-

views Foucault accepts this criticism of archaeology as fair. Since he continues to hold that archaeology is still a component of his type of historical investigation, he must believe that some version of it can overcome these difficulties. I argue below that Hacking's version of archaeology does provide us with one.

26 The empirical problem that I am alluding to is that it remains utterly obscure in *Discipline and Punish* how the panopticon escapes the prison and operates in all of modern society; no mechanism or account of this process is provided that explains the 'carceral society', or the generalization of the mechanisms of the prison. The analogy between prisons, factories and schools is empirically deficient, as Foucault realizes when he appeals to contingent events like the invention of the rifle.

27 Ian Hacking first develops this conception of truth candidates in 'Language, Truth and Reason', in M. Hollis and S. Lukes (eds), *Rationality and Relativism* (Cambridge, MIT Press, 1982), pp. 48–66; he develops his notion of 'styles of reasoning' further in 'Style for Historians and Philosophers', *The History and Philosophy of Science* 32:1 (1992), pp. 1–20. His own Foucauldian analysis of an actual case using these concepts is *The Emergence of Probability* (Cambridge: Cambridge University Press, 1975). Terrence Kelly and I have explored the ways in which the notion of a truth candidate can help Habermas avoid the pitfalls of Davidsonian transcendental arguments against relativism in our paper, 'Comparing Rationalities: The Rationality Debates in the Social Sciences Revisited', presented at a conference on Revising Rationality at the University of Southern Illinois at Carbondale, March 1993.

28 See Habermas, *The Theory of Communicative Action*, vol. 1, p. 116.

29 Donald Davidson, 'Problems in the Explanation of Action', in P. Pettit, J. Norman and R. Sylvan (eds), *Metaphysics and Morality* (Oxford: Blackwell, 1987), p. 47. For Davidson, we may use 'our norms' as a reliable basis for understanding actions, except in cases of hidden causation. That our beliefs must be largely true is the basis for his 'principle of charity' in interpretation. For a fuller account of these problems of rational interpretation, see my *New Philosophy of Social Science: Problems of Indeterminacy* (Cambridge: Polity Press; Cambridge, Mass.: MIT Press, 1991), ch. 3.

30 Habermas, *The Theory of Communicative Action*, vol. 1, p. 116.

31 Hacking, 'Language, Truth and Reason', p. 64.

32 Hacking, 'Style for Historians and Philosophers', p. 12.

33 Paul Veyne, *Did the Greeks Believe Their Myths?* (Chicago: University of Chicago Press, 1986). If Davidson is right, then we could not answer the question as Veyne does in the book: neither a simple yes nor a simple no. If Habermas describes evaluation as 'taking a yes/no position', such phenomena (such as what the Greeks believed about the gods and historical writing) show the necessity of modality of belief in interpretive social science.

8

HABERMAS AND THE
QUESTION OF ALTERITY

Diana Coole

In both *The Philosophical Discourse of Modernity* and in his essay
'Modernity: An Unfinished Project', Habermas adopts an uncompro-
misingly hostile approach towards poststructuralism/postmodernism.
My aim is to consider the reasons for that hostility and to suggest
that it is misplaced in so far as his concerns lie with emancipation.
Broadly, my argument will be as follows. Habermas rejects poststructuralism because in his view – a view I agree with – it depends on an
appeal to the Other. He is unable to attribute any emancipatory
potential to alterity, or otherness, however, because his basic ideas
concerning communicative reason and an emancipatory project of
modernity are predicated on its exclusion. I will support this argument in the first part of the chapter. In the second part, I will outline
various approaches to alterity in order to argue both that it necessarily continues to circulate within modernity, and that an emancipatory politics must operate on this level. My conclusion will be that
communicative reason and discursive democracy need supplementing
by an appreciation of the prediscursive and non-discursive levels on
which power and alterity circulate, such that postmodern decodings
and strategies are an essential dimension of any emancipatory
politics.

Postmodern Discourses and Alterity

In *The Philosophical Discourse of Modernity*,[1] a number of different
discourses are at work. First, but remaining in the background, there
is the philosophy of the Enlightenment which is broadly associated
with Kant. Habermas is more interested in its critiques, and especially
in a discourse of counter-Enlightenment that runs from Hegel and
Marx through the first generation of critical theorists. He is sympath-

etic to this particular modern approach and it is indeed the one from which his own thinking emerges, but he finds it flawed. For on the one hand, it fails to escape the subjectivist foundations of the Enlightenment, while on the other it succumbs to a virtually postmodern rejection of reason, since it finds it wholly reduced in late modernity to instrumentalism. When Habermas explores the affinities between Adorno's negative dialectics and Derrida's deconstruction, he classifies both as approaches to reason's Other.

Poststructuralism is the third discourse with which Habermas is concerned and he locates its origins in Nietzsche. If romantic critics of the Enlightenment gradually purged the aesthetic of cognitive-instrumental and moral-practical reason, Nietzsche took this purification further, associating the aesthetic with archaic forces modernity has renounced: with an experience of non-discursive excitement and self-oblivion, a route to reason's Other. In this 'aesthetically inspired anarchism', as Habermas calls it, what had been moments of aesthetic judgement and therefore able to command rational consensus in Kant, now become a frenzy outside reason, ecstatic rather than self-conscious. Worse, as far as Habermas is concerned, this aesthetic overflows its boundaries to impose its particular validity claims on cognitive and moral reason, such that truth and value become matters of taste.

It is then this 'postmodern' heritage that Habermas traces through Heidegger, Derrida, Bataille and Foucault, seeing the first three at least as caught up in a Dionysian escape route from reason. It is their appeal to the Other that unites them, according to this account, although that otherness takes a variety of forms: 'ecstatic sovereignty or forgotten Being ... bodily reflexes, local resistance, and the involuntary revolts of a deprived subjective nature' (*PDM*, p. 58). This conflation allows Habermas to level the criticisms he makes of Heidegger at poststructuralism, as if they were all of a piece. Heidegger is accused of pursuing Nietzsche's Dionysian messianism, where reason is a forgetting and Being's truth is reclaimed not by reflection, but by surrender to its authority, a mystical ecstasy which Habermas condemns as immune to any criterion of validity. It is, then, this mysticism of which he goes on to accuse Derrida, finding in the latter's archewriting only another name for Being. 'In the metaphor of the archewriting and its trace,' he writes, 'we see again the Dionysian motif of the god making his promised presence all the more palpable to the sons and daughters of the West by means of his poignant absence' (*PDM*, pp. 180–1). Once this equation is made, Derrida is vulnerable to accusations of closet messianism and inverted foundationalism; of making a mystical appeal to an absent god.

For Bataille, it is the heterogeneous and excessive which is Other and subversive of modern instrumentality. Again we find an appeal to the archaic, something prior to reason and immune to it yet retrievable through transgressive experiences which would extinguish the rational subject. What Habermas is suggesting, then, in placing Nietzsche and his successors in one camp, is that they all equate the Other with some prediscursive, primordial referent which precedes reason and which might be retrieved, by non-rational strategies, as a way of reinvigorating (post)modernity. He equates it with some unspeakable and undifferentiated excitement which, he remarks, is now fashionably labelled feminine (*PDM*, p. 307). Unlike the Romantics' aesthetic, this Other is not then a split-off and suppressed part of reason, but is temporally related to something preceding it, something allegedly authentic and archaic. Dionysus, Being, arche-writing or sacrifice are presented as merely different names for this primordial and mysterious Other.

Having established this commonality, it is not difficult for Habermas to write postmodernism off as an appeal to mystical, apolitical and irrational forces which would replace reason and truth with an undifferentiated chaos. Even if it secretly nourishes a modernist vision of aesthetic emancipation, as Habermas believes it does, its effects are resolutely non-emancipatory and unsupportable. Although he is rather more sympathetic to Foucault, he finally charges him too with the performative contradiction that postmodernists' alleged celebration of the irrational entails.

Habermas's antipathy towards poststructuralism thus rests on his denial of any emancipatory role to alterity. It is not just the case, then, as his critics often suggest, that he read Derrida et al. with insufficient care or thoroughness. In fact many of Habermas's comments on their appeals to alterity are extremely perceptive. But the logic of his theory already condemned such appeals as irrational, anachronistic and out of step with history's evolution, such that Habermas could never have accepted postmodernism as a radical or progressive discourse. This is why he condemns the postmoderns as 'young conservatives' whom he sees retreating into antimodernism, the archaic and an alliance with premodernists.[2] Their dismissal was already prefigured, regardless of the specific aporias to be discovered within postmodern texts. Rather than the details, it is the whole flavour, or project, of the two discourses that fundamentally distinguishes them.

The overall strategy of *The Philosophical Discourse* is to show how both Critical Theory and postmodernism have failed to recognize in modernity an unfinished emancipatory project which reason might yet complete. For by reducing it to its instrumental forms, or dismissing it altogether, they ignore reason's authentic, communicative aspect. Thus we arrive at a fourth discourse, which is Habermas's own and allegedly the only one to salvage reason by avoiding subjectivism. Here, communicative rationality, oriented towards learning about and cooperatively disclosing the world, is distinguished from an instrumentalism geared to strategic success. It is the relationship between these two rationalities that gives back to modernity its dialectical structure. The struggle *within* modernity is not for Habermas between reason and non-reason, but between communicative and instrumental reason, lifeworld and system, emancipation and reification. It is between different forms of reason and modes of rationalization and not between reason and its Other. The latter struggle only occurs for him in the transition from premodernity to modernity. An overview of Habermas's work, such as I will offer in the following section, then suggests that he does not merely find postmodernism inefficacious and contradictory, but that his entire project is predicated for its emancipatory claims on the *exclusion* of that alterity to which postmodernism appeals.

Habermas and the Eclipse of Alterity

If within modernity there remain distortions of the mutual understanding that originates in speech acts, these are blamed by Habermas on one-sidedly rationalized and *delinguistified* steering media, not on any lacunae at the heart of *language* itself. If communicative capacity is menaced, it is by the wrong sort of reason rather than by a non-reason resistant to communicative recuperation. Similarly, while our *lifeworld* might outrun attempts at total retrieval, nothing there is in principle immune, according to Habermas, to discursive redemption. Finally, *history's* schematic evolution into modernity is, like that of the *subject* into maturity, reconstructed as a process of eliminating – that is, rationalizing away – any otherness that might have played within traditional cultures or immature ego-development. My claim is that these accounts of language, lifeworld, history and subjectivity are systematically biased against the alterity whose evocation postmodernists practise.

Language is central to Habermas's theory because it is the communicative promise inherent in speech acts that guarantees a historical momentum towards rational intersubjectivity culminating in modernity. He grounds the idea of a universal communicative reason in a formal analysis of such speech acts. Even the most simple of these conveys a will to communicate something about a shared lifeworld and to reach a common understanding about it. It is this intersubjective will to communicate, rather than the subjective will to dominate, which is found in any competent speaker's pre-theoretical grasp of linguistic rules. However, only in modernity does this universal rationality become explicit, turning back on the lived but unreflected consensus of tradition to attempt discursive agreement. The latter emerges from rational discourse among equals who are motivated to reach agreement according to the force of the better argument, through testing its validity claims according to criteria of truth, rightness and truthfulness. Habermas writes: 'What counts as rational is solving problems successfully through procedurally suitable dealings with reality.'[3] As a vanishing point, he envisages an ideal speech situation where minds meet in undistorted meaning or intent, such that rational agreement on universal principles might be achieved.

In this context, Habermas criticizes Derrida for failing to recognize the various functions of language, among which the communicative aims of everyday speech acts and specialist discourses are pre-eminent. But Derrida's point is that no language, no matter how purposeful and communicative its usage, can achieve the unequivocal and transparent form reconstructed in speech-act theory. It is not just that contingent distortions usually impede the ideal, but that ordinary language is intrinsically riven by slippages, metaphors, absences, deferrals, desire and chance associations which mean that it always communicates both more and less than conversationalists intend. It is always abnormal and inevitably harbours excessive, unconscious, innovative, subversive and power-laden meanings that intervene to derail and enrich attempts at mutual understanding.

The attempt at fixing meaning in universal concepts and representing the world through linguistic clarity is itself for Derrida a violent metaphysical project. However, the alterity it tries to suppress, and which deconstruction would invoke, is not some mystical or primordial Other, as Habermas suggests, but the fault-lines and ruptures, the differences, which structure language itself. Derrida insists: 'This unnameable is not an ineffable Being which no name could approach: God, for example. This unnameable is the play which makes possible nominal effects, the relatively unitary and atomic structures that are called names in which, for example, the nominal effect *différance* is itself *enmeshed*, carried off, reinscribed.'[4] *Différance*, or what Habermas calls archewriting, is intrinsic to language's ability to express meaning at all; it cannot be wholly suppressed and exercises a constant resistance such that purified communication inevitably fails. Thus meaning is nowhere present within language but is always (spatially) displaced and (temporally) deferred, such that language creates meaning through its diacritical play. Communication is therefore a problem endemic to linguistification, rather than being guaranteed by it. If *différance* operates as a radical alterity here, however, it marks only the possibility (and impossibility) of meaning and not some alternative register. It might be invoked by certain aesthetic and deconstructive strategies in order to disclose the limits of lucidity, but Derrida never proposes it as an alternative symbolic.

Habermas's criticisms of Derrida's alleged mysticism and foundationalism in *PDM* thus seem somewhat disingenuous, but in any case
Derrida's motif of *différance*, and the post-Saussurean linguistics on
which it is based, cannot be countenanced by Habermas because they
are the ruin of his claims for communicative reason and discourse
ethics, suggesting as they do that even the most rational discourses
will remain charged with alterity – an alterity that is denied by the
very reconstruction of universal pragmatics. Moreover, as Richard
Bernstein has pointed out, Habermas does have an other, but it is
only our co-communicative partner, who has the right to question
validity claims, and the whole emphasis is on reciprocity, symmetry
and successful understanding.[5] There is no place, and certainly no
radical role, for disruption and transgression in this process. For
Habermas, failings in communication can only signify a distortion to
be overcome, never a salutary challenge to the hubris of reason.

Similar values and orientations are built, I will now claim, into
Habermas's understanding of the *lifeworld* and its fate in modernity.
The lifeworld is for him a milieu of coexistence, where reason is
already implicit in intersubjective communication. It is 'the sphere of
what is daily taken for granted, the sphere of common sense'. It is
constraining because we inhabit it as embodied and situated, yet it is
its dense texture which is the source and target of communicative
interpretation and renewal. Habermas insists that there is nothing in
the lifeworld which is resistant to thematization as such, although
'this context cannot be objectivated in toto.'[6] Thus there is no
dimension of Habermas's lifeworld that is immune in principle to
discursive retrieval,[7] and indeed the lifeworld is defined as fundamentally linguistic.

According to Habermas, the standards of rationality implicit in
communicative action are increasingly used reflexively rather than
intuitively and this process corresponds with a 'developmental logic'
of historical lifeworlds.[8] Grammatical speech allows cultures to move
to higher forms of communication and begin the process of differentiation which culminates, in modernity, in communicative action
becoming the means, rather than simply the medium, of consensus
formation. Modernity is thus both a historical and a theoretical
notion and is marked by rationalization and differentiation. My
argument here is that the narrative/formal reconstruction Habermas
unfolds posits too sharp a break between modernity and premodernity, with the former in crucial but mistaken ways *defined* by its
impossible purging of alterity from its lifeworld.

An analogous logic can be discerned in Habermas's account of
subjectivity – unsurprisingly in so far as the subject's maturing
recapitulates social development. Habermas gives subjects privileged
communicative access to their inner selves such that, despite commu-

nicative blockages, there is in principle nothing immune to rational self-communication: no structured unconscious, primary repression or resistance. The presymbolic stages which would be the psychic equivalent of the historically archaic, and wherein poststructuralists like Julia Kristeva locate irreducible sources of alterity, are to all intents and purposes ignored.

Returning now to history: although communicative reason evolves within the lifeworld, the latter undergoes fundamental changes within modernity. It cannot disappear, but it does shrink significantly. This is in part due to the pathological aspects of rationalization, whereby systems destroy and colonize it. And at the same time, expert cultures split off and find it increasingly difficult to communicate on a lifeworld level. But the sort of intuitive, background knowledge associated with both lifeworld and tradition is also increasingly thematized and formalized, such that 'the zones of what is unproblematic shrink.'[9] Although the lifeworld still defines general ethical patterns even in modernity, it 'gets cut down more and more'[10] as reflection replaces custom. Habermas acknowledges that the 'lifeworld concept of society finds its strongest empirical foothold in archaic societies,' the latter remaining undifferentiated, homogeneous and merging into the lived.

The merely lived thus yields to a constant, reflexive, critical and cooperative revision of culture, wherein lies for Habermas modernity's emancipatory promise. However, as I will contend shortly, this seems seriously to overestimate the rationalizing process, which is why Habermas largely ignores the non-systemic, non-discursive processes of power and politics that continue to circulate within the lifeworld even in modernity. The transition from premodernity to modernity corresponds for him with a shift from the sacred to the profane. This distinction between the sacred and the profane operates as an important opposition. For on the one hand it signifies those only potentially rational, still archaic cultures where irrational rituals and magical and theological notions dominate; the sacred, Habermas says, is 'immune from discursive examination'.[11] On the other hand, the opposition identifies modernity with the discursive and differentiated rationality that allows such otherness to be translated into intersubjectively comprehensible and verifiable claims. The sacred is then doomed precisely because its validity claims remain undifferentiated and unredeemable, such that its passing marks a transition from the irrational to the rational, from ritual to argumentation, from a stage where language is 'on holiday' to linguistification. In other words, the sacred is here a code for alterity, and my argument is that it is precisely because postmodernists appeal to an alterity that Habermas associates with the sacred, or archaic, that he is so reluctant to allow their invocations of the Other to infiltrate modernity, especially in the guise of a radical politics. He sees them appealing to historically obsolete, mystical and unverifiable beliefs, because he believes that the very meaning and triumph of modernity lies in its transcendence of such alterity.

In fact, Habermas occasionally acknowledges the force of what for him must be premodern intrusions into modernity, but they are either safely contained there – 'explosive experiences of the extraordinary have migrated into art that has become autonomous'[12] – or they are just temporarily out of step with the rationalizing process, as when he also associates the 'extraordinary' (a 'shattering and subversive intrusion' into 'ordinary, profane' life) with religion. Since postmetaphysical philosophy has by his own admission lost touch with this dimension, Habermas acknowledges that it will be temporarily unable to repress or replace a religious language whose 'content eludes (for the time being?) the explanatory force of philosophical language and continues to resist translation into reasoning discourses'.[13]

But is this continuing concern with alterity simply reducible to art or religion: two forms which Habermas is able to dismiss as apolitical because they are respectively separate from everyday experience or anachronistic? Is its fate really to succumb to marginalization or disappearance in the face of reason? What if the sacred were only another name for the Other, and religion but one of the extraordinary discourses that evoke it, using an undifferentiated mix of rational and aesthetic expressions to elicit what necessarily remains non-discursive and even non-linguistic? Perhaps alterity is not then simply a legacy of the archaic but necessarily continues to circulate within modernity – as, for example, Derrida's 'motif' of *différance* suggests that language both relies on, and is subverted by, the diacritical rhythms that yield meaning, or as psychoanalysis suggests that consciousness draws on, yet is disturbed by, unconscious processes.

Before concluding this section, I want to turn finally to Habermas's views on the aesthetic, since if he were to allow alterity any fecundity or emancipatory zeal within modernity and thus within his own thinking, we might expect it to be located here. It is the aesthetic, the third component of Habermas's trinity of validity claims, which is most downplayed by him and whose rationality is most problematic within his schema, yet it is here that the most dramatic lifeworld interventions might be made within an increasingly rationalized modernity. In considering Habermas's references to the aesthetic, my contentions are both that it is problematic for him precisely because of its association with alterity, and that his more recent concerns with it do suggest a greater recognition of a continuing vitality of otherness within modernity.

Because communicative reason and lifeworld are intertwined, it is not surprising that they should be structurally homologous in terms of reason's differentiations. If modernity means a differentiation of reason into science, morality/law and art, this triptych is already prefigured in speech acts, where speakers can take up a first (I) second (you) or third (they, it) person position, thus yielding the standard forms of speech acts (propositional, illocutionary, expressive). Instead of reifying the impersonal and objectifying logic of the third-person observer, Habermas's account emphasizes fungible co-speakers who communicate. The consensus they aim at arises not from recognizing a Truth 'out there', but from negotiating on the basis of certain procedures and formal validity claims. The latter then correspond to the positions available to speakers: claims of empirical validity (from a third-person perspective); claims of normative rightness and legitimacy regarding shared norms and group relationships (addressed to 'you' others); claims to sincerity, authenticity and truthfulness (on the part of the expressive self). These differentiated validity claims then yield three types of knowledge: cognitive-instrumental (objective, scientific); moral-practical (social, normative, moral/legal, interpersonal, relating to justice, solidarity); aesthetic-expressive (subjective, dramaturgical, oriented to agreement on taste, mutual trust, aesthetic harmony and individual autonomy/authenticity) .

We thus inhabit three worlds simultaneously, each with its own rationality and validity structure: the objective, the social and the subjective. In orienting themselves to each, rational individuals adopt the appropriate attitude (objectivating, norm conforming, expressive). Each world then contributes its own background certainties (intuitive knowledge, group solidarity/traditional practices, and skills/ know-how/body-centred complexes, respectively). Language intervenes to reproduce them all: it reproduces cultures, renews social integration and socializes the young, although each has its own potential pathology too: loss of meaning, anomie and psychopathology. Each world is thus lived and, in modernity, reflected upon. Only with the latter are differentiations clear, yielding the three types of validity claim which promise consensus, but also expert cultures (science, jurisprudence, art criticism) whose separation from the lifeworld is an unhealthy dimension of rationalization. Habermas is most insistent that this differentiation of reason should remain and that it is crucial for emancipation, but he would also like to see its three aspects (somehow) reintegrated in a balanced way within the lifeworld, to yield 'a non-reified, communicative practice of everyday life'.[14] It is the relationship between the three parts of this triad, with especial reference to the aesthetic, that I want to discuss now.

It is not at all clear how the aesthetic relates to the other two realms, or how it might evolve to become communicatively rational.[15] In fact, the aesthetic emerges as a rather piecemeal category containing anything that might broadly be classified as subjective: art, individual psychology and aesthetic experience more generally. Art criticism is the most obvious candidate for communicative reason, as an expert culture where judgements of taste and authenticity might be made by way of the proper logic of argumentation,[16] but clearly there is more to the aesthetic than this.

The second constituent relates to the expressive self. The equivalent of a validity claim here is conformity between intention and action, manifested in behaviour that is consistent and thus a sign of authenticity, trustworthiness, sincerity. The (psychically healthy) subjects who express themselves in this way are those who have unified and coherent identities and who can express themselves truthfully because their inner, private language can be made public. I have already mentioned reservations towards this account.

Thirdly, there is a more general sense of the aesthetic realm, and the one that comes closest to accommodating some gesture towards otherness. In this context, Habermas discusses the avant-garde movement of modernism and the related aesthetic experiences whose emancipatory potential has been vaunted by Romantics, surrealists and Bataille. The inclusion of the latter is significant because Habermas classifies Bataille among the postmoderns, while he explicitly associates postmodernists' Other with 'the contents of aesthetic experience' (PDM, p. 337). Thus avant-garde and postmodernist practices are almost synonymous for him.

It is indeed interesting that Habermas presents aesthetic expression in two ways. At one time he focuses on the consensus, harmony, a 'balanced and undistorted intersubjectivity'[17] art promises, seeing it as opening up the *familiar* to us. This seems to be the romantic appeal of art in reintegrating the lifeworld, in the spirit of Kant's Third Critique and aesthetic discourses of counter-Enlightenment generally. Postmodernists like Lyotard have remained sceptical regarding the 'unity of experience' it could yield.[18] However, elsewhere Habermas describes aesthetic experience in a far more postmodern way as relating to a transformed subjectivity which is decentred and unbound: transgressive, open to the unconscious, the fantastic, the mad, the feminine, the bodily – in short, it is touched by what is non-discursive, wild, and what Habermas himself summarizes as the Other (it is less aesthetic than sublime).

Habermas's attack on postmodernism is in many ways identical to his critique of the avant-garde here: he thinks the aesthetic is inappropriate to bring normative changes (which must occur through rational discussion) and inadequate as a challenge to the hegemomy of instrumentalism – the collapse of art into life would only disperse and nullify its effects.[19] Moreover, although he acknowledges that avant-garde artists saw themselves as doing something radical – 'exploring hitherto unknown territory, exposing [themselves] to the risk of sudden and shocking encounters, conquering an as yet undetermined future' – this is not the interpretation that Habermas puts on their activity. Their anticipation is in fact, he argues, but an exaltation of the present where the valorization of 'the transitory, the elusive and the ephemeral' actually discloses only 'the yearning for a lasting and immaculate present'.[20] But this is precisely Habermas's criticism of postmodernism: conservatism fostered in the name of rebellion and a paradoxical revolt against the normative while actually harbouring unstated ideals (of aesthetic modernism) (*PDM*, p. 275). It vaunts the second, sublime and disruptive, sense of the aesthetic rather than the first, harmonious and conciliatory one, while mistakenly believing it thereby pursues the emancipatory goals of the latter. Such undertakings, he concludes, 'can be seen today as nonsense experiments'.[21] One might reply: well, precisely, but this does not mean strategically insignificant, since meaning and power continue to unfold within such 'nonsense', or non-rational, realms.

In some of his more recent work, Habermas actually seems more sympathetic to these other dimensions, where he distinguishes between the pathological expertise of the art critic and a 'radical' manner of experiencing art by relating 'aesthetic experiences' to 'one's own life problems', which relate them more to questions of truth and justice. Once an aesthetic experience 'is related to problems of life or used in an exploratory fashion to illuminate a life-historical situation', it enters a different language game: 'it not only revitalizes those need interpretations in the light of which we perceive our world, but also influences our cognitive interpretations and our normative expectations, and thus alters the way in which all these moments *refer back and forth* to one another.'[22] Here, then, is the radical aesthetic of everyday life, and it goes some way to capturing the radicalism I am claiming for postmodernism. I am less sure what it does to the modern project of communicative reason, but it is important that the aesthetic should not be a *model* of an alternative, harmonious subjectivity or politics here (although some identities may be closer to it) but a *mode* of subversive/creative intervention – one that operates on prediscursive levels. It seems to me that Habermas still favours the first over the second and so his aesthetic cannot accommodate the sort of postmodern strategies that would engage modernity's pre- or non-discursive blockages after all. It is this latter category that I will address in the next section.

The Other and the Politics of Alterity

The implications of my claims thus far are that modernity cannot be defined as the transcendence of alterity and that reason and non-reason (or profane and sacred) cannot be simply opposed. Two important questions then arise. First, what are the implications of this recalcitrant alterity for a Habermasian discursive politics? And second, does this enduring dimension of otherness itself have political implications which might call for quite different emancipatory strategies? I have argued that the communicative imperatives and logic of history to be found in Habermas's work close up the fissures from which alterity might leak, while modernity is itself defined by its exclusion, or transcendence. In this second part of my chapter I will explain why I think this is a misunderstanding of modernity and one which yields an inadequate politics. This will entail three stages of argument: first, I will contend that otherness is irrepressible, regardless of historical development; secondly I will show how it is irreducibly associated with power and thus political; and finally I will explain why the postmodern discourses and strategies that engage with alterity on this level constitute crucial supplements to any communicative politics.

I will begin by citing two theories, one phenomenological and the other poststructuralist, that establish the ineliminable resistance of alterity to rationalization or discursive lucidity. This is important in response to Habermas's claim that nothing within the lifeworld or psyche is in principle immune to discursive retrieval and thus resistant to the project of modernity.

The first theory is that of Merleau-Ponty, who fits well in this context since like Habermas he deploys the notion of a lifeworld, while like poststructuralists he is influenced by Saussurean linguistics. As for Habermas, Merleau-Ponty's lifeworld harbours no absolute alterity in so far as it is always meaningful for us. But it is first meaningful for us as embodied beings, where our primary relation to the world is perceptual and perceptual significance remains prereflective and precognitive. Subsequent thematizations, as well as language itself, always retain the characteristics of their perceptual origins, as ambiguous, contingent and open. Merleau-Ponty, then, both retains a primary dimension of lived meanings – meanings to which we have access via the body but which do not pass by way of reflection – and suggests that thematization retains the equivocalness and opacity of the prereflective within it. Although Habermas acknowledges that the body situates and thus contextualizes our knowledge, his discursive redemptions are never the result of an embodied knowing in this way and so reason's incarnate legacy is not acknowledged by him.

Moreover, while there is nothing alien to us in Merleau-Ponty's lifeworld either, structures of meaning are for him intrinsically lined with alterity (with invisibility), such that there is always an interweaving of reason and non-reason, consciousness and corporeity, sense and nonsense, visible and invisible. For perceptual significance is, like a work of art, experienced rather than known, as a preconceptual unity whose parts cohere and are assimilated according to an overall existential style. The perceptual *gestalt*, like language, has meaning due to a diacritical play of differences (where perception is 'structured as a language'[23]), where parts have a contingent affinity in an open but structured whole and their internal logic is aesthetic. An operative rationality is thus already found prior to reflection, with the process of rationalization being an always menaced linking of parts into more comprehensive clusters, and the process of verification being a 'crossing out' of dissonant elements or closed forms. Social structures and historical forms are also first assimilated according to their existential style and lived significance, whose thematization remains hazardous and provisional.

Finally, language according to Merleau-Ponty is both used in attempts to articulate this inexhaustible primordial significance (its manifest meaning) *and* participates in it (its latent significance): 'language as well as music can sustain a sense by virtue of its own arrangement, catch a meaning in its own mesh.'[24] Again, it retains an irreducible existential significance, conveyed according to its physiognomy, its diacritical organization, the relationship to the world exemplified by it. It coordinates perceptions and orients us to an environment on a precognitive level, which is why Merleau-Ponty must, although on somewhat different grounds, agree with Derrida that language always retains a poetic dimension. His lifeworld is an effulgence of meaning in which language also participates and in which it never achieves complete ideality. Despite their intersubjectivity, Habermas's discursive participants remain individually, in comparison, too confident in their use of language and capacity to thematize. Like poststructuralists, Merleau-Ponty insists that non-reason is no archaic past but must continuously line all meaning, although, unlike them, he also contends that it is patterned and so already offers up latent, if ambiguous, meaning which is not endlessly deferred.

Merleau-Ponty's account of the lifeworld thus suggests, *contra* Habermas, that there remains a latent alterity there, in so far as its lived and corporeal significance cannot be rendered discursive without residue, while its thematizations, together with the language they rely upon, both retain an existential ambiguity – a significance that continues to operate beneath the level of consciousness – and participate in the structuration of all meaning, where alterity (*qua* the spaces between terms, differences) is interwoven with, and a condition of, sense. This does not challenge a project of rationalizing the lifeworld, but it places irreducible limits on its ability to render all meaning discursive and fundamentally opposes and subverts any such attempt. Moreover, although Merleau-Ponty's ontology has an affinity with Heideggerian Being and Derridean *différance*, he can in no way be accused, as those others are by Habermas, of mystifying social problems. He makes clear the importance of describing an ontology pervaded by alterity; a politics that eschews the violence inherent in rationalist ideologies, whether Marxist or Kantian. But if like Habermas he emphasizes intersubjectivity and rationality in politics, then these centre around the precarious processes of meshing substantively different perspectives in the light of ambiguity, embodiment and contingency, rather than pursuing consensus through undistorted communication. Risk, audacity and creativity necessarily accompany reason.

What is nevertheless missing from Merleau-Ponty's account is any real appreciation of power as it is lodged within this generation of meaning, and this is what postmodernists provide. The second, and more obviously postmodern, appeal to the Other I want to cite is made by Julia Kristeva when she associates postmodern writing with an attempt to 'expand the limits of the signifiable', by pushing the boundaries of language, communication, sexual identity, sociality and experience to the limit. Far from wanting to use rational communication to resolve normative questions, she sees a realigned language, capable of signifying the body, desire, the semiotic, able to evoke the presymbolic, pulverize meaning and confront psychosis through borderline experiences, as the basis for a reconfigured subjectivity and ethics. Against pressures to conformity, postmodern writing sets out 'to blaze a trail amidst the unnameable'; to elicit the 'darkest regions' where language originates.[25] Kristeva herself suggests that postmodernism takes over the exploration of what was previously called the sacred: it finds an analogy in 'mystical traditions', although this 'exploration of the limits of meaning' has never before taken place in so unprotected a way – that is, without religious or mystical justification.[26]

Contrary to Habermas's project then, the aim is for a politics of transgression which intervenes where the lifeworld sinks into non-discursiveness and where meaning and subjectivity themselves evolve, where power, sacrifice, exclusions and repressions already operate. I have suggested that Habermas's theory is directed against this sort of disruptiveness, especially via appeals to the non-rational, but it is difficult to see how communicative reason could be effective here. It simply operates on a different level.[27]

Having argued for the recalcitrance of alterity in all meaning and communication, I come now to the second part of my argument, which concerns the power relations involved in its movements and hence its political implications. In suggesting the senses in which alterity is political, I will make two claims. First, in a broader sense, the very suppression of the Other is an act of violence in which non-rational meanings, experiences and actors are suppressed. Alterity operates here within an opposition between openness and closure which broadly corresponds to that between liberation and domination. Secondly, and more specifically, the exclusion of otherness especially affects groups who are associated with it, or who forge their identities and life forms along these lines. They are marginalized, yet the processes by which these identifications and exclusions occur remain largely prediscursive, lodged within the horizons of the lifeworld where they are continually reproduced. Since meaning and identity continue to evolve at a lifeworld level even in modernity, a politics supplementary to the more formal procedures of discourse ethics is surely required. My contention is then that modernity cannot afford to turn its back on this politics, since it operates beneath and within processes of rational negotiation, where it affects, even constructs, the capacities and opportunities of actors who would participate in the free and equal manner that discursive democracy requires, as well as protecting modern lifeworlds against rationalist closure.

Alterity in these contexts is therefore ambiguous: associated with both an openness to be invoked and a closure to be subverted. It is broadly synonymous with the non-rational, the pre- or non-discursive, with that which is not, or cannot conclusively be, reflected upon or perhaps even rendered linguistic and subjected to formal validity claims. The political in this context is then associated with relations of power, in particular as these circulate within the unfolding of meaning itself. Postmodern practices intervene at this level, both opening dimensions immune to rational redemption and shifting representations that reproduce relations of privilege and exclusion.

To take up the broader claims being made here, first: Western, and especially modern, orientations to knowledge suppress the body and emotions, senses and desire, imagination and intuition, the merely lived and perceived – that is, what I am calling the non-discursive, or Other – in the sense that meanings which circulate in these dimensions are dismissed as irrational. In so far as they are considered retrievable, it is precisely by translating them into rational discourse. This is not, however, the same as evoking their own order of signification, their internal rhythms and economy, which may only be approached by mimetic or aesthetic means.

Now, such claims are not exclusive to postmodernists: feminists, Romantics and critical theorists, all of whom might be situated within the modernist discourse of counter-Enlightenment, also advance them, although they do not play much of a role in the story Habermas tells. Where they differ, however, is in the political goals and strategies they associate with rationalism's exclusions. In critical modern discourses, otherness is more likely to be romantically associated with substantive and harmonious forces which are identified as both resistant to instrumental reason and its domination, and an alternative to its existential impoverishments. Influential here is Kant's introduction of aesthetic judgement as a bridge between pure and practical reason, where the aesthetic suggests a harmonious logic that is without purpose and that obeys laws other than those of causality or deductive subsumption. It is this notion of an other order which speaks to the senses as well as to reason which Schiller developed and that Marcuse took up, now combining it with a Freudian description of the primary processes that yield meaning, but not reason, according to the logic of the pleasure principle. The harmony of aesthetic lawfulness without law, the synthesis of mind and body and the subversiveness plus emancipatory potential of an only basically repressed unconscious were therefore claimed for critical theory in the name of an alterity whose logic suggested both refusal (of one-dimensional rationalism) and a new sensibility.

In these critical modern discourses then, alterity suggests a non-rational logic which might both disrupt the narrowness of rationalism and suggest an alternative choreography for the rhythms of meaning-generation, existence and coexistence. Its attraction for radical social theorists lies precisely in its suggestion of an outside to the closures wrought by rationalization in the form of capitalism, bureaucracy and patriarchy. The problem with this solution is, however, that the Other is vulnerable to increasing systemic colonization, and culminates in the sort of political impasse to which pre-Habermasian critical theory and much radical feminism succumbed. I think Habermas and poststructuralists share this recognition and embark on a similar solution in so far as they both insist that the whole, while riddled with power, cannot be completely impervious to what we might call, following Foucault, practices of liberty. In Habermas's case it is open to communicative action and thus to another rationality, but for poststructuralists it is the location of alterity itself that is shifted, from an outside of power to an irreducible process within it. In this sense, poststructuralists continue a radical tradition that invokes alterity against closure, but they abandon its association with harmonious forces of reconciliation and focus instead on its transgressive, negative qualities, which are discovered not outside the given but as its very possibility.

At this stage, I want to try to be more specific about alterity and, in particular, to insist that far from being some primordial and archaic anachronism which represents a throw-back to the premodern, it suggests an inescapable dimension of any culture. Since its exponents are generally agreed that it cannot be named, defined or fixed, it does seem paradoxical – perhaps a performative contradiction – that so much should have been written about the Other. Indeed to the extent that otherness suggests an other language, or dimension of meaning, from that which rational communication can utilize or convey, it is often dismissed literally as nonsense. For if the Other cannot be represented, neither does its own alleged logic seem capable of signifying anything that is intersubjectively comprehensible.

However, suggestions are rarely made that a countersymbolic, the language and register of the non-rational, should or could replace reason. It is true that alterity is best invoked by practices broadly summarized as aesthetic, which communicate a sense that does not pass by way of lucidity or reason. But at the same time, such strategies can themselves be reflected on and their purposes discussed using rational argument. In this latter sense, poststructuralists never turn their backs on enlightenment.[28] Rather, advocates of alterity tend to deploy both aesthetic means (which may be linguistic, as in the case of avant-garde poetry, or non-linguistic, as in the case of the visual arts) and philosophical discourses. Even in the case of language and discourse, and *contra* Habermas, however, they insist on limits to what can be clearly and rationally said. For otherness cannot be translated into rational terminology without remainder, while linguistic and discursive forms also bear within themselves opaque and ambiguous dimensions of alterity.

This otherness is associated by postmodernists with mobility, fluidity, heterogeneity; with the ruin of all stability, certainty and reification; with a process rather than any thing. They incite the unnameable, the unknown, in order to disclose its resilience to discursive translation rather than to overthrow reason as such, as Habermas suggests. They alert us to the policing of boundaries that rationalization entails in its efforts to keep the non-rational at bay; to processes of exclusion, marginalization, silencing, repression and oppression that operate within the apparently neutral project of articulating meaning and reflecting upon it. They perceive modernity as an attempt to eliminate the unrepresentable by squeezing it into representational form, where any recalcitrant residue is denied significance or violently (mis)named. From this perspective it is not just purposive-instrumental reason that colonizes and subjugates, but a metaphysical will to lucidity as such. Irruptions of alterity are a means of opening spaces through which the unnameable and hence uncolonizable might be glimpsed, as a strategy subversive of reason's closures, not a leap into the irrational. Deconstructing the binary oppositions which it sees sustaining metaphysical thinking, postmodernism cannot set up a reason/non-reason dichotomy and invert it, but instead transgresses, plays along, its boundary, such that the non-rational irrupts into reason to destabilize without replacing it. It is the subversive thrust of this process which renders postmodernism political. If it has a more affirmative side, it lies precisely in its opening a space for other voices and their particular representational styles which reason would suppress or translate.

Having considered a general antirationalist politics, I want now to move to the final, and most important, stage of my argument, to consider what happens at a lifeworld level prior to its discursive retrieval, that is within the pre- (although not necessarily non-) discursive. Are there not power relations operative at this level, and thus a certain politics, which do not go via reflection and which perhaps are unamenable to discursive negotiation? In this context I will consider two dimensions of power which are underplayed in Habermas's account of modernity. The first concerns the translation of meaning from the prereflective lifeworld into discursive form. The second relates to processes which remain prediscursive even in modernity.

When lifeworld structures are experienced as constraints, then their thematization is motivated. This process has the following trajectory. A situation – a context of relevance – is thrown into relief as constraints emerge and it is then problematized, such that what had formerly been taken for granted is rendered thematic. That is, a merely tacit lifeworld knowledge becomes reflective and, as such, subject to discourse. Such is the process of rationalization. The lifeworld can be 'arbitrarily' thematized 'at will', although its interpretation must itself be a source of communicative debate within a context of formal validity claims.[29]

Foucault, however, alerts us to the power relations already operative within this process of problematization and thematization in a way that Habermas does not.[30] Here there is significant disagreement over the meaning of discourse. For Habermas it signifies rational argumentation oriented towards consensus; for Foucault power is inherent within discourse and not excluded by it. Such power operates for him within the very heart of meaning-generation, where phenomena are problematized (or not) and rendered discursive according to an economy of privilege and exclusion. The passage from the prediscursive to the discursive is not simply a transition to reason, occurring via communicative action, but a process wherein certain themes or persons are silenced, constituted, displaced, controlled, modified, etc.[31] Many existentially problematic aspects of the lifeworld remain unthematized and so excluded from discursive remedy, either because certain persons are disempowered, or because lifeworld (epistemic) horizons render them literally inconceivable. At the same time, phenomena that are problematized-thematized become saturated with power in the process. The process of thematization does not therefore reduce the stock of prediscursive circuits of power, since these are continually reproduced within discourse itself.

This feeds into my second concern. The lifeworld provides the content on which speaking and acting subjects impose their rules. But although they may organize their validity claims according to formally universal linguistic structures, they enjoy only a limited freedom regarding the content elicited, since they remain products of their traditions, norms and socialization. Habermas himself acknowledges these limits: if communication opens up traditions and defences, 'it can never completely illuminate the implicit, the prepredicative, the not focally present background of the lifeworld' (PDM, p. 300). It is precisely here, then, that processes are at work through which meanings and subjects are produced prior to their participation in communicative reason. Lodged within them are operations of power that engender and exclude alterity and the life forms associated with it: the Other and others. For Habermas, however, emancipation can only operate within those dimensions that have already been rendered discursive and so he can offer no politics to deal with exclusions that remain stubbornly operative within the prediscursive.

Otherness is associated here with others: with those groups and identities which, in Habermas's terms, reveal different (essentially premodern) life forms and lifeworlds. Clearly alterity cannot be reduced to the more sociological category of others, but there are important links. To be cast as Other here is to be marginalized and subjugated as a group (for instance, in the sense in which de Beauvoir describes women's designation as Other, the Second Sex), yet the defining otherness of such groups turns out to be the very syndrome associated with alterity as such (they are condemned as unruly, irrational even mad, dangerously subversive and fleshy, etc.). Those who are defined as other are precisely the ones who do not share modernity's canonical hierarchy between mind and body, conscious and unconscious, culture and nature, reason and non-reason. While the empowering of such marginalized others is part of what postmodernists see as their own democratizing credentials, this cannot be accomplished simply by admitting them to fair and equal discussion. It is also necessary to engage in a deconstructive cultural politics that subverts the oppositions on which a prior exclusion operates.

Now, Habermas is aware of the limits to discursivity when it comes to life forms: 'No one can reflectively agree to the form of life in which he has been socialized.' Life projects are chosen in more complex, arbitrary and obscure ways, while questions about the good life cannot 'be decided by standards of normative rightness'.[32] However it is not just difference but exclusion that is at issue here, and because Habermas can only grant political efficacy at a discursive level, he either has to ignore this dimension of power or suggest, as he subsequently has, that modernity is after all replacing lifeworld difference with discursive difference: 'rigid lifeforms succumb to entropy'; 'The accelerated change of modern societies bursts the mould of all stationary lifeforms. Cultures survive only if they draw the power for self-transformation from criticism and secession.'[33]

Yet this is surely to render the evolution of identity too rationalistic and to ignore the power that already structures choices and identities. If the historical trajectory of rationalization Habermas traces is away from a merely customary consensus and towards a negotiated one, the subject-modes and solidarities of the lifeworld must still remain significantly unquestioned and reproduced even *within* modernity, and thus below the threshold of communicative reason. This is less because they are normatively opaque than because cultures are thoroughly encoded with hierarchies of privilege and marginalization.

While impartial procedures, constitutional democracy and ethical discourses (would) mark a significant emancipatory coup for modernity, then, they surely cannot exhaust the question of others and the politics that circulates among them at a lifeworld and at a discursive level. Habermas lacks any theory of power operative within the modern lifeworld other than that of system intrusions, and he fails to acknowledge that even in modernity, pre- or non-discursive intersubjective relations operate within realms of alterity and according to practices that are communicative yet non-rational. Moreover, although such acknowledgement would yield only a supplementary politics, its effects are critical for democracy because it is here that needs, interests, identities, interpretive biases, exclusions, disempowerments, more open or closed group identifications – that is, the content for, and competencies of players within, democratic negotiations – are already forged. In closing, I will offer two illustrations of the sorts of processes I have in mind here.

The first occurs in descriptions of cultural imperialism offered by Iris Marion Young in her *Justice and the Politics of Difference*. Young describes how group oppression occurs in a prediscursive manner where habitual and group aversions are manifested through body language – gestures, avoidance of eye contact, tone of voice, nervousness, etc. These are immediately and non-discursively dismissive, but they also subvert more explicit commitments to egalitarianism. Because such motivations and expressions do not pass by way of consciousness, they avoid normative resolution. Women's oppression, for example, is 'clearly structured by the interactive dynamics of desire, the pulses of attraction and aversion, and people's experiences of bodies and embodiment.'[34] Thus racism, sexism, homophobia, ageism and ableism operate 'underground, dwelling in everyday habits and cultural meanings of which people are for the most part unaware'.[35]

Young draws on Kristeva's concept of abjection to associate the unconscious motivations for such behaviour with deep-rooted insecurities regarding the self and its boundaries, where certain groups are culturally associated with separation anxieties because they are equated with the body. Those whom we define as other remind us of the otherness within ourselves, of our ambiguous and hazardous subjectivity. Indeed Young argues that any group associated with the body in our rationalist culture risks being perceived as dangerous and repulsive and therefore other. A shift in the mind/body dualism, as well as in other oppositions structuring Western culture in a hierarchical way, is then needed. Although Young herself would try to resolve the problem with consciousness-raising techniques, precisely to render them amenable to discursive negotiation, the psychoanalytic work on which she draws emphasizes the importance of avant-garde aesthetic practices, both in alerting us to the uncanniness within the self, in order that we might become more attuned to otherness, the foreign and the alien, and in subverting the cultural dualisms on which such fears and exclusions draw.[36]

A further illustration of what I have in mind as a non-discursive politics concerns representations of gender. Feminists refer to it as a politics of vision, or representation. Visual, as well as linguistic, dimensions of culture reproduce norms and encode representations with sexual difference (for example in images of the female body). Additionally, an economy of vision is at work, distributing pleasure and desire. 'In a world ordered by sexual imbalance, pleasure in looking has been split between active/male and passive/female. The determining male gaze projects its phantasy onto the female figure which is styled accordingly.'[37] Such systems of meaning sustain relations of power that are communicated below the threshold of consciousness. Of course, theories like psychoanalysis allow them to be reflected upon and so subjected to discourse, as feminism demonstrates. But it seems impossible that such knowledge could exhaust or eliminate these processes, with their subliminal aesthetic and unconscious resonances. A more appropriate intervention can be made aesthetically: postmodern feminist art aims not to reconcile, but 'addresses the presence of the sexual in representation – to expose the fixed nature of sexual identity as a fantasy and, in the same gesture, to trouble, to break up, or rupture the visual field before our eyes'.[38] Such art thus challenges the conditions of desire and its displacements through problematizing, subverting and shifting images. Feminist deployments of postmodern tactics deconstruct the very process of signification; they 'politicize desire in their play with the revealed and the hidden, the offered and the deferred'.[39]

In one sense, this contesting of traditions and habits renders this politics thoroughly modern in Habermas's terms: 'the radical task of postmodernism is to deconstruct apparent truths, to dismantle dominant ideas and cultural forms and to engage in the guerrilla tactics of undermining closed and hegemonic systems of thought.'[40] It is also utilized as part of a modernist, emancipatory project – feminism – and guided by its discourses. Yet at the same time, it deconstructs feminism's agents and beneficiaries; it operates on an aesthetic level where communication is intersubjective but not rational or linguistic; it points to dimensions where power operates below the level of consciousness and remains immune to full discursive retrieval; it challenges reason and language, as well as vision, as sites where power is fundamentally inscribed and irremediably reproduced, and it defies appeals to validity claims or normative consensus. Modernity emerges here then as a paradoxical, rather than a merely unfinished, project.

This politics of alterity, and the aesthetic 'emancipatory' interventions within it, thus proliferate on a level that is quite alien to Habermas's aspirations for mobilizing the unfinished project of modernity, yet it is difficult to see how that project as he presents it could engage in these circuits of the non-rational. Indeed, I have suggested that his entire theory is predicated on an exclusion of this dimension of the Other and therefore of the postmodern, aesthetic interventions which are targeted there. At the same time, it seems that Habermas's acknowledgement of the persistence of the lifeworld calls attention to this prediscursive realm and to the limits of discourse, but it is a domain which seems increasingly to shrink in modernity as he describes it. Yet whatever the emancipatory potential of discursive ethics, this still cannot, and never will, exhaust other levels of intersubjectivity in which a supplementary politics is required, since otherness and its exclusions are continually reproduced at both lifeworld and discursive levels. If modernity remains an unfinished project, then there can in principle be no prospect of its completion.

NOTES

1 Jürgen Habermas, *The Philosophical Discourse of Modernity* (Cambridge: Polity Press; Cambridge, Mass.: MIT Press, 1987), hereafter cited as *PDM*.
2 See 'Modernity: An Unfinished Project', chapter 1 above.
3 Jürgen Habermas, *Postmetaphysical Thinking* (Cambridge: Polity Press, 1992), p. 35.
4 J. Derrida, '*Différance*', in *A Derrida Reader: Between the Blinds*, ed. P. Kamuf (Hemel Hempstead: Harvester-Wheatsheaf, 1991), p. 76.
5 R. Bernstein, *The New Constellation: The Ethical/Political Horizons of Modernity/Postmodernity* (Cambridge: Polity Press, 1991), p. 229, n49.
6 Jürgen Habermas, 'Questions and Counterquestions', in R. Bernstein (ed.), *Habermas and Modernity* (Cambridge: Polity Press, 1985), p. 215; 'Remarks on the Concept of Communicative Action', in G. Seebass and R. Tuomela (eds), *Social Action* (Dordrecht: D. Reidel, 1985), p. 165; and *Postmetaphysical Thinking*, p. 50.
7 Habermas, *Postmetaphysical Thinking*, p. 38.

8 Jürgen Habermas, *The Theory of Communicative Action*, vol. 2 (Cambridge: Polity Press, 1987), p. 145.
9 Ibid., p. 183.
10 Ibid., p. 154.
11 Ibid., p. 145.
12 Habermas, *Postmetaphysical Thinking*, p. 51.
13 Ibid., pp. 51, 145.
14 Habermas, 'Questions and Counterquestions', p. 210.
15 See Martin Jay, 'Habermas and Modernism', in Bernstein (ed.), *Habermas and Modernity*, pp. 137f.; David Rasmussen, 'Communicative Action and the Fate of Modernity', *Theory, Culture and Society* 2.3 (1985), p. 141.
16 Habermas, 'Questions and Counterquestions', p. 200.
17 Ibid., p. 202.
18 J.-F. Lyotard, 'What is Postmodernism?', in *The Postmodern Condition* (Manchester: Manchester University Press, 1984), pp. 72–3.
19 See p. 49 above.
20 See p. 40 above.
21 See p. 49 above.
22 See p. 51 above.
23 M. Merleau-Ponty, *The Visible and the Invisible* (Evanston: Northwestern University Press, 1968), p. 126.
24 Ibid., p. 153.
25 J. Kristeva, 'Postmodernism?', *Bucknell Review* 25, part 2 (1980), pp. 137, 140.
26 Ibid., p. 141.
27 Habermas himself acknowledges the limits of discursiveness: 'Negotiated descriptions of situations, and agreements based on the intersubjective recognition of criticisable validity-claims, are diffuse, fleeting, occasional and fragile'; see 'A Reply to My Critics', in J. Thompson and D. Held (eds), *Habermas: Critical Debates* (London, Macmillan, 1982), p. 235. If traditional consensus is prereflective but assured, modern agreements remain exceptionally hazardous (Habemas, 'Remarks on the Concept of Communicative Action', p. 171; Jürgen Habermas, *The Theory of Communicative Action*, vol. 1 (Cambridge: Polity Press, 1984), pp. 340ff.) and it is precisely lifeworld know-how that operates as a background tacit intuition underwriting efforts to agreement here. For it provides a shifting matrix of familiar and taken-for-granted assumptions operative below the level of consciousness and therefore of argumentation. 'It is an *implicit* knowledge that cannot be represented in a finite number of propositions; it is *holistically structured* knowledge, the basic elements of which mutually define one another; and it is a knowledge that *does not stand at our disposition*, inasmuch as we cannot make it conscious and place it in doubt as we please' ('Remarks on the Concept of Communicative Action', p. 166).
28 Cf. Michel Foucault, 'What is Enlightenment?' in P. Rabinow (ed.). *The Foucault Reader* (Harmondsworth: Penguin, 1984).
29 Habermas, *The Theory of Communicative Action*, vol. 2, pp. 122ff.
30 See Foucault's remarks on problematization, for example in Kritzman (ed.), *Politics, Philosophy, Culture* (London and New York: Routledge, 1988), p. 257.
31 See, for example, Michel Foucault, *The History of Sexuality*, vol. 1 (Harmondsworth: Penguin, 1981), p. 23.

32 Habermas, *The Theory of Communicative Action*, vol. 2, pp. 109–10.
33 Jürgen Habermas, 'Struggle for Recognition in Constitutional States', *European Journal of Philosophy* 1:2 (1993), p. 143.
34 I. M. Young, *Justice and the Politics of Difference* (Princeton: Princeton University Press, 1990), p. 123.
35 Ibid., p. 124.
36 See J. Kristeva, *Powers of Horror: An Essay on Abjection* (New York: Columbia University Press, 1982) and *Strangers to Ourselves* (New York and London: Harvester-Wheatsheaf, 1991).
37 L. Mulvey, 'Visual Pleasure and Narrative Cinema', *Screen* 16.3 (Autumn 1975), p. 11.
38 J. Rose, *Sexuality and the Politics of Vision* (London: Verso, 1986), pp. 227–8.
39 L. Hutcheon, *The Politics of Representation* (London and New York: Routledge, 1989), p. 154.
40 J. Wolff, 'Postmodern Theory and Feminist Art Practice', in R. Boyne and A. Rattansi (eds), *Postmodernism and Society* (London: Macmillan, 1990), p. 190.

9

THE CAUSALITY OF FATE: MODERNITY AND MODERNISM IN HABERMAS

Jay M. Bernstein

A Suppressed Dialectic

In *The Philosophical Discourse of Modernity*[1] Habermas argues that the rationalization processes of modernity are essentially ambiguous: rationalization involves both a real increment in rationality and a distortion of reason. The real increment in rationality can only be comprehended from the perspective of 'communicative' rationality; while the distortions of rationality are best comprehended as illegitimate extensions of subject-centred reason into an intersubjectively constituted lifeworld. In engaging with the distortions of reason and rationality the philosophical discourses of modernity that are the target of Habermas's critical history – the writings of Heidegger, Bataille, Derrida, Foucault, Adorno and Horkheimer – commit a metonymic fallacy, taking subject-centred reason as the whole of reason. Such totalizing critiques of enlightened reason involve an inevitable recoil, leaving them without any possible rational foundation or ground, any place from which their critique can be lodged. As a consequence, these writers are forced to generate an 'extraordinary discourse' that *claims* to operate outside the horizon of reason without being utterly irrational' (*PDM*, p. 308).

Because the writing of these philosophers is distinctive, 'extraordinary', and because the claims of this writing are to be sustained by specific practices of writing, I shall denominate the object of Habermas's critique 'philosophical modernism', its practitioners 'philosophical modernists'. This is a presumptive, and partial, classification; its *raison d'être* is to provoke a consideration of the connection between artistic modernism and a self-conscious philosophical discourse that has become extraordinary.

Philosophical modernism cannot be said to be unaware of the communicative rationality that Habermas contends provides the sole basis for enlightening reason about itself. On the contrary, Habermas's strategy in *The Philosophical Discourse of Modernity* turns on revealing communicative rationality as the road not taken by Hegel (*PDM*, pp. 27–30, 37–40), Marx (pp. 62–5), Heidegger (pp. 136–7), and Derrida in his discussion of Husserl (pp. 168–72). And because the road of communicative reason was not taken, because the difference between the dominating reason of the philosophy of consciousness and the reason of communicative action oriented towards establishing intersubjective agreement was not heeded, then either subject-centred reason comes to aporetically invade, recoil upon, the very discourses lodging a critique of it (pp. 151, 274), or the force of critique is voided (pp. 183–4, 237). Manifestly, this same point cuts the other way; if Hegel, Heidegger, Derrida and Adorno had the option of communicative rationality and refused it, then perhaps what Habermas claims for it is not truly available, or not available in the way he thinks it to be.[2] And this supposition would gain force if it were discovered that the duality between subject-centred reason and communicative reason was not either unambiguous, or absolute or exhaustive. What if communicative rationality, as Habermas conceives of it, is itself a product of subject-centred reason, is itself a distortion of reason? What if the social logics of subject-centred reason (systems integration) and communicative reason (social integration) are never pure; the espousal of their purity a mask for their (constitutive) interdependence?[3] What if there is more to reason and rationality, a form of reason and rationality, that is neither subject-centred nor communicative as Habermas understands these terms?

Habermas contends that 'we need a *theoretically constituted perspective* to be able to treat communicative action as the medium through which the lifeworld . . . is reproduced' (*PDM*, p. 299). The theoretically constituted perspective is that of the ideal speech situation (p. 323), which corresponds to, is a theoretical articulation of, 'the capacity of responsible participants in interaction to orient themselves in relation to validity claims geared to intersubjective recognition' (p. 314). While this theoretical articulation is not the consequence of transcendental reflection seeking intuitive insight into self-consciousness – the form of analysis consonant with subject-centred reason – but rather a product of the reconstructive sciences that bring to light the implicit rule-knowledge actually exercised in the generation of utterances (pp. 297–8), it is none the less the case that the perspective attained allows, for validity claims, a moment of absolute transcendence that ' "blots out" space and time' (p. 323). In *PDM*, more than previously, Habermas gestures at the social and historical embedding, the contextual constraints, that form the other side of validity claims. Despite these gestures, it remains the case that the theoretical perspective articulated through the deployment of the reconstructive sciences is of an ideal speech situation; and it is through the consideration of claims in terms of the ideal speech situation that their putative validity is one that transcends spaces and times. It is this universality, ideality and transcendence which has consistently been the target of Habermas's critics.[4]

Philosophical modernism's totalizing critique eschews procedural rationality and universality, conceiving them as figures of domination; its extraordinary discourses presumptively[5] leaving behind the claim of enlightened rationality for the sake of an apparently blind, normless particularism. Habermas, in contrast, wants to salvage the claims of enlightenment through the reconstructive sciences, operating as analogues of transcendental reflection and legislation. A choice between these extremes – philosophical modernism's immanence and particularism, and Habermas's transcendence and universalism – is less than inviting. Can we not recognize in these extremes of universal and particular a fateful dialectic at work? A sundering of the very comprehensive reason for which Habermas takes himself to be spokesman? Can we not recognize in philosophical modernism's particularity a substantiality that has forgotten that it is also subject? Can we not recognize in Habermas's ideal speech situation a subjectivity that has forgotten its substantiality? Are these two extremes not but two halves of an integral freedom to which, however, they do not add up? Can we not recognize ourselves in the dialectical belonging and separation of these conflicting positions?

In what follows I want to pursue this suggestion through an examination of the truth claims of philosophical modernism and Habermasian modernity independently of their reflective comprehension of their respective projects. In concrete terms, this means following through the suggestion that the philosophical discourses of modernity are modernist, their claims discursive analogues of one aspect of artistic modernism's claim of being the 'other' of reason (*PDM*, p. 96). The appropriateness of such a focus derives directly from the oft-noted disanalogy between the cognitive status of aesthetic judgements and the validity claims of truth and rightness within Habermas's tripartite scheme;[6] and the fact that this tripartite scheme only comes into view through the abandonment of the perspective (level) of judgement (p. 312). The claims of art and aesthetic judgement signify within the tripartite scheme the claims of what is abandoned when the level of judgement, the ontic fundament, the lifeworld is abandoned. These claims return in philosophical modernism. The latter, then, come to stand to Habermas's account of truth and normative rightness as Kant's third Critique, which was to bridge the gulf between knowledge and moral worth, stands to his first and second Critiques.[7] What is abandoned and excluded from,

marginalized within, philosophical modernity is the claim of comprehensive reason. This claim comes into view, claims us, through the
operation of the causality of fate.

From Fallibilism to Modernism

Let me begin obliquely. In a long and nervous footnote (*PDM*, pp.
408–9) to his excursus 'On Leveling the Genre Distinction between
Philosophy and Literature', Habermas addresses the question of
philosophical modernism from a diagnostic angle; not, that is, in
terms of its aporetic comprehension of reason and modernity, but
rather in terms of its rhetoric and writing. The note appears as an
'after-worry', a worry that in his systematic critique he had not quite
come to terms with the motives underlying the extraordinary discourse of philosophical modernism.

Habermas chides the philosophical modernists for their naiveté in
thinking that a special sort of writing is necessary to avoid metaphysics – the systematic gathering of foundations, presence, self-presence
and certainty. Systematic philosophy, with its claims for closure,
completeness, determinacy and uniqueness, which together would
make the world fully present to self, and the self fully present to
itself, is, Habermas contends, a straw man. Philosophy has long since
followed the path of the sciences and given up the ideal of systematic
closure, thereby acknowledging the fallibilistic character of its pursuits. Nowadays 'we reckon upon the trivial *possibility* that they [our
truth claims] will be revised tomorrow or someplace else.' It is
because they have failed to see that this is the case, because 'they still
defend themselves as if they were living in the shadow of the "last"
philosopher,' the philosophical modernists get caught in the paradox
of self-referentiality, the aporia of totalizing critique.

Now it would be odd if the philosophical modernists had been
twisting and contorting their discourse because they had failed to
notice that philosophy had become fallibilistic. Odder still to adopt
complex strategies of writing to avoid the claims of closure, completeness and certainty if these claims are, as they contend them to be,
non-satisfiable. Why struggle to avoid what you acknowledge as
impossible to achieve either in fact or in principle? Habermas's
contention that Heidegger, Adorno and Derrida (three writers who
self-consciously prioritize art and attempt, in some sense, to render
philosophical discourse 'aesthetic') confuse the universalist problematics that remain in a fallibilist context with long since 'abandoned
status claims' rings hollow against the background of *acknowledged*
aporia and a concern for alterity that mark all three writers'
discourses. Does fallibilism really capture what philosophical mod-

ernism resists of modernity? Or does fallibilistic self-consciousness repress the problematics of aporia and alterity motivating philosophical modernism?

No help in answering this will come from the excursus to which the note in question is appended. There Habermas defends a thesis, viz., that from the perspective of ordinary usage the genre distinction between philosophy and literature cannot be levelled, that, so far as I am aware, Derrida never denies.[8] What Derrida suggests is rather that dominant philosophical understandings of the distinction misconstrue it, fixing it and purifying it in ways that belie the connectedness and interdependency of the items distinguished.[9] And what better way of demonstrating this could there be than revealing the feint, trope, excess underpinning presumptive demonstrations of purity? That this might matter, in general, is something that Derrida cannot demonstrate, nor would he want to; mattering being strictly parasitic upon the mattering, the claims, of the text being deconstructed.

However, some headway can be made here if we examine briefly some of Habermas's comments on Foucault. Habermas avers that if one attempts to elicit the norms tacitly appealed to in Foucault's indictment of disciplinary power 'one encounters familiar determinations from the normativistic language games that he has explicitly rejected' (*PDM*, p. 284). So we rediscover in Foucault the 'asymmetric relationship between powerholders and those subject to power, as well as the reifying effect of technologies of power, which violate the moral and bodily integrity of subjects capable of speech and action' (ibid.). If we but rediscover in Foucault a reaffirmation of what we already believe, why does he bother to reject the language game of norms? And how are we to understand the appeal, the demand of his writing?

In fact, Habermas elegantly answers these questions for us, without, however, quite seeing the consequences of his own points. In Foucault, he claims, 'power'

> preserves a literally aesthetic relation to the perception of the body, to the painful experience of the mistreated body . . . The asymmetry (replete with normative content) that Foucault sees embedded in power complexes does not hold primarily between powerful wills and coerced subjugation, but between processes of power and the bodies that are crushed within them. It is always the body that is maltreated in torture and made into a showpiece of sovereign revenge; that is taken hold of in drill, resolved into a field of mechanical forces and manipulated; that is objectified and monitored by the human sciences, even as it is stimulated in its desire and stripped naked. If Foucault's concept

of power preserves for itself some remnant of aesthetic content,
then it owes this to his vitalistic, *Lebensphilosophie* way of
reading the body's experience of itself. (*PDM*, p. 285)

After quoting the closing peroration of *The History of Sexuality* in
which the dream of another economy of the body and its pleasures is
offered, Habermas comments that this

> *other* economy of the body and of pleasures, about which in the
> meantime – with Bataille – we can only dream, would not be
> another economy of power, but a postmodern theory that
> would also give an account of the standards of critique already
> laid claim to implicitly. Until then, resistance can draw its
> motivation, if not its justification, only from the signals of body
> language, from that nonverbalizable language of the body on
> which pain has been inflicted, which refuses to be sublated into
> discourse. (*PDM*, pp. 285–6)

One might well ask after the evidence for the thesis that in the
realization of the dreamed-of new *economy* of the body and its
pleasure Foucault believes that employed but unstated norms of
critique will suddenly become available. Put this query aside. What
needs illuminating first is the force and significance of the thesis that
the relation between power and the experience of the body in
Foucault is 'literally aesthetic'. How does this thesis connect with
Foucault's overt rejection of the language game of norms in a context
where his writing continues to affirm the 'content' of those norms?
And are these connections really best understood in terms of a
Lebensphilosophie way of reading the body's experience?

If we are to follow through on the aesthetic connection between
power and the perception of the body, then we need first to remind
ourselves of an inner connection between aesthetic judgement and
modernist art. Aesthetic reflective judgements begin with a consideration of the presentation of a particular; the consideration is 'autonomous' and disinterested in that it is made apart from epistemic,
practical (moral) and sensible interests one may have in the object or
state of affairs presented. Disinterested reflection renders the presentation autonomous from the network of cognitive, practical and
sensible ends or purposes in which it is otherwise implicated. Judgements issuing from disinterested reflection are themselves 'autonomous' because although the presentation judged is reflectively
articulated, the judgement itself is not the subsumption of the object
under any normative or epistemic concept.

Analogously, we describe a work of art as 'autonomous' just in
case its forms, and hence the integrity of the work itself, are not

derived from concepts and forms – religious, cultic, moral, political, etc. – external to the work itself. A work's intelligibility is a product of its internal working, without this working being beholden to purposes or ends external to the work. The self-conscious pursuance of autonomy, the awareness that aesthetic sense-making cannot rely on anything external to the work itself, informs the practice of artistic modernism. It is this awareness that underlies the more typical reflective characterization of modernism as the interrogation of art concerning its own nature.

What Habermas fails to notice, or take sufficient account of, in Foucault is the close inner connection between the body and writing, between the non-verbalizable language of the body inflicted with pain, which refuses to be sublated in discourse, and a writing of that body, a discourse that refuses the language game of norms. However skewed Foucault's own comprehension of his amnesiac objectivity, his happy positivism, against the background of the project of artistic modernism his deployment of power, power complexes, the play of differential forces and the like becomes intelligible as the generation of counterconcepts, non-logical (albeit economic) forms whose aconceptuality allows for the possibility of a sense-making resistant to given regimes of sense-making, for a kind of purposefulness (of writing) without (external) purpose, and hence for a kind of non-teleological history. Power, we might say, permits a writing that still harbours 'an archaic unity of logic and causality'.[10] In brief, the claim of Foucault's discourse must be comprehended as a philosophical internalization of whatever we take the claim of artistic modernism to be.

Before taking up the claim invoked by this idea of sense-making, to be elaborated in the next section, three comments are in order. First, it is no accident that Foucault should take the body as a recurring focus of his investigations. The role of the body in Foucault, as in Nietzsche, must be understood both substantively and strategically. The body signifies, as writing does in Derrida, the suppressed other of reason, language, *logos*, universality. As such, it further signifies the claim of particularity against universality; a particularity that would hence be further violated if its history and suffering were inscribed in a history generated in the very terms responsible for its suppression. The body can be given voice, its suffering made visible, only if its singularity is, in some sense, respected.

This helps explain two distinct if interconnected features of Foucault's writing: its strong reliance on images and set pieces (the grand confinement, the panopticon, the scene of torture, the confession, the surgical body, etc.), and a writing that continually disclaims itself, refusing the discursive consequences (the implied norms, for example) of its analyses. Foucault is implying that if one cannot judge that *here* is subjugation and domination, that *this* is a violation of the integrity of the body, the person, then there can be no claims worth heeding: or better, any further heeding must acknowledge *this* if that heeding is not going to be a brute refusal of the claims of individuals and their bodies. This is not a defence of intuitionism or decisionism; on the contrary, those gestures of the tradition are themselves products of looking elsewhere for justification for judgement, of not recognizing the other in their concrete particularity, as if it were the concept (law, rule, universal) that made the violation a violation rather than being an expression of it. And this is to say that Foucault's work is not cryptonormative (*PDM*, pp. 282–4), but just normative otherwise, 'internally' normative perhaps. The charge of cryptonormativism presupposes that normativity is the deriving of judgements from universal premises or procedures, and hence that the force of normative judgements is derived from the general (the Categorical Imperative, the Utilitarian Calculus, the Ideal Speech Situation); but of course it is this subsumption model of the force of norms that Foucault's 'aesthetic' discourse is challenging. Hence a concept of power that definitionally built the judgement of domination into it would defeat the point of employing it as a non-concept.

Finally it follows from all this that the aesthetic content of Foucault's relating of body and power does not derive from any *Lebensphilosophie* way of reading the body's experience of itself. That aesthetic content is the content of artistic modernism with respect to both autonomous judgement and autonomous work. Each of Habermas's three charges against Foucault – presentism, relativism, and cryptonormativism, whatever their validity from the perspective of discursive reason and the universalist problematics still maintained by philosophy, dissimulate and disengage the actual validity claims of Foucault's discourse. Foucault's presentistic procedure is the attempt to render his discourse, in the relevant sense, 'autonomous', to sustain the preponderance of intuition against concept, and hence make his writing a work to be judged rather than a discourse to be redeemed. It is the discursive, philosophical analogue of 'aesthetic' autonomy and not value freedom or empiricist purity that is the issue here. Hence, Foucault's work cannot claim the status it seeks for itself without undermining that status; like the modernist work of art it can say what it wants to say only by not saying it.[11]

If the non-discursive, because non-demonstrable, judgement of the body inflicted with pain provides motivation for resisting domination, this can be no idle point for Habermas, since a perpetual difficulty for his theory has been the absence of a motivational base for taking up the claims of communicative reason.[12] And what better evidence could we want for the existence of an aporia concerning the relation of particular and universal than the division between a discourse perpetually refusing itself, and a reflective theory without a motivational base?

Modernism and Local Reason

It is usually argued that a break in Foucault's trajectory occurs after *The Order of Things*, that he moves from a conception of language informed by a modernist thematics of writing which operates a refusal of representation and an acknowledgement of the non-discursive sources of meaning, to a theory of power. Prior to his writing on power Foucault had let the significance of his work be governed by the modernist idea of writing, such that it, and not philosophy, was the repository for our understanding of modernity. Hence art and literature generally, and modernist writing in particular, were conceived as meta-epistemic, 'allegories of the deep arrangements which make knowledge possible'.[13] The continuity in Foucault becomes visible if we read the significance of modernist art, against Foucault, in the manner of Adorno; treat power in the double register of a force of social structuration and an aconceptual form for writing; and notice the coincidence of Foucault's turning away from literature with the drying up of the critical force of artistic modernism in the 1960s. Philosophy, then, could no longer be parasitic on modernist art, be the self-effacing saying of art's saying by not saying, as Adorno had attempted it; but it had, as it were, to make those claims, those sayings through not saying, its own, make them come from it. Philosophical modernism had to attempt to secure for itself the kind of autonomy that had previously been the prerogative of modernist art. For categorial reasons this project is even more fraught, more difficult, more aporetic than the project of critical artistic modernism.

Before limning these categorial restrictions, we need first to ask after the substance of the project. Earlier I suggested the thesis that the writing of modernist philosophy was geared towards producing a form of sense-making that remained at a distance from discursive reason, reason as subsumption, entailment, inference, et al., that is, reasoning as governed by forms whose force is indifferent to content. Of course, it is surely the case that, as a matter of fact, most concepts we employ are non-topic-neutral (unlike the logical constants and such terms as 'several', 'most', 'although', etc.), and therefore are not and cannot be governed by pure (logical) forms. Most concepts 'have their own informal logical powers which can only be understood from coming to know their own distinctive uses and employments'.[14] However, we might say, and Habermas might agree (*PDM*, p. 350), that rationalization tendentially brings the operative force of the central concepts of particular domains within the orbit of a procedural governance that weakens, to the point of disappearance, their reliance on practice for their sense. And this has the consequence of making the sense (the logical powers) of indefinitely more expressions dependent on forms whose functioning is a material equivalent of the functioning of syntactical and logical forms for topic-neutral terms. In other words, one way of reading rationalization would be to claim that it renders increasingly more terms *effectively* topic-neutral.

Aesthetical sense-making, the drive for autonomy, is centrally concerned with the possibility of making the coherence, intelligibility and claim of a work remaining irrefrangibly local, a product of the internal connections among the elements of the work, and hence inexponible. In Kant, the possibility of aesthetic 'provincialism' was dependent on aesthetic ideas, inexponible products of the imagination which induce 'much thought, yet without the possibility of any definite thought whatever, i.e. *concept* being adequate to it, and which language, consequently, can never quite get on level terms with or render intelligible'.[15] As aesthetic ideas were increasingly drawn within the governance of enlightened reason their capacity to inhibit interpretation and conceptual articulation weakened; traditional works, including premodernist autonomous works, were drawn level with language by an increasingly self-confident critical community. Modernist art hence had to disabuse art of its reliance on these ideas and turn inwards on to its own productive forms. These forms, again, were not purely logical forms, but still harboured 'an archaic unity of logic and causality'. Power, differance, et al., are non-concepts in just this way; they are for the sake of localizing discourse, which can, thus, 'induce much thought' without any concept being able to subsume the discourse and hence generate conceptual closure.

Philosophy was late in absorbing the lessons of modernism; which is perhaps why it receives denominations – 'poststructuralism', 'postmodernism' – drawn from different histories, different temporalities; and equally why it has proved so difficult to perceive that the claims of philosophical modernism, however its practitioners understand them, are best understood as the progeny and continuers of the project of critical artistic modernism.

This project involves the elaboration of the interconnection of three elements: local reason and rationality, sensual particularity (non-identity, alterity, otherness, the body), and judgement. Roughly, the logic at work here is that non-identity (of object with concept) is threatened by rationalization, which is metaphysics come of age, metaphysics become modern. Methodologism is to scientific discourse what proceduralism is to philosophy, and system is to the lifeworld. In each case constitutive concepts and meanings are rendered effectively topic-neutral. The claims of practice and the other can only be rendered visible through the instauration of a local reason working against the claims of abstract reason; for only within the ambit of a local reason is discriminatory judgement possible, judgement which, while supported by context, is none the less resolutely particular.

Without relying on the employment of non-concepts, but with a strong claim for the place of rhetoric in writing, the 'Introduction' to *Negative Dialectics* provides a defence of philosophical modernism as the interweaving of these three elements.[16] Philosophy now, Adorno maintains, must concern itself with what philosophy has traditionally shunned, 'nonconceptuality, individuality, and particularity – things which ever since Plato used to be dismissed as transitory and insignificant, and which Hegel labeled "lazy Existenz"' (*ND*, p. 8). The goal of negative dialectics is to change the direction of conceptuality, to block the movement of subsumption, the 'rationalized rage at nonidentity' (p. 23) implicit in idealism as the *summa* of the history of philosophy, and give conceptuality 'a turn toward nonidentity' (p. 12). To release the 'coherence of the nonidentical, the very thing infringed by deductive systematics' (p. 26) is possible only through a reliance on writing and language, a writing, then, that refuses to halt, stop, name: 'The determinable flaw in every concept makes it necessary to cite others; this is the font of the only constellations which inherited some of the hope of the name' (p. 53). 'Constellation' is Adorno's name for the entwinement of particular and context in philosophical thought (pp. 162–3). Constellations are philosophical 'compositions' (p. 165), philosophical 'works'. Because unsupported by reason, logic, foundations, such philosophizing must rely on 'the consistency of its performance, the density of its texture' (p. 35) as its guarantor. Such writing requires and leads to judgement, discrimination, 'that which escapes the concept' (p. 45). Only in judgement is the (rational) 'elective affinity between knower and known' (ibid.) realized and sustained.

If philosophy is to go in the direction of non-identity, it must refuse closure; and that does not mean merely certainty (as the contrary of fallibilism), but more centrally, full conceptual articulation.

> instead of reducing philosophy to categories, one would in a sense have to compose it first. Its course must be a ceaseless self-renewal, by its own strength as well as in friction with whatever standards it may have. The crux is *what happens in it, not a thesis or a position* – the texture, not the deductive or inductive course of a single line of reasoning. Essentially, therefore, philosophy is not expoundable. If it were, it would be superfluous; the fact that most of it can be expounded speaks against it.[17]

The 'what happens' in a discourse as opposed to a 'thesis or a position' specifies the space separating the judgement of local reason from the discursive redemption of claims. In *Aesthetic Theory* Adorno goes on to acknowledge, and indeed insist upon, the fragility of the truth of modernist works; their capacity to resist the effort of interpretation and criticism is only ever temporary – 'Neutralization is the social price art pays for its autonomy.'[18] And, equally, neutralization must be the social price that modernist philosophical works pay for their autonomy. Local reason is powerless to resist indefinitely the claims of universality; its claims depend on context, on the fine-grained texture of the non-topic-neutral powers of its concepts, powers generated and released by the contextualization provided by the density and texture of writing. Once its claims are removed from that context, they evaporate: its writing becomes presentism; its localism aporetic and self-defeating; its immanent standards pseudonormative. Their 'temporal substance' makes the truths of philosophical modernism 'suspended and frail' (*ND*, p. 34), ever subject to neutralization. 'The transcendent moment of *universal* validity [that] bursts every provinciality asunder' (*PDM*, p. 322), that ' "blots out" space and time' (p. 323), is their death.[19]

Reason: Divided and Distorted

The claims of local reason cannot be heard by Habermas for the very precise reason that his communication theory becomes visible and operative only when the analytic level of judgement is abandoned (*PDM*, p. 312); and worse, once the level at which communicative rationality manifests itself is attained its form of transcendence entails a virtual silencing of the claims of local reason and its objects, the others of universalist reason – nature, the human body, desire, the feelings, sensuous particularity. None the less, Habermas might still argue that this rationality and intelligibility has been placed so far outside what we now recognize as reason that its claims do not just appear as muted, silent; they are non-claims because there is no possible, non-utopian way in which local reason and universalist reason can be reconciled.

This thesis depends on Habermas's contention that local reason operates on the basis of an 'exclusion model' (*PDM*, p. 306) whereby what has been suppressed and denied by instrumental rationality is the sheer other of reason and not a form of latent rationality. In opposition to this he supports a 'diremption model' of reason in which the other of subject-centred reason is 'the dirempted totality, which makes itself felt primarily in the avenging power of destroyed reciprocities and in the fateful causality of distorted communicative relationships' (ibid.). In order, then, to resist Habermas's silencing of local reason it is first necessary to demonstrate that the diremption model and the exclusion model are not themselves exclusionary; that the dirempting of (comprehensive) reason can at the same time be an excluding and a silencing.

The difficulty facing us here is that Habermas distinguishes between what he regards as a legitimate disarticulation of substantial reason from the diremption of reason. This distinction leads to an overburdened conception of modernity in which the comprehension of the ambiguity of rationalization processes is partially constituted by the non-diremptive disarticulation of reason. Hence, what would need to be shown in order to demonstrate the compatibility of the diremptive and exclusionary models is that there is diremption where Habermas perceives disarticulation; that the overcoming of diremption, and with it the claims of comprehensive reason, occurs – slightly – elsewhere than Habermas avers; and that the positive claims of modernity can be detached from Habermas's strong theory of communicative rationality. While the demonstration of all these theses would be an elaborate and extensive affair, the central markers for such a set of propositions are readily available.

Habermas contends that latent within Kant's conception of formal, differentiated reason is a theory of modernity. Roughly, Habermas reads the Kantian disarticulation of substantive rationality into the three procedurally legislated domains of objective knowledge, moral-practical insight, and aesthetic judgement to be the philosophical crystallization of the Weberian theory of rationalization whereby, through value intensification, there develop the differentiated value spheres of science, morality and art.[20] Habermas gives this account a further twist in contending that the three value spheres that are philosophically written in terms of the trisection of reason represented by the three Critiques are just the three primordial functions of language that come into view when we abandon the level of judgement (PDM, p. 312). The components representing the three fundamental linguistic functions – the propositional component for representing states of affairs; the illocutionary component for taking up personal relationships; and the components that express the speaker's intentions – are mutually combined and interwoven in elementary speech acts (ibid.).

It is the binding of the Kantian-Weberian account of modernity to speech-act theory that overburdens the former. The thrust of my argument to here has been that philosophical modernism is best understood in terms of the claims and aporia of Kantian aesthetic judgement; claims and aporia that are equally those of modernist art. What these aporetic claims amount to is the thesis that one branch of trisected reason, viz. aesthetic judgement, when realized in the value sphere of art, discovered its autonomy, its separation from cognition and moral rightness, to be a distortion of it which, *a fortiori*, entailed the distortion of reason in its non-aesthetic forms.[21] Nor is this surprising since, on reflection, it becomes difficult to see what the dirempting of aesthetic judgement and its objects from considerations of truth and rightness could be if not a silencing of it and them. And how could this silencing make its experience of diremption speak if it has been constituted through the silencing of its claims; and if procedural reason in its cognitive and moral forms has been constituted as procedural and universalistic through the exclusion of judgement, through the reduction of judgement to aesthetic judgement and art to autonomy? Hence, when aesthetic judgement does try to speak, as it does in philosophical modernism, its speech is paradoxical and aporetic. Still, there are claims being made in such discourse, cognitive, moral and reflective claims, and we can only begin to come to a comprehension of the diremption of reason by heeding those claims.

Recognition and Communication

In engaging with claims similar to the ones I've been forwarding, Habermas has been content to concede the thesis that works of art have a 'truth potential' which does not correlate with any one of the three validity claims constitutive of communicative rationality; but goes on to follow Wellmer in thinking of this potential as something to be released *into* the lifeworld, and not as an actual dismantling of the trisection of reason.[22] But a dismantling of the trisection is tentatively broached in the passage from Wellmer that Habermas quotes:

> We can explain the way in which truth and truthfulness – and even normative correctness – are metaphorically interlaced in works of art only by appealing to the fact that the work of art, as a symbolic formation with an aesthetic validity claim, is *at the same time an object of life-world experience, in which the three validity domains are unmetaphorically intermeshed.* (emphasis added)

Having conceded art's silencing, it follows that claims for truth and moral rightness can enter into art works, as art works, only metaphorically. What happens to these very same claims when they issue from a work of philosophy? Are they still just metaphorical? Is philosophical modernism's work of undoing the purified categorial distinction between literal and metaphorical discourse itself literal or metaphorical? Might it be neither as a claim of local reason, but become neutralized and so become a 'merely' metaphorical, albeit categorial, denial of the distinction between literal and metaphorical when taken up by universal (trisected) rationality? What if, to paraphrase Habermas (*PDM*, p. 199), the presupposed idealizations that transcend any particular language game are what deform reason because they are idealizations that transcend, because they press local reason into saying what it does not want to say, silencing its (categorially) transgressive movement? How is categorial transgression possible? How can philosophy eschew its own categorial placement without contradicting itself? What might the lifeworld's unmetaphorical intermeshing of validity claims token for philosophy? Can philosophy judge?

Wellmer's statement attempts to blunt the sting of aporia while acknowledging its force. If art works are 'at the same time' objects of the lifeworld, then either the silencing of judgement and local reason has not really occurred, or it has occurred, cannot be undone, but the effects can be mitigated through the transmissions of mediators and interpreters. In opting for the latter alternative Habermas now appears to have conceded that diremption and exclusion are compatible models; without, however, seeing how his theory of communicative rationality colludes with the very diremption of reason it now seeks to undo by taking up the position of interpreter on behalf of the lifeworld.[23] Of course, the adoption of the position of an interpreter on behalf of the lifeworld is paradoxical since it assumes *both* the position of comprehensive reason, now understood as the claims of the lifeworld, and the position of enlightened reason that regards the trisection of reason as the cognitive achievement of modernity. Habermas avoids paradox and aporia only by refusing to examine his competing accounts at the same time.

Wellmer states, and Habermas by implication appears to concede, that the three validity domains are unmetaphorically intermeshed in the lifeworld. This is a systematically ambiguous claim; how ambiguous it is becomes apparent, however, only in the light of an examination of what I believe to be the unacknowledged constitutive theme of Habermas's thought: the fate of the causality of fate.

From 'Labor and Interaction' to the Freud chapters of *Knowledge and Human Interests* through to *The Philosophical Discourse of Modernity* (pp. 26–30, 306, 316, 324–5), Habermas has been attempting to preserve what he regards as the fundamental validity of Hegel's model of the causality of fate.[24] Using Hegel's example of a criminal and his punishment in 'The Spirit of Christianity and its Fate', Habermas depicts the operation of the causality of fate in these terms.

A criminal who disturbs such ethical [*sittlich*] relationships by encroaching upon and oppressing the life of another experiences the power of the life alienated by his deed as a hostile fate. He must perceive as the historical necessity of fate what is actually only the reactive force of a life that has been suppressed and separated off. This force causes the one at fault to suffer until he recognizes in the annihilation of the life of the other the lack in his own self, and in the act of repudiating another's life the estrangement from himself. In this causality of fate the ruptured bond of the ethical totality is brought to consciousness. This dirempted totality can become reconciled only when there arises from the experience of the negativity of divided life a longing for the life that has been lost – and when this experience forces those involved to recognize the denial of their own nature in the split-off existence of the other. Then both parties see through their hardened positions in relation to one another as the result of detachment, of abstraction from their common life-context – and in this context they recognize the basis of their existence. (*PDM*, pp. 28–9)

The problematic of modernity, and with it the force of the diremptive model and the critique of subject-centred reason, are together best understood in terms of a heightening of the operation of the causality of fate to the historical and collective level. The individual act that sets the operation of the causality of fate into motion in antiquity becomes the categorial deformation of the ethical totality in modernity: 'This act of tearing loose from an intersubjectively shared lifeworld is what first *generates* a subject–object relationship' (*PDM*, p. 29; see also p. 315).

   According to Habermas, because Hegel 'indissolubly' associated the force of the ethical totality with popular religion, on the one hand, and on the other hand came to recognize in civil society a new form of social organization which fundamentally breaks with the models of antiquity (and underlines the achievement of self-consciousness in modernity), he could not sustain the full movement of the causality of fate as an analysis and comprehension of the modern predicament (*PDM*, pp. 30–1). If one could separate the force of ethical totality from the claims of popular religion, it then would become possible to use the model of the causality of fate as the early Hegel had done. This detachment of ethical totality from popular religion would count as a detachment, and not as a transplantation, if it could acknowledge reason's altered – self-grounding, time-conscious – status. These two desiderata – holding on to the model of the causality of fate while acknowledging the claims of dis-enchanted reason – define Habermas's project exactly: the comprehension of language as communicatively structured is to take up the burden of the intersubjective and hence social mediation of the subject; while the establishment of communicative rationality, with its quasi-transcendental status, is there to acknowledge the 'reflective concept of reason developed in the philosophy of the subject' (p. 30).

As stated in this way, it appears evident that the *force* of ethical totality, whose unifying power Hegel collected under the titles of 'love', 'life', and, more complexly, 'faith', has, as it were, been divided, dirempted, in Habermas into the claims of the lifeworld itself, without which there would be no causality of fate, no 'world', for example, for money to 'de-world' when it is introduced as a universal medium of exchange (*PDM*, p. 350); and into the claims of communicative rationality, without which the achievements of reflective reason would remain unacknowledged. And this severing into two of the force of ethical totality correlates with a noted systematic ambiguity in Habermas's use of communicative action: first, as signifying actions that operate through explicit or implicit intersubjective consensus about norms, values and practices; and secondly, as signifying actions which are geared explicitly to establishing norms, truths and the like through dialogically achieved consensus.[25]

This duality is further underwritten by Habermas in his claim that there are 'two heritages of self-reflection that get beyond the limits of the philosophy of consciousness': rational reconstruction, which is directed towards anonymous rule systems; and methodologically carried out self-critique, which is related to totalities as deformed by the operation of quasi-causal mechanisms (*PDM*, pp. 298–300). These two programmes respond to starkly different needs. While the project of the rationally reconstructed sciences is a replacement programme for transcendental reflection, securing for communicative reason, however fallibilistically, a quasi-transcendental right, methodologically carried out self-critique responds to the fact that in modernity the force of the causality of fate is experienced in symptomatic and displaced ways, ways that correspond to the fact that the act of diremption that sets the causality of fate into motion is a collective act, 'an involuntary product of an entanglement that . . . communicative agents would have to ascribe to communal responsibility' (p. 316).

What Habermas's argument reveals, despite itself, is that the model of the causality of fate can, and indeed must, be operative independently of communicative rationality as strongly (transcendentally) interpreted. The modern subject, enlightened subjectivity and hence subject-centred reason are the *fate* of substance. The becoming subject of substance does not entail the disappearance of the latter, but only, and precisely, its deformation and occultation. While the occultation of substance allows for the indubitable cognitive achievements of modernity, those achievements are misrecognized if not recognized as products of deformation and occultation. Habermas misidentifies the precise nature of the achievement, and hence fails to attend to the incommensurability between communicative reason and the logic of the causality of fate. The governing rationale behind the causality of fate as a philosophical trope is to suggest that it is only in virtue of its workings, its avenging forcing (even, especially, when muted, occluded) that we come to recognize that 'any violation of the structures of rational life together, to which all lay claim, affects everyone equally ... [that] "betrayal of another is simultaneously betrayal of oneself; and every protest against betrayal is not just protest in one's own name, but in the name of the other at the same time."'[26]

To concede this is to make the lifeworld, ethical totality, into a 'comprehensive reason', an unmetaphorical intermeshing of the three validity claims. But this argument does not do, nor am I claiming that it does do, all that is necessary to resurrect the claims of the causality of fate. For what is perspicuously absent is the *force* of the claim of the lifeworld; the force which was located in (the faith in) popular religion, which Hegel thematized in terms of 'recognition', 'love' and 'life'; and which Habermas himself acknowledged the need for in his writing on Freud under the headings of transference and 'a passion for critique'.[27] But the best analysis of the disappearance of this force from the lifeworld, the revelation that the very lifeworld which is the ground and repository of our collective life has been as lifeworld systematically 'de-worlded', suggests that rationalization has distorted and deformed reason *intrinsically* by trisecting it, by categorically disallowing where needed an unmetaphorical intermeshing of validity claims. More precisely, the structures of the lifeworld have been distorted such that they appear, almost always and nearly everywhere, to accord with the claims of subject-centred reason. Which is to say, communicative action, in the weak sense, has been constituted by power relations that render invisible the operation of the causality of fate; and thereby defuse the claims of reciprocity that its avenging power is said to reveal.

Habermas's strong analysis of communicative reason is there not only to take up the claims of subject-centred, reflective reason, but equally, it is there to make up, albeit in rationalist terms, the affective deficit left by the systematic rationalization of the lifeworld. But this, of course, it cannot do. The *ground* for our orienting ourselves towards establishing validity claims through intersubjective recognition is intersubjective recognition. *The claims of others register as claims only in so far as we already recognize them as other selves (persons).* It is only in virtue of our recognizing that the refusal of the other is equally a refusal and betrayal of oneself that leads one to orient oneself to establishing validity claims through consensus and intersubjective recognition. Communicative reason can express this recognition once made, but cannot ground it. If the force of ethical totality could be grounded, in universal norms, say, becoming thus an obligation deriving from such a norm, then there would be no avenging force acting back upon the subject. That there is such a force, no matter how displaced and defused, marks the entwinement of passion and (re-)cognition, the very entwinement foreclosed by the duality between philosophical modernism and enlightened modernity.

Universality, Speculation and Politics

The recognition of the self in (absolute) otherness cannot be established so quickly. After all, the recognition of the other is the recognition of an other self or person; and these terms carry a weight of universality, a weight as to what does and what does not count as a moral criterion (of personhood); what is and is not relevant to being a self or person. There is a long and complex history behind the fact that now gender, race, nationality, language or religion are not criterially relevant here; that our communicative practices provide implicit recognitions even where they are overtly denied. Again, however, the avenging force of the causality of fate is more oblique, more difficult to detect, speaks in a quieter voice, or in the non-verbalizable language of the body inflicted with pain. In this context this thought entails the opposite of what it has up to now. If the trisection of reason has silenced local reasons, the claims of sensuous particularity and the public acknowledgement of individual needs, it has equally emptied universality of substantiality, either reifying it into a transcendental form or, what is nearly the same thing, transforming it into an abstract procedure presumptively expressive of reason itself. In Kant's moral philosophy, transcendental form and procedural rationality become indissolubly entwined. Habermas follows Kant down this path.

If elsewhere Habermas separates what needs uniting, here he identifies what needs separating. In the communicative retrieval of the claims of subject-centred reason, in the communicative transformation of procedural reason, Habermas runs together two quite distinct features of reason in modernity: universality and rational reflection. The rights of reason, as it were, are recognized when implicit claims become subject to the demands of discourse oriented towards reaching agreement. The claims of universality, however, can never be read off from the procedural forms through which claims are validated. On the contrary, to steal a trope from Marx, it seems more correct to say that there is a conflict between the substantive content of universalistic claims and the procedural inscription of them, between, that is, the forces and relations of universality.

The point is not either that claims have to be 'raised here and now and be de facto recognized' (*PDM*, p. 322) if they are to be able to serve the purposes of effective cooperation; or that such claims necessarily always have a temporal core (p. 300). It is rather the case that what is meant by universality is in each case substantive, responsive to the particular requirements of a situation. Which is to say that universality is best understood as a critical and not a procedural or formal concept; and that the appearance of 'bursting every provinciality asunder' (p. 322) derives from its critical operation. Universality always works against a provincialism, a restriction of validity, an exclusion; that is why the claim is raised, the point of raising it. In being raised in this way the appearance is given out that local restrictions have been surpassed, and hence a real, absolute universality achieved – a universality free from the charge of provincialism. But the force of the claim of universality derives not from its utter universalism, but rather from the fact that it acknowledges claims which existing universality suppresses; the new universality reveals past universality to be the non-acknowledgement of implicit claims, the reification of an inessential particularity. What is thus entwined in such a movement is not the real communication community with an ideal one (p. 323); but the present community with a potential future community.[28]

In order to substantiate a thesis of this kind one would need to point to the variety of 'provincialisms' against which universality claims have been raised: religious authority in early modern science, restrictions of class, gender, race et al. in political life, restricted meaning- or participant-oriented conceptions of the understanding of social life, and so on. And then continue to reveal how the reification of the universalist critical claim led to difficulties and disasters whose correction involved the acknowledgement of new provincialisms, such as the local laws of a natural habitat or ecological system, or the role of local and non-rationalized paradigms in scientific research; the claims of particular groups and communities against the bias of neutral equality ('all rights are rights to inequality'); the interpretive perspective from which 'objective' features of social life come into prominence; and so on. This dialectic is quite different from Habermas's dialectic of contexts of justification and contexts of discovery (*PDM*, pp. 323–4); that dialectic looks to the material interests in which validity claims are raised, and leads to ideology critique. The dialectic I am pointing to is not for the purpose of unmasking, however relevant that might be, but for the purpose of revealing the actual material content of universalist claims.[29] The temptation to secure universality from the threat of substantiality by making it formal and procedural does not alter the dialectic, but only makes its operation more difficult to detect.

Communicative rationality is equally substantive, equally a counter to restrictions and silencings in particular contexts and circumstances. Its force is, bluntly, the claim of a radical and participatory democratic polity against the silencing and neutralization of democratic ideals consequent upon the rationalization of the economy together with the cutting of ethical life into public and private spheres that reiterate the trisection of reason.[30] Once upon a time, Habermas demonstrated how the bourgeois norms of personhood, reciprocity, justice and equality expressed in the conception of a juridically constituted state were not mere ideological protections for an exploitative economy, as Marxists were wont to argue. Rather, the force of these norms and ideals were tied to their capacity to protect and nourish a public sphere in which truly public opinions could be formed. Only in the absence of such a sphere do these norms take on ideological colouring, do they become mere ideals, abstract norms whose very abstractness and universality serves to reinforce rather than inhibit or diminish domination and exploitation.[31]

Autonomous public spheres, however, are the voice and the claim of the lifeworld against the demands of system (*PDM*, p. 364). It is not only money and power which cannot buy or compel solidarity and meaning (p. 363); procedural reason cannot obligate solidarity and meaning. Solidarity and meaning are the claims of the lifeworld, claims which precede whatever mechanisms are deployed in order to acknowledge those claims. Autonomous public spheres would be the precipitates of a political love which both felt the suffering of the lifeworld through acknowledging the movement of the causality of fate, and simultaneously took up the standpoint of modernity by allowing us to adopt the perspective of a participant in a radicalized democratic polity.[32] But this is to say that the claims of the lifeworld, the claims of philosophical modernism (local reason), and the claims of modernity are, in distorted forms, the same claim. That the debate between modernity and modernism remains a theoretical or philosophical debate over the fate of reason in modernity represses the absent politics of which both the local reason of philosophical modernism and the universalist reason of philosophical modernity are distorted recognitions.

No reader of *The Philosophical Discourse of Modernity* can fail to be struck by the marginalization of the political in both Habermas and his adversaries. Discussion of politics, the fate of politics, the fate of the public sphere does not enter centrally into Habermas's discussion of philosophical modernism, but arises only in the context of his analysis of relations between lifeworld and system in the final chapter. This marginalization, this absence of the political *is* the philosophical discourse of modernity, not, as it were, wilfully or by avoidance, but fatefully. 'Philosophy, which once seemed obsolete, lives on because the moment to realize it was missed' (*ND*, p. 3). Living on, which is neither the realization of philosophy nor its overcoming, is the ambiguous state, the aporia, of a philosophy that can neither be itself nor fail to be itself; which sustains itself through its relation to non-philosophy, through, say, its relation to art or sociology; or by being non-philosophy, by attempting to occupy the space of its other, to hold it as its own. The figure of living on falters, however, when it forgets that that is what it is doing, that living on is, perhaps always, the realization and non-realization of philosophy. And we understand both living on and its faltering when we see in the trisection of reason and the postures of philosophy identifying itself with one of its broken moments the inscription of an absent politics.

This is the fate speculatively recognized by comprehensive reason: faith, love, judgement without universality is blind; universality without love and recognition is empty. This statement is not the prelude to a philosophical synthesis, but the recognition of the fate of subject and substance in modernity. In recognizing it we recognize ourselves in otherness; acknowledging thus the avenging force of the causality of fate, our collective betrayal and responsibility. Perhaps, if we were not as moderns so constitutionally optimistic or pessimistic, sanguine or stoical, idealistic or cynical, we would perceive this recognition for what it is: a tragic understanding of modernity. Perhaps remembering at the same time that the acceptance of tragedy, the understanding of life in a tragic mode, is a necessary condition for the possibility of, is contemporaneous with, a politics no longer under the aegis of metaphysics or reason.

NOTES

1 Jürgen Habermas, *The Philosophical Discourse of Modernity* (Cambridge and Cambridge, Mass. 1987), hereafter also cited as *PDM*.

2 See, for example, Jacques Derrida, 'Signature Event Context', *Glyph* 1 (Baltimore, 1977), pp. 172–97.

3 On this see Thomas McCarthy, 'Complexity and Democracy, or the Seducements of Systems Theory', *New German Critique* 35 (Spring/Summer 1985), pp. 27–33; and in the same place, Nancy Fraser, 'What is Critical about Critical Theory? The Case of Habermas and Gender', esp. pp. 103–11.

4 For a summary of these objections see Thomas McCarthy, *The Critical Theory of Jürgen Habermas* (London, 1978), pp. 101–2, 182–92; and J. B. Thompson and D. Held (eds), *Habermas: Critical Debates* (London, 1982), essays 4, 7, 8.

5 See now Michel Foucault, 'What is Enlightenment?' in Paul Rabinow (ed.), *The Foucault Reader*, (New York, 1983). Nowhere does Adorno disown the ideals of the Enlightenment.

6 See Thomas McCarthy, 'Reflections on Rationalization in the Theory of

Communicative Action', *Praxis International* 4:2 (1984), pp. 77–91; D. Ingram, 'Philosophy and the Aesthetic Mediation of Life', *Philosophical Forum* 18:4 (Summer 1987), pp. 329–57; John McCumber, 'Philosophy as the Heteronomous Center of Modern Discourse: Jürgen Habermas', in Hugh Silverman (ed.), *Philosophy and Non-Philosophy since Merleau-Ponty* (New York and London, 1988), pp. 211–31; and my 'The Politics of Fulfilment and Transfiguration', *Radical Philosophy* 47 (Autumn 1987), pp. 21–9.

7 On this see my *The Fate of Art: Aesthetic Alienation from Kant to Derrida and Adorno* (Cambridge, 1989).

8 Habermas takes himself to be arguing against J. Culler here, which leaves the relation between Culler's position and Derrida's moot.

9 This is nearly the central theme of Rodolphe Gasché's *The Tain of the Mirror* (Cambridge and London, 1986).

10 T. W. Adorno, *Aesthetic Theory*, trans. C. Lenhardt (London, 1983), p. 199.

11 Ibid., p. 107.

12 A point Habermas does not dispute.

13 On Foucault's trajectory see John Rajchman, 'Foucault, or the Ends of Modernism', *October* 24 (Spring 1983), pp. 37–62. My quote is from p. 51.

14 Kai Nielsen, 'Rationality and Relativism', *Philosophy of the Social Sciences* 4 (1974), p. 320.

15 I. Kant, *The Critique of Judgement*, trans. J. C. Meredith (Oxford, 1952), p. 314.

16 Theodor W. Adorno, *Negative Dialectics*, trans. E. B. Ashton (London, 1973), hereafter cited as ND.

17 ND, pp. 33–4. For a comparable account of Foucault's practice of writing see Charles Scott's *The Language of Difference* (Atlantic Highlands, 1987), pp. 89–119.

18 Adorno, *Aesthetic Theory*, p. 325.

19 Or immortality. The point at issue here is the relation between traditional philosophical ambitions and human finitude. How are we to keep doing philosophy, whose project has depended upon its departure (either directly as in Plato, or analytically as in Kantianism) from the empirical, from the world of life and death, and keep our inquiry immanent? Fallibilism is indeed a 'trivial' acknowledgement of finitude and mortality.

20 See, for example, Jürgen Habermas, 'Philosophy as Stand-In and Interpreter', in K. Baynes, J. Bohman and T. McCarthy (eds), *After Philosophy* (Cambridge and London, 1987), pp. 298–9; and *The Theory of Communicative Action*, vol 1, trans. T. McCarthy (Cambridge, 1984), pp. 140–1, 233–42. My *The Philosophy of the Novel: Lukács, Marxism and the Dialectics of Form* (Minneapolis, 1984) attempts an indirect demonstration of this thesis.

21 See notes 6 and 7 above.

22 Jürgen Habermas, 'Questions and Counterquestions', in R. J. Bernstein (ed.), *Habermas and Modernity* (Cambridge, 1985), pp. 202–3.

23 Habermas, 'Philosophy as Stand-In and Interpreter', pp. 312–13.

24 See my 'Self-Knowledge as Praxis: Narrative and Narration in Psychoanalysis', in C. Nash (ed.), *Narrative in Culture* (London, 1989).

25 Fraser, 'What is Critical about Critical Theory?', pp. 102–3.

26 PDM, pp. 324–5. Habermas is quoting from K. Heinrich, *Versuch über die Schweierigkeit nein zu sagen* (Frankfurt, 1964), p. 20.

27 Jürgen Habermas, *Knowledge and Human Interests*, trans. J. J. Shapiro (Cambridge, 1972), pp. 234–6.

28 The theory of substantive universals employed here is, of course, Marcuse's: *One-Dimensional Man* (Boston, 1964), pp. 105–6. For an elaboration see Andrew Feenberg, 'The Bias of Technology', in R. Pippin et al., *Marcuse: Critical Theory and the Promise of Utopia* (London, 1988), pp. 244–8.
29 Again, see Fraser, 'What is Critical about Critical Theory?' pp. 128–9.
30 I elaborate this argument in my 'The Politics of Fulfilment and Transfiguration'.
31 Jürgen Habermas, *Strukturwandel der Öffentlichkeit* (Neuwied, 1962).
32 See my 'The Politics of Fulfilment and Transfiguration', pp. 25–9; and McCumber, 'Philosophy as the Heteronomous Center of Modern Discourse', pp. 230–1.

10
THE SUBJECT OF JUSTICE IN POSTMODERN DISCOURSE: AESTHETIC JUDGEMENT AND POLITICAL RATIONALITY

David Ingram

the person who is addressed and remains silent, clothes himself or herself in an aura of indeterminate significance and imposes silence. For this, Heidegger is one example among many. Because of this authoritarian character, Sartre has rightly called silence 'reactionary'.
Jürgen Habermas, 'Transcendence from Within, Transcendence in this World'.

In the *différend* something 'asks' to be put into phrases and suffers from the wrong of not being able to at that instant. Thus, humans who believed that they used language as an instrument of communication learn through this feeling of pain that accompanies silence (and from the pleasure that accompanies the invention of a new idiom), that they are summoned by language not in order to increase the quantity of communicable information in existing idioms for their benefit, but in order to recognize that what there is to be phrased exceeds what they can presently phrase, and that they must be allowed to institute idioms that do not yet exist.
Jean-François Lyotard, *Le Différend*

It is surprising that *The Philosophical Discourse of Modernity* mentions Lyotard only in passing.[1] After all, Lyotard *is* the leading exponent of the postmodernism Habermas criticizes, and his objections to Habermas's own project confirm this. Simply stated, Lyotard wonders why the pluralizing effects of self-reflexive, self-transcending reason underwrite – rather than undermine – the autonomy and identity of persons living in late modern societies. This objection, in turn, directly challenges the legitimacy and justice of those enlightenment ideals defended by Habermas. For Habermas, justice consists in permitting all persons to participate freely and equally in conversations aimed at reaching consensus on norms regulating their conduct. So construed, norms are legitimated by a universal consensus whose own legitimacy is demonstrably grounded in conditions of rational speech. Taken together, these ideals of justice and legitimation anticipate a democracy whose citizens shape their mutually intertwined identities through collective deliberation on common ends. Lyotard, by contrast, denies the necessity and desirability of unconstrained consensus as a goal of rational speech. He holds that consensus is only one of the possible goals of rational speech and he opposes to it other goals, such as the invention of deviant vocabularies and the assertion of differences. For him, dissensus wrought by invention is preferable to consensus, since it alone subverts the modern trend towards totalitarian homogeneity and majoritarian tyranny.

Rather than disputing the disagreement between Lyotard and Habermas over the justice and legitimacy of rational speech, I propose to use it as a basis for exploring their deeper understanding of the preconditions underlying a more fundamental kind of rationality: the *clinical* judgement of philosophers and political agents engaged in bringing about conditions of global well-being suitable for fostering autonomous agency and integral identity. Such judgement requires drawing essential distinctions between different types of rational comportment, deliberation and discourse. Its guiding idea is not political justice narrowly conceived but the idea of a community in which distinct spheres of rational comportment – such as those operant within science, economics, politics, law, morality and aesthetics – communicate with one another in a *just* or non-hegemonic manner.

The problem of hegemony indicated here becomes important when we examine the dialectic of enlightenment which comprises the background of their respective philosophies (section I below). Both philosophers hold that the pluralizing dynamics of social rationalization encourage forms of specialization that threaten to impoverish lay persons' capacities for autonomous moral reflection. Habermas thinks there are countervailing tendencies within modern culture that offset this inequality (section II); Lyotard does not – unless, of course, this culture is seen as transcending its own logic (section III). However, regardless of their stance on this issue, both believe that the dynamics of postindustrial capitalism exacerbate the problem of a one-sided cultivation of rational competences in that it encourages the growth of one aspect of rationality – the scientific and technological – at the expense of the moral and expressive. The economic and administrative expansion that fuels this growth in turn disrupts the biopolitical integrity of environment and community requisite for autonomous selfhood.

Criticism of such rational one-sidedness necessitates clinical judgement; discrimination of the proper harmony and felicitous interaction between types of rationality must be guided by an idea – at once descriptive and normative – of their unity. For reasons that will become clear, Lyotard and Habermas eschew the dialectical (conceptual) solution to this problem developed by Hegel, preferring instead the aesthetic solution provided by Kant's account of reflective judgement (section IV).

Now our examination of this feature of their thought will require revising certain misconceptions about their respective views of rationality as well (section V). Contrary to the assumption – held by Habermas among others – that Lyotard is a radical contextualist (or conservative?) who rejects universal ideas of justice, I will argue that the *agreement to disagree* that he appropriates from Kant represents an idea which he and Habermas both find compelling.[2] This idea, he insists, must be conceived *minimally*, as regulative for social critique but not prescriptive of any concrete goal achievable through concerted political action – an injunction he believes Habermas violates.

Lyotard, I believe, simply misunderstands that Habermas's procedural notion of justice is only intended to clarify how certain categories of rights – those implicit in the freedom and reciprocity comprising the moral point of view – are deeply implicated in rational speech. Lyotard's contention is also misplaced when directed against Habermas's other appeal to justice – his call for a completed enlightenment as a yardstick for a well-balanced, non-hegemonic community of rationalization complexes. Habermas's recent concession that 'there are no metadiscourses' and no definite criteria of rational unity governing our clinical judgement about pathological forms of rationalization suggests that the idea of community informing such judgement is regulative, not prescriptive. Likewise his staunch opposition to a 'dialectics of reconciliation' and his support for a 'plural, non-integral and yet non-separatist' concept of reason suggests that the kind of communal integrity he endorses is far removed from the harmonistic totality that Lyotard criticizes.[3]

In conclusion I argue that neither Lyotard nor Habermas provides us with a wholly satisfactory account of the legitimacy and justice of reason *qua* integral phenomenon. Lyotard fails because of his extreme deference to the anarchism of communication; Habermas because of his equally extreme deference to its idealism. Indeed, it may well be that the grand narrative which they inherit from Kant and that forms the backdrop to their problematic – the dialectic of enlightenment – is incapable of any resolution one way or the other. Yet even if we reject this narrative as an unsatisfactory interpretation of modernity we are still confronted with the problem of cultural hegemony and the problem of reasonably adjudicating spheres of justice, as Michael Walzer puts it. Judgement here necessarily involves *metaphorically* commensurating what appear to be incommensurable types of distributive criteria or – to borrow a phrase from Habermas and Lyotard – incommensurable types of reasons. Given that the judgement in question mediates between conflicting types of criteria instead of being determined by any one of them separately, it cannot be – as Kant correctly observed – discursively demonstrated. At best, it can be indirectly shown – by appeal to more global intuitions and 'ways of seeing' that *feel* authentic to us.

Contrary to Habermas, then, the postmodern critic's refusal to offer propositional support in lieu of narrative interpretation or aesthetic representation does not *ipso facto* involve commission of a performative contradiction. Moral and expressive judgements combine *determination* of particular instances along with *reflexive* articulation of the rules under which they are subsumed. Thus they mediate between indeterminate ideas of reason and determinate contexts of experience in ways that undermine the modernist's and postmodernist's insistence on rational incommensurability and purity.

I

A superficial reading of Habermas and Lyotard might lead one to suppose that modernism and postmodernism are radically opposed movements – the former celebrating rational form and function, the latter condemning it. On closer inspection these philosophers endorse a more complicated view that sees postmodernism as the 'nascent' and 'constant' state of a modernism that has broken radically with convention (Lyotard); become aware of its own radical temporality, complexity and reflexivity; and continually recreates its own normative criteria out of itself (Habermas) (*PC*, p. 79; *PDM*, p. 7).

In their opinion Kant was the first philosopher to have perceived, however dimly, the legitimation crisis set in motion by the self-transcending power of rational reflection. On one hand, by showing how cognitive reflection on the totality of objective conditions issues in self-referential paradox (antinomy), he initiated the end of premodern metaphysics and its dogmatic foundationalism. On the other hand, by showing how transcendental reflection on the totality of subjective conditions redeems the universal validity of knowledge, morality and taste as *distinct* deployments of reason, he placed in doubt the unitary basis of his own reflection, thereby anticipating the postmodern rupture of reason with itself.

Following Weber's lead, Lyotard and Habermas reconceptualize this dialectic as a *social* process. For Weber, the *cultural* value spheres of knowledge, morality and aesthetics implicated in Kantian transcendental psychology acquire public institutionalization in scientific, legal and artistic disciplines. These disciplines in turn anchor capitalist economy, bureaucratic administration and private household. Cultural and social 'rationalization' subjects the organic unity of traditional society to disenchantment in a manner no less rigorous than Kant's own critique of traditional metaphysics. Yet, from Weber's standpoint, rationalization can only assume the *unemancipated* form diagnosed by Nietzsche. Crushed between the millstones of technological efficiency and bureaucratic hierarchy on one side and amoral hedonism on the other, the vocational ethic of capitalism commands not autonomy, but ceaseless toil, authoritarian self-abnegation and slavish consumption.

By confining rationality to value-free procedures of preference ranking, consistency testing and instrumental calculation of the sort deployed by individual utility maximizers, Weber was even less successful than Kant in extricating himself from the nihilistic implications of reason. Kant had hoped that the critique of cognitive reason – the limitation of its deployment to causal events in space and time – would restore faith in the transcendent commands of moral reason. The romantic – and essentially communitarian – *counterdiscourse* that followed in the wake of Kant's critical philosophy, and that serves as the main nemesis opposing Habermas and Lyotard's revival of it, was much less hopeful. For Hegel – whose own speculative philosophy culminates this discourse – the critical delimitation of theoretical and practical reason is emblematic of the very problem it ostensibly solves, and ultimately portends disastrous consequences for both science and morality.

Looking ahead to Weber and the twentieth century, Hegel seemed to fathom the perverse affinity between totalitarianism and abstract individualism that would eventually emerge from the mass dynamics of modern society. In his opinion, the events culminating in the Reign of Terror clearly attest to the moral impoverishment of a truncated enlightenment wherein utilitarian heteronomy and fanatical virtue – now secularized and emancipated from otherworldy religion – confront one another as opposed 'moments' of reason. Only the promise of reconciliation vouchsafed by dialectical reason, he thought, could redeem the spiritual and secular intentions of religion from rational diremption; only it could show how abstract morality and abstract need are sublated in the ethical community of a modern *Rechtsstaat*.

The dialectic of enlightenment recounted by Hegel remains the dominant *leitmotiv* in the writings of Lyotard and Habermas. Like their Frankfurt School predecessors, they warn of the total(itarian) assimilation of the individual to a unified, technological-scientific system in which questions of normative legitimacy are reduced to questions of efficient adaptation, and in which the hegemony of 'performativity', as Lyotard puts it, all but extinguishes the need for moral community founded on mutual freedom and equality.[4]

If they reject Hegel's appeal to dialectical reason as a solution to this problem it is because they find its yearning for organic wholeness to be as potentially totalitarian as its emancipatory antithesis (*PDM*, pp. 23–50; *PC*, pp. 32–7). Drawing on Hegel's own logic, they note the impossibility of effecting a complete synthesis of reason's dirempted aspects. For Hegel, rational reflection moves between circular completion (*Vollendung*) and indefinite progression. Reflection is progressive in so far as it assimilates its own limits (ends) as ideas of thought. Overcoming and surpassing all limits, reason contains within itself its 'other' – material reality. Hence the commensurability of reason's distinct aspects with(in) the indefinitely dense contexts of language, law and desire.

So much for the dissolution – or deconstruction – of reason celebrated by postmodernists. For Hegel, however, this is not the whole story. Reason's self-overcoming – its *particularistic* concretion and determination vis-à-vis its other – becomes a moment of further reflection. The movement of reality is then but a reflection of a reflection – a complete circle that moves within one and the same universal Idea. In the course of reflecting on its dialectical progression, reason affirms (returns to) itself as certainty of its own unconditioned, absolute – and therefore, incommensurable – identity. This affirmation of an identity that is simultaneously universal and concrete is possible only if reason fully encompasses the totality of possible ends, conditions and determinations. Yet, as Lyotard – and Habermas to a lesser degree – note, reason cannot *fix* its ends without again surpassing them. That is, it cannot reflect on its object without once again changing it. Since this object is a reflection of itself, reason is condemned to eternally re-experience its own otherness, or historicity. Having exploded its own totality, modern teleology issues once again in postmodern progression.

Far from dissolving the problem of critical philosophy, the failure of absolute idealism to close the circle of reflection only reinstates it at a higher register. The potential reunification of theoretical and practical reason thus remains to be demonstrated. Although Lyotard and Habermas warn against integrating science, art and morality in a total(itarian) ideology – the Lysenkoist science of Stalinist Russia and the moralizing art propaganda of the Third Reich being notable examples of this kind of integration – they none the less acknowledge that totalitarianism is at least partially abetted by the fragmentation of reason and its nihilistic acquiescence in authority. Hence each in his own way seeks to contain (if not reverse) such fragmentation. The moral integrity of the community no less than that of the individual depends on reintegrating cognitive, moral and expressive aspects of life into a community of reason.

As we shall see, there are resources within critical philosophy itself for generating just this possibility. Kant's notion of reflective judgement accounts for metaphorical identifications – or family resemblances, to use Wittgenstein's phraseology – between faculties of reason that are otherwise conceptually incommensurable. By retrieving this notion of judgement, Habermas and Lyotard hope to accomplish two goals intrinsic to critical theory: *description* of the *actual* interdependencies between cognitive, moral and aesthetic types of reasoning *within* broader genres of rational discourse – scientific, legal, political, etc. – and *criticism* of hegemonic imbalances between these genres with reference to *possible* states of communal integrity and justice.

I will begin by sketching Habermas's response to Weber's paradox. Unlike his earlier attempt to develop a model of undistorted communication in conjunction with the programme of ideology critique, Habermas's theory of communicative action proffers a model of identity formation critical of social reification. In order to criticize selective processes of social rationalization that assimilate spheres of familial and public life essential to the development of moral identity to systems of economic exchange and administrative regulation aimed at strategic domination and functional adaptation, Habermas must rebut Weber's neo-Kantian reduction of reason to scientific cognition. He does this by showing the *priority* of communicative rationality as a set of normative expectations *common* to *all* spheres of rational discourse. This demonstration proves too much and too little – too much in so far as the unity of reason is gained at the expense of reducing it to a cognitive orientation towards consensus that fails to do justice to fundamental differences between political, moral, evaluative and therapeutic discourses; too little in that the unity in question instantiates only a formal idea of democratic fairness and not a holistic idea of societal well-being. Only when Habermas turns to the aesthetic theories of Kant and Schiller to retrieve a metaphorical unity of experience does he succeed in explaining the *substantive* interdependencies linking incommensurable domains of rational validity and discourse. And only then does he appeal to the aesthetic idea of a 'free interplay' – 'uninhibited and balanced' – between mutually interpenetrating cognitive interpretations, moral expectations, expressions and evaluations of the sort capable of grounding the critique of reification.[5]

II

Habermas's critical philosophy seeks to justify modernity in the face of Weber's paradoxes: the relativism of rational value spheres that ostensibly gives rise to social pathology and the identification of social rationalization with capitalism. This defence hinges on reject-

ing philosophy of consciousness in favour of philosophy of communication. By privileging the cognitive relationship between the
self-centred knower and his or her object, the former equates
rationality with the objectifying reduction of nature to laws of motion
fungible for efficient prediction and control. Restricted to instrumentality and deprived of reflexivity, social rationality aims at *individual*
dominion over others (strategic action) or *totalitarian* dominion over
hostile environments (system integration).

Habermas hopes to redeem social rationality by privileging the
communicative relationship foundational for intersubjectivity.
Hegel's dialectic is transformed by conceiving reason (reflection) as a
process of *real dialogue with others* in which mutual recognition
requisite for self-identity is procured through *argumentative justification* of claims to truth, moral rightness and sincerity that accompany every genuine speech act. Since reflection no longer moves
within the interiority of a self-contained Subject (*Geist*), it escapes
the paradox of a totalizing reason that expressively objectifies itself
(*PDM*, p. 298).

By conceiving of *all* learning processes as a *collective* effort of
impartial criticism, Habermas is able to extract a universal core of
communicative rationality – the anticipation of a consensus reached
by all freely and fairly – that rebuts Weberian scepticism and
relativism. Furthermore, since this normative ideal is understood to
be a precondition for knowing, acting and expressing, it *ostensibly*
constitutes a unitary basis for resisting the one-sided growth of
economy and bureaucracy endemic to capitalism. Individual strategic
action and impersonal systemic adaptation thus find their limit in
those areas of public and private life that foster democratic participation, communal solidarity, decentred subjectivity and complex
identity.[6]

Just how compelling is Habermas's resolution of Weber's paradox?
Habermas's appeal to communicative intersubjectivity apparently
enables him to avoid the most serious implications of the dialectic of
enlightenment – the equation of reason with instrumental domination
and the equation of social rationalization with capitalism. Yet
residual problems concerning the unity of communicative rationality
have not been satisfactorily answered.

First, even if we accept Habermas's claim that there are *exactly*
three validity claims that *necessarily* accompany *every* speech act and
that these correspond to recognizable types of rational argumentation
– theoretical and practical with respect to truth and moral rightness,
evaluative and therapeutic with respect to aesthetic appropriateness,
sincerity and authenticity – there remain significant discrepancies
between these types of argumentation concerning the *scope* of the
anticipated consensus and the moral symmetry of the interlocutors.

For instance, Habermas concedes that participants in evaluative discourses raise claims that are not strictly universal, as in the case of practical and theoretical discourse. And he concedes that the relationship of transference binding analyst and analysand in therapeutic discourse deviates from dialogic assumptions of mutual equality and freedom.[7]

Second, consensus might not be a necessary feature of practical discourse – moral or political. Although valid moral rules must satisfy universal interests, this fact, as Kant correctly noted, can only be hypothetically determined in the form of a *simulated* dialogue. Dialogue with others is no doubt indispensable for cultivating correct moral character, but justification of universal rules is a private matter.[8] More importantly, moral reasoning does not primarily involve justifying moral rules at all, but normally involves justifying exceptions to rules that are taken for granted. Here again, while our interpretations of particular dilemmatic situations in which exceptions arise no doubt benefit from criticism obtained in conversations with others, they are ultimately – and radically – situated with respect to our own unique set of personal circumstances.[9]

Unlike moral rationality, political rationality necessitates real discourse, since here the aim is to justify specific public policies that have been formulated abstractly – without reference to the multitude of concrete situations in which they will be individually applied. Furthermore, because the rules in question are punitively sanctioned, not voluntarily and privately self-imposed, such discourse must be democratic – allowing for full and equal participation on the part of all affected. Yet, here again, the analogy to consensus-oriented, theoretical discourse is weaker than Habermas supposes. Although he may be right that participants in political discourse ought to *seek* consensus, he is wrong to think that consensus is necessary for legitimation. He is on firmer ground when he ties the legitimation of a law to the fairness of its ratification procedures. Yet, even when political consensus is reached, it is often of a very different kind than that which is reached in theoretical discourse between scientists. Although Habermas claims that semantic consistency is a pragmatic assumption which all participants in discourse – practical or theoretical – tacitly accept as a consensual condition for possible communication, it functions only as a logical requirement in *normal* scientific discourse.[10] Unlike scientists, citizens may agree on proposals for sometimes conflicting reasons, and what passes for common linguistic usage in political debates often conceals deeper incommensurabilities rooted in heterogeneous world-views.

In all fairness to Habermas, I feel compelled to add that the general thrust of these criticisms coincides with his own deepening understanding of the complexity of political discourse in liberal democracy.

In his most recent work on this subject, *Faktizität und Geltung* (1992), he distinguishes four types of discourse – moral, ethico-political, pragmatic and juristic – that enter into the process of rational deliberation at various levels of public discussion, legislation, adjudication and administration.[11]

Public and parliamentary negotiations aimed at reaching fair compromises on non-generalizable interests do not conform to the consensual model of moral discourse, since the reasons underwriting the agreement – reflecting as they do competing constellations of power – vary among the consenting parties.[12] The mandated representation of conflicting interest positions in legislative bodies, however, must be qualified, in turn, by the *un*mandated, critical reflection on basic values and goals that occurs in formal and informal ethico-political discourses aimed at hermeneutically explicating the authentic identity underlying a given community's traditional self-understanding.[13] Unlike strategic compromises, such existential discourses are indeed consensual in nature but in a manner, as we shall see, that is sustained by common experiences, not context-independent beliefs. Only when ethical debate enters the cosmopolitan framework of moral discourse on universal principles of justice – the limits within which all legitimate authority must operate – do the reasons underwriting consensus become context-independent.[14]

Ultimately, the results of these mutually interlocking discourses culminate in acts of legislation that need to be concretized in the form of efficient policies and determinant judgements by administrators and judges involved in pragmatic and juristic discourses. In each case the reasons underwriting consensus vary depending on the discourse under consideration: the rational choice of techniques and strategies or the complete and impartial description of cases.[15]

As we shall see, Lyotard finds this web of irreducibly heterogeneous types of argumentation to be far more problematic for a coherent, consensual model of political rationality than Habermas would ever concede. But let us momentarily leave aside the accuracy of Habermas's theory of argumentation as a *description* of such communication and address its potential for generating a standard of criticism. Granting Habermas's account of the procedural unity of dialogic argumentation, it still remains incumbent on him to prove its usefulness in guiding the critique of social reification.

Now social reification occurs whenever the proper balance between cognitive and moral rationalization within society favours the former more than it should, and whenever rational specialization has gone too far in empowering experts and impoverishing lay critics. On Habermas's understanding of the matter, criticism of reification involves a clinical judgement of *health*, or of the right mixture of cognitive, practical and aesthetic competencies requisite for cultivating happy – well-integrated and evenly developed – moral identities.[16] Unfortunately, he nowhere shows that health is a rationally defensible value on a par with truth, justice and sincerity, all of which find a secure niche in communicative action. Since he says that critical theory must limit its assessments of society to those aspects of reason that *do* find such a niche, he can ground *at most* ideology critique, which derives its standard of truth from the notion of a just, unconstrained consensus.[17] Yet Habermas now thinks that the critique of reification should be the proper task of critical theory.[18]

Thus far I have argued that Habermas's account of the procedural unity of rational discourse fails both as a description of the possible integrity of rational comportment and as a normative ground for criticizing reification. However, some of Habermas's tentative remarks about the intertwinement – or, if one prefers, impurity – of aspects of validity and rationality within so-called purely differentiated types of rational discourse suggest a rather different set of possibilities.[19] The same applies with respect to his speculative pronouncements on aesthetic truth.

The question of impurity can best be approached by recalling a difficult section of *The Theory of Communicative Action* where Habermas argues that different aspects of validity complement one another in grammatically articulated speech. On the one hand, locutionary, illocutionary and expressive functions are logically irreducible. For example, you cannot infer that a person sincerely believes something from the mere fact of his having asserted it to be true; nor can you infer that she ought to do something from the fact that she has factually promised to do it. On the other hand, intermodal transitions between first-, second- and third-person perspectives clearly reveal structural linkages between locutionary, illocutionary and expressive functions. First-person expressions of intent or obligation ('I promise you that p') are in principle convertible into third-person ascriptions ('He promises him that p'). Thus, the asymmetrical conversion of first-person expressives and performatives into third-person assertions implies a *non-reductive structural unity* that makes possible the rational preservation and criticism of context-independent claims. However, such conversion possibilities say nothing about the potential rationality of everyday speech since, on Habermas's interpretation, such speech still manifests a certain disregard for logical distinctions.[20] Thus, we typically infer that persons *do* sincerely (truthfully) believe what they merely assert to be true.

Rational argumentation (discourse) disallows such leaps in logic. In addition to excluding the metaphorical conflation of validity claims (taking truth claims as claims for truthfulness), it regiments both type and sequence of reasoning in accordance with a logic specially adapted to a *dominant* validity claim. However, as Habermas notes, the capacity to reflect on the *practical* presuppositions underlying *theoretical* knowledge, the capacity to reflect on the *theoretical* presuppositions underlying *practical* self-understanding and the capacity to reflect *therapeutically* on the viability of our language as a medium of discourse unconstrained by ideological distortion suggest that specialized discourses are no less impure when taken to radical extremes.[21] Even when not taken to such extremes, specialized discourses, he observes, typically implicate the full range of validity claims and discursive logics. For instance, moral arguments aimed at justifying general principles frequently raise factual and evaluative questions about the adequacy of case descriptions and the probable satisfaction of genuine needs; and aesthetic critiques aimed at evaluating the authenticity of works of art similarly raise issues pertaining to appropriate descriptions and moral values.[22]

These impurities are even more pronounced in the case of those specialized discourses, such as philosophy and art criticism, that serve to communicate the highly technical insights of the arts and sciences in a more colloquial language accessible to the lay person. This potential for mediation can serve to mitigate one of the pathological tendencies associated with the diremption of modern reason: the splitting off of elite subcultures. The resolution of this problem requires not only disseminating technical knowledge relevant to democratic decision-making but also restoring to ordinary citizens critical competencies that have been lost in the cul-de-sacs of specialized discourses. If citizens cannot become experts, they can at least acquire the knowledge and critical skills necessary for holding them accountable. Philosophy and literary criticism can facilitate the critical mediation of technical expertise and everyday language because they are at once discursive (specialized with respect to single validity aspects, like expert discourses) and colloquial (deploying rhetorically and metaphorically charged expressions that violate the cognitive demand for clarity and semantic consistency) (*PDM*, p. 209).

The importance of metaphorical language in mediating aspects of validity and rationality assumes even greater importance in Habermas's discussion of the critical power of art to illuminate social reification resulting from the colonization of a communicative lifeworld by the economy and the administrative system. Indeed, works of art represent a specially significant illustration of the intermeshing of validity claims and rationality aspects in as much as they function simultaneously as arguments and as idealized anticipations of integral experience. In short, modern art

reaches into our cognitive interpretations and normative expectations and transforms the *totality* in which these moments are related to one another. In this respect, modern art harbors a utopia that becomes a reality to the degree that the *mimetic powers* sublimated in the work of art find resonance in the *mimetic relations of a balanced and undistorted intersubjectivity of everyday life.*[23]

Elsewhere, Habermas links the mimetic disclosure of an integral and balanced utopia to Kant's notion of a *sensus communis*, or unconstrained communication between faculties of the sort implicated in aesthetic judgement. In the Schillerian appropriation of this notion

> art operates as a catalyst, as a form of communication, as a medium within which separated moments are rejoined into an *uncoerced totality.* The social character of the beautiful and of taste are to be confirmed solely by the fact that art 'leads' everything dissociated in modernity – the system of unleashed needs, the bureaucratized state, the abstractions of rational morality and science for experts – 'out under the open sky of common sense'. (*PDM*, p. 50)

If critical theory is called upon to judge the felicitous balance between system and lifeworld and the integrity of rationalization complexes, then art itself can offer a presentiment of the complete, integral life experience that serves as an intuitive yardstick in these matters. But what is the rationale underlying this kind of aesthetic criticism? Clinical judgements regarding the global well-being of personal and societal identity do not comprise a class of recognizable validity claims in the sharply demarcated taxonomy of arguments presented in *The Theory of Communicative Action.*[24] In that work, aesthetic and evaluative discourses are defined rather narrowly, in terms of the redemption of expressive claims regarding the sincerity of speakers or the authenticity of needs. Confined to justifying claims pertaining to just one dimension of experience – the subjective – such discourses seem uncongenial to the justification of judgements of *global* well-being implicating the integrity of all dimensions, moral and cognitive included.[25]

A different view of the matter emerges, however, in the account of ethical-political discourse given in *Faktizität und Geltung* and in earlier pronouncements about a kind of aesthetic rationality, or truth. In the former Habermas connects ethico-political discourses treating questions concerning authentic, collective identity with clinical recommendations regarding exemplary ways of life that integrate diverse values freely and without distortion.[26] In the latter, he talks about the *poetic* function, or illuminating power, of language and art in disclosing 'anew an apparently familiar reality'.

The validity claim accompanying this disclosure 'stands for a *potential* for "truth" that can be released only in the whole complexity of life experience'. As such, it 'may not be connected to (or even identified with) one of the three validity claims constitutive for communicative action'. On the contrary, since works of art symbolize a 'lifeworld experience' in which 'the three validity claims are unmetaphorically intermeshed,' their own truth and truthfulness could only be metaphorical. The rationale underlying such claims – for Habermas steadfastly insists that works of art *do* function as arguments – would not be simply discursive, but would be rhetorically compelling in some experiential or intuitive sense.[27] Descriptions might supplement evaluations and prescriptions, but no set of criteria would *determine*, or compel, agreement in these matters. Indeed, we might have to resort to perlocutionary effects – such as emphatic pointing, poetic rhapsodizing, or even gazing (or listening) in mute *silence* – to get others to *feel* the same way we do about a work of art. By the same token, the judgement of health and harmony (or lack thereof) proffered by the critical theorist – or the participant in ethico-political discourse – convinces only to the extent that she or he can bring about agreement in feelings and experiences as well as agreement in judgements.

Habermas's appeal to aesthetic truth no doubt explains the possibility of reunifying aspects of validity and rationality that his own critical philosophy has shown to be conceptually incommensurable. In this respect it follows the same logic as Kant's third Critique. But Kant, of course, understood that aesthetic ideas can symbolize sublime incommensurability as well as beautiful harmony. Hence, the question-begging nature of Habermas's appeal to aesthetics – an appeal aptly queried by Lyotard:

> Is the aim of [Habermas's] project of modernity the constitution of sociocultural unity within which all the elements of daily life and of thought take their places as in an organic whole? Or does the passage that has to be charted between heterogeneous language games – those of cognition, of ethics, of politics – belong to a different order from that? ... The first hypothesis, of a Hegelian inspiration, does not challenge the notion of a dialectically totalizing *experience*; the second is closer to the spirit of Kant's *Critique of Judgment*; but must be submitted, like the *Critique*, to that severe reexamination which postmodernity imposes on the thought of the Enlightenment, on the idea of a unitary end of history and of a subject. (*PC*, pp. 72–3)

We have already answered part of Lyotard's query: Habermas's modernism places him squarely on this side of the Kant/Hegel divide.

But the 'completion of modernity' he and Kant propose as a practical task remains questionable from the standpoint of postmodernism. If, as Lyotard maintains, discourse is always potentially in a state of crisis, if it is always on the verge of transcending its 'own' internal logic and unitary end – literally losing its determinate identity by becoming a different kind of discourse – then would it not be more accurate to talk about its tendential disintegration into conflicting norms (goals) than about its tendential harmony in accordance with a dominant one?

III

These last reflections take us to the heart of Lyotard's postmodern alternative. The fluidity and complexity of this alternative defy easy translation into fixed philosophical categories. Lyotard is a thinker who finds equal merit in the biologism of Nietzsche and Freud, the contextualism of Aristotle and the Sophists, the anarchism of Feyerabend, *and* the idealism of Kant.[28] Moving freely across boundaries separating rationalism from antirationalism, universalism from particularism, idealism from materialism, his 'critical rationalism' owes more to Adorno's 'micrologies' than to Kant's tribunal of reason.[29] Like Habermas, Lyotard rejects philosophy of consciousness in favour of a theory of speech action based on Wittgenstein's model of language games. However, the result is more consistent with Wittgenstein's own dismissal of his earlier attempt to found language on truth-functional logic. For the late Wittgenstein, postulation of a transcendental metarule governing the application of rules succumbs to Russell's paradox – if the metarule is a member of the class it regulates it ceases to be ultimate; if it is not then it ceases to be a rule. Lyotard and Wittgenstein avoid this antinomy by conceiving linguistic rules as local practices subject to continual reinterpretation (*PC*, p. 10).

Where Lyotard differs with Wittgenstein is over the primacy of consensus and convention. Lyotard stresses the unconventional, agonistic inventiveness of 'moves' (*coups*) within language games. Like another philosopher with whom he has much in common – Donald Davidson – he pushes this principle of linguistic *uncertainty* to the point of endangering the very concept of rule-governed language.[30] Yet, unlike Davidson, Lyotard vigorously protests the *literal* intertranslatability of different language games. In his opinion, language games may share rigidly designating names – inscrutability of reference notwithstanding – and they may share metaphorical complicities that ease transitions between them, but they are – for all that – essentially incommensurable.

At the same time, the nominal and metaphorical links between language games infect them with external impurities. The difference between Lyotard and Habermas on this score is striking. Habermas concedes linguistic impurity up to a point – he says, for example, that the ideal constraints implicit in consensual speech are superimposed over success-oriented aims; that the hortatory rhetoric of political discourse combines consensual and strategic orientations; that the opening up and preservation of communicative interaction often depends on the unannounced power, or indirect influence, of *perlocutionary effects*; and that different orientations towards validity are metaphorically interlaced in discourse as well as in everyday communication. But he insists that such impurity is mostly contingent and contained by the dominant consensual orientation.[31] In principle, such impurities could be eliminated from theoretical discourse entirely and from practical discourse to the extent that action constraints are bracketed or kept subordinate.

Lyotard disagrees. Although he shares Habermas's view that scientific discourses strictly speaking are oriented towards consensus and abide by canons of logic in a way that distinguishes them from everyday conversations, he denies that consensus orientation and logic exhaust their function and structure. Of course, the logical distinction between object language and metalanguage disqualifies badly formed – but colloquially acceptable – sentences of the sort 'This statement is false' from science. But, as we saw in the case of Habermas, scientific discourse allows for practical, aesthetic and therapeutic reflections on the core concepts regulating accepted paradigms that violate this distinction. This possibility resides in its mixing of metaprescriptives (rules of logic), prescriptives (paradigmatic axioms), denotations (observations) and heteromorphous combinations of prescriptive and denotative assertions (laws). In Lyotard's opinion, such reflexivity and impurity conspire to generate 'paralogies' (Heisenberg's Uncertainty Principle, Gödel's Theorem, etc.) as well as anomalies and surprises. Thus, conflict, dissensus, 'the winning strategy' and novelty are as much a part of the aim of science as consensus (*PC*, pp. 64ff.).

Needless to say, this view of language has ominous consequences for the idea of subjectivity. What we have is not the decentration of a transcendentally unified subject of speech, as in Habermas's model, but the dissolution of a subject caught in the midst of a chain of speech acts and positioned with respect to multiple and sometimes conflicting roles, realities and expectations (*PC*, p. 40). According to Lyotard, the referent, meaning, addressor and addressee 'presented' by any phrase (speech act) are determined by the phrase that follows. Now phrases belong to different *regimens* (or language games), such as ostension, description, prescription and interrogation. Regimens are *not* commensurable; you cannot translate prescriptions into descriptions; and the former cannot be offered in lieu of the latter when the game in question is just describing. However, different regimens can be linked to one another in more complex language games called *genres*. For example, it is normally acceptable to link a description to an act of ostension (denoting the described object's spatio-temporal location) in scientific discourse. The ostensive phrase, in turn, might be offered in response to a question, command or request for information. In any case the universe of a descriptive phrase P varies depending on subsequent phrases. It could be a response to a question; but it could also be a warning, a command, or a request. Most importantly, its sense at least partially depends on the response it elicits; proclaimed authorial intent does not always carry final authority in these matters. My intended use of P as a signal for assistance can be overridden by my interlocutors, who understand it as an offhand remark, a description awaiting further qualification, and so forth.

This last point is decisive for understanding the sorts of conflicts that arise in everyday communication. Unlike the rules governing regimens, the rules governing genres do not determine a specific response. What they determine is an overall aim: truth in the case of science; unconditional obligation, in the case of morality, etc. A problem arises, however, in as much as phrases provide occasions for linking heterogeneous regimens *and* genres. Thus a certain injustice, or *différend*, occurs whenever the aim of a phrase is suppressed and superseded by that of its successor.

More precisely, a *différend* occurs 'whenever a plaintiff is deprived of the means of arguing and by this fact becomes a victim', as in the case where the settling of a conflict between two parties 'is made in the idiom of one of them in which the wrong (*tort*) suffered by the other signifies nothing' (*DF*, pp. 24–5). As distinct from litigation, 'a *différend* would be a conflict between (at least) two parties which cannot be adjudicated equitably for lack of a rule of judgement applicable to the two arguments' (*DF*, p. 9). A *différend* occurs, for example, when the silence of holocaust survivors – say, in response to the revisionist historian's 'scientific' demand that evidence be given to prove the existence of death camps – is interpreted as a denial of such evidence. Indeed, the very existence of holocaust survivors – which the historian's cognitive discourse demands as proof – seems to undermine the proof itself. Here the survivor is deprived of the means of argumentation and reduced to silence.

Although historian and survivor seem to be communicating with one another rationally – in Lyotard's Kripkean way of putting it, they both use the same names (Auschwitz, Treblinka, etc.) to rigidly designate a simple (empty) referent, and they both have equal opportunities to make and rebut arguments pertaining to this referent

– they have positioned themselves in different universes of discourse. The names mean something different to the survivor; they do not designate determinable, historical facts about which one could argue and on which one could reach consensus. Rather, they signify suffering of such indeterminable, inhuman magnitude that they can only be thought in silence.

The contractualist language of market exchange marks the site of another *différend*, in this case between labour and management. The legal terms specified in the contract require that labourers define their labour as alienable exchange value (remunerable in terms of some monetary equivalent) – not as the living expression of their very personality. If it were defined as a power of expression and self-actualization, its articulation would carry us into the moral and political discourse of democratic self-determination – a sphere of discourse whose criterion of justice would require nullifying the split between labour, management and (perhaps) ownership presupposed in the labour contract.

The example of the labour contract illustrates how a discursive process – which necessarily tends towards a definition of terms – issues in exclusion, suppression, hegemony and ultimately political domination. Yet despite whatever sympathy we might feel for the workers, it would be wrong to think that this kind of *différend* is merely incidental to the process of communication, and could be eliminated in a just, democratic order. Indeed, for Lyotard, all political discourse – including democratic dialogue – suffers from a profound legitimation crisis centring around innumerable *différends*. For, he tells us, the latter 'is not a genre; it is the multiplicity of genres, the diversity of ends' – the very 'threat of the *différend*' itself (*DF*, p. 200).

Like Habermas, then, Lyotard departs from the premise that democratic political reasoning comprises a complex web of pragmatic, ethical, moral and juristic genres of discourse that qualify one another in various ways. Although his specific account of the typology and connection of genres differs from Habermas's in minor details, what is important for us to note is the antithetical way in which this 'unity' is described: not as a relatively coherent and hierarchically ordered process, but as a symmetrical chain of suppressions and injustices.

In Lyotard's model, the genre initiating democratic discourse is ethical, and its characteristic interrogation begins by asking: what should we be? (*DF*, p. 213). In this phrase the 'we' that is obligated might be 'humanity', if what is enjoined upon us is realization of our universal personality as bearers of certain fundamental rights. Or, it might be 'we Americans (Germans, French, etc.)', if what is enjoined upon us is the realization of our national identity. In any case, the question of what legitimates this obligation already suggests a kind of *différend*. If it is just ourselves – we authorize (democratically) the authority (constitution, idea of humanity, nation) that authorizes us – we produce a vicious circle.[32] Morally speaking, the one who authorizes (addressor) and the one who is authorized (addressee) cannot be identical. Otherwise the *limits* imposed on the one who is authorized by the one authorizing are no longer limits (that is, normative obligations), and injustices (*différends*) in the name of The People against the people will occur. Hence, the idea of democratic *self-determination* (the absolute sovereignty of the people) ought to be qualified by a healthy respect for pre-political rights (*DF*, pp. 206ff.).

Perhaps this can be achieved by grounding, as Habermas does, the idea of a democratic constitution in something preceding the will of the people: practical discourse. However, this strategy, Lyotard suggests, again involves the commission of a *différend*. A universal, *indeterminate idea* (of humanity, nation, etc.) is thought to be binding in some *determinate* way. But this can happen only if certain persons (such as the Founding Fathers) presume to speak on behalf of the universal – a clearly illegitimate and paradoxical usurpation of authority that effectively silences political opposition (*DF*, pp. 209ff.).

Let us leave aside the *différend* that occurs at the founding moment. Once the supreme ethical question is answered, the next asks: what should we do? The prescribers of determinate policies (laws) act in the name of indeterminate ideas, but the abyss between prescription and idea cannot be bridged without doing violence to the latter. The bureaucrat's prescription usurps the Founder's idea. Moreover – as paradoxes of collective choice amply attest – since 'The People' simply does not exist as a representable or realizable phenomenon, Habermas's hope that an amorphous, popular consensus on ethical identity can be translated without loss into legislative proposals, and that these, in turn, can be translated without loss into concrete policies and judgements, appears to be without foundation.[33] The impersonal form of the law conceals the partisan nature of its prescriptive content (*DF*, p. 214).

This *différend* is followed by another, which involves the trumping of the moral genre by the cognitive. Since 'ought' implies 'can', the addressee of an unconditioned command – the expert delegated the task of implementing the policy – is now required to consider it as factually conditioned and potentially revocable. However, actuality does not exhaust possibility. So, cognitive discourse must be trumped, in turn, by the 'irreal' narrative of imaginable achievements. The appeal to speculative history returns us to the question of political ends. At this point, someone must 'adjudicate' between conflicting ends. But who has the right to judge and by what authority?

It should be clear by now that everyone has the right to judge, yet no one has the authority to do so. To begin with, judgement is not legitimated by consensus on universal interests. Nor is it legitimated by consensus on the rules of the game; the latter remains subject to shifts in signification and authorization that accompany *différends* in political discourse. Indeed, Lyotard fears that, by linking legitimation to the consensual regularization of moves within a language game rather than to their agonal contestation, Habermas comes dangerously close to abetting the kind of systemic closure he himself opposes. The danger is only magnified by his talk of a universal subject of history (humanity, or the human species) whose emancipation remains linked to a universal consensus on true needs. Like all *grands récits* of the Enlightenment, Habermas's appeal to universal history (or developmental psychology as analogue for social evolution) regresses behind the contingent standpoint of decentred dialogue to the speculative standpoint of *Geist*-centred dialectic. To cite Lyotard: 'the cause is good, but the argument is not' (*PC*, p. 66).

A better argument, Lyotard thinks, links legitimation to popular justice ('give the public free access to the memory and data banks') and to the paralogical creation of new moves – a view that reflects the fact that systems are always on the verge of breaking down under the weight of their own internal complexity. Of course, such crises are not inevitable. By seeing the contestable *communicative* network in which 'autonomous' subsystems interact with their environments as part of their internal complexity, Lyotard and Habermas open a space for critical interventions aimed at theoretically enlightening functionaries within those systems about the practical limits of the cognitive regime under which they labour.[34]

We are back to our original problem: critically judging the rightful boundaries separating cognitive from moral discourse. In a major interview conducted in 1979 Lyotard offered what appeared to be a 'modern' response to this problem.[35] Determination of the fairness of moves relative to the rules of a particular language game (the multiplicity of justices) was said to presuppose determination of the autonomy of incommensurable language games (the justice of multiplicities). The problem arises concerning the status of this latter justice: what entitles philosophy to adjudicate boundary disputes between other language games? Indeed, can there be a judgement that doesn't arbitrarily impose order – and commit a *différend* – in the name of some partial law?

IV

Lyotard's answer to this question hinges on finding an *aesthetic* rationale for philosophical criticism that avoids the paradox of the 'great prescriber': the presumption of judicial authority that acts in the name of law at once determinate (local) and transcendent (universal). His point of departure is Kant's *Critique of Judgment*. Judgement, for Kant, involves subsuming a particular intuition under a universal concept. In the case of *determinant* (*bestimmend*) judgement the universal is immediately given along with the particular it subsumes. The category of substance, for example, is immediately thought along with an intuition of a particular object; the categorical imperative is likewise determinant for the lawful prescriptivity of a particular maxim. Yet, as Hegel pointed out – and as Lyotard's own analysis of the *différend* confirms – a prescription that is purely rational (unconditional) *and* determinant is oxymoronic.

To circumvent this aporia Lyotard proposes an account of critical rationalism that comports with Kant's notion of *reflective* (*reflektierende*) judgement. Unlike a determinant judgement, a reflective judgement *discovers* a universal in the purposive presentation of a particular.[36] There is no single criterion (or rule) that demonstrably determines *apriori* the judgement in question. Now reflective judgements come in two varieties: judgements of natural and historical *teleology*; and *aesthetic* judgements of the beautiful and of the sublime.[37] This taxonomy is not rigid. Lyotard's own postmodernism, for example, draws him to Kant's interest in the sublime as a figure of historical progress(ion).[38]

Like judgements of beauty, judgements of sublimity are grounded in shared *feeling* (*sensus communis*) or, more precisely, experience of pleasure arising from the free (playful) harmony (*Zusammenstimmung*) of incommensurable faculties – either between the imagination and the understanding, as in the case of judgements of beauty, or between the imagination and reason, as in the case of judgements of the sublime. In both instances pleasure arises from reflectively comparing understanding (or reason) to the pure form (or formlessness) of a representation given *disinterestedly* to imagination, apart from any *aposteriori* gratification or conceptual determination.[39] Hence the impossibility of rationally deducing – or discursively 'legitimizing' – judgements whose exemplary validity and universality alone depends on the mere communicability of subjective feelings.[40]

Now the pleasure associated with the sublime is mixed with pain, owing to the peculiar complexity of the judgement in question. Unlike judgements of beauty, in which the imagination apprehends a formal representation in a way that harmonizes with (is purposive with respect to) the understanding, the imagination here apprehends a representation as so *unlimited* and *exceeding all form* that it discloses not the harmony, but the utter inadequacy (*Unangemessen-*

heit), of intuition with respect to Idea. In the case of the *mathematical* sublime, the imagination's attempt to completely represent an infinite *magnitude* discloses a *disharmony* between imagination and *theoretical* reason. In the case of the *dynamical* sublime, the imagination's attempt to entertain the infinite *power* of raw nature or divinity reveals a disharmony between imagination and *practical* reason. Yet judgements of sublimity also reflect a *harmony* between our finite capacity to resist nature and our infinite, rationally destined empowerment over nature in a manner analogous to the painful/pleasurable feeling of moral respect (*Ehrfurcht*).[41]

This tension between harmony and disharmony, unity and disunity in judgements of sublimity is emblematic of the kind of metaphorical complicity linking incommensurable regimens and genres – in this instance those of aesthetics and morality – that Lyotard finds so appealing. Such complicity explains Habermas's speculative temptation to judge unconditional moral prescriptions *as if* they were cognitive truth claims susceptible to consensual adjudication. It also explains the metaphorical resemblance linking free, disinterested judgements of taste with our moral capacity to 'think from the standpoint of everyone else' enjoined by 'common human understanding'.[42] The metaphorical link between the 'truth' of a poem as an event of secular illumination, the 'truth' of its moral content, the 'truth' of our description of it, and the 'truth(fulness)' of its expression of authentic experience comprises a syndrome that is as compelling to literary critics as it is to lay persons. But the syndrome by no means eliminates the literal incommensurabilities (disanalogies) separating these distinct senses of truth. That sublimely infinite gap reflects critically on the *felt* disparity between our *presentiment* of a vibrant life lived with full integrity (Dewey) and the *reality* of a life dispersed into opposed moments – a disequilibrium, if you will, that also marks an injustice.

If we follow Lyotard's own analogy between philosophical and critical judgement, the judgement dispensed by the critical rationalist concerning the justice of multiplicities mediates abstract idea and concrete intuition as well as the diverse spheres of reasoning, but not with prescriptive authority. It is like the judgement dispensed by Kant's guardian in *The Strife of the Faculties*, who is not a neutral tribunal issuing final, impartial verdicts. In Lyotard's judgement, Kant's guardian – far from legally adjudicating the conflict of *genres* – listens for the silences that betoken *différends* so as to let the suppressed voice find its proper idiom within a community of reason.

The idea regulating this community is nothing other than *an agreement to disagree;*[43] its basis is aesthetic *feeling*, its symbol is the field (*Feld*), or as Lyotard puts it, the archipelago – a sea of discourse islands traversed by a floating judgement which, having no aim but to present (communicate) to one island the offerings of commerce or war destined to it by the others, is without an island of its own (*DF*, p. 190).

With this appeal to the oceanic it would appear that Lyotard's thought once again slips back into the dark void of the singular, the fluid and the prediscursive. Transcending the stable, background consensus on traditional norms and values supportive of communicative interaction, the free-floating idea of community to which his judgement appeals lacks sufficient ground (*Grund*) for discrimination. Hence the suspicion that his judgement amounts to little more than an unprincipled, sophistical rhetoric of provocation, forever mutable with respect to context – aesthetic performance rather than reasoned criticism.

Yet perhaps there is another way to read Lyotard here. His postmodern patchwork of paganism (Aristotle) and modernism (Kant) suggests that *determinant* and *reflective* judgements are abstractions of a single movement of deliberation.[44] Judgements determine the regulative content of ideas by applying them to particular cases, while prejudgements – originating in tradition – determine the process of judging itself, apart from *thematic* reflection. This process, however, is not deterministic. Both instances engage a prethematic reflection in which particular and universal, judge and (pre)judgement, interpret one another dialogically – *not* discursively. Only in the course of this dialogue do the identity of the judge, the criteria on which she or he relies and the facts on which she or he judges acquire mutual definition. And – to recall the problem of sufficient reason – only in the course of this dialogue do the historical community requisite for sustaining legitimate expectations over time and the rational community requisite for criticizing illegitimate prejudices *determine* one another in a manner conducive to judgement. If judgements presuppose agreement in contextual sensibility – to paraphrase the early Lyotard, *discours* is no substitute for *figure* – they remain free and indeterminate with respect to an ideal, open-ended future.[45]

Contrary to Habermas, we may conclude that refusal to offer standard sorts of reasons in ethico-political discourse need not entail commission of a performative contradiction. Since discourse in this instance involves getting one's interlocutor(s) to enter the hermeneutic circle in which one's own highly situated life's experience is intimately implicated, the reasons offered in support of a judgement will not be exhausted by illocutionary claims to truth, justice and the like, but will necessarily include such things as experiences, which we indirectly indicate through perlocutionary acts. And if – after all is said and done – no such common experience emerges, we might then rightly choose to remain silent.

V

The endless spectacle of *différends* – indeed, of boundless formlessness – cannot arouse the sort of sublime enthusiasm and sense of
rational finality that Kant, as disinterested historical spectator, man-
aged to feel about the French Revolution, despite all its injustices. It
cannot do so because unity and finality – humanity progressing
towards perpetual peace – are alien to it. But can we rest satisfied
with a response that amounts to little more than the modest demand
that 'politics cannot have for its stake the good, but would have to
have the least bad' (*DF*, p. 203)?

Answering this question would require adjudicating the *différend*
between Habermas and Lyotard – an impossible task. Instead I
propose an immanent criticism of their respective views. I have
already noted the tensions in Habermas's modernism. *Within* the
logical and semantical limits of practical discourse as Habermas sees
it, one cannot infer a procedural idea of justice without committing
certain fallacies: the fallacy of inferring a normative phrase from a
transcendental one; and the fallacy of inferring a transcendental
phrase from a factual one. Habermas's attempt to account for the
quasi-transcendental, *quasi*-prescriptive nature of rules of argumentation that are neither strictly compelling (necessary) nor strictly
discretionary (susceptible to violation without performative contradiction) shows that he is cognizant of the former difficulty. His
attempt to ground rational reconstructions in the considered judgements reached by philosophers, social scientists, psychologists and
test subjects in a reflectively equilibrated dialogue shows that he is
cognizant of the latter. Contrary to Lyotard, neither difficulty speaks
against the possibility of practical discourse *per se* but only against
the possibility of a discourse that insists on suppressing the metaphoricity of reason behind the rigid exterior of logical incommensurabilities. By the same token, they do not preclude the raising of
fallible truth-claims so long as their meaning and validity are not
assumed to be finally determined.

Finality would make sense *only if* we could purify unitary form of
the multiplicity of local contents. Habermas's own 'fudging' of
boundaries separating *literally* incommensurable phrasal regimens
and genres amply testifies to the impossibility of such purification.
Thus the integrity of reason can be conceived only if its contextual
impurity and *metaphoricity* are factored in. Habermas's account of
the integrity of both specialized and everyday discourse – as well as
his recent claims about the *informal* (intuitive and aesthetic) rationality governing judgement – are compatible with this position;[46] his
insistence on the finality and – above all – formal rationality of justice
is not.[47] For, if Habermas's idea of democratic procedural justice

intentionally lacks the institutional specificity that Lyotard – fearing totalitarian democracy – thinks it does, it also intentionally lacks the utopian feel for integral happiness that Habermas – fearing social reification – wishes it might have.

This last point brings us to similar tensions in Lyotard's account of the *différend*. The *différend* presupposes incommensurability between different genres and regimens. This all-too-modern presumption of pure, rational types threatens to degenerate into a radical pluralism of unrelated phrases whose external interaction cannot even begin to explain the mere possibility of communicative linkage.[48] In order to account for the latter, Lyotard must qualify the extent to which phrases and genres are literally incommensurable, without abandoning the idea entirely. Like Habermas, he does this by introducing the notion of aesthetic judgement, which reflects the metaphorical commensurability of literally incommensurable language games. In effect, both philosophers concede that the strict opposition between rational argumentation and aesthetic judgement falls to the ground.[49]

Now I shall argue that Habermas's idea of rational community is preferable to Lyotard's, if for no other reason than that it explains why one ought to resist hegemonic injustice. Put simply, health (integrity) is a more attractive aesthetic idea to fight for than sublimely endless distraction.

The preference for Habermas becomes clearer when we examine the limits of the *différend* as a cypher for justice. Lyotard nowhere clearly distinguishes the *différend* that occurs between the camp survivor and the revisionist historian from the *différend* that necessarily occurs in any speech. Although the former plainly constitutes a wrong, the latter does not. (Indeed, does it not seem bizarre to describe as *injustice* a condition whose continual interruption of hegemonic closure supposedly redeems our faith *in* justice?) In fact, Lyotard takes great pain to show that the *différend* is a class of injustice totally *unlike* our customary notions of political injustice.

At this juncture I feel compelled to raise an objection that goes directly to the heart of the problem Lyotard and Habermas inherit from German Idealism: the problem of choosing between total(itarian) unity or total(itarian) anarchism. I am sympathetic to Richard Rorty's suspicion that these thinkers are scratching where it does not itch. Surely, the source of hegemony – if indeed there is hegemony – is nothing as murky as the diremption or selective cultivation of reason. At first blush, it seems closer to the kind of injustice Michael Walzer talks about when he criticizes the wrongful hegemony of one sphere of goods over another – a hegemony without which political injustice (class domination, or monopoly over dominant goods) wouldn't be a problem in the first place.[50] Like Walzer, Lyotard argues that questions of justice must be resolved in accord-

ance with the 'common understandings' that persons in a given
society share regarding the distribution of specific types of goods.
Specific *criteria* of justice are thus validated with respect to the
popular narratives (or *petits récits*, as Lyotard puts it) that persons of
specific societies recount to one another about these goods. In the
Hindu narratives of traditional Indian caste society, for example,
blood descent dictates a *simple* criterion for distributing all goods –
education, power, wealth and prestige. In the modern democracies of
the West the criteria for distributing each of these goods are *complex*:
need entitles one to basic medical care and education, but not to
political office; market success entitles one to unequal shares of
commodities, but not to unequal education, medical care or political
power.

Since the dominance of money in capitalist democracies threatens
the autonomy of the other spheres of justice and violates what
Lyotard calls 'the justice of pluralities' and what Habermas, under
the very different rubric of health, designates the 'integrity of a form
of life', its influence must at least be curtailed or confined more
thoroughly to the sphere of commodity exchange than it presently is.
Here it should be noted that Lyotard's call for universal access to
information in 'non zero–sum' democratic games confronts the
hegemonic pretensions of business and administrative elites with a
demand for *political* justice that is no less urgent than Habermas's
(*PC*, p. 67).

Yet, as our examination of Lyotard and Habermas has shown, one
could hardly justify democracy as a *universal* and *pure* type of
political rationality. Even if the *structural* combination of ethical,
moral and pragmatic criteria underwriting political discourse comprises an integral whole and not a *différend*, something of the latter
still persists in the mediation of more substantive ethical and moral
interpretations. Contrary to Walzer and Habermas, our 'common
understanding' of the *concrete* meanings of distributional criteria vis-
à-vis specific assortments of goods is, if anything, *un*common. Being
grounded neither in *the* reason of things (Habermas) nor in stable,
coherent traditions (Walzer), its sense fluctuates depending on the
conflicting 'stakes' intersecting our political discourse.

To take an example from American constitutional law, the republican interest in insulating democracy from the inegalitarian influence
of money, knowledge and power opposes the federalist interest in
retaining a marketplace of ideas and lifestyles in which unequal
capacities for participation inevitably develop. If the former interest
cedes priority to democratic majorities, the latter's respect for minorities does not – at least, not without the protection of judicial review.
This tension must be borne in mind when considering Lyotard's
alleged hostility to democracy. Given his fear of manufactured

consensus in mass democracy ('majority does not mean large number, but great fear'[51]), it is no accident that some commentators have seen his postmodern call for political justice as centring on 'neo-liberal, interest group pluralism' and 'free, flexible, contractual arrangements'.[52] Yet Lyotard's federalist suspicion of majoritarian tyranny is consonant with the spirit of dualist democracy.[53] The separation of powers that Kant opposed to absolute democracy and that Lyotard seems to endorse as a necessary antidote to Jacobin Terror has the advantage of preserving – against the whims of *transient* legislative majorities who lack popular mandate – the hard-fought advances in higher law-making brought about by the masses.

However, no dual democratic vision 'harmonizing' republican and federalist aims can overcome all injustice. No single criterion of justice – be it procedural (pertaining to decision rules), structural (pertaining to distributive rules), or libertarian (pertaining to civil rights) – suffices to legitimate legal institutions.[54] At best, appeal to such criteria in proper combination serves to mitigate the injustices perpetrated by each separately.

Having momentarily strayed into the dense thicket of postmodern political justice, we can now safely assert that the problem of judging hegemony remains even after we jettison the dialectic of enlightenment as our point of reference. These same considerations suggest that judgement can never achieve the rational integrity towards which it aspires. Habermas's acknowledgement of the 'tortuous routes along which science, morality, and art communicate with one another' reminds us that judgement here may well be mixed with tinctures of the kind of sublimity attested to by Lyotard.[55] Yet unlike him, he refuses to exaggerate this dissonance. In his opinion, the inability to 'link meaning and validity, meaning and intention, and meaning and accomplished action', as well as the inability to effect 'intermodal transfers' of validity within a communication setting, is nothing less than pathological.[56]

Contrary to some of Lyotard's more extreme formulations, there must be some integrity in our capacity to *judge*. The *manner* in which we switch from one mode of argumentation to another within a specific type of discourse, from one phrasal regimen to another within a mode of argumentation and from one perspective (modality) to another within a phrasal regimen must be regulated in advance by the logic of the discourse in question, even if the transition (or translation) between otherwise incommensurable modalities is metaphorical, not logical. As Habermas puts it, '*whether* and *when* we are supposed to accomplish it depends on the faculty of judgement inherent in communicative action itself.'[57] If this is the case – and all our previous inquiries suggest that it is – then the rationale guiding this faculty must be intuitive, aesthetic and prediscursive. Again, to

cite an earlier example, one might question my judgement that P
sincerely believes what she says, but whether or not my inference is a
good one surely depends on my experience in dealing with her. At
some point it becomes silly for me to offer any further reasons in
support of my judgement, a view amply confirmed in my ultimate
retort: 'You don't know P the way I do!'. The ensuing silence once
again marks the *rational* limits of reasoned justification. No one
better states the case for it than Habermas himself when he reminds
us that 'there are no metadiscourses for this [judgement]' – indeed
'no metadiscourses whatsoever' – since 'every discourse is . . . equally
close to God.'[58]

This same aesthetic rationality also regulates clinical judgements
about ethico-political identity. Absent any consideration of universal
history, the critical – and ultimately democratic – discourses in which
these judgements figure would be meaningless. Such narratives – and
here I include Habermas's own analogy between individual moral
development and social evolution – may well be legitimate. If so, we
might think of them in the same way we think of other *grands récits*
of enlightenment – as transcendental illusions possessing a *non-
cognitive* rationale. Such 'myths' enable us to *think as if* 'we'
individual, decentred subjects possessed a *rational* identity pointing
us in the direction of an emancipated democracy. In the words of
Lyotard, they provide *ideas* that might mitigate despair (and perhaps
inspire hope) but could not serve as determinate prescriptions –
without incurring the risk of ideological distortion – apart from their
concrete articulation in public opinion.

The latter merits a more detailed discussion than can be given here,
but two points are worth noting. First, grand narratives are indispensable for engaging in debates about the larger questions of justice
raised by Lyotard, Walzer and Habermas. The struggle against
totalitarianism is conducted on multiple fronts, each centred on some
specific *lingua franca*. The meanings and distributive criteria attached
to these goods change, as do the boundaries delimiting the language
games in which they are staked. Interpreting them therefore requires
engaging a grander narrative about who we are – whence we have
come and whither we are going – as part and parcel of a more
encompassing community of judgement.

The second point qualifies the first. In contrast to the guardedly
optimistic, problem-solving orientation of progressive, modernist
narratives, Lyotard's *différend* reminds us of the inherent limits and
unavoidable injustices that come with trying to impose any simple *or*
complex schema of justice. Indeed, it reminds us of the peculiarly
tragic nature of our dirempted (post)modern condition; the aims of
truth, honesty, equality, freedom and happiness that enter into our
complex reasoning are not reconcilable in a way that could do justice

to them all. Such a reminder entails conservative cynicism just as much (or as little) as its opposite – optimistic idealism – entails revolutionary totalitarianism. Should it perchance encourage piece-meal amelioration of suffering and injustice in the name of liberal compassion, so much the better. If this is the price we democrats must pay for justice, then *silence* – or the 'great refusal' – may well be as justified as unremitting participation in a 'dialogue' whose promise for redemption – however illusory – still remains our only hope.

NOTES

Epigraphs from J. Habermas, 'Transcendence from Within, Transcendence in this World', in D. S. Browning and F. S. Fiorenza (eds), *Habermas, Modernity and Public Theology* (New York: Crossroad, 1992), p. 226, and J.–F. Lyotard, *Le Différend* (Paris: Éditions de Minuit, 1983), p. 30.

1 J. Habermas, *The Philosophical Discourse of Modernity*, trans. F. Lawrence (Cambridge: Polity Press; Cambridge, Mass.: MIT Press, 1987), p. xix; hereafter cited as *PDM*.

2 J.-F. Lyotard, 'Reponse à la question: qu'est-ce que le postmoderne?', in J.-F. Lyotard, *Le postmoderne expliqué aux enfants* (Paris: Galilee, 1986), p. 16; in English as 'Answering the Question: What is Postmodernism?', in J.-F. Lyotard, *The Postmodern Condition: A Report on Knowledge*, trans. G. Bennington and B. Massumi (Minneapolis: University of Minnesota Press, 1984) (hereafter cited as *PC*), p. 73. Habermas links Lyotard's more recent work, *Le Différend* (Paris: Éditions de Minuit, 1983) (hereafter cited as *DF*), to Rorty's own 'radical contextualism', which rescues from idealism 'moments of the non-identical and the non-integrated, the deviant and heterogeneous, the contradictory and conflictual, the transitory and accidental'. See J. Habermas, *Nachmetaphysisches Denken* (Frankfurt: Suhrkamp, 1988), p. 153; and R. Rorty, 'Habermas and Lyotard on Postmodernity', in R. Bernstein (ed.), *Habermas and Modernity* (Cambridge: Polity Press, 1985), pp. 162, 164. For Habermas's own concession to contextualism, see note 47 below.

3 J. Habermas, 'A Reply', in A. Honneth and H. Joas (eds), *Communicative Action* (Cambridge, Mass.: MIT Press, 1991), pp. 222, 226.

4 Cf. T. Adorno and M. Horkheimer, *Dialectic of Enlightenment* (New York: Herder and Herder, 1947); J. Habermas, *PDM*, pp. 105–30; and *The Theory of Communicative Action*, vol. 1: *Reason and the Rationalization of Society*, trans. T. McCarthy (Cambridge: Polity Press, 1984), esp. part IV; Lyotard, *Le postmoderne expliqué*, pp. 97ff.

5 Habermas, 'A Reply', p. 225.

6 Habermas, *The Theory of Communicative Action*, vol. 1, pp. 243–72.

7 Ibid., pp. 15ff.

8 J. Habermas, 'Justice and Solidarity: On the Discussion Concerning "Stage 6"', *Philosophical Forum* 21:1–2 (Fall–Winter 1989–90), p. 41.

9 Cf. A. Wellmer, *Ethik und Dialog: Elemente des moralischen Urteils bei Kant und in die Diskursethik* (Frankfurt: Suhrkamp, 1986), pp. 54–112.

10 Habermas's invocation of the logical rule, proposed by Robert Alexy, that 'different speakers may not use the same expression with different meanings'

would have the paradoxical result of discouraging debate between (say) anti-abortion activists, who appeal to a religious conception of family values with its attendant emphasis on the *natural* rights of the unborn foetus *qua* moral person, and pro-abortion activists, who appeal to utilitarian justifications of reproductive rights with its attendant de-emphasis on the personhood of the foetus. Cf. J. Habermas, *Moral Consciousness and Communicative Action* (Cambridge: Polity Press, 1990), p. 87.

11 J. Habermas. *Faktizität und Geltung: Beiträge zur Diskurstheorie des Rechts und des demokratishen Rechtsstaats* (Frankfurt: Suhrkamp, 1992), pp. 201ff; in English as *Between Facts and Norms: Contributions to a Discourse Theory of Law and Democracy*, trans. William Rehg (Cambridge: Polity, 1996).

12 Habermas, *Faktizität und Geltung*, p. 205.

13 Ibid., pp. 222ff.

14 Ibid., p. 200.

15 Ibid., pp. 229ff.

16 Habermas, *The Theory of Communicative Action*, vol. 1, pp. 73–4.

17 According to Habermas, critical theory must refrain from 'critically evaluating and normatively ordering totalities, forms of life and cultures, and life-contexts and epochs *as a whole*'; *The Theory of Communicative Action*, vol. 2: *System and Lifeworld*, trans. T. McCarthy (Cambridge: Polity Press, 1987), p. 383.

18 Habermas argues that 'in place of the positive task of meeting a certain need for interpretation by ideological means, we have the negative requirement of preventing holistic interpretations from coming into existence' (ibid., pp. 354–5). Yet he also notes that 'in place of "false consciousness" we today have a "fragmented consciousness" that blocks enlightenment by the mechanism of reification.'

19 The following remarks touch on no fewer than *six* problems of mediation: (1) the mediation of expert cultures and the everyday lifeworld; (2) the mediation of rationalization complexes with one another; (3) the mediation of distinct aspects of validity in everyday speech; (4) the mediation of distinct aspects of validity in specialized discourse; (5) the formal unity of argumentation common to all discourses; and (6) the mediation of discourse and action. Problems 1–5 are especially pertinent to this paper. (5) is problematic even by Habermas's standards, and is explicitly rejected by Lyotard. (3) and (4) are given summary treatment by Habermas but comprise, as we shall see, the very core of Lyotard's postmodernism.

20 Habermas, *The Theory of Communicative Action*, vol. 2, pp. 62ff.

21 J. Habermas, 'Wahrheitsteorien', in *Vorstudien und Ergänzungen zur Theorie des kommunikatives Handelns* (Frankfurt: Suhrkamp, 1984), pp. 174–6.

22 Habermas, *The Theory of Communicative Action*, vol. 2, p. 398.

23 J. Habermas, 'Questions and Counterquestions', in Bernstein (ed.), *Habermas and Modernity*, p. 203, emphasis added.

24 Habermas, *The Theory of Communicative Action*, vol. 1, pp. 252–3.

25 Ibid., pp. 16–20.

26 Habermas, *Faktizität und Geltung*, pp. 199ff.

27 Habermas, 'Questions and Counterquestions', p. 203.

28 Lyotard's defence of a pagan, postmodern Kantianism is given in J.-F. Lyotard and J.-L. Thébaud, *Just Gaming* (Manchester: Manchester University Press, 1986), pp. 89–90; original French edition, *Au Juste* (Paris: Christian Bourgeois, 1979).

29 Lyotard, *Le postmoderne expliqué aux enfants*, pp. 97ff, 107ff, 114.

30 It is true that Lyotard sometimes invokes consensus on linguistic rules to emphasize Wittgenstein's point about the public (or social) nature of language *games* as a prior constraint on and condition of the personal (or *subjective*) choice of words. To this extent, he *seems* less radical than Davidson, who deploys Quine's model of radical translation to account for the context-specific understanding of malapropisms and other highly person-alized and original usages. Appearances notwithstanding, Lyotard no less than Davidson rejects the idea that linguistic convention is an *absolute*, external constraint on individual creativity. Hence, contrary to Habermas, no rules – not even those governing rational discourse – are immune to change. However, whereas Davidson, deploying Tarski-style T-sentences as a basis for reconstructing radically localized 'passing theories' of behav-ioural meaning, generalizes the condition of radical translation and innova-tion – literally eliminating any conception of linguistic convention – Lyotard holds that innovative changes in the rules of the game occur mainly at the fringes of linguistic usage, and always presuppose at least some consensus on other linguistic rules. Cf. D. Davidson, 'A Nice Derangement of Epitaphs', in E. Lepore (ed.), *Truth and Interpretation* (Oxford: Blackwell, 1986), pp. 433–46.

31 Habermas, 'A Reply', pp. 245, 254.

32 Derrida's deconstruction of the Declaration of Independence plays on the same *paradox of authorization*. For a comparison of this deconstruction with Lyotard's own deconstruction of the Declaration of the Rights of Man, see David Ingram, *Reason, History, and Politics* (Albany: SUNY Press, 1995), pp. 346–53; and J. Derrida, 'Declarations of Independence', *New Political Science* 15 (1986), pp. 7–15.

33 The differences between Habermas and Lyotard on the subject of popular sovereignty and consensus have been exaggerated. Given the pluralism of liberal democracy, Habermas, too, voices scepticism about 'the people' as a placeholder for democratic self-determination. For him, consensus on formal constitutional provisions – in their abstract rather than concrete form – is practically all that remains of our shared identity; yet the 'subjectless' process of democratic dialogue still remains initially oriented towards reaching agreement on substantive ends, especially as these figure in the concrete meaning of constitutional provisions. Habermas, *Faktizität und Geltung*, p. 365.

34 *PC*, pp. 61–3; *Faktizität und Geltung*, pp. 74ff.; and J. Habermas and N. Luhmann, *Theorie der Gesellschaft oder Sozialtechnologie – Was Leistet die Systemforschung* (Frankfurt: Suhrkamp, 1971).

35 Lyotard, *Au Juste*, pp. 182ff.

36 I. Kant, *Critique of Judgment*, trans. J. H. Bernard (New York: Macmillan, 1951), pp. 15ff.

37 Ibid., p. 30.

38 I. Kant, 'An Old Question Raised Again: Is the Human Race Constantly Progressing?', part 2 of 'The Strife of the Faculties', in Kant, *On History*, ed. L. W. Beck (Indianapolis: Bobbs-Merrill, 1963), p. 143.

39 Kant, *Critique of Judgment*, pp. 123–38.

40 Ibid., p. 120.

41 Ibid., pp. 82ff.

42 Ibid., pp. 136–7.

43 'As regards aesthetic feeling, the partisan of the universality of the beautiful demands a consensus that is identical to that obtainable for the true, and his adversary, in showing that it is impossible (because there is no concept corresponding to the aesthetic presentation), seems to renounce any universality whatsoever. The Kantian solution appeals to the feeling itself that one and the other necessarily experience, without which they would not even be able to agree that they were in disagreement. This feeling proves that there exists a bond of "communicability" between them' (*DF*, p. 243).

44 Lyotard, *Au Juste*, p. 52.

45 Ibid., p. 150.

46 Habermas, *The Theory of Communicative Action*, vol. 2, p. 398.

47 Habermas thinks that speech-act theory ought not to sacrifice *universal* significations on the 'altar of contextualism' ('A Reply', p. 236). But when speaking of the 'heterological' impurity of everyday discourse (p. 263), he concedes that 'argumentational games do not form a hierarchy' that would enable us to adduce 'final reasons', since this would entail 'freez[ing] the context in which we here and now consider a certain type of reason to be the best' – in effect prematurely closing an inherently open process of dialogue (p. 248).

48 Lyotard's appeal to both rational purity (modernism) and aesthetic impurity (postmodernism) reflects a tension between two different critical standpoints. The *transcendental* standpoint presumes to offer *determinant* (prescriptive) judgements about the limits determining the valid deployments of specific types of reasoning. It therefore seeks to preserve the *autonomy* (incommensurability) of morality vis-à-vis science. The *immanent* standpoint, by contrast, modestly denies such spectatorial distance; immersed in the sea of speech, its judgement is as impure, contextual and metaphorical as the genres and regimens it mediates. Since it lacks the requisite autonomy to adjudicate the rights of other language games, it must resign itself to feeling the inevitable injustices and paralogies perpetrated by unbounded language games. In my opinion, both standpoints, when taken to their *logical* extremes, are incoherent. The transcendental standpoint proffers conditional (determinant) judgements *as if they were* unconditional assertions. Its own autonomy is purchased at the expense of abandoning any unitary basis from which to regulate conflicting discourses. The immanent standpoint proffers disinterested (reflexive) judgements *as if they were* partial and prejudiced. Its immersion in the impure contexts of speech is purchased at the expense of its critical autonomy (hence paralogical disruptions of hegemonic injustice are indistinguishable from hegemonic violations of autonomy). I contend that the only way around this dilemma is to deny the premise – common to both sides – that reason and aesthetics are purely opposed types.

49 Cf. notes 47 and 48 above. Habermas appeals to Davidson in criticizing the idea of *literally* incommensurable conceptual schemes. I argue – with Kuhn and against Davidson – that this idea is partially defensible (at least with respect to core concepts) and doesn't speak against the possibility of *metaphorical* commensurability. This means that *rational* dialogue between speakers inhabiting literally incommensurable conceptual schemes (worldviews, etc.) is possible, so long as such dialogue allows for non-literal and non-univocal linguistic usage. It therefore means that logical criteria of literalness and univocity that play a valid role in *normal* scientific discourse might not apply in the *extraordinary* discourses characteristic of science in

the throes of revolutionary crisis or in other multicultural contexts. Cf. J. Habermas, *Erläuterung zur Diskursethik* (Frankfurt: Suhrkamp, 1991), pp. 213–18; D. Davidson, 'On the Very Idea of a Conceptual Scheme', in D. Davidson, *Inquiries into Truth and Interpretation* (Oxford: Oxford University Press, 1985, pp. 183–98; and Ingram, *Reason, History, and Politics*, ch. 8.

50 M. Walzer, *Spheres of Justice: A Defense of Pluralism and Equality* (New York: Basic Books, 1983), pp. 3–30.

51 Lyotard, *Au Juste*, p. 188.

52 Some support for ascribing this *simple* view of justice may be found in Lyotard's reference to the temporary contract as an ambiguous tendency throughout all domains of life and his assertion that 'one must maximize as much as possible the multiplication of small narratives' (Lyotard and Thébaud, *Just Gaming*, p. 59). Cf. S. Benhabib, 'Epistemologies of Postmodernism: A Rejoinder to Jean-François Lyotard', *New German Critique* 33 (Fall 1985), p. 124; and S. K. White, *Political Theory and Postmodernism* (Cambridge: Cambridge University Press, 1991), p. 136.

53 For a defence of a dual-democratic vision within the American context, see B. Ackerman, *We The People: Foundations* (Cambridge, Mass.: Harvard University Press, 1991).

54 Cf. J. Fishkin, *Tyranny and Legitimacy: A Critique of Political Theories* (Baltimore: Johns Hopkins University Press, 1979).

55 Habermas, *The Theory of Communicative Action*, vol. 2, p. 398.

56 Habermas, 'A Reply', p. 226. Habermas discusses certain varieties of systematically distorted communication that bear a striking resemblance to the sorts of *différends* mentioned by Lyotard. One such variety involves covertly switching the context and meaning of an argument, so that, for example, it ceases to be about a cognitive assertion and becomes a justification for a moral prescription. See J. Habermas, 'Überlegung zur Kommunikationspathologie', in Habermas, *Vorstudien und Ergänzungen*, pp. 255–6; 267–9.

57 Habermas, 'A Reply', p. 226.

58 Ibid.

INDEX